T5-DHA-615

Aggression in Children and Youth

NATO ASI Series

Advanced Science Institutes Series

A Series presenting the results of activities sponsored by the NATO Science Committee, which aims at the dissemination of advanced scientific and technological knowledge, with a view to strengthening links between scientific communities

The Series is published by an international board of publishers in conjunction with the NATO Scientific Affairs Division

A	Life Sciences	Plenum Publishing Corporation
B	Physics	London and New York
C	Mathematical and Physical Sciences	D. Reidel Publishing Company Dordrecht and Boston
D	Behavioural and Social Sciences	Martinus Nijhoff Publishers The Hague/Boston/Lancaster
E	Applied Sciences	
F	Computer and Systems Sciences	Springer-Verlag Berlin/Heidelberg/New York
G	Ecological Sciences	

Series D: Behavioural and Social Sciences – No. 17

Aggression in Children and Youth

edited by

Robert M. Kaplan

Associate Professor
Department of Community Medicine
School of Medicine
University of California at San Diego
San Diego, California, USA

and

Director, Center for Behavioral Medicine
San Diego State University
San Diego, California, USA

Vladimir J. Konečni

Professor
Department of Psychology
University of California at San Diego
San Diego, California, USA

Raymond W. Novaco

Associate Professor
Program in Social Ecology
University of California at Irvine
Irvine, California, USA

1984 **Martinus Nijhoff Publishers**
The Hague / Boston / Lancaster
Published in cooperation with NATO Scientific Affairs Division

Proceedings of the NATO Advanced Study Institute on Aggression in Children and Youth, Maratea, Italy, June 17-28, 1981

Library of Congress Cataloging in Publication Data

(nato advanced science institutes series. series d, behavioural and social sciences : 17)
''published in cooperation with nato scientific affairs division.''
includes index.
1. aggressiveness in children--congresses.
2. adolescent psychology--congresses. 3. aggressiveness (psychology)--congresses. i. kaplan, robert m.
ii. konecni, vladimir j. iii. novaco, raymond w.
iv. north atlantic treaty organization. scientific affairs division. v. title. vi. series: nato advanced. science institutes series. series d, behavioural and social sciences : no. 17.
bf723.a35n37 1981   155.4'18   83-22113
isbn 90-247-2903-3

ISBN 90-247-2903-3 (this volume)
ISBN 90-247-2688-3 (series)

Distributors for the United States and Canada: Kluwer Boston, Inc., 190 Old Derby Street, Hingham, MA 02043, USA

Distributors for all other countries: Kluwer Academic Publishers Group, Distribution Center, P.O. Box 322, 3300 AH Dordrecht, The Netherlands

Printed in The Netherlands

PREFACE

Human aggression is a fascinating research topic, but it is of much more than academic importance. To a large extent, the quality of life and perhaps even world survival depend on an adequate understanding of human aggression. Family violence (child battering and spouse abuse), rape, assault, armed robbery, murder, terrorism, and war are all instances of various types of aggression. The ability to regulate and control such acts could have a crucial contribution to the improvement of the quality of life.

Aggressive acts in children and youth need to be understood for three major reasons. First, most Western cultures are witnessing an increasing involvement in violence by youths. Second, the aggressive dispositions formed early in life may set the tone for or contribute to adult aggression. Third, the quality of childhood and the formation of personality are influenced by both the expression and inhibition of aggression. The regulation and control of aggression in children and youth can have a profound effect on the institutions of the family and the educational system as well as on society at large. Most societies are dedicated to maintaining harmony and to providing nonviolent solutions to human problems and social conflict.

A substantial amount of knowledge has accumulated about aggression and its regulation from empirical research, theory, and clinical sources. Because of the social importance of aggression, the study of human aggression in children and youth has become a popular area for scientific research. Knowledge in the area of human aggression has grown considerably in the past decade and very recent research in both Europe and the United States has forced major changes in thought about the development and control of human aggression. Further, there have been major methodological advances which have changed our thinking about the meaning of scientific data.

In order to explore the topic of aggression in children and youth, the North Atlantic Treaty Organization (NATO) sponsored an Advanced Study Institute which brought together recognized experts from 6 countries, and was held in Maratea, Italy, between June 17 and 28, 1981. The format for the Institute included formal lectures, group and panel discussions, and informal discussions. The chapters in this book are revisions of the formal lectures presented at the Institute and reflect the fact that the contributors' ideas changed as a function of interacting with their colleagues.

In addition to the faculty of the Institute, 43 participants from 10 countries attended the meetings. Their names are listed in Appendix 1.

Many people contributed to the completion of this volume. Connie Toevs provided many forms of assistance to the Institute Director. Linda Friend, Paige Gilman, and Sherry Merryman labored at the computer terminal to complete the typing and endless correspondence. Dori Joyner also provided valuable editorial assistance. Without their efforts, the entire project would not have been possible. In addition, we would like to thank the many people who contributed to the success of the Advanced Study Institute. These include Mario DiLullo, Director of the Advanced Study Institute Program, Tilo and Barbara Kester of International Transfer of Science and Technology, and A. Guzzardi of the Villa del Mare Conference Center in Maratea.

We are most grateful to NATO for supporting the meeting. Also we very much appreciate the additional support contributed by the University of California, Irvine, Los Angeles, and Riverside campuses.

Robert M. Kaplan
Institute Director

Vladimir J. Konečni
Institute Co-Director

Raymond W. Novaco
Institute Co-Director

TABLE OF CONTENTS

IV. MASS MEDIA EFFECTS AND EPIDEMIOLOGICAL APPROACHES

I. METHODOLOGICAL AND THEORETICAL ISSUES

METHODOLOGICAL ISSUES IN HUMAN AGGRESSION RESEARCH

Vladimir J. Konečni

University of California, San Diego

It is generally assumed in the philosophy of science that the quality of conclusions one can legitimately draw from research largely depends on the quality of the methodology that was used. In other words, "answers" are only as sound as "questions" that led to them. In an empirical science, whether of the hypothetico-deductive or inductive variety, an extremely close relationship between theory and method is assumed to exist; with some justification, one could go as far as to claim that the methodological and theoretical aspects of research fully constrain and complement each other, sometimes blending to the point of being indistinguishable.

For the purpose of this chapter, methodological issues can be outlined as follows: (a) "Conceptual translation" of theoretical ideas dealing with the causes of the phenomenon under investigation into concrete experimental operations, designated as independent variables ("operationalization" procedures); (b) choice of subjects, research settings, and experimental design; (c) the definition and measurement of the phenomenon in question, that is, of its observable or inferable manifestations, designated as dependent variables; and (d) the various relationships between the above three sets of issues, including, for example, questions of reliability and validity.

When one thinks of methodological issues in aggression research, social psychology and its practitioners spring readily to mind. First of all, social

1

Kaplan, R.M., Konečni, V.J., Novaco, R.W. (eds.) Aggression in Children and Youth
© 1984, Martinus Nijhoff Publishers, The Hague/Boston/Lancaster
ISBN 90-247-2903-3. Printed in The Netherlands

psychologists have undoubtedly been one of the most active groups doing aggression research, at least on humans. Furthermore, they can reasonably be claimed to have been on the cutting edge of methodological astuteness and sophistication in psychology, and unusually sensitive to intricate connections among methodology, design, statistical analysis, and theoretical conclusions. Their contributions range from experimenter-expectancy issues (Rosenthal, 1969), and complicated aspects of experimental design (Campbell & Stanley, 1963), to a major contribution by Webb, Campbell, Schwartz, and Sechrest (1966) on "nonreactive measurement", perhaps the soundest advice that social scientists have given each other for a safe passage through the analogue of the quagmires Heisenberg outlined in physics in his "uncertainty principle".

However, perhaps as a function of the otherwise very impressive diversification of social psychology, the work on aggression has not profited from the methodological advances as much as could have been expected, and one of the purposes of this chapter is to drive that point home. Another major objective is to provide a classification of independent and dependent variables used in human-aggression research.

The remainder of the chapter is organized as follows: (1) A classification of independent variables and a brief examination of the rationale for their operationalization; (2) a classification of dependent variables; and (3) a discussion of a number of past and present controversies and theoretical/experimental problems in the aggression literature which could have been avoided had the methodological issues been approached with more precision and less naivete.

Independent Variables

An attempt to classify the independent variables that have been used over the years in the research on human aggression is presented in Table 1. Criteria that governed the inclusion of variables in this table are briefly discussed first.

The table reflects an emphasis on studies which deal with the experimentally-manipulated precursors of aggressive behavior, rather than its organismic, demographic, psychodynamic, or personality-trait alleged causes. Despite these constraints, the variables included come from studies whose authors have been inspired by a relatively broad variety of theoretical ideas about aggressive behavior, including the revised frustration-aggression hypothesis (e.g., Berkowitz, 1969), social learning (e.g., Bandura, 1973), the excitation-transfer hypothesis (e.g., Zillmann, 1971), the bidirectional-causality anger-aggression model (e.g., Konečni, 1975a), attribution-theory-inspired research on aggressive behavior (e.g., Rule, Ferguson, & Nesdale, 1978; Rule & Nesdale, 1976), and other positions.

Independent variables which satisfied the criteria for inclusion were then divided into groups (columns in Table 1) primarily on the basis of the neo-Jamesian theories of emotion and arousal (e.g., Konečni, 1975a; Mandler, 1975; Schachter, 1964; Zillmann, 1971), and the relationship between various emotional states and aggressive behavior (e.g., Konečni, 1975a; Zillmann, 1971), especially anger (Averill, 1978; Buss, 1961; Donnerstein & Wilson, 1976; Konečni, 1979a; Zillmann, 1971). In this context, the classificatory scheme also reflects the writer's bias toward: (a) an emphasis on facial and postural cues as determinants of emotional states in addition to the arousal and cognitive-labeling issues stressed by other neo-Jamesian theories; and (b) an emphasis on bi-directional causal effects between internal states (the level of arousal, the degree of an emotion, such as anger), on one hand, and the behavioral manifestations of aggression, on the other, which results in a feedback-loop model that deals with emotional states and aggressive behavior in the same unified causal sequence and pays attention to both the antecedents and consequences of aggression, and for both the (human) target of aggression and for the aggressor. [These ideas on the perception and judgment of emotion in oneself and others, on aggressive behavior, and the relationships between them have been elaborated in other papers (e.g., Konečni, 1975a, 1975b; 1978; 1979a, 1979b].

3

TABLE 1

INDEPENDENT VARIABLES IN HUMAN-AGGRESSION EXPERIMENTS

I Arousal only	II Arousal and emotional state other than anger	III Arousal and aggression- relevant context	IV Arousal and Aversiveness
Complex melodies (at comfortable listening level, e.g., 70-73 dB)	Erotic stimuli (written passages; slides films, etc.)	Aggression- related stimuli (aggressive films, aggressive models aggressive sports, aggressive car- toons, aggressive stories, weapons)	Fear-inducing stimuli (threat of shock, noise, immersion in cold water)
White noise (60-70 dB)	Humorous stimuli (car- toons, films, etc.)	Presence of an angry confederate	Melodies/ noise at loud listening levels (over 90 dB)
Mild shock	Videotaped interactions inducing mirth/disgust	Aggressive play	High ambient temperature (92-95° F)
Exciting films with neutral content	Presence of a euphoric confederate		Nonsocial frustration (goal blocking)
Physical exercise	Alcohol		Nonarbitrary severe shock
Cognitive tasks with arousal- raising potential	Marijuana		
Frustration-free competitive play			

(V through VII continues on next page)

TABLE 1 (continued)

INDEPENDENT VARIABLES IN HUMAN-AGGRESSION EXPERIMENTS

V	VI	VII
Arousal and Aversiveness and the cognitive label of anger	Consequences to the anger instigator	Facial configuration manipulations
Noise, shock, arbitrarily administered	Instigator is hurt/not hurt by the subject	Instructions to assume facial configurations indicative of an emotion (without mentioning emotional labels)
Socially-induced frustration	Instigator is hurt/not hurt by someone else	Instructions to imagine scenes varying in emotional content
Insults	Instigator has a positive/ negative experience	Instructions to suppress or exaggerate felt emotion (pain, mirth, disgust)
	Instigator is exposed to the subject's verbal aggression	Instructions to mimic videotaped emotional expressions
	The subject engages in aggressive fantasy or aggression against a substitute target	

The classificatory scheme is meant to summarize some of these considerations and not represent a complete and exhaustive list of every independent variable that fits the criteria.

In the first column of Table 1 is a list of variables whose effects have been shown (or may be expected) to be limited to increases in the level of physiological arousal (marked changes in systolic and diastolic blood pressure, heart rate, respiration rate, and so on, and recorded by the customary psychophysiological procedures), without having other relevant effects. The point here is that although a perceptible change in the subject's physiological system occurs (detectable by measurement devices and, in some cases, perceivable by observers or the subjects themselves), these changes are not of the type or magnitude (or both) that would lead the subjects (a) to regard the situation and/or the resultant internal state as aversive, and (b) to be able to report (if querried) a clear unambiguous emotional label (such as anger or fear) for the resultant state.

For example, complex computer-generated melodies (9.17 bits per tone) used by Konečni, Crozier, and Doob (1975) have been found to raise the level of physiological arousal, but do not result in any reportable emotional state. Nor are they found by the subjects to be aversive: The subjects do not verbally label them as aversive; they do not learn melody-terminating (escape) responses when given a chance; and the melodies are listened to, in a free-choice situation, as much as the less arousing, simple melodies (4.00 bits per tone). Similar statements can be made about the effects of hammering nails, squeezing a wrist-strengthener, pounding a lever arm with a mallet, or riding an exercise bicycle for a few minutes (e.g., Holmes, 1966; Hornberger, 1959; Konečni & Wood, 1982; Ryan, 1970; Zillmann, Katcher, & Milavski, 1972), about 60 dB white noise (Donnerstein & Wilson, 1976), and about exciting films with neutral content (track competition events) used in some of the studies by Berkowitz and Geen (e.g., Berkowitz & Geen, 1966). Very mild electric shock, cognitive tasks with arousal-raising potential, and frustration-free competitive play (no prizes, declared winners, etc.) can reasonably be expected to have similar effects (e.g., Konečni & Day, 1977; Konečni & Sargent-Pollock, 1976).

Experimental variables which have been shown, or may be expected, to induce not only an increase in the level of physiological arousal, but also an unambiguous, reportable, emotional state--other than anger--are listed in the second column of Table 1. These

6

variables include erotic stimuli, which result in high arousal and sexual excitation (e.g., Baron & Bell, 1977; Donnerstein, Donnerstein, & Evans, 1975; Malamuth, Feshbach, & Jaffe, 1977; Zillmann, 1971) and humorous stimuli, which lead to raised arousal and feelings of mirth and amusement (e.g., Baron, 1978; Leak, 1974; Mueller & Donnerstein, 1977). It would seem that analogous effects may result from the subject's exposure to the emotional behavior of another person, such as a (live) euphoric confederate (Schachter, 1964) or the high-activity, emotional (positive and negative), videotaped interactions between a mother and her child (used by Konečni and Franco, 1974; in different, skillfully-acted sequences, the mother plays joyfully with, or severely physically punishes, her 6-year-old child).

The subject's consumption of alcohol and marijuana (e.g., Lang, Goeckner, Adesso, & Marlatt, 1975; Mariaskin, Lupfer, & D'Encarnacao, 1976; Shuntich & Taylor, 1972; Taylor & Gammon, 1975; Taylor, Vardaris, Rawtich, Gammon, Cranston, & Lubetkin, 1976) has also been classified in Column II, but tentatively. The precise effects of these drugs on arousal are still somewhat unclear, and whether the euphoria and other mood changes that they produce are genuine emotions is open to debate. Possible alternative candidates are Columns I and IV; the latter is the poorer of the two, because the dosages administered in the cited experiments were too low to produce aversive effects in regular users (all of the subjects were).

Experimental operations which are more directly aggression-relevant than those in Columns I and II are presented in Column III. They include the presentation of live or filmed aggressive models (e.g., Bandura, Ross, & Ross, 1961, 1963; Hanratty, Liebert, Morris, & Fernandez, 1969; Hicks, 1965; Parton & Geshuri, 1971), aggressive cartoons (e.g., Hapkiewicz & Roden, 1971; Lövaas, 1961; Mussen & Rutherford, 1961; Osborn & Endsley, 1971), aggressive stories (e.g., Larder, 1962), aggressive films (e.g., Berkowitz, 1965; Berkowitz & Geen, 1967; Berkowitz & Rawlings, 1963; Doob & Climie, 1972; Doob & Kirshenbaum, 1973; Feshbach, 1961; Geen & Berkowitz, 1966, 1967; Hartmann, 1969; Kuhn, Madsen, & Becker, 1967; Steuer, Applefield, & Smith, 1971; Walters & Thomas, 1963) and other aggressive displays, including aggressive sports, such as football and ice-hockey (e.g., Arms, Russell, & Sandilands, 1977; Goldstein & Arms, 1971), as well as the presence of weapons in the experimental setting (e.g., Berkowitz & LePage, 1967; Page & Scheidt, 1971; Turner & Simons, 1974), and the presence of an angry, malevolent confederate (Schachter, 1964; the confederate's state was, however, neither caused by, or directed at, the subject). In other studies, children were allowed to engage in aggressive play (e.g., Feshbach, 1956; Kenny, 1953; Mallick & McCandless, 1966), and adults to punch boxing bags (e.g., Konečni & Wood, 1982), or participate in a vigorous contest (Ryan, 1970).

The magnitude of the effects of these variables presumably depends on the details of the operationalization, but it is probable that they all: (a) Raise the level of arousal (e.g., Doob & Climie, 1972; Doob & Kirshenbaum, 1973; Osborn & Endsley, 1971); (b) are not perceived as aversive by the subjects; (c) increase the probability that the subjects will view the experimental setting as one where aggressive behavior is sanctioned, or, in behaviorist parlance, bring aggression closer to the top of the hierarchy of behavioral alternatives ("disinhibition" and "facilitation" of aggression, but see Konečni and Ebbesen, 1976, for a discussion of different meanings of the term "disinhibition"); and (d) do not result in an unambiguous reportable, emotional label, at least not the label of anger. In summary, variables in Column III have components of those listed in Columns I and II, and, in addition, introduce an aggression-relevant or aggression-sanctioning context.

Procedures and stimuli which, unlike those in Columns I-III, have been shown, or may be expected, to be both arousing and aversive, are listed in Column IV. They include: Threats of physical suffering [e.g., the possibility of hearing extremely loud bursts of noise (Konečni, 1979a, Experiment 6) and the possibility of limb-immersion in even colder water than what the subject had already experienced (Konečni & Frank, 1977)]; considerable physical discomfort [complex melodies and white noise at over 90 dB, as in Konečni (1975b), and Donnerstein and Wilson (1976), respectively, and high (92-95 ° F) ambient temperature, as in Baron and Bell (1976) and Bell and Baron (1976); these stimuli are administered as a "part of the experiment" and thus not attributable to a cruel or capricious human source]; psychological discomfort (nonsocial frustration or goal-blocking not easily attributable to a malevolent human source; cf. Buss, 1961; Kulik & Brown, 1979); and actual pain (induced by, for example, electric shock, but again received, as in the control conditions of Berkowitz and Geen, 1966, and Holmes, 1966, as a "part of the experiment", and not easily attributable by the subject to a capricious human source).

All of these procedures are clearly arousing and aversive, and would result in avoidance or escape responses if the subjects were given an opportunity.

8

Some (such as the threat of pain) led the subjects to experience the emotion of fear, whereas others resulted in acute discomfort or pain (whether pain should be considered as emotion is debatable; my personal bias is against such a classification); but despite the arousal and aversiveness, none presumably led the subjects to consider themselves angry. The reason for this is that the aversive stimuli were not administered by an arbitrary, malevolent, obnoxious, aggressive human being, but rather "clinically", as "part of the experiment", for "scientific objectives".

The emotional impact (or lack of it) of an aversive stimulus has been repeatedly shown to be dependent on its source, the source's perceived ulterior motives, and the general context in which it is administered (e.g., Konečni, 1975a, 1975b; 1979b; Nickel, 1974; Pastore, 1952; Rule, Dyck, & Nesdale, 1978; Rule, et al, 1978). Moreover, the same aversive stimulus may result in different negative emotions, depending on the estimated utility of various behavioral alternatives to which these emotions lead (for example, a 12-year-old-boy, physically threatened by his father, would presumably experience fear and engage in escape behavior; the identical threat uttered by a 6-year-old neighbor would probably result in anger, and possibly aggression; thus the emotion-labeling process is assumed to take into account the consequences of emotion-congruent behavior).

In Column V are listed procedures which are, except for insults, identical to those in Column IV, with the important difference that the subject can blame their administration not on "science", but on an arbitrary and obnoxious person (usually an experimental confederate or experimenter; e.g., Hanratty, O'Neal, & Sulzer, 1972; Hokanson & Burgess, 1962a; Kulik & Brown, 1979; Mallick & McCandless, 1966; Turner, Simons, Berkowitz, & Frodi, 1977; Zillmann, 1971). For this reason, these procedures are not merely arousing and aversive, but also lead to anger, and thus highly increase the probability and intensity of the subject's aggression against both the anger instigator and substitute targets (e.g., Frost & Holmes, 1979; Konečni & Doob, 1972).

An insult is a prototypic social aversive event and leads to all three consequences that define Column V. Some experimental procedures (for example, the one used by Doob and Wood, 1972, Konečni and Doob, 1972, Konečni, 1975a, 1975b, and Konečni and Ebbesen, 1976, in which a well-trained confederate repeatedly insults the subject over a 7-minute period in a face-to-face situation) are no less physiologically arousing than

9

are very painful physical stimuli; this procedure results in considerably more anger and dislike of the confederate (by self-report measures), and physical aggression against this person (by behavioral measures, such as the number of "electric shocks" delivered) than is the case in control conditions. A set of very pronounced physiological, emotional, behavioral, and attitudinal changes takes place as a consequence of the insults uttered by a complete stranger over a brief period.

Column VI contains experimental procedures that manipulate what happens to the person (e.g., a confederate) who had instigated the subject's anger. Typically, these independent variables are administered in the second phase (after anger induction) of aggression experiments dealing with one or another aspect of "catharsis". The subjects are, for example, given an opportunity to deliver a fixed number of "electric shocks" to the confederate in the course of a pseudolearning task, indeed are forced by the instructions and the confederate's (programmed) errors to do so (e.g., Konečni & Doob, 1972; in the control condition, the subjects have no opportunity to "hurt" the confederate after being insulted by this person). In other experiments, the subjects viewed the experimenter deliver "shocks" to the confederate (Doob & Wood, 1972), or read a derogatory letter written about the insulting person (Fromkin, Goldstein, & Brock, 1977). In an experiment by Bramel, Taub, and Blum (1969), the subjects watched a videotape in which the annoying confederate was portrayed as experiencing either a bad or a pleasant drug-related experience some time in the past. Finally, the subjects were given an opportunity to aggress against the anger instigator verbally, usually through a written communication (e.g., de Charms & Wilkins, 1963; Kahn, 1966; Pepitone & Reichling, 1955; Rosenbaum & deCharms, 1960; Thibaut & Coules, 1952; Worchel, 1957). However, whether the subjects considered the confederate even psychologically "hurt" by their behavior in these experiments is dubious. Also, on the reasonable assumption that few psychotic or delusional subjects had been used, it must have been perfectly clear to the subjects provided with an opportunity to engage in aggressive fantasy (e.g., Baker & Schaie, 1969; Berkowitz, 1960; Feshbach, 1955; Hokanson & Burgess, 1962b; Hornberger, 1959) that their behavior had no effect whatsoever on the anger instigator. The same is presumably true of studies in which the subjects were given an opportunity to aggress physically against a person other than the anger instigator (e.g., Gambaro & Rabin, 1969; Frost & Holmes, 1979; Hokanson, Burgess, & Cohen, 1963; Holmes, 1966; Konečni & Doob, 1972; Konečni & Spees, 1977).

As it turns out, the events that befall the obnoxious confederate (especially when the subject himself does the hurting, and it is physical) have a considerable impact on the subject's arousal, emotions, and subsequent behavior, especially aggression. An angry person, who has been given an opportunity to "hurt" the anger instigator, subsequently aggresses less against this person, feels less angry, and is less aroused (in comparison to the appropriate control conditions). His/her attitudes about the confederate do not change, however: That person continues to be disliked. These findings are discussed at length by Konečni (1975a) and form the basis of one part of the bidirectional-causality anger-aggression model.

Precisely what an angry subject does in control conditions of these and similar experiments (i.e., when (s)he is not given an opportunity to hurt the confederate) is also very important for the purpose of predicting the amount of subsequent aggression, especially if the interpolated activity has an effect on the level of arousal (and therefore on the degree of anger, since the arousal provides the physiological justification for the emotion, in the neo-Jamesian view). In various experiments, angry subjects in control conditions have worked on mathematical problems or waited idly (Konečni, 1975a; Mallick & McCandless, 1966), given shocks to an innocent third person (Frost & Holmes, 1979; Konečni & Doob, 1972; Konečni & Spees, 1977), performed "aggressive" actions against inanimate objects, such as throwing darts at targets (e.g., Mallick & McCandless, 1966), and so on, or were, alternatively, exposed to manipulations listed in Columns I-III. Generally speaking, interpolated activities and procedures which raise the level of arousal increase the amount of subsequent aggression of subjects who had been angered; arousal-decreasing procedures have the opposite effect on the aggressive behavior of such subjects.

Finally, Column VII of Table 1 deals with experimental procedures designed to alter the subject's facial expression--for the effect that the proprioceptive feedback from the facial musculature has on a person's judgment of his/her emotional state and its intensity, rather than for what different facial expressions communicate to others.

Laird (1974) developed a procedure in which the subject is instructed to contort or relax certain facial muscles and thus, in effect, adopt a facial expression indicative of an emotion (anger, joy), without these labels being explicitly mentioned (in order to minimize the experimenter-demand contamination

11

of the dependent measure, which was a self-report of emotion experienced while watching relatively neutral slides). This procedure was subsequently used by Konečni and Zellensky (1976) in conjunction with the anger manipulation; among other results, angry subjects, who had been instructed (indirectly) to adopt a frowning face during the dependent-measure phase, administered more punishments to the anger instigator than did subjects in the various control conditions.

In another condition of the Konečni-Zellensky experiment, angered and non-angered subjects were asked to imagine scenes with different emotional content (i.e., events that had recently made subjects angry or happy). This procedure, originally used by Schwartz (1976) to test the notion that emotional imagery is detectable by electromyographic measurement of facial muscles, produced results--in the Konečni-Zellensky experiment--analogous to those obtained by using Laird's procedure (e.g., angry subjects imagining annoying events delivered more "shocks" than controls).

The remaining two procedures listed in Column VII have not been used in aggression experiments proper, but are nevertheless relevant (self-report of emotional state, including anger, was one of the dependent measures in some of the experiments in question). Lanzetta, Cartwright-Smith, and Kleck (1976) found that instructing subjects to suppress or exaggerate facial expression of pain in response to electric shocks decreased and increased, respectively, both physiological arousal and the subject's experience of pain. In her doctoral dissertation, Sargent-Pollock (1978) obtained analogous results with other emotions (mirth, disgust).

Konečni and Sargent-Pollock (1977) used a "facial shadowing" task ("shadowing" in the sense that the term is used in the dichotic-listening paradigm in cognitive psychology) to study the effects, on the subjects' emotional state, of mimicking for 30 seconds a videotape of a person whose face gradually changes from neutral to the peak of an emotion (e.g., anger) and back to neutral. The original videotapes were made by professional actresses facially acting out different emotions in the neutral/peak/neutral sequence, in accordance with a "facial-muscle-activation script" given to them by the authors. "First-generation" subjects mimicked these tapes and were themselves videotaped while doing so; the facial expressions on their tapes were mimicked by the second-generation subjects, and so on. This "facial rumor" paradigm was used to study the selective disappearance/augmentation of facial expressions across generations of mimickers "shadowing" a particular emotional state, such as anger, as well as other questions of theoretical importance. One of the findings of the Konečni/Sargent-Pollock study that is relevant here was that subjects mimicking an angry facial expression reported feeling significantly more angry than did subjects who merely watched the same tape.

In summary, various procedures designed to manipulate a subject's facial expression, notably that indicative of anger, seem to have similar effects, and, when the question has been addressed experimentally, seem to increase the amount of aggressive behavior performed by an angry individual--presumably by augmenting the degree of anger through the proprioceptive feedback from the facial musculature.

Dependent Variables

The rationale underlying the classification of dependent measures in aggression experiments, presented in Table 2, is self-evident.

Three methods of measuring direct physical aggression are described in Column I. One employs the familiar "aggression machine" (Buss, 1961; Milgram, 1961, has made a claim of independent discovery), which has been used in literally hundreds of experiments by Berkowitz, Geen, R. A. Baron, E. Donnerstein, Zillmann, their colleagues, and countless other researchers. The subject is forced by the instructions to press one of 10 levers on each of a number of trials, and his/her choice consists of which level of punishment to deliver. The average intensity of "shocks" or "blasts of noise" (on a scale from 1 to 10) supposedly delivered by the subject to the confederate is usually reported, often separately for blocks of 3-10 trials; occasionally, average and/or total duration of shocks is also computed and reported.

13

TABLE 2

DEPENDENT VARIABLES IN HUMAN-AGGRESSION EXPERIMENTS

I Direct physical aggression	II Displaced physical aggression	III Aggression against inaminate objects	IV Direct verbal aggression
"Shocks" or "blasts of noise" using the Buss "aggression machine" (duration, intensity) administered by the subject to the anger instigator	"Shocks" using the Doob-Konečni pseudo-creativity task (number, duration), administered by the subject to a person other than the anger instigator	Beating up Bobo doll	Verbal analogue of the Buss "aggression machine"
"Shocks" (intensity) administered by the subject in the course of Taylor's pseudo-reaction-time task	Knocking down the opponent's towers of building blocks	Slamming down tele- phone receiver	Written or oral comments with potential negative con- sequences for the anger instigator
"Shocks" or "blasts of noise" using the Doob-Konečni pseudo-creativity task (number, duration) administered by the subject to the anger instigator	Pressing a button which "slows down" the opponent's progress on a task	Shooting toy gun while playing "soldiers"	
	Frequency of high voice- responses (yelling) in reading a text to the opponent	Throwing a wet sponge at a carnival clown	
		Horn honking	

(V through VII continued on next page)

TABLE 2 (continued)

DEPENDENT VARIABLES IN HUMAN-AGGRESSION EXPERIMENTS

V	VI	VII
Displaced verbal aggression	Physiological indices	Miscellaneous
Written or oral comments without negative consequences for the anger instigator (including projective-test responses)	Systolic and/or diastolic blood pressure	Self-report of own emotional/ arousal state (rating-scale, questionnaire, and interview responses)
	Heart rate	Amount of tip
	Pulse rate	Alcohol consumption
	Skin conductance	Performance on the digit-symbol task
	Finger temperature	Choice between complex and simple computer-generated melodies
	Respiration rate	

The procedure used by Taylor (1967) is a derivative of the one developed by Buss; the average intensity of the subjects' shocks over trials (in response to an ascending series of shocks received from the confederate) is reported, by blocks of 5-6 trials, and usually compared to the intensity of the subject's first, unprovoked, shock to the confederate, which serves as the baseline for an experimental condition.

The third procedure in Column I has been used extensively by Doob, Konečni, and others (e.g., Doob & Wood, 1972; Frost & Holmes, 1979; Konečni, 1975a; Konečni & Doob, 1972) and involves a pseudo-creativity task. On each of many trials (25-50), the subject reads aloud a word from a list provided by the experimenter. The confederate is supposed to give a "creative" one-word response within three seconds (these responses are preprogrammed and of mediocre creativity). The subject's task is to judge the creativity of each answer (no criteria are provided) and press the "shock" (or "noise") button if (s)he judges it to be uncreative. It is the differential harshness of the subjects' criteria of what constitutes a "creative" response that sharply distinguishes the experimental conditions; the number, and occasionally, the average or total duration, of shocks (or blasts of noise) are reported.

Common and essential to all three methods is the experimenter's hope that the subjects do not see through the deception (no shocks are actually delivered to the confederate). [In fact, the subjects' perceived certainty that the shocks are delivered to the confederate was experimentally manipulated by Konecni and Manley (1977); moreover, this factor—the certainty that a "blow" has actually "landed" on, and hurt, the intended target—is formally a part of Konecni's bidirectional-causality anger-aggression model (a decrease in certainty is expected to weaken the arousal-decreasing effect of angry persons' physical aggression)].

In this line of research, no effort is therefore spared to increase the effectiveness of the deception and to minimize the subjects' suspicion, including extensive pretesting, the use of elaborate and convincing cover stories, the recruitment of experimentally-naive subjects (including high school students), and in-depth, "funnel" postexperimental interviews.

Some examples of "displaced" aggression (where the subjects' actions are directed at someone other than the anger instigator) are listed in Column II. The first entry refers to one of the conditions in the

16

Konečni-Doob (1972) study and its subsequent replications by Konečni and Spees (1977), and by Frost and Holmes (1979); after being angered or treated neutrally, and aggressing against the anger instigator or waiting idly, subjects had the opportunity to deliver shocks to another confederate (while working on the previously described pseudo-creativity task).

The second entry in Column II is more problematic for classification purposes. It refers to a study by Rocha and Rogers (1976) in which an unobstrusive measure of aggression consists of a child's knocking over of an opponent's tower of building blocks. The action differs from those listed in Column III in that the tower clearly belongs to the opponent, and from those in Column I, in that the opponent is not directly physically hurt. It is a relatively rare analogue in the aggression literature of what must be a very frequent real-life behavior-- deliberate and malicious destruction (or theft) of an enemy's property.

The third entry in Column II is also difficult to classify. In one of the experiments by Mallick and McCandless (1966), the dependent measure was the subjects' pressing a button which supposedly slowed down the anger instigator's progress on a task. Thus, the behavior affects the opponent directly, and in a negative way, but, unlike the actions in Column I, the effect is not physically injurious or painful. As in the preceding case, one could easily think of many real-life counterparts of this dependent variable.

The final entry in Column II is conceptually similar to the one just described. Fitz and Stephan (1976) used the frequency of subjects' high voice-volume responses as the main dependent measure. High voice volume could apparently somewhat interfere with the opponent's performance, but certainly not physically hurt him. [Since the subjects were asked by the experimenter to read the text (on which occasion the voice volume was measured), and since this text had nothing to do with the opponent, I have not classified the subjects' behavior as an instance of either direct or displaced verbal aggression (Columns IV and V).]

Column III contains examples of high-magnitude behaviors which have been termed "aggressive" in various studies, presumably because of their morphological similarity to aggressive actions; however, no one gets hurt and no opponent's or anger instigator's property gets damaged. These actions range from children "beating up" a Bobo doll in the well-known Bandura et al. (1961) studies (this activity was termed "aggressive play" by Kaplan and Singer, 1976) to slamming down the

17

telephone receiver on a confederate who refuses to comply to the subjects' plea for a charitable donation (Kulik & Brown, 1979; it would seem from the report that although subjects put the receiver down harder when they were frustrated, they did so at the natural end of the conversation, not in order to terminate it; this behavior should not, therefore, be regarded as an instance of direct aggression, intended by the subject to cause even psychological harm to the confederate). In another experiment (Feshbach, 1956), shooting a toy gun while playing "soldiers" was one of the dependent measures of aggression--an impure case of aggression against inanimate objects, but clearly related to the aggressive-play measure used in the Bandura et al. studies.

The final two examples in Column III are difficult to classify and were only tentatively placed in this column. It is not clear to what extent throwing a wet sponge at someone (Turner et al., 1977) is aggression, as opposed to being a playful behavior expected at a carnival, and to what extent a deindividuated, nonreactive clown's head can be considered a real, as opposed to a somewhat inanimate target (hence the placement in Column III). The meaning of horn-honking at a stalled pick-up truck (Turner et al., 1977) is also ambiguous, and for several reasons. Were the horn-honking motorists aware that the truck was stalled deliberately? Was the intent of the horn-honking aggressive or merely communicative (we are waiting behind you)? If the intent was aggressive, what sort of damage does this behavior produce? Would it have been more reasonable to classify it together with insults, as causing psychological harm?

It should be noted that the instances of "aggression" against inanimate objects which are listed in Column III differ somewhat from activities that used to be employed in Kleinian "aggressive play" therapies; there, a "hyperaggressive" child was frequently encouraged to attack a symbolic object (e.g., use a pair of scissors on a doll named the same as the child's brother or sister).

Columns IV and V are analogous to I and II, except that verbal aggression is involved (written or orally expressed comments or ratings). What I have classified as direct verbal aggression includes: (a) A verbal attack which the subject knows (or believes) is communicated to the target, thus having at least the potential of causing psychological harm through its negative or insulting nature; and (b) a verbal attack or negative evaluation which though communicated to a third party, may subsequently (or so the subject believes) be

18

conveyed to the intended target, or otherwise adversely affect that person (e.g., (s)he may lose the job by virtue of the third party acting upon the subjects' negative performance evaluation). The two instances may be called "insult" and "malicious gossip", respectively. A clear example of the former is the verbal analogue of the Buss "aggression machine" used by Goldstein, Davis, and Herman (1975), in which the subjects call out remarks from an escalating series of insults to the confederate (instead of pushing buttons on an ascending shock-intensity scale). Examples of the latter (verbal aggression via a third party) are found in studies by Bramel, Taub, and Blum (1968) and Kahn (1966), in both of which the subjects were led to believe that their negative evaluations may have adverse effects on their antagonist (in terms of his job standing, etc.).

In contrast, the overwhelming majority of subjects whose behavior is referred to in Column V would be very hard pressed to imagine how their verbal behavior could conceivably affect their target in an adverse way. For this reason, I have labeled these measures "displaced" verbal aggression, although "verbal expression of negative feelings without consequences for any target" is more accurate ("displaced" aggression implies a substitute target, which is not the case here). The measures range from projective-test "aggressive" responses (e.g., Buss & Foliart, 1958; Kenny, 1953) and "aggressive stories" involving the antagonist, to a host of different formats of negative verbal ratings and evaluations of experimenters and confederates who managed to cross the subjects (e.g., Berkowitz, 1960; Berkowitz, Green & Macaulay, 1962; deCharms & Wilkins, 1963; Feshbach, 1955; Hornberger, 1959; Pepitone & Reichling, 1955; Rosenbaum & deCharms, 1960; Thibart & Coules, 1952; Worchel, 1957). This is a very incomplete list and, moreover, contains only studies in which verbal aggression (via evaluations, etc.) was the main dependent measure. Literally hundreds of other studies in which a human being had been used to induce anger or frustration in subjects also employed verbal-aggression measures--as "manipulation checks", in addition to the main dependent variable(s).

Some of the physiological indices that have been most commonly used in aggression experiments as main dependent measures are listed in Column VI. The use of these measures reflects the fact that many of the theoretical issues in human aggression have traditionally been couched in emotional/motivational or physiological-arousal terms. Among the indices used: Systolic blood pressure (e.g., Baker & Schaie, 1969; Doob & Kirshenbaum, 1973; Frost & Holmes, 1979;

19

Hokanson & Burgess, 1962a; 1962b; Hokanson, Burgess & Cohen, 1963; Hokanson & Edelman, 1966; Hokanson & Shetler, 1961; Holmes, 1966; Kahn, 1966), diastolic blood pressure (e.g., Frost & Holmes, 1979; Gambaro & Rabin, 1969; Hokanson & Edelman, 1966; Holmes, 1966; Kahn, 1966), heart rate (e.g., Hokanson & Burgess, 1962a, 1962b; Hokanson & Edelman, 1966; Holmes, 1966), pulse rate (Baker & Schaie, 1969; Frost & Holmes, 1979), skin conductance and finger temperature (Kahn, 1966), and respiration rate (Baker & Schaie, 1969). Following these early studies, many subsequent ones have used the same or similar physiological indices. However, the tendency has been to use them as auxiliary measures, in conjunction with the behavioral ones, or, more importantly, as a means of scaling the impact and/or the timecourse of certain (especially arousal-related) experimental variables, either in pretesting or in the experiment proper (for example, in the work of Donnerstein, Konečni, Zillmann, and others). Such work has sometimes made possible a reconciliation of seemingly contradictory findings from earlier studies which had ignored the changing impact of experimental variables (on the level of arousal, etc.) over time.

Finally, some other behaviors that have been used as dependent variables in aggression experiments are listed in Column VII. This list is by no means exhaustive and is only meant to illustrate the diversity of measures that have been used. The variables listed range from self-report measures of own emotional/arousal state, used in countless studies, and naturalistic alternatives to the verbal/evaluative measures, such as the size of tip given to a frustrating taxi driver (Fromkin, Goldstein, & Brock, 1977), to a miscellany of behaviors which have in common a responsiveness to anger- and aggression-induced fluctuations in the level of arousal, including alcohol consumption (Marlatt, Kosturn & Lang, 1975), performance on the digit-symbol task (Doob & Climie, 1972; Worchel, 1957), and choice between complex and simple melodies (Konečni, et al, 1975). These diverse measures are, in a sense, a reflection of attempts to integrate aggression phenomena into more general theoretical frameworks that relate emotional and physiological processes to behavior.

Implications

Perhaps the first thing that might strike one looking at Tables 1 and 2 is the relatively large number of columns and entries in each column. For the independent variables, this variety would appear healthy--presumably indicative of an active, well-researched field, in which multiple causes of the

20

phenomenon in question ("aggressive behavior") have been established. However, a close scrutiny of the bewildering variety of dependent measures challenges any such optimistic conclusion about independent variables and is worrisome in its own right. The use of numerous different measures of the (allegedly) "same thing", both within a single study and across studies, is an excellent strategy in the Webb et al. (1966) "triangulation" sense, if one is lucky enough that they all come out in such a way as to isolate a common, central core of the phenomenon (Webb et al. unfortunately have nothing to say about the cases where this does not happen and the measures suggest different, nonoverlapping conclusions, cf. Konečni and Ebbesen, 1979). As it happens, when one goes through the human-aggression literature study by study, more often than not there are discrepancies among the different dependent measures within single studies which had not been predicted by the theories that motivated the studies; moreover, when different dependent measures are used in different studies, and the results, collectively, come out such that they cannot be explained by any one theory, it becomes impossible to compare these studies, or to think of the results and the studies as a cumulative building-block type of scientific effort. In addition, of course, by no means has every independent variable from Table 1 been used in combination with every dependent variable from Table 2. For reasons of convenience, tradition, and lack of foresight, researchers have tended to use only certain independent and dependent variables together. Thus, researchers from different theoretical orientations have relied on different "slices" of Tables 1 and 2, which further complicates any meaningful comparison of theories, lines of research, or even of the work coming out of different laboratories. It is partly for this reason that every "grand" theory of aggressive behavior has been pronounced dead or moribund by some other school, and perhaps for good reason, since few of these theories have much to say about the clustering of various dependent variables, nor can they--in their pure form, and with few parameters--explain a sizeable number of findings in the literature.

In the rest of this section, I will attempt to give specific examples of how the neglect of methodological details--alluded to above in very general terms--has obfuscated theoretical issues, clouded the validity of applications of basic research, and needlessly sapped research efforts. The objective is to provide a concise listing of illustrative examples, rather than an exhaustive and detailed analysis that would utilize all features of the classification of independent and dependent variables in the previous two sections.

The list is composed of three parts: (a) methodological problems specifically related to the administration of independent variables; (b) methodological
problems related to the nature and collection of dependent variables; and (c) combined problems.

(a) <u>Methodological</u> <u>problems</u> <u>related</u> <u>to</u> <u>independent</u>
<u>variables</u>.

<u>1</u>. <u>Order of</u> <u>administration of</u> <u>independent</u> <u>vari-</u>
<u>ables</u>. Among the numerous examples that could be given
here, perhaps the clearest involves the placement of
the anger/frustration manipulation relative to watching
an aggressive display. In Bandura's early studies, the
frustration always followed the exposure to the aggressive model; no rationale for this was given, presumably
either because the social-learning theory could not say
anything about order effects, or because these were
implicitly thought to be substantively irrelevant. In
the work of Berkowitz and many others, the anger manipulation always preceded the aggressive film, again
with no explicit rationale. Conclusions about the combined effects of anger and observed aggression were
thus being drawn in literally many dozens of studies
without this issue being even acknowledged as one of
theoretical and interpretive importance, let alone
examined experimentally. Yet, when finally it was submitted to experimental scrutiny (Donnerstein, Donnerstein, & Barrett, 1976), it turned out that the two
different orders of inducing anger and exposing subjects to an aggressive film produced very different
results, thus casting doubts on years of previous
effort by paying attention to a seemingly minor methodological detail. The arousal-related and cognitive
factors (summarized by terms such as distraction,
attentional shift, cognitive labeling, excitation
transfer) which underlie the mentioned order effect
have subsequently been incorporated into the theoretical thinking and experimental work of Donnerstein,
Konečni, Novaco, and Zillmann, among others.

<u>2</u>. <u>Taking</u> <u>into</u> <u>account</u> <u>that</u> <u>a</u> <u>variable</u> <u>may</u> <u>have</u>
<u>more</u> <u>than</u> <u>one</u> <u>effect</u>. This issue is related to 1.
above. It consists of the researchers' failure to
realize that some of the independent variables they use
are not unidimensional, that a variable may have more
than one type of impact (especially cognitive and physiological; see Table 1) on the subject, and that these
different effects, in the most unfortunate case, may
"pull" the behavior in opposite directions (e.g., a

22

film may raise arousal, but also be an emotion- and behavior-attenuating source of distraction or "attentional shift"). One of the many consequences of the neglect of this issue had been the repeated failure to include a no-film condition in the design of "media violence" experiments (as first noted by Weiss, 1969, all of the previous studies included only a nonaggressive-film control). Again, when the issue was finally experimentally tackled by Zillmann and Johnson (1973) and Donnerstein et al. (1976), a very different interpretation of all of the previous findings developed. Conversely, the Bandura et al. 1961 studies used only a no-model control. When a nonaggressive, but highly active, model condition was included in a subsequent study (Bandura et al., 1963b), it was found that watching the aggressive model did not increase novel aggressive responses in comparison to this new control condition.)

3. Taking into account the timecourse of an effect. Remarkably little experimental work has been done on the timecourse of the effects of various independent variables (either in the pretesting or experimental phases), presumably because the arousal aspects of the variables have been either ignored or not understood in their complete psychophysiological sense, that is, as subject to the action of homeostatic mechanisms which are correlated with the passage of time (see Table 1). In the few studies in which the duration of the administration of an independent variable was explicitly manipulated (e.g., Konečni, 1975a), or the length of the delay in the collection of the dependent variable was treated as a factor (e.g., Doob & Climie, 1972; Zillmann & Bryant, 1974), the arousal-related timecourse of a variable's effect proved to be singularly important.

In many studies, the fact that the effects of different variables may have different timecourses is implicitly taken into account, but not (a) explicitly acknowledged, (b) incorporated into theoretical statements, or (c) subjected to pretesting. For example, Geen & O'Neal (1969) first exposed the subjects to an aggressive film and then to 60 dB noise. Presumably, they felt that the effect of the film on aggressive behavior would be longer-lasting than the effect of the noise, but nothing was said about this, nor is there any mention of pretesting. [For that matter, these authors did not even pretest the physiological impact of 60 dB noise (only verbal ratings of the noise were obtained); this low level has--quite reasonably--been used in other studies (e.g., Donnerstein & Wilson, 1976) as a control condition.]

23

4. Taking into account the arousing, aversive, and anger-inducing potential of a variable (or lack of it). This is a somewhat different aspect of the issue discussed under 2. above, and refers to the material presented in Columns I, IV, and V in Table 1. Ignoring--through a lack of pretesting and proper control groups--the precise "ingredients" of an independent variable, in terms of its arousingness, aversiveness, and anger-inducing potential, is probably both one of the most common and most serious methodological problems in the human-aggression literature. The rationale for drawing these distinctions, their predictive utility, and their theoretical importance have been discussed in conjunction with Table 1 and need not be reiterated here. The number of studies in which these distinctions were ignored when making the predictions is quite large and the readers should have little difficulty in coming up with their own examples. Suffice it to say that studies in which the main independent variable simply raises the level of arousal, or produces high arousal and aversiveness (but not anger), typically have weak and/or irreplicable effects (in terms of behavioral aggression), in comparison to studies in which acute anger is induced. In the former set of studies, the effect is sometimes strengthened by including particularly effective examples from Column III of Table 1 (creating an aggression-sanctioning experimental context); but, this is often at the expense of external validity (at both the independent- and dependent-variable side) and sharply reduces the percent of variance of real-life aggression that the variable in question could possibly account for (cf. Kaplan & Singer, 1976).

5. Taking into account what the subjects consider the consequences of their behavior to be for the target of aggression. This point is in reference to items in Column VI of Table 1, where the independent variable consists of an opportunity (or lack of it) for the subject to "express aggression" toward a confederate (the anger instigator). What form this aggression takes, and the consequences for the target, have been treated rather casually by most researchers, presumably because this issue had not formally been a part of the theoretical positions which inspired their studies. Yet, as it turns out, the very performance of an aggressive act, the form it takes (e.g., physical vs. verbal vs. fantasy), and the consequences for the target (e.g., pain, loss of job, no consequence) have been shown empirically (e.g., Konečni & Manley, 197 ; Konečni & Wood, 1982) to make a great deal of difference and to affect the aggressor (his/her arousal level, emotional state, and the amount of subsequent aggressive behavior), as well as the target.

24

These factors are an explicit part of the bidirectional-causality anger-aggression model (e.g., Konečni, 1975a) which stresses the importance of the emotion-behavior-emotion feedback loop. The conclusions from previous studies (discussed in conjunction with Table 1), in some of which the mode of the subject's aggression appears to have been almost randomly decided upon, and which ignored the subject's thoughts about the consequences (if any) of their behavior for the target (and the effect of these thoughts on the subjects' arousal and emotional state), need to be seriously reexamined.

(b). Methodological problems related to dependent variables.

1. External and construct validity of dependent measures. Perhaps the most frequent, and potentially the most damaging, criticisms of human-aggression research in general have had to do with the types of dependent measures that had been used. Such criticisms can usually be reduced to issues of external or construct validity of the measures, or both.

Considering the number of such criticisms and the airing that they have received, even a mere summary of the issues involved would necessitate a whole article, so I will leave this can of worms alone. However, I am convinced that even a reader only casually glancing at the entries in Table 2 will come to the conclusion that some of the criticisms must be correct. Many of the behaviors that have been used as dependent variables are so esoteric as to strain both credibility and the logic that links them to theoretical ideas supposedly being tested in the experiments in question [some recent claims to the contrary, for example, by Berkowitz and Donnerstein, 1982, notwithstanding]. (For example, what is the purpose of dependent measures which are merely "expressive", in that neither the anger instigator nor anyone else is harmed in the slightest? Presumably, aggressive behavior would not have become such a research focus if the term referred merely to people muttering to themselves, fantasizing, and harmlessly flailing about when no one is in sight, unless these behaviors are highly correlated with the probability of inducing physical, emotional, or economic harm in others--and that remains to be demonstrated.) And the number of empirical attempts to obtain correlations among even the most popular measures (not to mention systematic attempts to examine the external and construct validity of such measures) remains to date woefully small (Shemberg, Leventhal, & Allman, 1968, and Williams, Meyerson, & Eron, 1967, are the only--and rather modest--exceptions).

2. Taking into account the extent to which sub-jects have a choice not to aggress at all. Dependent measures that have been used differ in an important, but frequently unrecognized or unacknowledged, way--namely, in the extent to which subjects have a choice not to aggress at all. This factor may well affect the subjects' behavior when it is examined across blocks of trials. For example, in the Buss procedure, the subject--short of discontinuing his/her participation in the experiment--must aggress, by delivering an elec-tric shock to the confederate on each trial, and the question is just one of the intensity (shock level) that is chosen. The meaning of a dependent measure of aggression in a situation where refraining from aggres-sion altogether is not one of the choice alternatives becomes debatable. Moreover, the escalation over blocks of trials that is frequently observed in studies using the Buss procedure may well be an artifact, or at best a spurious by-product of the fact that the choice not to aggress had been eliminated (cf. Konečni & Ebbesen, 1976). In contrast, in the Doob-Konečni pro-cedure (see Table 2), although there is perhaps an implicit pressure to aggress in that some of the confederate's "creative" responses are so poor that they would not meet anyone's criterion of creativity (and, so, that at least some shocks are in order), the subjects are nevertheless free not to give any shocks at all, and some indeed do not.

3. Sequential collection of dependent measures. Many studies of aggressive behavior have used more than one dependent measure, either in the same mode (e.g., two different verbal measures) or in a different mode (e.g., a verbal and a behavioral measure, or a behavioral and a physiological measure). Since the different measures in most cases have had to be col-lected sequentially, the issue that arises is whether the subject's behavior on one measure changes his/her behavior on the subsequent measure, over and above the effect that the independent variable has on the second measure. The problem is an almost direct extension of Heisenberg's original formulation of the "uncertainty" principle in physics--the effect that the measurement of a particle's position has on its velocity and its measurement (and vice versa).

Just as most theories of aggressive behavior have been insufficiently developed to predict complicated patterns across a multitude of dependent measures, so have investigators remained silent on the topic of order effects (order in the sense of collection of dif-ferent dependent measures, rather than administration

26

of independent variables). This is odd, given that studies using more than one measure are the rule, rather than an exception; thus, the order of collection must have been either randomly chosen in the various studies, or the investigators have had implicit theories about its effects that they could not, or have not wished to, verbalize in their experimental reports. When the order-of-collection was systematically examined [by Konečni and Wood (1982), for one behavioral (physical aggression) and two verbal (ratings of self, ratings of the confederate) measures], it proved to be highly important, both statistically and interpretively.

There are several straightforward solutions to the order-of-dependent-measures problem. The simplest way out is to collect secondary measure(s), or "checks on the manipulation", after the main measure, and not read too much into the meaning of such checks or secondary measures (because of their possible "contamination" by the collection of the main dependent measure). A preferable solution is to obtain secondary measures (e.g., physiological ones) and checks on the manipulations in extensive pretesting or in separate experimental conditions in which the main dependent measure is not collected. The best solution clearly is to treat the order of collection of dependent measures as an explicit experimental variable and to formally incorporate this variable in one's theoretical model of aggressive behavior. All of this seems elementary but is unfortunately often ignored.

In some studies, a related, and potentially even more serious, methodological blunder is committed. In part because of the difficulties associated with operationalizing the opportunity to (a) express verbal aggression and (b) fantasize aggressively as independent variables, the distinction between independent and dependent variables is blurred in these studies, raising a host of interpretive problems. What is claimed to be an independent variable (one group of subjects does something, whereas the control group does not) is, in fact, not that, because each subject assigned to the group which supposedly receives the treatment (does something, for example, aggresses verbally, or fantasizes aggressively) is allowed to perform as much as he wishes (i.e., receive the treatment ad libitum), which is, of course, a characteristic of dependent variables. In other words, each subject assigned to a treatment condition decides on the "dosage" he is to receive, which leads not only to a greater variability within groups, but also--more seriously--precludes meaningful comparisons of groups (both within and across studies) which have allegedly received identical

27

treatments.

Examples from some landmark studies are as glaring as those that can be found in countless more humble efforts buried in the human-aggression literature. In a study by Berkowitz (1960), a "check or the manipulation" was first obtained--a measure of the subject's liking for a person who had attacked them (the same rating was used as the baseline for the second measure of liking obtained later). Subjects were then randomly assigned to either a TAT-fantasy or a self-descriptive questionnaire condition, and this was treated as one of the two main independent variables; yet, in both conditions, the subjects were allowed to behave on an ad libitum basis (e.g., fantasize what and as much as they wanted; respond in whichever way they wanted on the questionnaire). Finally, a second measure of liking was obtained and reported as a change score from the first measure. In an experiment by Feshbach (1955), the subjects' ad libitum TAT fantasy (vs. work on a neutral intellectual task) was similarly treated as a major independent variable and the examination of its effects on the subsequently collected verbal measures (the subjects' opinion of the insulting experimenter expressed through a sentence-completion task and an attitude questionnaire) was the chief objective of the study. Worchel's (1957) insulted subjects were allowed to express as much verbal aggression as they chose (to the insulting experimenter or his assistant), and the effect of this "independent" variable on the main dependent measure (the subjects' performance on the digit-symbol task) was compared to a control condition (talking to the experimenter about a neutral topic). The insulted subjects in an experiment by Thibaut and Coules (1952) were either given or not given an opportunity to send a note back to the insulting person (in the former case the subjects could include as much or as little aggressive content as they pleased) before another verbal dependent measure was collected. Finally, in another often-cited experiment by Berkowitz, Green, and Macaulay (1962), subjects first received either six shocks or one shock from a "fellow-subject", and then either evaluated that person's performance on a task (by giving him shocks ad libitum) or had no opportunity to give shocks. This procedure was both explicitly labeled as a "check or the manipulation" (of the 6- vs. 1-shock variable), and treated as an independent variable expected to affect the two subsequently collected dependent measures (ratings of the "fellow-subject's" friendliness and ratings of own state).

Most of these five classic studies (and many others) had the order-of-collection problem, in addition to confusing the notion of an independent and a dependent variable: Their results, from a strict philosophy-of-science standpoint, are uninterpretable. Moreover, they have collectively established an unfortunate methodological precedent in the aggression literature.

(c). Combined (independent/dependent-variable) methodological problems: The "catharsis" controversy.

For several reasons, the issue of "catharsis" can easily be claimed to have occupied a central position in the human-aggression research of the last 45 years. I do not say this lightly, and certainly not because the thinking about this issue can be judged--with the benefit of hindsight-- to have been terribly profound or correct, starting with the "classical" positions (Aristotle, Plato), and on to the "Renaissance" (Freud), the "Reformation" (the Yale group, 1939-41), the "Romantic" period (Feshbach, 1955-61), the "Neoclassical" period (Berkowitz, 1962-69, Geen, Hokanson, Holmes, Kahn), and the various "moderns" (e.g., A. N. Doob, Konečni, Zillmann). Nor do I think that the folk wisdom regarding catharsis, and its derivatives in political, anthropological, psycho-historical, legal, psychotherapeutic, social, journalistic, and other kinds of thinking have been particularly illuminating or socially beneficial.

Rather, the facts of the matter are: Catharsis (a) has been at some point addressed by just about every researcher who has published an article on human aggression, (b) has been implicated in literally a dozen of other dominant themes in the human-aggression research (ranging from the effects of media violence, and portrayals and availability of erotica, on aggressive and criminal behavior, to the short- and long-term effects of participation in body-contact sports), and, most importantly, (c) has been associated with a three-stage experimental design (induction of frustration-anger/expression of aggression/measure of residual aggression) that can be used to summarize effectively the purpose and the results of literally hundreds of studies in the human-aggression literature.

In large part, the popularity of the concept stems from its long standing as a research issue. Moreover, since almost everyone interpreted "catharsis" to mean some sort of reduction in something vaguely anti-social (aggression, heightened drive, etc.), it became the researchers' social duty to comment on this method of "control" of undesireable emotions, drives, and behaviors, and to have a strong stand--for or against-

29

-its "truth" and effectiveness.

It is precisely the popularity (or, rather, the notoriety) of the concept of catharsis that makes it a good candidate for illustrating how closely the methodological and theoretical issues are intertwined in the human-aggression research--especially with regard to the combined independent/dependent-variable methodological problems.

The catharsis controversy can be understood in large part by realizing that at its core lie the various researchers' staunch, though most often unacknowledged, allegiances to either the Platonic or the Aristotelian versions of the catharsis hypothesis. These two versions are radically different, however, and the differences lie precisely in what the relevant independent and dependent variables are thought to be, and, above all, what the outcome of putting them together would be.

Aristotle (in Poetics) was of the opinion that watching the performance of tragedies--which have the ability to arouse pity, anger, and fear--would purge such emotions in the spectators and provide a healthy relief. In modern terms, the observation of violent displays should lead to a decrease in arousal level and the degree of negative emotions.

Plato (in The Republic) had this advice for men made angry: "(I)f one man is angry with another, he can take it out of him on the spot, and will be less likely to pursue the quarrel further"--a far more sophisticated (and accurate) statement. Thus, the performance of aggressive actions, provided that one is angry, against the anger instigator, will decrease the probability of further violent actions.

The entire three-stage catharsis paradigm is outlined here: (1) an independent variable dealing with the induction of an aggression-relevant emotional state; (2) another independent variable specifying the type of "expression of aggression" that is relevant (aggression against a particular target); and (3) a specific dependent measure--behavioral aggression, again with the appropriate target specified (the original anger-instigator).

Note the differences between Aristotle and Plato in terms of the independent and dependent variables considered to be relevant, and in the predictions of what would happen when they are brought together. It is my contention that much of the catharsis controversy could have been avoided had the researchers not confused these two positions and their various ramifications in their theoretical thinking and experimental efforts (especially in the operationalization of the independent and dependent variables). Given this confusion and the formulation of various esoteric theoretical spin-offs, it is not surprising that what appears to be a mind-boggling mishmash of results was generated over the years. [The interested reader can consult Tables 1 and 2 for specific examples of esoteric operationalizations. A detailed discussion of the various versions of the catharsis hypothesis, and of the results and conclusions stemming from the research efforts which these different versions have inspired, are provided in Konečni (1975a) and need not be reiterated here. The same article also outlines--on the basis of empirical evidence--the bidirectional-causality anger-aggression feedback model; this model appears to be capable of accounting for most of the divergent results by making use of theoretical ideas that underlie the classifications in Tables 1 and 2 of the present paper.]

Discovering precisely why the confusion of Aristotle's and Plato's positions has occurred and tracing the history of the controversy--why, for example, researchers expected the manipulation of Aristotelian independent variables to produce a decrease in Platonic dependent measures (most "media-violence" studies can be thus characterized)--could be the subject of an entire paper. One reason for the confusion was undoubtedly the fact that both positions predicted a reduction--in terms of measures that (incorrectly) appeared to many to be interchangeable or synonimous. Another, and probably more important, reason may have been Freud's involvement with the concept. More specifically, one way to unify (or, rather, confuse) Aristotle's and Plato's positions was to assume that the internal (intrapsychic/physiological) mediator linking the Aristotelian independent and dependent variables was the same as that linking the inputs and outputs in Plato's model, namely, a "hydraulic" or "boiling pot" mechanism (which has always been associated with Freud, and subsequently with Lorenz). Yet, neither Aristotle's nor Plato's position necessarily requires such a mediator (cf. Konečni, 1975a); furthermore, both can be accounted by the anger-aggression feedback model which does not make any use of fluid mechanics.

In conclusion, I realize that some would claim that methodological and theoretical controversies and debates are healthy and that they advance science. Perhaps so--in the long run, and provided that the research efforts are cumulative. Whether the rather

elementary methodological and theoretical confusions
that have characterized the research or catharsis can
be thus described is a moot point. Moreover, I think
that the catharsis controversy has needlessly expended
valuable research efforts and exposed social
psychology's dirty linen (to the general public, the
funding agencies and Senator Proxmire), by virtue of
the fact that the various participants in the catharsis
debate have decided to make (confused and premature)
recommendations for changes in public policy, to tes-
tify in front of congressional committees, and so on.

In fact, the catharsis controversy is a good example both of the numerous links that exist among methodology, experimentation, theory, generalizations from
research, public policy, and the funding of science,
and of how these connections can become muddled.

Summary

The main purpose of this article was to demonstrate the remarkably close connections between the
methodological and theoretical issues in the human-
aggression research, and the extent to which the methodological negligence and naivete have needlessly
expended research efforts and led to time-wasting controversies and debates. A secondary objective was an
attempt to provide relatively elaborate classifications
of independent and dependent variables, respectively;
this attempt was guided mainly by the bidirectional-
causality anger-aggression feedback model and the
related theoretical positions. The implications of
these classifications for a variety of experimental and
theoretical issues, including several controversies of
long standing, were also discussed. When possible,
suggestions for avoiding common methodological, experimental, and interpretive pitfalls were made.

References

Arms, R. L., Russell, G. W., & Sandilands, M. L.
    Effects of viewing aggressive sports on the hostil-
    ity of spectators. Unpublished manuscript, Univer-
    sity of Lethbridge, Alberta, Canada, 1977.

Averill, J. R. Anger. Nebraska Symposium on Motiva-
    tion. Lincoln: University of Nebraska Press, 1978.

Baker, J. W., II, & Schaie, K. W. Effects of aggressing "alone" or "with another" on physiological and psychological arousal. Journal of Personality and Social Psychology, 1969, 12, 80-86.

Bandura, A. Aggression: A social learning analysis. Englewood Cliffs, N. J.: Prentice-Hall, 1973.

Bandura, A. Influence of a model's reinforcement contingencies or the acquisition of imitative responses. Journal of Personality and Social Psychology, 1965, 1, 589-595.

Bandura, A., Ross, D., & Ross, S. Transmission of aggression through imitation of aggressive models. Journal of Abnormal and Social Psychology, 1961, 63, 575-582.

Bandura, A., Ross, D., & Ross, S. Imitation of film-mediated aggressive models. Journal of Abnormal and Social Psychology, 1963, 66, 3-11. (a)

Bandura, A. Ross, D., & Ross, S. Vicarious reinforcement and imitative learning. Journal of Abnormal and Social Psychology, 1963, 67, 601-607 (b).

Baron, R. A., The influence of hostile and nonhostile humor upon physical aggression. Personality and Social Psychology Bulletin, 1978, 4, 77-80.

Baron, R. A., & Bell, P. A. Aggression and heat: The influence of ambient temperature, negative affect, and a cooling drink on physical aggression. Journal of Personality and Social Psychology, 1976, 33, 245-255.

Baron, R. A., & Bell, P. A. Sexual arousal and aggression by males: Effects of type of erotic stimuli and prior provocation. Journal of Personality and Social Psychology, 1977, 35, 79-87.

Bell, P. A., & Baron, R. A. Aggression and heat: The mediating role of negative affect. Journal of Applied Social Psychology, 1976, 6, 18-30.

Berkowitz, L. Some factors affecting the reduction of overt hostility. Journal of Abnormal and Social Psychology, 1960, 60, 14-21.

Berkowitz, L. Some aspects of observed aggression. Journal of Personality and Social Psychology , 1965, 2, 359-369.

Berkowitz, L. The frustration-aggression hypothesis

33

revisited. In L. Berkowitz (Ed.), Roots of aggression: A re-examination of the frustration-aggression hypothesis. New York: Atherton Press, 1969.

Berkowitz, L., & Donnerstein, E. External validity is more than skin deep. American Psychologist, 1982, 37, 245-257.

Berkowitz, L., & Geen, R. G. Film violence and the cue properties of available targets. Journal of Personality and Social Psychology, 1966, 3, 525-530.

Berkowitz, L., & Geen, R. G. Stimulus qualities of the target of aggression: A further study. Journal of Personality and Social Psychology, 1967, 5, 364-368.

Berkowitz, L., Green, J. A., & Macaulay, J. R. Hostility catharsis as the reduction of emotional tension. Psychiatry, 1962, 25, 23-31.

Berkowitz, L., & LePage, A. Weapons as aggression-eliciting stimuli. Journal of Personality and Social Psychology, 1967, 7, 202-207.

Berkowitz, L., & Rawlings, E. Effects of film violence on inhibitions against subsequent aggression. Journal of Abnormal and Social Psychology, 1963, 66, 405-412.

Bramel, D., Taub, B., & Blum, B. An observer's reaction to the suffering of his enemy. Journal of Personality and Social Psychology, 1968, 8, 384-392.

Buss, A. H. The psychology of aggression. New York: Wiley, 1961.

Buss, A. H., & Foliart, R. Role-playing aggression and the catharsis hypothesis. Unpublished manuscript, 1958. (Cited in Buss, 1961.)

Campbell, D. T., & Stanley, J. C. Experimental and quasi-experimental designs for research on teaching. In N. L. Gage (Ed.), Handbook of research or teaching. Chicago: Rand McNally, 1963.

deCharms, R., & Wilkins, E. J. Some effects of verbal expression of hostility. Journal of Abnormal and Social Psychology, 1963, 66, 462-470.

Donnerstein, E., Donnerstein, M., & Barrett, G. Where is the facilitation of media violence: The effects of nonexposure and placement of anger arousal. Journal of Research in Personality, 1976, 10, 386-

398.

Donnerstein, E., Donnerstein, M., & Evans, R. Erotic stimuli and aggression: Facilitation or inhibition. Journal of Personality and Social Psychology, 1975, 32, 237-244.

Donnerstein, E., & Wilson, D. W. Effects of noise and perceived control on ongoing and subsequent aggressive behavior. Journal of Personality and Social Psychology, 1976, 34, 774-781.

Doob, A. N., & Climie, R. J. The delay of reinforcement and the effects of film violence. Journal of Experimental Social Psychology, 1972, 3, 136-142.

Doob, A. N., & Kirshenbaum, H. M. The effects on arousal of frustration and aggressive films. Journal of Experimental Social Psychology, 1973, 9, 57-64.

Doob, A. N., & Wood, L. Catharsis and aggression: Effects of annoyance and retaliation on aggressive behavior. Journal of Personality and Social Psychology, 1972, 22, 156-162.

Ebbesen, E. B., Duncan, B., & Konečni, V. J. Effects of content of verbal aggression on future verbal aggression: A field experiment. Journal of Experimental Social Psychology, 1975, 11, 192-204.

Feshbach, S. The drive reduction function of fantasy behavior. Journal of Abnormal and Social Psychology, 1955, 50, 3-11.

Feshbach, S. The catharsis hypothesis and some consequences of interaction with aggressive and neutral play objects. Journal of Personality, 1956, 24, 449-462.

Feshbach, S. The stimulating vs. cathartic effects of vicarious aggressive activity. Journal of Abnormal and Social Psychology, 1961, 63, 381-385.

Fitz, D., & Stephan, W. G. Effects of direct or displaced cathartic aggression on subsequent aggression. Psychological Reports, 1976, 39, 967-973.

Fromkin, H. L., Goldstein, J. H., & Brock, T. C. The role of "irrelevant" derogation in vicarious aggression catharsis: A field experiment. Journal of Experimental Social Psychology, 1977, 13, 239-252.

Frost, R. O. & Holmes, D. S. Displaced aggression by

35

annoyed and nonannoyed subjects: Its effect on physiological arousal and subsequent aggression. Journal of Research in Personality, 1979, 13, 221-233.

Gambaro, S., & Rabin, A. I. Diastolic blood pressure responses following direct and displaced aggression after anger arousal in high- and low-guilt subjects. Journal of Personality and Social Psychology, 1969, 12, 87-94.

Geen, R., & Berkowitz, L. Name-mediated aggressive cue properties. Journal of Personality, 1966, 34, 456-465.

Geen, R., & Berkowitz, L. Some conditions facilitating the occurrence of aggression after the observation of violence. Journal of Personality, 1967, 35, 666-676.

Geen, R. G., & O'Neal, E. C. Activation of cue-elicited aggression by general arousal. Journal of Personality and Social Psychology, 1969, 11, 289-292.

Goldstein, J. H., & Arms, R. L. Effects of observing athletic contests or hostility. Sociometry, 1971, 34, 83-90.

Goldstein, J. H., Davis, R. W., & Herman, D. Escalation of aggression: Experimental Studies. Journal of Personality and Social Psychology, 1975, 31, 162-170.

Hanratty, M. A., Liebert, R. M., Morris, L. W., & Fernandez, L. E. Imitation of film-mediated aggression against live and inanimate victims. Proceedings of the 77th Annual Convention of the APA, 1969. Pp. 457-458.

Hanratty, M. A., O'Neal, E., & Sulzer, J. L. Effect of frustration upon imitation of aggression. Journal of Personality and Social Psychology, 1972, 21, 30-34.

Hapkiewicz, W. I., & Roden, A. H. The effect of aggressive cartoons on children's interpersonal play. Child Development, 1971, 42, 1583-1585.

Hartmann, D. P. Influence of symbolically modeled instrumental aggression and pain cues on aggressive behavior. Journal of Personality and Social Psychology, 1969, 11, 280-288.

Hicks, D. J. Imitation and retention of film-mediated aggressive peer and adult models. Journal of

Personality and Social Psychology, 1965, 2, 97-100.

Hokanson, J. E., & Burgess, M. The effects of status, type of frustration, and aggression on vascular processes. Journal of Abnormal and Social Psychology, 1962, 65, 232-237. (a)

Hokanson, J. E., & Burgess, M. The effects of three types of aggression on vascular processes. Journal of Abnormal and Social Psychology, 1962, 64, 446-449. (b)

Hokanson, J. E., Burgess, M., & Cohen, M. F. Effects of displaced aggression on systolic blood pressure. Journal of Abnormal and Social Psychology, 1963, 67, 214-218.

Hokanson, J. E., & Edelman, R. Effects of three social responses on vascular processes. Journal of Personality and Social Psychology, 1966, 3, 442-447.

Hokanson, J. E., & Shetler, S. The effect of overt aggression on physiological arousal level. Journal of Abnormal and Social Psychology, 1961, 63, 446-448.

Holmes, D. S. Effects of overt aggression on level of physiological arousal. Journal of Personality and Social Psychology, 1966, 4, 189-194.

Hornberger, R. H. The differential reduction of aggressive responses as a function of interpolated activities. American Psychologist, 1959, 14, 354.

Kahn, M. The physiology of catharsis. Journal of Personality and Social Psychology, 1966, 3, 278-286.

Kaplan, R. M., & Singer, R. D. Television violence and viewer aggression: A reexamination of the evidence. Journal of Social Issues, 1976, 32, 35-70.

Kenny, D. T. An experimental test of the catharsis theory of aggression. Ann Arbor: University Microfilms, 1953.

Konečni, V. J. Annoyance, type and duration of postannoyance activity, and aggression: The "cathartic effect." Journal of Experimental Psychology: General, 1975, 104, 76-102. (a)

Konečni, V. J. The mediation of aggressive behavior: Arousal level vs. anger and cognitive labeling. Journal of Personality and Social Psychology, 1975, 32, 706-712. (b)

Konečni, V. J. Perception and labeling of emotional states in oneself and others. Paper presented in the symposium "New perspectives in the research on emotion" at the 86th Annual Convention of the American Psychological Association, Toronto, Canada, 1978.

Konečni, V. J. Determinants of aesthetic preference and effects of exposure to aesthetic stimuli: Social, emotional, and cognitive factors. In B. Maher (Ed.), Progress in experimental personality research (Vol. 9). New York: Academic Press, 1979 (a).

Konečni, V. J. The role of aversive events in the development of intergroup conflict. In W. G. Austin & S. Worchel (Eds.). The social psychology of intergroup relations. Monterey, CA: Brooks/Cole 1979 (b).

Konečni, V. J. Crozier, J. B., & Doob, A. N. Anger and expression of aggression: Effects on aesthetic preference. Scientific Aesthetics/Sciences de l' Art, 1976, 1, 47-55.

Konečni, V. J., & Day, J. Competition and aggression. Unpublished manuscript, University of Califonia, San Diego, 1977.

Konečni, V. J., & Doob, A. N. Catharsis through displacement of aggression. Journal of Personality and Social Psychology, 1972, 23, 379-387.

Konečni, V. J., & Ebbesen, E. B. Disinhibition vs. the cathartic effect: Artifact and substance. Journal of Personality and Social Psychology, 1976, 34, 352-365. (a)

Konečni, V. J., & Ebbesen, E. B. External validity of research in legal psychology. Law and human behavior, 1979, 3, 39-70.

Konečni, V. J. & Franco, L. A test of Valins's reinterpretation of the Schachter-Singer results using visually-presented false heart-rate feedback and videotaped emotion-inducing sequences. Unpublished manuscript, University of Califonia, San Diego, 1974.

Konečni, V. J. & Frank, C. Effects of current and anticipated physical stress, and proprioceptive feedback from facial expression, on judgments of own emotional state. Unpublished manuscript, University of Califonia, San Diego, 1977.

Konečni, V. J. & Manley, J. The effects of anger, and the level of certainty that the anger instigator has been hurt, on aggressive behavior. Unpublished manuscript, University of California, San Diego, 1977.

Konečni, V. J. & Sargent-Pollock, D. A "facial-shadowing" (mimicking) procedure for studying the judgment of own emotional state in a "facial rumor" paradigm. Unpublished manuscript, University of California, San Diego, 1977.

Konečni, V. J. & Sargent-Pollock, D. Choice between melodies differing in complexity under divided-attention conditions. Journal of Experimental Psychology: Human Perception and Performance, 1976, 2, 347-356.

Konečni, V. J. & Spees, F. W. A comparison of effects of physical aggression, physical activity, and exposure to noise on subsequent aggression, with special attention to temporal and sequence parameters. Unpublished manuscript, University of California, San Diego, 1977.

Konečni, V. J. & Wood, S. The effects of aggressive and nonaggressive physical exercise on aggressive behavior. Unpublished manuscript, University of California, San Diego, 1982.

Konečni, V. J. & Zellensky, D. Effects of socially-induced emotional state and proprioceptive feedback from facial expression on aggressive behavior. Unpublished manuscript, University of California, San Diego, 1976.

Kuhn, D. Z., Madsen, C. H., & Becker, W. C. Effects of exposure to an aggressive model and "frustration" on children's aggressive behavior. Child Development, 1967, 38, 739-745.

Kulik, J. A., & Brown, R. Frustration, attribution of blame, and aggression. Journal of Experimental Social Psychology, 1979, 15, 183-194.

Laird, J. D., Self-attribution of emotion: The effects of expressive behavior on the quality of emotional experience. Journal of Personality and Social Psychology, 1974, 29, 475-486.

Lang, A. R., Goeckner, D. J., Adesso, V. J., & Marlatt, G. A. Effects of alcohol on aggression in male social drinkers. Journal of Abnormal Psychology, 1975, 84, 508-518.

Lanzetta, J. T., Cartwright-Smith, J., & Kleck, R. E. Effects of nonverbal dissimulation on emotional experience and autonomic arousal. Journal of Personality and Social Psychology, 1976, 33, 354-370.

Larder, D. L. Effect of aggressive story content on non-verbal play behavior. Psychological Reports, 1962, 11, 14.

Leak, G. Effects of hostility arousal and aggressive humor on catharsis and humor preference. Journal of Personality and Social Psychology, 1974, 30, 736-740.

Lövaas, O. I. Effect of exposure to symbolic aggression on aggressive behavior. Child Development, 1961, 32, 37-44.

Malamuth, N. M., Feshbach, S., Jaffe, Y. Sexual arousal and aggression: Recent experiments and theoretical issues. Journal of Social Issues, 1977, 33, 110-133.

Mallick, S., & McCandless, B. R. A study of catharsis of aggression. Journal of Personality and Social Psychology, 1966, 4, 591-596.

Mandler, G. Mind and emotion. New York: Wiley, 1975.

Mariaskin, M., Lupfer, M., & D'Encarnacao, P. The effects of alcohol and frustration on aggression and generosity. Paper presented at the 8th Annual Convention of the American Psychological Association, Washington, D. C. 1976.

Marlatt, G. A., Kosturn, C. F., & Lang, A. R. Provocation to anger and opportunity for retaliation as determinants of alcohol consumption in social drinkers. Journal of Abnormal Psychology, 1975, 84, 652-659.

Milgram, S. Behavioral study of obedience. Journal of Abnormal and Social Psychology, 1963, 67, 371-378.

Mueller, C., & Donnerstein, E. The effects of humor induced arousal upon aggressive behavior. Journal of Research in Personality, 1977, 77, 73-82.

Mussen, P., & Rutherford, E. Effects of aggressive cartoons on children's aggressive play. Journal of Abnormal and Social Psychology, 1961, 62, 461-464.

Nickel, T. W. The attribution of intention as a crucial factor in the relation between frustration and aggression. Journal of Personality, 1974, 42, 482-492.

Osborn, D. K., & Endsley, R. C. Emotional reactions of young children to television violence. Child Development, 1971, 42, 321-331.

Page, M. M., & Scheidt, R. J. The elusive weapons effect: Demand awareness, evaluation apprehension, and slightly sophisticated subjects. Journal of Personality and Social Psychology, 1971, 20, 304-318.

Parton, D. P., & Geshuri, Y. Learning of aggression as a function of presence of a human model, response intensity, and target of the response. Journal of Experimental Child Psychology, 1971, 11, 491-504.

Pastore, N. The role of arbitrariness in the frustration-aggression hypothesis. Journal of Abnormal and Social Psychology, 1952, 47, 728-731.

Pepitone, A., & Reichling, G. Group cohesiveness and the expression of hostility. Human Relations, 1955, 8, 327-344.

Rocha, R. F., & Rogers, R. W. Ares and Babbitt in the classroom: Effects of competition and reward on children's aggression. Journal of Personality and Social Psychology, 1976, 33. 588-593.

Rosenbaum, M. E., & deCharms, R. Direct and vicarious reduction of hostility. Journal of Abnormal and Social Psychology, 1960, 60, 105-111.

Rosenthal, R. Interpersonal expectations: Effects of the experimenter's hypothesis. In R. Rosenthal & R. L. Rosnow (Eds.), Artifact in behavioral research. New York: Academic Press, 1969.

Rule, B. G., Dyck, R., & Nesdale, A. R. Arbitrariness of frustration: Inhibition or instigation effects on aggression. European Journal of Social Psychology, 1978, 8, 237-244.

Rule, B. G., Ferguson, T. J., & Nesdale, A. R. Emotional arousal, anger, and aggression: The misattribution issue. In P. Pliner, K. Blankstein, & T. Spiegel (Eds.), Advances in communication and effect (Vol. 4). New York: Plenum, 1978.

Rule, B. G., & Nesdale, A. R. Emotional arousal and aggressive behavior. Psychological Bulletin, 1976, 83, 851-863.

Ryan, E. D. The cathartic effect of vigorous motor activity on aggressive behavior. Research Quarterly, 1970, 41, 542-551.

Sargent-Pollock, D. The effects of proprioceptive feedback from facial configuration on emotional experience. Unpublished doctoral dissertation, University of California, San Diego, 1978.

Schachter, S. The interaction of cognitive and physiological determinants of emotional state. In L. Berkowitz (Ed.), Advances in experimental social psychology (Vol. 1). New York: Academic Press. 1964.

Schwartz, G. E., Fair, P. L., Salt, P., Mandel, M. R., & Klerman, G. L. Facial muscle patterning to affective imagery in depressed and nondepressed subjects. Science, 1976, 192, 489-491.

Shemberg, K. M., Leventhal, D. B., & Allman, L. Aggression machine performance and rated aggression. Journal of Experimental Research in Personality, 1968, 3, 117-119.

Shuntich, R. J. & Taylor, S. P. The effects of alcohol on human physical aggression. Journal of Experimental Research in Personality, 1972, 6, 34-38.

Steuer, F. B., Applefield, J. M., & Smith, R. Televised aggression and interpersonal aggression of preschool children. Journal of Experimental Child Psychology, 1971, 11, 442-447.

Taylor, S. P. Aggressive behavior and physiological arousal as a function of provocation and the tendency to inhibit aggression. Journal of Personality, 1967, 35, 297-310.

Taylor, S. P. & Gammon, C. B. Effects of type and dose of alcohol on human physical aggression. Journal of Personality and Social Psychology, 1975, 32, 169-175.

Taylor, S. P. & Vardaris, R. M., Rawtich, A. B., Gammon, C. B., Cranston, J. W., & Lubetkin, A. I. The effects of alcohol and delta-9-tetrahydrocannabinol on human physical aggression. Aggressive Behavior, 1976, 2, 153-161.

Thibaut, J. W., & Coules, J. The role of communication in the reduction of interpersonal hostility. Journal of Abnormal and Social Psychology, 1952, 47, 770-777.

Turner, C. W., & Simons, L. S. Effects of subject sophistication and evaluation apprehension on aggressive responses to weapons. Journal of Personality and Social Psychology, 1974, 30, 341-348.

Turner, C. W., Simons, L. S., Berkowitz, L., & Frodie, A. The stimulating and inhibiting effects of weapons on aggressive behavior. Aggressive Behavior, 1977, 3, 355-378.

Walters, R. H., & Thomas, L. E. Enhancement of punitiveness by visual and audiovisual displays. Canadian Journal of Psychology, 1963, 17, 244-255.

Webb, E. J., Campbell, D. T., Schwartz,, R. D., & Sechrest, L. Unobtrusive measures: Nonreactive research in the social sciences. Chicago: Rand McNally, 1966.

Weiss, W. Effects of mass media of communuication. In G. Lindzey & E. Arouson (Eds.), The handbook of social psychology. Reading, Mass.: Addison-Wesley, 1969, Vol. 5.

Williams, J., Meyerson, L., & Eron, L. Peer-rated aggression and aggressive responses elicited in an experimental situation. Child Development, 1967, 38, 181-189.

Worchel, P. Catharsis and the relief of hostility. Journal of Abnormal and Social Psychology, 1957, 55, 238-243.

Zillmann, D. Excitation transfer in communication-mediated aggressive behavior. Journal of Experimental Social Psychology, 1971, 7, 419-434.

Zillmann, D. & Bryant, J. Effects of residual excitation on the emotional response to provocation and delayed aggressive behavior. Journal of Personal and Social Psychology, 1974, 30, 782-791.

Zillmann, D., & Johnson, R. C. Motivated aggressiveness perpetuated by exposure to aggressive films and reduced by exposure to nonaggressive films. Journal of Research in Personality, 1973, 7, 261-276.

Zillmann, D., Katcher, A. H., & Milavsky, B. Excitation transfer from physical exercise to subsequent aggressive behavior. Journal of Experimental Social Psychology, 1972, 8, 247-259.

THE MEASUREMENT OF HUMAN AGGRESSION

Robert M. Kaplan*

University of California, San Diego and
San Diego State University

INTRODUCTION

Most social psychology textbooks include a chapter on aggression. The chapters typically begin with a discussion of the
increase in the number of violent crimes and then proceed to
present psychological research which purportedly explains human
aggression. In this chapter I will examine the measures used in
this research and comment on the relevance of these approaches to
the understanding of the serious violent crime wave which has
caused concern in most western countries. The crux of this issue
is the definition and measurement of aggression.

The task of discussing the measurement of human aggression is
quite difficult because there are many different definitions of
aggression and investigators have employed many diverse techniques
for its measurement. Unfortunately it will only be possible to
provide a brief survey in the limited space provided here. Before
discussing specific measures, it will be necessary to provide an
overview of some of the basic psychometric issues associated with
measurement.

RELIABILITY AND VALIDITY

Measurement error occurs in almost all forms of observation.
For most qualities, there is a true score which we assume is

* The author gratefully acknowledges the comments of Neil
Malamuth, Rosaline L. Feierabend, and Howard Kushner on an earlier version of this paper.

44

Kaplan, R.M., Konečni, V.J., Novaco, R.W. (eds.) Aggression in Children and Youth
© 1984, Martinus Nijhoff Publishers, The Hague/Boston/Lancaster
ISBN 90-247-2903-3. Printed in The Netherlands

approximated by our measures. In most cases our observations or the observed score will not be exactly the same as the true score. The deviation of the observed score from the true score is measurement error. Reliability is the extent to which a score is free of measurement error.

Reliability is one of the most fundamental concepts in science. If measures of aggression are unreliable, it will be difficult to demonstrate that they correlate with other variables. Although this may seem obvious for advanced students of psychology, we will see many examples in which measures with poor or unknown relaibility are used in research settings.

More detailed discussions of reliability and the methods used to estimate it are available in a variety of text books (Anastasi, 1982; Kaplan and Saccuzzo, 1982; Lord and Novick, 1967; Nunnally, 1978).

The meaning of a measure of violence or aggression is established through the process of validation. In this process, we define the meaning of a particular measure through its correlation with other measures. For example, we would not assume that a test has any meaning until we could demonstrate that it behaved the way we would expect--it should correlate highly with other measures of aggression and it should not correlate highly with measures that are designed to measure some opposing behavior or characteristic.

There are different types of validity which are associated with different types of evidence for the meaning of a measure. Content validity refers to the extent to which the items on a measure are representative of the area of content the measure purports to represent. Criterion validity is the correlation between the measure and some well-defined outcome used as a conceptual anchor. If the criterion is measured at some future point, the correlation is a predictive validity coefficient and if it is obtained at the same point in time it is a concurrent validity coefficient. Often there is no specific criterion against which to evaluate the measure. Instead the measure is correlated with many different measures and the nature of the observed relationships is used to define the meaning of the measure. This process is called construct validation. Reliability and validity are intimately related. Poor reliability attenuates correlations. Thus it is impossible to demonstrate that an unreliable measure is valid.

MEASURES OF AGGRESSION

There has been considerable confusion and debate over the types of behaviors which should be classified as aggressive. Most of us would agree that aggression is behavior that results in harm to a person or his/her property. Much of the debate centers around the issue of intent. Dollard Doob, Miller, Mowrer, and Sears (1939) defined aggression as, "A response having for its goal the

45

injury of a living organism" (p. 11). This definition centers around intent to harm. Confusion often results from situations which result in injury to some individual when injury had not been the original goal. Consider the football lineman who, while attempting to block a kicked ball, breaks the kicker's leg. The intent was to deflect the ball and not to harm the kicker. A definition of aggression emphasizing behavior which resulted in harm would have captured this incident as an act of aggression. A definition including "intent to harm" as a necessary condition would not have tabulated this as an act of aggression. The difficulty with intent definitions is that they employ cognitive constructs which can not be directly observed.

Several authors have made the distinctions between different types of aggressive behaviors (Buss, 1961, 1971; Edmunds and Kendrick, 1980; Moyer, 1968, 1971). One of the most important distinctions--between instrumental and hostile aggression--was proposed by Feshbach in 1964. Instrumental aggression is aggressive behavior used in the pursuit of some non-aggressive goal. Aggression is an instrumental act leading to the attainment of some desired goal, such as money, sexual enjoyment,etc. In pure cases of instrumental aggression, anger and hostility are at a minimum. A wife who kills her husband solely in order to cash in his life insurance policy or a boxer who fights for titles and prizes may be exhibiting instrumental aggression. The act of injuring someone else is not a reinforcer for the behavior. Instead, the behavior is sustained by some other reward or its expectation.

Hostile aggression is motivated by anger or rage. Instead of aggression being an instrumental response to obtain nonaggressive reinforcement, aggression itself becomes reinforcing with the specific reinforcer being the perception of injury to the object of the anger. The goal is the infliction of pain or injury on another person, group, or object. A jealous husband who attacks his wife's lover or a frustrated boy who throws a rock at his schoolmate would exemplify hostile aggression (Feshbach, 1964).

Most aggressive acts contain elements of both hostile and instrumental aggression. Although either type rarely occurs in its pure form, the theoretical distinction is, nevertheless, quite useful.

Rating Scales

In their attempt to measure aggressive behavior, a great number of researchers and clinicians have chosen paper and pencil scales. Edmunds and Kendrick (1980) provided a comprehensive review of the available paper and pencil measures. These include the Iowa Hostility Inventory (Moldawsky, 1953), the Cook and Medley (1954) Hostility Scale, the Manifest Hostility Scale (Siegal, 1956), The Hostility Scale of the Autobiographical Survey (Sarason, 1958), the Green and Stacey Aggression and Hostility Questionaire (Green and Stacey, 1958), the Schultz (1954) Hostility

46

and Aggression Scales, the Zaks and Walters (1959) Aggression Scale, the Need Aggression Scale (Edwards, 1954), the Hostility and Direction of Hostility Questionare (Caine, Foulds and Hope, 1967).

After careful consideration of each of these scales, Edmunds and Kendrick (1980) concluded that few had sufficient validity. For example many of the aggression scales do not include items which adequately represent the domain of aggression (content validity). In addition, many of the aggression scales are validated against measures that do not appear to meaningfully describe instrumental or hostile aggression. The Iowa Hostility Inventory, for instance, was validated against the the rate at which college students learned "hostile" or "neutral" words (Smith, 1954). Few of the studies demonstrate that the scales are in any way predictive of observed aggressive behavior.

The scales mentioned in the last paragraph are rarely used in contemporary research. Today the two paper and pencil measures to receive the most widespead usage are the Buss-Durkee Inventory and the Myer-Megargee Inmate Typology. These two approaches will be considered briefly.

1. The Buss-Durkee Inventory. Some years ago, Buss and Durkee (1957) developed a scale which would classify different types of aggressive and hostile responses. Hostility was viewed as a verbal response expressing ill will or negative evaluation of people and events. The scale included seven subscales. The different subscales are designed to represent different forms of aggression. Assault and Verbal Aggression represent direct active aggression. Negativism was included to tap direct passive aggression. Indirect aggression represents active but indirect aggression, and Resentment and Suspicion are included to reflect hostility.

Buss and Durkee attempted to included items similar to those in several other paper and pencil measures to adequately sample content and they employed the care to control for social desirability. Still, the evidence for the Inventory's validity has not been impressive. Although some studies have shown that components of the Buss-Durkee Inventory may correlate with performance on some learning tasks, there is very little evidence that the scales correlate with observable aggressive behavior (see Edmunds and Kendrick, 1980). There is some evidence that the Inventory does correlate with other verbal measures (Geen and George, 1969).

Edmunds and Kendrick (1980) employed a variety of different questionaires including the Buss-Durkee in a massive validation trial. Their goal was to find the relationship between the Buss-Durkee Inventory and measures of aggressive behavior, ratings of aggression, involvement in criminal activities, and performance on laboratory aggression machines. In a large factor analysis of this battery they discovered two major factors for male respondents: aggressiveness and hostility. The results of factor

47

analysis for female groups were not as clearly interpretable.

The major finding of the study was that the paper and pencil scales were not related to observable aggressive or violent behaviors. In summary, paper and pencil scales of aggressiveness do not appear to be promising for the elucidation of the causes of real life aggressive behavior. This apparently is also the conclusion of many active researchers and journal editors. As a result, the use of paper and pencil scales has been on the decline in recent years.

2. The Meyer-Megargee Profile Megargee and his colleagues (Megargee and Bohn, 1979; Myer and Megargee, 1977) have performed a variety of multivariate studies on convicted criminals using the Minnesota Multiphasic Personality Inventory (MMPI). On the basis of these studies, Megargee has characterized the violent criminal as an "overcontrolled" individual who is capable of exploding with bursts of violent rage. He has also suggested that unique MMPI profiles distinquish reactive/aggressive criminals from those who might be prone to becoming victims. This information is useful to correctional staffs who wish to separate potentially assaultive criminals from those who might become their victims.

Despite widespread acceptance of Megargee's classification system by the American corrections community, there is still some doubt about the reliabity and validity of this approach. The instability of MMPI scores has been observed in many different studies (see Kaplan and Saccuzzo, 1982 for review). This general finding has been applied directly to the Megargee profiles. In one study, inmates at a Federal corrections institute in Memphis, Tennessee (USA), were tested and classified using the Megargee system. In nearly all (92%) an unambigious classification was obtained. Yet when these same inmates were retested on the average of 10 months later, only 28% retained their original classification (Simmons, Johnson, Grouvier, and Muzyczka, 1981). Although there is some evidence for the validity of the Megargee system (Megargee, 1977; Megargee and Bohn, 1979; Edinger, 1979), there is also reason for concern about the consequences of its use. The MMPI assumes that characteristics are stable over time. Prisoners classifed by the system may find themselves in particular circumstances (which might be difficult to reverse) on the basis of a personality test which may not reflect their current state of functioning. Further, the capability of the MMPI for predicting specific behaviors in the future is quite poor (Mischel, 1978).

In summary, paper and pencil measures have several limitations which may restrict their value in scientific investigations. In recent years, many investigators have selected laboratory measures of aggressive behavior as an alternative.

LABORATORY MEASURES

Aggression Machines

Perhaps the most widely used measure of aggression in laboratory studies is the Iowa Aggression Machine. The machine purportedly can be used to deliver electric shocks and has several levels associated with increasing intensities of shock. In the original experiments using the machine, a confederate and a subject arrived at the lab simultaneously. The experiment was described as an investigation of the effects of punishment upon learning. The confederate was assigned to be the learner in an experiment and the subject to be the teacher. Each time the confederate made an error, the subject was free to shock him or her and to choose what level of shock to deliver (see Buss, 1961 for details). Actually no shocks were given because the machine was not really hooked up. However, the subject believed the shocks reached their target.

Records are made of the intensity and the duration of the imagined shocks. In most experiments using the machine, social conseqences for aggression are absent. In many cases, the subject knows that his victim will not have a chance to retaliate. The subject is actually told to deliver shocks, and the measure is the frequency or magnitude.

There has been considerable debate about the validity of the Iowa machine as a measure of aggression. The machine has been used in an impressive number of studies which demonstrate that the same variables associated with aggression in real life settings are also associated with aggression as measured by the machine (Konecni, 1975). For example, many experiments clearly demonstrate that angry subjects will deliver more intense and longer duration shocks than non-angry subjects (Baron, 1977). Similarly, the majority of assaults and murders are associated with arguments (FBI Uniform Crime Reports, 1980). Although some experiments have shown that violent criminals will give higher intensity shocks than college students (Wolfe and Baron, 1971), other investigators have been unable to demonstrate similar relationships (Edmunds and Kendrick, 1980).

Attempts to validate the aggression machine against other measures of aggression have produced mixed results. Although some argue for the validity of the approach (Shemberg, Leventhal, and Allman, 1968) there is little empirical evidence on the issue. Shock measures seem to correlate reasonably well with similar laboratory measures (Walters and Brown, 1963) but may not correlate with self-ratings of anger or other forms of emotional expression (Liebowitz, 1968).

Tom Wylie, a San Diego State University student, recently summarized all laboratory studies of aggression reported in major journals over the last three years. In the process, Wylie recorded whether the author discussed the validity of the measure. He found that only two recent authors even mentioned validity and

49

no author provided any evidence that his or her measure supported any generalization beyond the laboratory. However, this did not preclude several of these authors from offering such implications. Berkowitz and Donnerstein (1982) proclaim that laboratory measures are valid but cite little new evidence to support their point. Although they did review some studies supporting the validity of the shock machine, they neglected to cite the ones supporting opposing conclusions (Edmonds and Kendrick, 1980).

Most experiments employing the aggression machine provoke subjects to anger and the experiment assesses the extent to which they believe they are retaliating via the machine. But is retaliation really aggression? One series of experiments suggests that retaliation may not be labeled as aggression by observers. In three experiments naive observers read descriptions of experiments in which the aggression machine had been used as the dependent measure. Upon reading these descriptions, observers only came to label acts as aggressive if the subjects returned more electric shocks than they had received from a provoker. However, in studies employing the aggression machine the mean number of shocks given by subjects is almost always lower than the number they had received. It appears that the behaviors which social scientists are quite willing to label as aggressive might not be identified as aggressive by naive observers (Kane, Joseph, and Tedeschi, 1976).

The debate about the meaning of scores from experiments using the aggression machine is certain to continue. However, the use of the machine may not. Today, well informed college students have typically seen a film about Milgram's (1974) obedience experiments that shows a similar use of deception. In addition, concerns about the rights of human subjects have led many investigators to abandon approaches that require deception.

The Bobo-Doll Measure

Perhaps the best known laboratory experiment was conducted by Bandura, Ross, and Ross (1961, 1963a, 1963b). In these experiments preschool children observed an adult aggressive model who performed either live (group 1) or on film (group 2). A third group watched a film of an aggressive cartoon character. No film was shown to a control group. In the live and film conditions, the adult model attacked a large Bobo-doll while screaming "Sock him in the nose...hit him down...throw him in the air..."and "pow" (p. 5). Over a series of experiments it was demonstrated that young children who had witnessed this scene either live or on film had a higher probability of attacking the doll themselves. This effect was particularly evident when the presentation included a segment in which the adult was rewarded for her attack on the doll (Bandura, Ross, and Ross, 1963c). These experiments are often taken as a demonstration that viewing TV violence causes aggressive behavior. That issue will be addressed in Dr. Singer's presentation (this volume). In this paper, I will focus only on the validity of attacks on an inflatable doll as a measure of aggression.

Aronfreed (1969), Feshbach and Singer (1971), Kaplan and Singer (1976), and many others have challenged the proposition that hitting a Bobo-doll (Bandura's measure of aggression) is representative of aggressive behavior. Neither the model nor the imitating child damages the doll. There is no damage to person or to property. Hitting a doll in the laboratory or playing with "aggressive" toys does not carry the same consequences as, for instance, hitting another child in a school yard. The behaviors observed in the imitation experiments might be better character- ized as solitary aggressive play.

In defense of the Bobo-doll measure, Hanratty, Liebert, Morris, and Fernandez (1969) claimed that attacks on dolls gen- eralize to live human beings. Children who had observed a model attack a nonreactive adult dressed in a clown costume which was designed after the Bobo- doll were subsequently more likely to assault the live costumed human. Although the Hanratty et al. results are suggestive, they must be interpreted cautiously. The presence of an adult dressed as a Bobo-doll may not have activated the ordinary social sanctions against aggression. In fact, it may have invited a playful "aggressive" response by signaling to the child that the adult would not retaliate against him. Clowns in circuses are often hit with no retalitory consequences as a sort of fun aggression. In addition, the level of aggression against the live Bobo was much less than that observed with the plastic doll.

The differences between the Bobo-doll measure of aggression and real destructive behavior are more clearly apparent in a doc- toral dissertation by Ross (1972). In this study, two measures of aggressive imitation were used to evaluate the effects of violent cartoons. Kindergarten boys and girls were shown either a violent cartoon, a nonviolent cartoon, or no cartoon. Observations of two categories of aggression were recorded separately. One category was normative aggression, such as hitting a Bobo-doll or pounding a hammer. This category describes behavior similar to that observed in the social learning experiments. The other category was "transgressive" aggression and involved destructive behaviors such as throwing a dart at a Bobo-doll. Although children who had seen violent cartoons scored higher on normative play, there were no differences between groups for transgressive aggression. The models in the cartoons, however, had engaged in inapppropriate aggressive behavior. Thus, Ross's data suggest that cartoon modeling may affect aggressive play but it may not generalize to any destructive behavior.

Other attempts to demonstrate that attacks on Bobo-dolls gen- eralize to other behaviors have similarly been unsuccessful. Leifer and Roberts (1972) attempted to replicate some of the early social learning experiments using a different measure of aggres- sion. Their measure was a response hierarchy which asked children which type of response was appropriate in a variety of provoking situations. A variety of statistical maneuvers were used to demonstrate that manipulation of the same independent variable would affect the new measure and the Bobo-doll measure in the same way. However, they were unable to demonstrate this relation. Which of the two measures (Bobo or response hierarchy) has greater meaning? Although it has been difficult to demonstrate that the Bobo measure correlates with other forms of aggressive behavior, the response hierarchy physical aggression scores correlate relatively well with teacher ratings for "overt aggression in the school environment". Thus there appears to be greater support for the external validity of the response hierarchy.

I do not want to diminish Bandura's extremely important demonstration that children learn novel behaviors through observation. In fact, cognitive social learning theory may be the best explanation for the acquisition of aggressive behavior. The difficulty is in using Bobo-doll assaults as the measure of aggression. There is very little evidence that data obtained with this measure can support the inferences we may be required to make about real life aggressive behavior. These statements may be better supported by research which employs naturalistic measures of aggression.

Naturalistic Measures

Rating scales, aggression machines, and Bobo-doll measures all appear to be unable to account for large portions of the variance of aggressive behavior outside of the laboratory. Because of these limitations, there has been a reawakening of interest in naturalistic measures of aggression. Naturalistic measures include behavioral observations of aggression in natural settings (Feshbach and Singer, 1971; Patterson, et al., 1967), self ratings of anger, likelihood of attack or aggression (Novaco, 1976; Olweus, 1980), and peer ratings of aggression (Eron, 1980). All of these approaches have considerable advantage over laboratory measurements because they require little generalization. However, we must consider some of the objections to the use of naturalistic measures.

Naturalistic measures of aggression come in many forms and before we can discuss specific issues it is necessary to delineate different forms they may take. Olweus (1980) distinguishes three types of data which are summarized in the following table:

Type of Data	Source
S data	self reports
R data	global rating by observer
T data	rated by observer in a Test situation

The major distinction between R data and T data is that the former refers to more general, often personality, judgments while the latter considers observations of specific behavior categories in either naturalistic or laboratory settings. One of the issues commonly raised in relation to the measurement of aggression is that such measures of aggression may not predict behavior in specific situations (Mischel, 1968). The issue of stability of personality has been considered in several recent papers (Bem and Funder, 1978; Epstein, 1979; 1980; Olweus, 1980).

One of Mischel's major criticisms is that behavior is not consistent from one situation to another. In addition, he was concerned that personality tests and ratings by observers (R data) may not be predictive of observed behavior in laboratory tests (T data). Because of these discrepancies, Mischel assumed that the test and rating data were defective. Based on these observations, Mischel suggested that measures which evaluate personality traits are without value. In support of this view, Mischel reviewed data showing that behavior in particular situations was difficult to predict.

Mischel's monograph had a major impact upon the field of personality assessment. Many personality researchers and clinical psychologists gave up measuring traits. However, within the last few years there has been a revival of interest in trait measures (Bem and Funder, 1978; Epstein, 1979, 1980; Olweus, 1973, 1980). One of the most important studies demonstrating the stability of personality was reported by Olweus (1973, 1974, 1977, 1980). Two hundred and three boys were rated on their tendency to start fights and on other characteristics of aggressive behavior. The ratings were obtained when the boys were in the sixth grade and then again three years later. In each case, at least 3 raters were used (and in some cases as many as ten were used). Aggressive behaviors were shown to be stable over the three year period (coefficient of stability = .66). When the effects of rater bias were statistically controlled the observed stability of aggressive behavior became even stronger (coefficient of stability = .80). These data suggest that aggressive behavior can be demonstrated to be a stable personality characteristic. The results are in conflict with Mischel and the reason for the discrepancy may be explained by traditional psychometric theory.

One of the reasons Mischel (1968) and others may have had so much difficulty demonstrating that personality measures do not predict behavior in particular situations is that the situational measures are not reliable. The more particular the situation the less representative it is of the domain it is purportedly sampled from. Simple laboratory tests might be thought of as analogous to one item tests. In other words, situational tests are unreliable personality measures. In a variety of different studies it has been shown that when larger samples of behavior are taken at several points in time or when scores from several types of observations are averaged together, the stability of personality estimates increases.

The problems of inconsistency across situations and of instability over time may both result from measurement error. More reliabile measures can be created by averaging together behavior across several situations. In addition, this average behavior from one point in time might be a good predictor of the average behavior (over the same situations) at another point in time. In a series of studies, Epstein (1979, 1980) has demonstrated that as measures of behavior are averaged over an increasingly larger group of behaviors, the stability of personality increases.

Olweus (1980) has shown that different types of data do not correlate highly with one another, but that there is a high degree of consistency within similar data types. Although S data may not be predictive of T data, there is a fair degree of stability of S data over the course of time. Similarly there is a fair degree of stability for T data and R data when each of these is reliably measured.

GENERAL VIOLENCE INDEXES

A number of general violence indexes have appeared in the literature. The most general of these are the indexes designed to evaluate the amount of violence on television. These include the Gerbner Index and other TV violence indexes. Other general violence indexes include indices of international violence and indexes of crime.

Gerbner's Violence Index

The Gerbner Violence Index is the best known and most widely discussed system for coding television violence. Gerbner has been active in this area for nearly fifteen years and his work has been very influential in the United States Congress. After hearing from the 1972 US Surgeon General's task force, Senator Pastore actually requested that the US Department of Health, Education and Welfare (now the the Department of Health and Human Services) publish the Gerbner index as a national statistic (Rubinstein, 1976).

Gerbner and his colleagues pride themselves on excluding subjective perceptions and dramatic subtleties from their analysis. Instead, they prefer to record, "...gross, unambiguous, and commonly understood facts of portrayal." They argue that these more gross measures are commonly understood among the heterogeneous public which composes the television audience (Gerbner, Gross, Jackson-Buck, Jeffries-Fox, and Signorielle, 1978).

Violence Defined. Gerbner and his colleagues define violence as, "The overt expression of physical force, with or without a weapon, against self or other, compelling action against one's will on pain of being hurt or killed, or actually hurting or killing" (Gerbner et al., 1978, p. 12). According to this view of violence, acts of aggression must; 1)be directed at a human being or human-like being, 2) hurt or kill or at least threaten to hurt or kill, and 3) be "clear unambiguous and overt physical violence."

Units. Gerbner's system, which he sometimes calls the Message Analysis System, reports three types of units for the analysis of television content: 1) programs, 2) violent action, and 3) characters. Programs refer to single fictional stories confined to a single television presentation. Violent action is some violence between persons shown in a particular scene. An act ends when a new violent character enters the scene or if there is some change in time. However, violent action interruped by a flashback or some other change of scene, is still counted as the same violent action if the script returns to the same scene. Characters in television drama are divided into two categories: major and minor. Major characters are those in "principal roles essential to the plot" while minor characters are all others in speaking roles. Nearly all of the analyses reported by the Gerbner group refer only to major characters.

Calculation of Index. The calculation of the violence index is relatively straightforward once certain terms are defined. The important terms are defined in Table 1.

Despite the care and effort which went into the development of the system, several methodological problems must be considered. The most important is that the components of the index are not independent. Rate per program and rate per hour, which are dependent upon one another, are both major components of the index. It would be unlikely that rate per program would be high while rate per hour would be low. The problem with including two components which are not independent is that any differences between networks are magnified. In effect, frequency (R/P) is counted and then it is counted again to the extent that frequency is represented in saturation (R/H). %P, Which is the other term in equation 1, is also not independent of frequency or saturation. For those programs in which there is no violence the rate per program and the rate per hour are, by definition, zero.

As shown in the first equation, the nonindependent terms for (R/P) and (R/H) are weighted by an arbitrary coefficient of 2. According to Gerbner et al. (1978) this is done to "raise their relatively low numerical value to the importance that the concepts of frequency and saturation of violence deserve" (p.21). The introduction of the weights represents an arbitrary judgement on the part of Gerbner and his colleagues. Apparently early data revealed that the rates per program and the rates per hour were low. In effect, the formula doubles the frequency of low probability events.

According to Gerbner et al., "the program score gives the greatest weight to the extent to which violence prevails at all in the programs, secondary weight is given to the frequency of violence and the saturation of the programs with violent action" (p. 21). The formula, however, supports the opposite of this assertion. Actually, the program score gives twice as much weight to the frequency and saturation measures as it does to the percentage of programs involved with violence. The reason for Gerbner's

Table 1

COMPONENTS OF THE GERBNER VIOLENCE INDEX

Term	Definition
Prevalence	Percent of all programs (broken down by network) containing any violence.
%P	An indicator of prevalence expressing percent of program hours containing violence.
Violent episodes	Scenes of violence confined to the same characters.
Rate per Program (R/P)	The number of violent episodes divided by the number of programs. This yields a measure of frequency.
Rate per Hour (R/H)	The number of violent episodes divided by the number of hours. This gives a measure of saturation.
%V	Percent of all characters involved in violence either as perpetrators or as victims.
%K	Percent of all characters involved in killings either as the killer or the killed.

Using these definitions, a program score is then calculated using the following formula:

$$PS = (\%P) + 2(R/P) + 2(R/H)$$

A character score (CS) is obtained as:

$$CS = (\%V) + (\%K)$$

The violence index is the sum of equations (1) and (2). It can be expressed as:

$$VI = CS + PS$$

$$= (\%P) + 2(R/P) + 2(R/H) + (\%V) + (\%K)$$

remark is apparently that the percentage of programs (%P) indicator usually obtains the highest numerical values.

The problems with independence which were apparent in formula (1) are even more obvious in formula (2). The terms (%V) and (%K) can in no way be viewed as independent. A character involved in killing is also involved in violence and is therefore counted in both categories. A closer look reveals that this nonindependence problem actually creates an arbitrary weighting system. The term (%V) or percent involved in violence can be decomposed into two subcomponents. Some of the characters have been involved in killing (%K) and others have not (%K'). So we can say that

$$\%V = \%K + \%K'$$

Substituting this into (2) we obtain

$$CS = \%K + \%K' + \%K$$

$$= 2\%K + \%K'$$

In words, the formula for CS is equivalent to weighting each character involved in killing twice as high as a character not involved in killing. Again this is an arbitrary weighting system which may or may not represent the way viewers conceptualize TV violence.

In summary, Gerbner's violence index is a composite which sums together nonindependent components. The program score and the character scores include some of the same components and these are weighted arbitrarily in the composite. The system, which is often noted as objective, depends upon a weighting system which is entirely arbitrary and subjective. In order to obtain scores for the different networks, the system is used on a single week sample of television programs. Applications of the system have met some strong objections because it does not make distinctions between different types of violent action. For example, family variety programs often receive high violence scores because of playful hits among characters.

Measures of International Violence

There have been a variety of attempts to quantify the amount of violence which occurs within a country. These indexes must depend upon archival data such as the events published in newspapers or events recorded in public documents. One of the difficulties with using public documents is that it requires combining many events which may be qualitatively different. For example, one country may have more assassinations but fewer political demonstrations. The decision as to whether the two countries differ in degree of political unrest depends upon frequency of events and the weights attached to them.

One approach to this problem uses a solution similar to that used in current versions of TV violence indexes. Feierabend, Feierabend and Nesvold (1972, 1973) built an elaborate system to evaluate cross-national patterns in political violence. In an impressive effort, they reviewed archival sources (such as Deadline Data on World Affairs and Encyclopedia Britannica Yearbooks) and tallied every act of political violence in each of 84 nations around the world. These events were combined into a violence score through several steps. First events were placed within ranges representing qualitative intensity of violence. Within these ranges, index scores were obtained by multiplying the frequency of events by a weighting factor and summing across the event categories. The weighting factors were determined in scaling studies using 7-point rating scales from 0 for events reflecting political stability to 6 for events reflecting political instability. The criteria for assigning these weights emphasized the amount of violence accompanying the action, the number of persons involved, the degree of expected political repercussions of the event for the society as a whole, and the duration of the situation. In all 16 characteristics of each event were recorded. Feierabend et al. report that the typical scale positions for the events were: 0 for a regularly scheduled election, 1 for the dismissal or resignation of cabinet officials, 2 for peaceful demonstration or arrest, 3 for assassination of non chief of state or sabotage, 4 for assassination of chief of state or terrorism, 5 for coup d'etat or guerrilla warfare, and 6 for civil war or mass execution. The reliability of the system has been evaluated in several studies. For example the correlation between ratings in the Feirabend's system and those obtained by Gurr (1968) from different sources was .70. The profiles do not appear to be dependent on a particular data source since profiles obtained from Deadline Data and from the New York Times Index correlate highly (r = .8). Finally there does not appear to be a bias toward large countries with more extensive news coverage. The correlation between population size and political violence was only .12 (Feierabend, et al., 1973). In summary, the system has been very successful for aggregating large masses of data, relating international incidents to substantive theory, and providing useful descriptions of cross- national political violence.

Crime Rates

Crime rates are the most common statistic used in criminology research. In the United States crime reports have become part of the daily news and most citizens have some familarity with the crime rates in their city or town. However, the fallibility of crime statistics is well known and widely documented (Douglas, 1967). Nearly all analyses are based on data from the Federal Bureau of Inventigation Uniform Crime Reports. This report summarizes the crimes tallied by local police units. Each year these reports demonstrate that the frequency of crime is on the increase. Since the reports began in 1933, the introductory sentence in each annual report suggests "This year major crimes reached a new high in the United States". The report also

58

includes a crime time clock telling how many crimes are committed each minute. Each year the clock ticks faster (Doleschal, 1979).

Reading the Uniform Crime Report would lead us to believe that the crime rate is excelling beyond any tolerable limit and that larger budgets are required for law enforcement. However, there are other explanations for the increases in crime. One of them is that crime reporting rather than actual crime which is increasing. In 1973 the United States Bureau of the Census began a large random sample survey of crime victims. The purpose of the survey is to determine the rate of various crimes in an unbiased fashion. Each year since 1973 the survey has shown that a large proportion of crimes (as many of 70%) do not get reported to the police and are therefore not part of the FBI reports. The most interesting finding is that since the beginning of the survey the rates of violent crimes have been remarkably stable. For example the rate of aggravated assault has been approximately 10 per 1,000 U.S. inhabitants (over the age of 12) since 1973. There appears to be no evidence of a large increase in crime and the more serious crimes also seem to be the most stable over years. The big increase has been in crime reporting. Similar findings have been obtained in Denmark, Sweden, Finland, and Norway (Doleschal, 1979).

Causes of increased crime reporting may sometimes be the paradoxical result of increased attention to law enforcement. For example, Campbell (1969) described the increase in arrests for larceny in Chicago before and after the introduction a new "tough on crime" police chief. Early analysis shoowed that larceny increased when the police got tough. However, after more detailed study, it was shown that the new chief caused a greater tendency to report the crime. Officers were encouraged to report all violations--including many they had formerly overlooked.

Another problem in the use of crime statistics is the failure to employ age adjustment. Most crimes are committed by persons within a defined age band. During certain periods there are more of these individuals available to commit crimes. Thus, the big increase in murder in the 1970's may simply reflect the fact that there were more individuals in the murder sensitive age range during that period. A more detailed discussion of this problem will be presented by Turner, et al. (this volume).

In summary, several general violence indexes have been proposed. The most general of these attempt to neatly summarize the amount of violence shown in television drama. Unfortunately many methodological issues must be resolved before data obtained with these methods can be taken seriously. These methods do show promise as a means of aggregating diverse sources of data, and similar approaches have met with some success as crude estimates of the amount of violence in cross-national studíes of political violence. Crime rates have not been shown to be reliable sources of information. However, random sample surveys of crime victims may provide more accurate data on probabilities of different

59

```
39 │ 1  Chile                    Homicide Per 100,000
38 │                             Stem and Leaf Display
37 │                                (units=tenths)
36 │
35 │
34 │
33 │
32 │
31 │
30 │ 0  Nicaragua
   ═
20 │ 5  Thailand
19 │
18 │
17 │
16 │
15 │
14 │ 4  Paraguay
13 │
12 │
11 │
10 │
 9 │ 24  USA, Argentina
 8 │ 6  Venequela
 7 │
 6 │
 5 │
 4 │
 3 │ 49  Bermuda, Cuba
 2 │ 2  Hungry
 1 │ 012223334467  Sweden, Japan, Peru, Egypt, West Germany, Italy, Poland, Iceland,
   │                 Austria, Luxembourg, Isreal, Phillipines
 0 │ 15567789  Iran, Denmark, Spain, Greece, Norway, Switzerland, Netherlands, Ireland
```

Fig. 1.   Stem and leaf display showing the murder rates for various countries. Data were obtained from the World Health Organization.

criminal offenses.

Measuring the Impact of Violence

The probability of being murdered is actually quite small. In the United States, there were approximately 20,000 murders last year. The United States is one of the most probable places to be murdered. Among NATO countries, our murder rate is not exceeded. Figure 1 is a stem and leaf display (Turkey, 1978) showing the number of murders in various countries around the world based on World Health Organization data. Notice that the murder rates tend to be similar in most European countries. The larger murder rates in the world tend to be in the Americas. The simple notion that murders occur more often in underdeveloped countries is not entirely supported by these data. In addition, there appear to be remarkably large differences between countries in the number of murders. If we believe these data, the chances of being murdered in Chile are 391 times as great as the chances of being murdered in Iran. Yet recent newscasts in the United States present Iran as a much more dangerous place to be.

One of the major problems with the use of the international classification of death data is that we have no assurance that physicians around the world apply uniform policy in certifying causes of death. This problem is well known to epidemiologists who have documented instances of changing certification practices (NIH, 1979).

Although the use of murder statisitics entails many problems, they are still the "hardest" data we have available on the incidence of aggression in various countries. In addition, the chances of being murdered appear to be a major factor in the quality of life for inhabitants of different communities. In the next section I will argue that the subjective probability of being murdered has a large unmeasured impact upon the quality of life.

Quality of Life

What are the chances of being murdered? In the United States these chances are greater than in all but a few of the countries in the world community. We are frequently labeled the "most violent society in the world" or a "brutal nation". Indeed these labels are supported by our relatively high murder rate. In light of this concern, it is worth asking how probable it is to be murdered in the United States. The answer is: quite improbable. Among the 1.8 million deaths in the United States last year, about 20 thousand were the result of murder. About forty-three percent of these murders were associated with quarrels between people who knew each other (42.9%). As I will argue, most citizen concern is about being murdered in the course of a robbery or being killed by someone with unknown motives.

How common is it to be the victim of a stranger with unknown motives? According to recent (1979) American FBI uniform crime

61

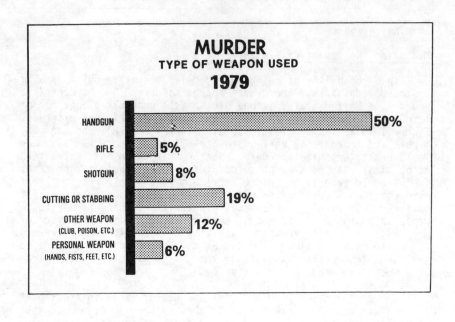

Fig. 2. Types of weapons used in murders.
         Source: FBI Uniform Crime Report, 1979.

Question: "Why did that person in your household buy a handgun or pistol?"

[Percent]

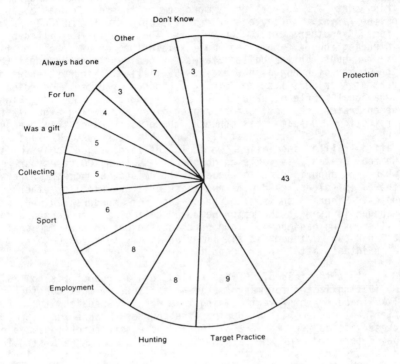

Fig. 3. Reasons gun owners list for owning a handgun or pistol in
         the United States.
         Source: Sourcebook of Criminal Justice, 1979.

statistics, 17.7% of 1979 murders were in this category. Among the 20,591 murders this comes to an estimated 3645 cases. Is this a large number? Probably not. As a cause of death, murders of this sort are only slightly more common than death due to cancer of the larynx. In any one year more people die from kidney infections. Another great concern is that we may be killed by an intruding robber. This fear may explain the great proliferation of handguns in the United States. Recent estimates suggest that the number of handguns now exceeds 55 million. Figure 2 shows the reasons Americans list for owning a handgun or pistol according to a national sample of handgun and pistol owners. As the Figure demonstrates, the most common reason given for owning a gun is for protection. Despite this concern, there is evidence that handguns are rarely used successfully for this purpose. In fact, the National Rifle Association, which is the largest gun lobby in the United States, is able to document less than 100 cases per year when a handgun is used to successfully defend a home. However, there is clear evidence that these guns are used for other purposes. Figure 3 shows the percentage of murders in which a handgun is used as the major weapon. Half of all murders are committed using handguns. A gun purchased to defend the home against an unknown intruder is six times as likely to be used to kill an acquaintance after an argument.

Since the fear of being killed by a robber is a major motivating factor for many American families, we must consider the likelihood of this event. Using 1979 data it appeared that 2163 Americans were killed during the course of robberies. Some of these victims were robbers, although the exact proportions can not be determined from the data. The chances of death resulting from a robbery are less than the chances of death from an infection of the subcutaneous tissue. Tuberculosis, which is considered by many public health officials as a nearly extinct disease, claims more lives per year than murders associated with robberies. Death from any type of murder is less probable than death due to cancer of the pancreas, which is considered to be a rare cite for malignant disease. Excluding murders involving intimate friends, the chances of being murdered in the United States are about the same as the probability of dying in an accidental fall. Suicide still surpasses homicide as a cause of death in nearly all NATO countries.

I do not want to suggest that we should be unconcerned about murder. Yet it does appear that fear of being murdered is exaggerated in the daily behavior of most American citizens. There is evidence that similar reactions are occurring throughout western Europe. In the next section I will suggest that this fear produces a disproportionate impact upon the quality of life.

A Health Index

During the last eight years some colleagues and I have developed a general quality of life measure in order to evaluate public health and medical programs (Kaplan and Bush, 1982; Kaplan, Bush and Berry, 1976, 1978, 1979). The Index classifies individuals into well defined levels of functioning for particular days. Then each state is weighted by the perceived desirability of the state in the eyes of random samples of community members. For example, people see being confined to the house because of illness as about .6 on a scale ranging from 0 to 1.0. In other words being confined to the house is about 60% of the distance between death (the bottom of the scale) and perfect functioning (the top of the scale). If a person is confined to bed for an entire year, then we would say that their life has been 40% (1.0-.6=.4) less desirable or that they have lost .4 years. Two people in a state rated as .5 for one year each have lost the equivalent of .5 years. Together they have lost the equivalent of 1 year of life. Using this system we have been able to estimate the number of well year equivalents various health programs produce.

The health index system might also be used to estimate the direct and the indirect effect of murder. For example, murder may be only as common as cancer of the pancreas, but it is more likely to occur early in the life cycle. With a mean age of 34 years murder victims lose an average of 41 years of life. This calculation is based on current life expectancy, conditional upon age, obtained from U.S. Vital Statistics. In contrast, cancer of the pancrease victims are typically struck later in life (mean = 61) and therefore lose only 18 years. Child and youth victims are most severely hit. Child abuse victims lose an average of 72 life years (based upon current life expectancy). These figures consider only deaths and not diminished quality of life associated with violence.

In an indirect way fear of victimization may contribute to decreased quality of life. A public opinion poll published by Newsweek (March 23, 1981) revealed that 64% of Americans report that they stay home at night in order to avoid being victimized. For sake of argument let us say that the quality of life for these approximately 140 million people is diminished by 10% because of their fear. This means that over the course of one year they might lose the equivalent of 14 million life years (.1 X 140,000,000=14,000,000/years).

For the sake of argument, let us suppose that we could implement a public policy which would reduce the fears by one half. This might alter the desirability of the lives of the affected individuals to 5% less desirable than optimal as a function of their concern. The net effect of this policy would be .05 X 140,000,000=7,000,000/years or the equivilant of 7 million life years.

What type of policy might have this sort of effect? One possibility is very strict regulation of handguns. The impact of a strict gun policy is difficult to evaluate. In one quasi-experimental evaluation, Pierce and Bowers (1981) examined the impact of the Bartley-Fox law which created a mandatory one year prison term for carrying a firearm in Massachusetts. The law resulted in a reduction in robberies in which the assailant used a gun. Robberies in which other weapons were used increased, but not enough to offset the decreases in gun robberies. Gun homicides decreased with no increase in other weapon homicides. Evaluations of other gun control laws, such as the District of Columbia's Firearms Control Regulations Act of 1975, also were favorable. Yet, the studies evaluating these laws had many methodological problems (Jones, 1981). Other mandatory sentencing for firearm violence laws have been evaluated less favorably (Loftin and McDowall, 1981). Within a large country, such as the U.S., people can move from jurisdiction to jurisdiction with little difficulty. Thus, an effective policy must apply to all jurisdictions.

One policy under consideration in the United States is the Kennedy-Rodino Handgun Crime Control Act. The bill has several provisions including: 1) a hault to the manufacture and sell of "Saturday Night Specials" which are 22 calibur pistols that have little or no value for hunting, 2) requiring a waiting period and check of handgun purchaser, 3) establishment of mandatory jail sentences for possession of a handgun, 4) improvement of handgun record keeping, 5) encouragement of states to pass licence-to-carry laws, 6) makes licencing of handgun manufacturing and distribution more difficult and expensive.

The costs of this policy are difficult to determine. Shields (1981), a major advocate of the law argues that most of the costs of the law would be born by the increased fees for licencing and manufacturing guns. The major administrative chores and costs would be given to the industry. Based on an analysis by Philip Cook of Duke University, Shields estimated that the net cost of the Kennedy-Rodino law from public sources would be $4.2 million (without considering inflation from 1981 dollars). This does not include costs of prison terms, but it also ignores the economic benefits of preventing murders and assualts. In order to be conservative and to include many costs ignored by Shields, this figure was multiplied by 5 to obtain a cost of $21 million. If the policy reduced the handgun murder rate by 10 percent, it would yeild approximately 10000 handgun victims X 41 (average years lost) = 41,000 years, without even considering quality of life. At a cost of $21 million this would produce a life year at $512. Thus, by even the most conservative standards, it sould be very cost/effective. If quality of life benefits are considered the cost per year ratio approaches zero. However, the public costs of this program may have been underestimated and the effectiveness overestimated. Skepticism about the efficacy of gun control legislation is plentiful (Kaplan, 1981). A truely effective policy might require a radical departure from current proposals.

In order for a gun control policy to be effective, it might be necessary to offer a bounty to recall the circulating guns. This could be done by offering $1000 for the return of any handgun--no questions asked. Such a program might actually serve as an incentive for criminals to steal guns from one another in order to retrieve the reward. Current data suggests that guns are stolen in a significant number of robberies (Moore, 1981). The cost of the program to reclaim 50 million guns would be 50 million X $1000= $50 billion dollars (plus administrative costs). This large sum is well less than one quarter of what the United States spends annually for defense.

Dividing the cost of the program by the number of years it produces gives the cost/effectiveness ratio. Suppose the program improved quality of life for fear victims by 10% and yeilded 7 million years. The cost/effectiveness ratio would be 50 billion over 7 million. The ratio reduces to $7143 to produce the equivilant of a year of life (Weinstein and Stason, 1977). In comparison to what is ordinarily spent on effective health care programs this is not expensive. Hypertensive screening, which is promoted as one of the most cost/effective preventive medicine measures, is estimated to cost $10,000 to produce the equivilant of a year of life. Renal dyalisis, which is a very effective medical treatment for kidney failure is estimated to cost $50,000 to produce the equivilant of a year of life. A radical public policy toward guns may actually improve the quality of life for many individuals to the point that it can be shown as cost/effective as many accepted public policies.

This analysis is highly speculative and depends upon many unverified assumptions. It might be argued that the possession of guns reduces fear for many individuals and that removing these arms may actually reduce rather than improve the quality of life. The point of this example is that it is worthwhile to think of indirect effects of violence and aggression in addition to the more direct and observable effects. After reviewing the literature on violence, a French commission concluded that the real impact of violence was the fear of victimization rather than actual harm done to citizens.

Conclusions

Aggression and violence remain major topics of behavioral research Although considerable effort has been devoted to the measurement of aggression, little consensus has emerged. Laboratory measures remain the most precise and reliable, yet serious questions have been raised about the validity of laboratory tasks, such as Bobo-doll assaults and shock machines.

Considerable evidence now supports the use of naturalistic observation of aggressive behavior in field settings. New evidence suggests that these observations can be valid, reliable, and may be used to demonstrate that aggressive behavior is stable over

67

the course of several years. Similar methods used to assess the amount of violence shown in film and television share common benefits, but have not been satisfactorily developed at present.

Although used as the major source of data for many investigations in criminology, crime rates and FBI statistics suffer from many problems. Increases in crime may actually reflect increases in crime reporting. Survey data on victimization are considered a better data source for scholarly investigations.

In addition to direct measures of crime, it is worth considering the impact of crime on other behaviors. For example, many individuals report alterations in their daily activities because they fear victimization. One of the major consequences of violence and aggression may be the fear it instills in the people. Policy analysis may benefit from a consideration of the health and quality of life impacts of violence.

REFERENCES

Anastasi, A. Psychological Testing, Fifth Edition. New York: Macmillan, 1982.

Aronfreed, J. The problem of imitation. In L. P. Lipsitt and H. W. Reese (eds.), Advances in Development and Behavior (Vol. 4). New York: Academic Press, 1969.

Bandura, A., Ross, D. and Ross, S. A. Transmission of aggression through imitation and aggressive models. Journal of Abnormal and Social Psychology, 1961, 63, 575-592.

Bandura, A., Ross, D. and Ross, S. A. A comparative test of the status envy, social power, and secondary reinforcement theories of identificatory learning. Journal of Abnormal and Social Psychology, 1963, 67, 527-534, a.

Bandura, A., Ross, D. and Ross, S. A. Imitation of film-mediated aggressive models. Journal of Abnormal and Social Psychology, 1963, 66, 3-11, b.

Bandura, A., Ross, D. and Ross, S. A. Vicarious reinforcement and imitative learning. Journal of Abnormal and Social Psychology, 1963, 67, 601-607, c.

Baron, R. A. Human Aggression. New York: Plenum, 1977.

Bem, D. J. and Funder, D. C. Predicting more of the people more of the time. Psychological Review, 1978, 85, 485-561.

Berkowitz, L. and Donnerstein, E. External validity is more than skin deep: Some answers to criticisms of laboratory experiments. American Psychologist, 1982 37, 245-257.

Buss, A. H. The Psychology of Aggression. New York: John Wiley, 1961.

Buss, A. H. Aggression pays. In J. L. Singer (ed.), The Control of Aggression and Violence. New York: Academic Press, 1971.

Buss, A. H. and Durkee, A. An inventory for assessing different kinds of hostility. Journal of Consulting Psychology, 1957, 21, 343-349.

Caine, T. M., Foulds, G. A. and Hope, K. Manual of the Hostility and Direction of Hostility Questionnaire (H.D.H.Q.). London: University of London Press, 1967.

Campbell, D. T. Reforms as experiments. American Psychologist, 1969, 24, 409-429.

Cook, W. W. and Medley, D. M. Proposed hostility and pharisaic-virtue scales for the MMPI. Journal of Applied Psychology, 1954, 38, 414-418.

Doleschal, E. Crime--some popular beliefs. Crime and Delinquency, 1979, 25, 1-6.

Dollard, J., Doob, L. W., Miller, N. E., Mowrer, O. H. and Sears, R. R. Frustration and Aggression. New Haven: Yale University Press, 1939.

Douglas, J. D. The Social Meaning of Suicide. Princeton: Princeton University Press, 1967.

Edinger, J. D. Cross-validation of the Megargee et al. MMPI typology for prisoners. Journal of Consulting and Clinical Psychology, 1979, 47, 234-242.

Edmunds, G. and Kendrick, D. C. The Measurement of Human Aggression. Chichester, England: Ellis Horwood Limited, 1980.

Edwards, A. L. Manual for the Edwards Personal Preference Schedule. New York: Psychological Corporation, 1954.

Epstein, L. The self-concept: A review and the proposal of an integrated theory of personality. In E. Staub (ed.), Personality: Basic Issues and Current Research. Englewood Cliffs, N.J.: Prentice-Hall, 1979.

Epstein, S. The stability of behavior. II. Implications for psychological research. American Psychologist, 1980, 35, 790-806.

Eron, L. D. Prescription for reduction of aggression. American Psychologist, 1980, 35, 244-252.

Federal Bureau of Investigation. Uniform Crime Statistics. Washington: Government Printing Office, 1980.

Feierabend, I. K., Feierabend, R. L. and Nesvold, B. A. Social change and political violence: Cross-national patterns. In I. K. Feierabend, R. L. Feierabend and T. R. Gurr (eds.), Anger, Violence, and Politics: Theories and Research. Englewood Cliffs, N.J.: Prentice-Hall, 1972.

Feierabend, I. K., Feierabend, R. L. and Nesvold, B. A. The comparative study of revolution and violence. Comparative Politics, 1973, April, 393-424.

Feshbach, S. The function of aggression and the regulation of aggressive drive. Psychological Review, 1964, 71, 257-272.

Feshbach, S. and Singer, R. D. Television and Aggression. San Francisco: Jossey-Bass, 1971.

Geen, R. G. and George, G. Relationship of manifest aggressiveness to aggressive word associations. Psychology Reports, 1969, 25, 711-714.

Gerbner, G., Gross, L., Jackson-Buck, M., Jeffries-Fox, S. and Signorielli, N. Violence Profile Number 9: Trends in Network Television Drama and Viewer Conceptions of Social Reality, 1967-1978. Philadelphia: University of Pennsylvania, 1978.

Green, R. T. and Stacey, B. G. The development of a questionnaire measure of hostility and aggression. Acta Psychologica,.

1967, 26, 265-285.

Gurr, T. A causal model of civil striff: A comparative analysis using new indices. American Political Science Review, 1968, 62.

Hanratty, M. A., Liebert, R. M., Morris, L. W. and Fernandez, L. E. Imitation of film-mediated aggression against live and inaminate victims. Procedures of the 77th Annual Convention of the American Psychological Association. 1969, 4, 457-458.

Hanratty, M. A., O'Neal, E. and Sulzer, J. L. Effects of frustration upon imitation of aggression. Journal of Personality and Social Psychology, 1972, 21, 30-34.

Jones, E. D., III. The District of Columbia's "Firearms Control Regulations Act of 1975": The toughest handgun control law in the United States--Or is it? Annals of the Academy of Political and Social Science, 1981, 455, 138-149.

Kane, T. R., Joseph, J. M. and Tedeschi, J. T. Person perception and the Berkowitz paradigm for the study of aggression. Journal of Personality and Social Psychology, 1976, 33, 663-673.

Kaplan, J. The wisdom of gun prohibition. Annals of the Academy of Political and Social Science. 1981, 455, 150-168.

Kaplan, R. M. and Bush, J. W. Health-related quality of life measurement for evaluation research and policy analysis. Health Psychology, 1982, 61-80.

Kaplan, R. M., Bush, J. W. and Berry, C. C. Health status: Types of validity for an index of well-being. Health Services Research, 1976, 11, 478-507.

Kaplan, R. M., Bush, J. W. and Berry, C. C. The reliability, stability and generalizability of a health status index. American Statistics Association, Proceedings of the Social Statistics Section. 1978, 704-709.

Kaplan, R. M., Bush, J. W. and Berry, C. C. Health status index: Category rating versus magnitude estimation for measuring levels of well-being. Medical Care, 1979, 5, 501-523.

Kaplan, R. M. and Saccuzzo, D. S. Psychological Testing: Principles, Applications and Issues. Monterey, C.A.: Brooks/Cole Publishing, 1982.

Kaplan, R. M. and Singer, R. D. Television violence and viewer aggression: A reexamination of the evidence. Journal of Social Issues, 1976, 32(4), 35-70.

Konecni, V. J. Annoyance, type, and duration of postannoyance activity, and aggression; The "cathartic effect". Journal of Experimental Psychology: General, 1975, 104, 76-102.

Leifer, A. D. and Roberts, D. F. Children's responses to television violence. In J. P. Murray, E. A. Rubinstein and G. A. Comstock (eds.), Television and Social Behavior (Vol. 2). Washington, D. C.: U. S. Government Printing Office, 1972.

Liebowitz, G. Comparison of self-report and behavioral techniques of assessing aggression. Journal of Consulting and Clinical Psychology, 1968, 32, 21-25.

Loftin, C. and McCowall, D. "One with a gun gets two": Mandatory sentencing and firearms violence in Detroit. Annals of the Academy of Political and Social Science. 1981, 455, 150-168.

Lord, F. M. and Novick, M. R. Statistical Theories of Mental Test

Scores. Redding, M.A.: Addison-Wesley, 1968.

Megargee, E. I. A new classification for criminal offenders. Criminal Justice and Behavior, 1977, 4, 107-216.

Megargee, E. I. and Bohn, M. J. Classifying Criminal Offenders: A New System Based on the MMPI. Beverly Hills: Sage, 1979.

Megargee, E. I. and Dorhout, B. A new classification system for criminal offenders, III: Revision and refinement of the classifitory rules. Criminal Justice and Behavior, 1977, 4, 125-148.

Milgram, S. Obedience to Authority. New York: Harper and Row, 1974.

Mischel, W. Personality and Assessment. New York: John Wiley, 1968.

Moldawasky, P. A study of personality variables in patients with skin disorders. Unpublished doctoral dissertation, State University, Iowa. Cited in A. H. Buss (1961) The Psychology of Aggression, 1953.

Moore, M. H. Keeping handguns from criminal offenders. Annals of the Academy of Political and Social Science, 1981, 455, 92-109.

Moyer, K. E. Kinds of aggression and their physiological basis. Community Behavior and Biology, 1968, 2, 65-87.

Moyer, K. E. The Physiology of Hostility. Markham Press, 1971.

Myer, J., Jr. and Megargee, E. I. A new classification system for criminal offenders, II: Initial development of the system. Criminal Justice and Behavior, 1977, 4, 115-124.

National Institutes of Health. Epidemiology of respiratory diseases: Task Force Report on State of Knowledge, Problems, Needs (N.I.H. Publication No. 81-2019). Washington: National Institutes of Health, 1979.

Novaco, R. W. Anger Control: The Development and Evaluation of an Experimenal Treatment. Lexington, M.A.: Lexington Books, 1976.

Novaco, R. W. The cognitive regulation of anger and stress. In P. Kendall and S. Hollon (eds.), Cognitive-Behavioral Interventions: Theory, Research, and Procedures. New York: Academic Press, 1979.

Nunnally, J. Psychometric Theory. New York: McGraw-Hill, 1978.

Olweus, D. Personality and aggression. In J. K. Cole and D. D. Jensen (eds.), Nebraska Symposium on Motivation 1972. Lincoln: University of Nebraska Press, 1973, 261-321.

Olweus, D. Personality factors and aggression: With special reference to violence within the peer group. In J. de Wit and W. W. Hartup (eds.), Determinants and Origins of Aggressive Behavior. The Hague: Mouton Press, 1974.

Olweus, D. Aggression and peer acceptance in adolescent boys: Two short-term longitudinal studies of ratings. Child Development, 1977, 48, 1301-1313.

Olweus, D. Familial and temporamental determinants of aggressive behavior in adolescent boys--a causal analysis. Developmental Psychology, 1980, 16, 644-660.

Patterson, G. R., Littman, R. A. and Bricker, W. Assertive behavior in children: A step toward a theory of aggression. Monographs of the Society for Research in Child Develooment,

1967, 32, (5) whole, No. 113.

Pierce, G. L. and Bowers, W. J. The Bartley-Fox Gun Law's short-term impact on crime in Boston. Annals of the Academy of Political and Social Science, 1981, 455, 120-137.

Rubenstein, E. A. Warning: The Surgeon General's research program mayy be dangerous to preconceived notions. Journal of Social Issues, 1976, 32, 18-34.

Ross, L. B. The Effect of Aggressive Cartoons on the Group Play of Children. Unpublished doctoral dissertation, Miami University, 1972.

Sarason, I. G. Interrelationships among individual difference variables, behavior in psychotherapy, and verbal conditioning. Journal of Abnormal Social Psychology, 1958, 56, 339-344.

Schultz, S. D. A differentiation of several forms of hostility by scales empirically constructed from significant items on the Minnesota Multiphasic Personality Inventory. Unpublished doctoral dissertation, Pennsylvania State College. Cited in A. H. Buss (1961) The Psychology of Aggression, 1954.

Shemberg, K. M., Leventhal, D. B. and Allman, L. Aggression Machine performance and rated aggression. Journal of Experimental Research in Personality, 1968, 3, 117-119.

Shields, P. Guns don't die--people do. New York: Arbor House, 1981.

Siegal, A. E. Film-mediated fantasy aggression and strength of aggressive drive. Child Development, 1956, 27, 365-378.

Simmons, J. G., Johnson, D. L., Gouvier, W. D., Muzyczka, M. J. The Myer-Megargee Inmate Typology: Dynamic or unstable? Criminal Justice and Behavior, 1981, 8, 49-54.

Smith, K. G. Influence of failure, expressed hostility, and stimulus characteristics on verbal learning and recognition. Journal of Personality, 1954, 22, 475-493.

Turkey, J. W. Exploratory Data Analysis. Redding, M.A.: Addison-Wesley, 1977.

Walters, R. H. and Brown, M. Studies of reinforcement of aggression, III: Transfer of responses to an interpersonal situation. Child Development, 1963, 34, 563-571.

Weinstein, M. C. and Stason, W. B. Foundations of cost-effectiveness analysis for health and medical practices. New England Journal of Medicine, 1977, 296, 716-721.

Wolfe, B. M. and Baron, R. A. Laboratory aggression related to aggression in naturalistic situations: Effects of an aggressive model on the behavior of college student and prisoner observers. Psychonomic Science, 1971, 24, 193-194.

Zaks, M. S. and Walters, R. H. First steps in the construction of a scale for the measurement of aggression. Journal of Psychology, 1959, 47, 199-208.

DEVELOPMENT OF AGGRESSIVENESS: A MOTIVATION THEORY PERSPECTIVE

H.-J. Kornadt

University of the Saar, Saarbrücken, West Germany

The empirical investigation and theoretical understanding of the general development of aggressiveness and of individual differences is a difficult and still unsolved task. Difficulties concern empirical, but mainly theoretical, problems.

Three major problems are:
- The definition of aggression and the question whether one has to differentiate between hostile and instrumental aggression, since they may not follow the same rules.
- The concept of aggressiveness: to understand individual differences one has to assume a specific and enduring disposition. The nature of this disposition is unclear. In many cases the term "aggressiveness" is used in the sense of a global, unspecified concept.
- Likewise, the developmental process and its influential factors are still unclear. For further research we need less global and more differentiated functional hypothesis.

In the first half of this paper I will deal with these general points from the perspective of a motivation theory of aggression.

Referring to aggression seven years ago Willard Hartup (1974) and Seymour Feshbach (1975) pointed out how little we know about its developmental process. In the meantime some important works have been published. One is the longitudinal study by Lefkowitz and coworkers (1977). Additionally there are the two important articles by Olweus (1979, 1980). In the first he shows the remarkable stability of aggressiveness, and in the second one--by method of path-analysis--he comes an important step nearer the understanding of causal relationships between familial and

73

Kaplan, R.M., Konečni, V.J., Novaco, R.W. (eds.) Aggression in Children and Youth
© 1984, Martinus Nijhoff Publishers, The Hague/Boston/Lancaster
ISBN 90-247-2903-3. Printed in The Netherlands

temperamental factors, and aggressiveness.

But nevertheless, the central problem pointed out by Hartup remains unsolved. That is the theoretical understanding of the ontogenetic developmental process which must be seen within the frame of a general developmental theory. For that purpose we need, what Hartup (1974) called a "functional analysis". As long as we don't know how a disposition to aggress works in detail and why or how certain factors influence the development of aggressiveness, no precise hypothesis can be formulated and tested; empirical studies will bring us no more than quantitative relationships. Without an adequate theory their interpretation remains difficult.

One example from Olweus' study (1980) is the question whether a causal relationship between the temperament of the boys and the negative attitude of their mothers exists and, in which direction. This cannot be inferred from correlation scores only.

Therefore a functional theory is needed. It should comprehend a differentiated concept of aggressiveness, taking into account that there cannot be a uniform, monolithic trait. We know that several elements are involved in aggressive behavior, e.g. affective reactions, attributive processes, values and the like, as well as situational factors. The theory should explain the functional relationships between these factors.

Likewise, the theory should be able to avoid too global a view of the factors influencing the development and their function. Not only the employment of punitive, inconsistent, or power-assertive methods as such may be influential, but the context of their use and the age of the child may be very important.

MOTIVATION THEORY OF AGGRESSION

As a point of departure which may be helpful in this context, I want to propose a motivation theory of aggression as described earlier (Kornadt, 1974, 1981). A motive theory conceives of the disposition to aggression in terms of a motive system (Olweus, 1974, 1978; Feshbach, 1974). Its elaboration implies particular assumptions concerning the function and internal structure of the motive.

Aggressive behavior--insofar as it is not instrumental--is understood as specifically motivated. This motivation is a function of the enduring aggression motive and of situational conditions as they are subjectively assessed. This function can best be expressed by applying the formula developed by Atkinson (1964) for the function of achievement motive:

$$\text{Motivat.}_A = f\ (M_A \times E_A \times I_A) - (M_{aA} \times E_p \times I_p)$$

That is: The motivation for a specific aggressive act is a

74

function of the enduring aggression motive (M_A), the expectancy of success for the specific act (E_A), and the incentive of the specific aggression goal (I_A), minus the enduring motive to avoid aggression (= aggression inhibition) (M_{aA}), the expectancy of punishment (by external punishment or by guilt) (E_p), and the negative incentive of the punishment (I_p).

This model is also relevant in respect to the person-situation controversy, interpreting the relationship as an interaction of both.

The function of the motive can be understood in more detail by analysing the behavioral sequence from the first relevant cue to the performance of the aggressive act and its termination.

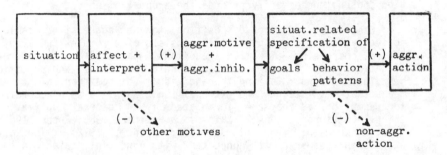

Fig. 1. Internal processes of aggression.

First, situational conditions which activate aggression-related affects must be given. These may be anger, but they can be positive affects, too.

Next, both--situation and affect--are cognitively structured and interpreted. If anger and/or aggression relevance is con-firmed, the enduring aggression motive becomes activated. This consists of an actualization of the generalized aggression goals and the stored capabilities of aggressive acts, of possible behavior patterns.

The next step is that these are specified according to the specific situation and that the incentives of several related acts are estimated. Let's take an example:

One may be travelling in a foreign country and may feel angered by somebody and intend to defend oneself. Thus, one has to decide what (aggressive) goal should be attained in the situa-tion, e.g. the person should become silent or polite and submis-sive or angry. One has to decide what kind of insulting state-ments, what specific words should be used as an instrumental act in order to reach the goal; and one has also to estimate whether one will be able to do this appropriately and successfully in the foreign culture.

75

Probably here the aggression inhibition comes in when possible negative incentives of the aggression goal are considered. These negative incentives may be connected with the expectation of retaliation by the other or with the subjective moral system which may lead to the judgment: aggression in general is stupid or unacceptable. The result can be a decision to act out this aggression, or another one, or not to be aggressive at all.

Since this sequence is similar to the model presented earlier in the conference by Konecni the difference between both models shall be underlined here.

First, in my conception, in addition to learned connections between situation and affect, also an innate, biologically rooted connection is assumed: a cognitive interpretation of the situation does not necessarily precede the arousal of anger.

Second, an enduring disposition to be aggressive, called motive-system, is assumed. It consists of a complex individual system, comprising affective reactions, patterns to interpret situations, aggressive goals and their incentives, and specific behavior patterns. Calling the individual disposition a motive means that its internal and external functioning is seen according to assumptions as they are formulated in a general motivation theory (Atkinson, 1964; Atkinson & Feather, 1966; Fuchs, 1963, 1976; Heckhausen, 1968, 1973, 1980; Weiner, 1972). Thereby, aggression research is connected with and integrated in the broader field of general motivation theory and research.

In addition, I want to underline, like Brandon Rule points out in her paper (1981), that the cognitive processes mentioned in the model are not to be seen as conscious; and that such processes may not be as time consuming as they appear.

This brief description shows that in the motivation theory aggressiveness is not treated as a simple trait, but as a complex system. It consists of two motive components:

On the one hand the approach component which I call the aggression motive. This is defined primarily by the intended goal: of hurting or impairing somebody, of violent removal of one's sources of frustration. Anticipating and attaining such goals is connected with positive emotional changes.

On the other hand the avoidance component, which I call the aggression inhibition. This is defined by the goal of avoiding aggression since aggression is connected with negative emotions like fear or guilt.

Each of these two components consists of many elements: situation-affect connections, attribution style for the interpretation of frustrations, generalized goals with positive, or sometimes negative incentives, stored aggressive behavior patterns, to mention only a few. Furthermore, the motive system does not by

76

itself induce aggressive behavior; it becomes effective only in interaction with situational conditions.

INDIVIDUAL DIFFERENCES IN AGGRESSIVENESS

Individual differences between high and low aggressive persons can therefore by analysed in a more differentiated way. In principle, they can exist in each of the two components: aggression motive and aggression inhibition.

Low overt aggressive behavior is ambiguous: it can be the result of a low aggression motive or of the combination of high aggression motive and high aggression inhibition. In this case the result will be high aggression conflict, as in the overcontrolled persons described by Megargee (1966). Individual differences as well can exist in each of the before-mentioned elements. Since this is important for understanding the development of aggressiveness I want to briefly mention some details.

Following the different steps of the sequence just mentioned:

At first a great interindividual variance in kind and number of cues eliciting anger, and in intensity of the affective reaction can be predicted. This is confirmed for instance in Olweus' study of bullies and whipping boys (1978). To the statement:

"I get angry with other people easily"

bullies agreed significantly more often than others.

Secondly, one can predict a great variance in preferred attribution styles for the interpretation of situation and affect. If one tends to interpret frustrations as caused by bad intentions of others as compared to interpreting them as harmless or funny, many more situations are viewed to be aggression relevant. These hypotheses have been confirmed by my own data (Kornadt, 1982).

Furthermore, variances in the generalized aggression goals and aggressive behavior patterns can be predicted. E.g.: For some people it is quite unlikely if not nearly impossible to set the goal of physically hurting another person. They would prefer goals like injuring other persons' self-esteem. For others, physical attack is not only much more likely, it may be almost the only goal they can imagine.

Aggression goals are moreover related to aggression relevant values and belief systems. The following items from Olweus (1978) may serve as an example:

"When a boy teases me I try to give him a good beating".
"Fighting is often the best way to solve conflicts".

Bullies accept these statements significantly more often than

others. Aggression behavior patterns comprise all motoric, verbal, and other behavior patterns which might be instrumental for
obtaining aggressive goals. They comprise skills to reach aggressive goals, such as physical strength and/or an appropriate verbal
repertoire. They comprise as well the degree of self-confidence
in using these skills successfully.

Furthermore, a variance in the related factors constituting
the inhibition component, especially negative values, can be
predicted. Examples from Olweus are statements like:

> "I think getting angry doesn't pay".
> "I think fighting is silly".

These items differentiate between aggressive boys and others, too.

Finally, as mentioned before, there is not only anger
involved as aggression related affect. Aggression can as well be
experienced as pleasurable, and therefore, a situation can elicit
positive expectations of being aggressive. An example from Olweus
could be:

> "I often think it is fun to make trouble".

DEVELOPMENT OF AGGRESSIVENESS

These assumptions about several functional elements of the
aggression motive system and of individual differences have very
important consequences for the question of how the motive system
will be developed generally and how its individual differences
will be manifested.

General Assumptions

These consequences can be formulated in terms of a few general assumptions:

1. The motive systems cannot exist in its complexity from the
    very beginning of the individual development. It must
    develop gradually according to the general process of per-
    sonality development.

2. There has to be a much simpler structure at the beginning of
    the developmental process. Its starting point must consist
    of quite a simple affective reaction (anger) to certain cir-
    cumstances (aversive events), which does not yet constitute a
    motive.

3. Different stages of the general development may be specifi-
    cally relevant for forming certain elements of the motive
    system. Therefore some elements will be developed earlier
    than others (e.g. affect conditioning vs formation of
    values).

4. The developmental processes in different stages follow predominantly different theoretical principles (e.g. conditioning vs concept formation). All these different theoretical principles are relevant for the aggression motive system and its theoretical explanation.

    That makes the motive theory an integrative approach. That is, it can comprise biological, conditioning, and cognitive processes, for example, in a systematic way.

5. According to which processes are predominant in various developmental stages, the function of the same influential factor will differ from age to age.

6. Though the developmental processes which form various elements of the aggression motive system primarily take place at different ages, the elements do not develop completely independently from each other. Elements developed at earlier developmental stages influence the later processes.

    In the following, I want to describe roughly the most important steps of development of the aggression motive.

Stages and Processes of Development

1. The point of departure for the development of aggressiveness must be seen in the first affective reaction to "frustration" or perhaps more to aversive events in the early childhood. Here, I assume an inherited, inborn, and biologically rooted connection, which most likely has individual differences. Later on learned connections occur, too. In this stage the aggression related behavior consists of simple affective reactions which can be called anger, maybe in temper tantrums, too (Hamburg & van Lawick-Goodall, 1974; Feshbach, 1970).

2. The next step will be a phase where simple anger-connected behavior patterns and their effects will be learned. The processes should be learning through conditioning by experiencing positive or negative consequences of affective reactions like in temper tantrums, in hitting, crying, kicking, biting or the like, especially, between children (Lambert, 1974; Hartup, 1974). It is not unlikely that these learning processes are facilitated by inherited specific "learning dispositions" (Eibl-Eibesfeldt, 1974). The effect of these processes can be seen as the first simple form of "aggressive behavior" (see also Turner's paper, 1981). Perhaps it should be better called "proto-aggressive" behavior, since its organization consists of more or less simple conditioned reactions, and an intention to hurt. A motive, according to our definition, is not yet developed; but there exist already aggression specific elements. According to Feshbach's (1964) differentiation, this is the stage of "hitting" and not yet "hurting".

3. An important cognitive development should take place together
    with the learning of first behavior patterns:
    The formation of a first, very diffuse but basic belief sys-
    tem concerning the person-environment-relationship: This
    should be very emotionally based. One either feels the world
    to be friendly and secure so that it can be trusted, or one
    feels the world to be unfriendly and hostile so that it has
    to be mistrusted; one is afraid and feels insecure, and
    learns somewhat later that one has to watch oneself and be
    ready for defense. Later, these feelings become a very
    important basis for the interpretation of events like frus-
    tration.

4. In order to develop the first real aggression motive,
    specific cognitive development steps are necessary. The gen-
    eral ability to understand events as the effect of one's own
    actions and to anticipate and to intend them is necessary but
    not sufficient. Insofar as aggression comprises acts aimed
    at hurting somebody, the following cognitions have to be
    developed too:

    - Understanding how harmful effects of one's own behavior can
      occur to other persons (by empathy; role taking).
    - Choosing just this effect, since it is somehow rewarding.
    - Understanding that aggression can be a means to remove
      frustrations or to solve conflicts.

5. In connection with these processes certain patterns of inten-
    tion attribution will be developed (Rule et al., 1974;
    Nickel, 1974; see also Rule's and Sarason's papers (1981).
    This presupposed cognitive abilities to attribute intentions
    to others and to interpret their behavior accordingly.

    Thereafter instrumental and hostile (motivated) aggression
    can and have to be differentiated. The earlier developed
    behavior patterns can be used as instruments to attain
    intended aggression goals as well as the goals of other
    motives. Insofar as these behaviors are similar, they may be
    called aggressive; but each is differently motivated and will
    therefore follow different rules (see Kornadt, 1982, p. 296).

6. From here the next step--the moral development--becomes
    important. Behavior labeled as aggression becomes an object
    of moral evaluation. The result is certainly not always to
    judge aggression as bad. At a certain stage of moral
    development aggression will be seen as a matter of just bal-
    ance, of restoring equity (e.g. revenge as in "an eye for an
    eye and a tooth for a tooth" (c.f. Feshbach, 1974). At
    another stage aggression may be judged as a justified method
    of getting things one is entitled to have, of defending one's
    own rights, or maybe of defending law and order or even moral
    principles.

The moral system with its individual differences in developmental stages and in the content of what is seen as "good" and "bad" is a part of the aggression motive (Feshbach, 1974). But the moral evaluation, based on empathy, role-taking and identification, will especially support the development of aggression inhibition even when the aggression motive is previously developed.

Stepwise Increasing Complexity

The development of the aggression motive system is therefore a long and complicated process, which leads gradually to an increasing complexity of the disposition. In this process the earlier developmental processes will influence the later ones. This effect will be twofold:

Direct effects occur as former processes are a basis for the next developmental stage, e.g. many anger outbursts as compared to a few constitute a different condition for learning of patterns of affective reactions, of behavior patterns, and of cognitive systems. A basic belief in a hostile world will facilitate the development of a moral system which justifies aggression.

Indirect effects occur when the behavior of the child influences the kind of social interaction between the child and its environment. E.g. many and severe anger outbursts may increase the probability of positive reinforcement and thus increase the learning of aggressive reactions. This, in turn, may evoke more unfriendly reactions of the care-taker, which, in turn, may later decrease the identification and intensify the development of a tendency to interpret frustrations as caused by bad intentions of others.

DEVELOPMENT OF INDIVIDUAL DIFFERENCES

The development process in the various stages will be influenced by several environmental conditions. According, the elements developed during these stages will differ in intensity and quality.

In the following diagram (see Figure 2), some examples are given and summarized of factors which may contribute to the development of high or low aggressiveness in different developmental stages. In the theoretical model it is easy to understand that the same influential factor will have different effects at different age-levels. One example may be:

Maternal rejection will probably increase aggressiveness more, the earlier it occurs. It should facilitate the forming of many cue-anger connections, specific patterns of emotional reaction and the belief in a hostile world in which one has to be prepared to defend oneself. And vice versa--maternal acceptance and unlimited warmth in the earliest childhood may minimize

81

anger-conditioning and prevent the child from forming a basically mistrustful, threatening and suspicious person-environment-relationship (Hamburg & van Lawick-Goodall. 1974; Bowlby, 1973). However, at a later age level, if warmth occurs in the form of maternal permissiveness, it may increase the aggression motive by giving the child too much experience of positive reward for aggression (Olweus, 1980).

But one may ask whether there exists a most critical period and whether neglecting the child earlier than this period, perhaps before the first attachment is formed, may lead more to depressive than to anger reactions. This is a matter of empirical studies.

Another example will be:

If a child is forced too early to behave according to high moral principles which it cannot yet understand, this may improve aggressiveness. Such child-rearing may be felt as unjust and as cold and rejecting. However, in later years this kind of child-rearing may form negative incentives of aggression and therefore improve the development of aggression inhibition.

The relationship between "influencing factors" and the motive development should not be misunderstood as mono-causal and uni-directed. Those influences (external and internal) further or enhance certain developmental processes, but even at a low developmental stage individual differences in the reaction as well as in the activity of the children are relevant and specific patterns of social interaction will be established (Murray, 1979).

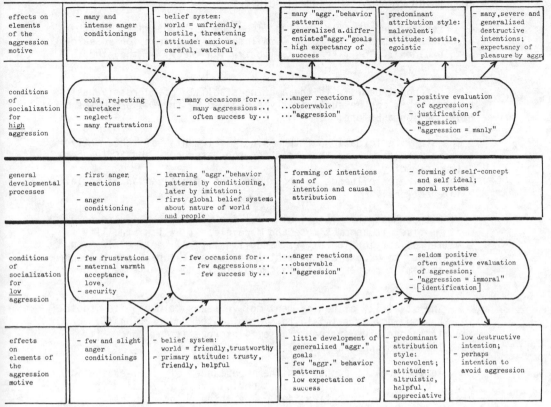

Fig. 2. Schematic diagram: Process of development of aggression motive and influencing factors.

CONCLUDING REMARKS: FURTHER HYPOTHESES

Let me end by indicating two points concerning further hypotheses. They have to do with integrating aggression research into broader fields like general motivation theory or the study of personality.

One point deals with the amazing stability of aggressiveness. Perhaps this can be sufficiently explained by the two processes I have mentioned before:

- The stepwise formation of the single elements of the motive where the former is the basis for the later ones and influences them directly.
- The indirect influence by the increasing stabilization of social interactions.

But perhaps this is not all. In the development of achievement motive, it becomes more and more clear that its stability is a matter of attribution styles and finally of self-evaluation. These seem to become a fundamental aspect of the self-concept and self-esteem in respect to one's own ability and excellence in general.

The stability of achievement motive seems to have its roots in the tendency to maintain this complicated and emotionally very important cognitive system of self-interpretation, once it is established (Heckhausen, 1981).

In the area of aggression the importance of self-evaluation could be quite similar. It is obvious that aggression is also closely connected to self-esteem. The threatening of self-esteem can be conceived as a main cause for aggression.

The specific cognitive system and attribution styles constituting the aggression motive have been much neglected so far. But should these not be a central part of its development? The specificity of aggression motive has to do with a particular aspect of the relationship between person and enrivonment and of social interaction: such as attack, threat and defense, removal of frustration and conflict-solving by violence. Could it not likewise be that the basic cognitive structure of aggressiveness lies in the fundamental way of self-interpretation and -evaluation in respect to one's ability and in the (perceived) necessity of coping with threat, of solving social conflicts, and of self-defense? Everybody is facing those problems. The need to cope with them is also universal. Therefore, in this respect a universal and fundamental aspect of the self-concept of every growing personality must exist. The ability of that coping will have central importance. Thus it could become the core of the motive system, and pecularities, once established, could produce also a tendency to stabilize this system.

The subjective importance of aggression as compared to other

84

means of coping is then dependent on individual developmental conditions and on the opportunity to learn coping by means of aggression.

In a high aggressive person a kind of feed-back system may be established, consisting of: a general belief in a hostile world, many primary anger connections, high abilities to be successful by aggression, self-confidence in respect to the ability to "solve" social problems violently, low identification, low empathy, low emotional ties, aggression supporting value-systems, nearly no non-aggressive alternatives (see Sarason's paper 1981; Kornadt, 1982).

This first point shows that it is necessary to broaden the view by analyzing the development of aggression within the context of personality development.

My second point follows the same line. Starting from the just mentioned idea of a basic cognitive-affective structure forming the core of aggressiveness I think aggression might be understood better when also studying non-aggressive reactions and the conditions for their development. In principle, there are many situations where non-aggressive reactions will evoke positive (and that means: satisfactory) effects, as well as or even more than, aggression. Consequently, there should be some "critical" developmental stages for forming a differentiation between pro- and anti-social motives. In this respect one might conceive of helping behavior as a kind of "symmetric" counterpart to aggression. It would be worthwhile to study the contrasting conditions which promote the forming of pro-social motives as compared to aggressiveness, as Norma Feshbach has done in her interesting studies about empathy (N. Feshbach, 1973, 1974).

To conclude, I hope that I was able to demonstrate the fruitfulness of motivation theory to integrate various theoretical principles as well as to produce differentiated hypotheses for the development of aggressiveness. Of course, most of what I have pointed out so far, is speculative for the moment. But this is not meant to substitute empirical research; on the contrary, it should stimulate such research in order to test the hypotheses and to refine the theory.

REFERENCES

Atkinson, J.W. An introduction to motivation. Princeton, NJ: van Nostrand, 1964.
Atkinson, J.W. & Feather, N.T. A theory of achievement motivation. New York: Wiley, 1966.
Bowlby, J. Attachment and loss. II: Separation. New York: Hogarth Press, 1973.
Eibl-Eibesfeld, I. Phylogenetic adaptation as determinants of aggressive behavior in man. In J. de Wit & W.W. Hartup

(Eds.), Determinants and origins of aggressive behavior. The Hague: Mouton, 1974.

Feshbach, N. The relationship of child rearing factors to children's aggression, empathy and related positive and negative behaviors. In J. de Wit & W.W. Hartup (Eds.), Determinants and origins of aggressive behavior. The Hagge: Mouton, 1974.

Feshbach, N. & Feshbach, S. The relationship between empathy and aggression in two age groups. Developmental Psychology, 1969, 1:102-107.

Feshbach, S. The function of aggression and the regulation of aggressive drive. Psychological Review, 1964, 71:257-272.

Feshbach, S. Aggression. In P.H. Mussen (Ed.), Carmichael's Manual of Child Psychology (Vol. 2). New York: Wiley, 1970.

Feshbach, S. The development and regulation of aggression: Some research gaps and a proposed cognitive approach. In J. de Wit & W.W. Hartup (Eds.), Determinants and origins of aggressive behavior. The Hague: Mouton, 1974.

Fuchs, R. Funktionsanalayse der Motivation. Zeitschrift für experimentelle und angewandte Psychologie, 1963, 10:626-645.

Fuchs, R. Furchtregulation und Furchthemmung des Zweckhandelns. In A. Thomas (Ed.), Psychologie der Handlung und Bewegung. Meisenheim am Glan: Hain, 1976.

Hamburg, D.A. & van Lawick-Goodall, J. Factors facilitating development of aggressive behavior in chimpanzees and humans. In J. de Wit & W.W. Hartup (Eds.), Determinants and origins of aggressive behavior. The Hague: Mouton, 1974.

Heckhausen, H. Achievement motive research: Current problems and some contributions towards a general theory of motivation. In J.W. Arnold (Ed.), Nebraska symposium on motivation. Lincoln, NB: University of Nebraska Press, 1968.

Heckhausen, H. Intervening cognitions in motivation. In D.E. Berlyne & K.B. Madsen (EDs.), Pleasure, reward, preference. New York: Academic Press, 1973.

Heckhausen, H. Motivation und Handeln. Berlin: Springer, 1980.

Heckhausen, H. Attributionsmuster für Leistungsergebnisse-- individuelle Unterschniede, mögliche Arten und deren Genese. In F.E. Weinert (Ed.), Metakognition, Motivation und Lernen. Stuttgart: Kohlhammer, 1982 (in press).

Konecni, V. Experimental Methodologies. Paper, presented at the NATO ASI Aggression in children and young, Maratea, Italy, 1981.

Kornadt, H.-J. Toward a motivation theory of aggression and aggression inhibition. In J. de Wit & W.W. Hartup (Eds.), Determinants and origins of aggressive behavior. The Hague: Mouton, 1974.

Kornadt, H.-J. Aggressions-Motiv und Aggressions-Hemmung (2 Vols.). Bern: Huber, 1982.

Kornadt, H.-J. Outline of a motivation theory of aggression. Arbeitsbericht aus der Fachrichtung Erziehungswissenschaft der Universität des Saarlandes. Saarbrücken, 1981b.

Kornadt, H.-J. Die Entwicklung der Frustrations--und der Aggressionsforschung. In H.-J. Kornadt (Ed.), Aggrression und Frustration als psychologisches Problem (Vol. I). Darmstadt:

Wissenschaftliche Buchgesellschaft, 1981a.

Lambert, W.W. Promise and problems of cross-cultural exploration of children's aggressive strategies. In J. de Wit & W.W. Hartup (EDs.), Determinants and origins of aggressive behavior. The Hague: Mouton, 1974.

Lefkowitz, M., Eron, L., Walder, L. & Huesman, L. Growing up to be violent. New York: Pergamon Press, 1977.

Megargee, E.I. Undercontrolled and overcontrolled personality types in extreme antisocial aggression. Psychological Monographs: General and applied, 1966, 80(3, whole No. 611):1-29.

Murray, A.D. Infant crying as an elicitor of parental behavior: An examination of two models. Psychological Bulletin, 1971, 86:191-215.

Nickel, T.W. The attribution of intention as a critical factor in the relation between frustration and aggression. Journal of Personality, 1974, 42:282-292.

Olweus, D. Personality factors and aggression: With special references to violence within the peer group. In J. de Wit & W.W. Hartup (Eds.), Determinants and origins of aggressive behavior. The Hague: Mouton, 1974.

Olweus, D. Aggression in the schools: Bullies and whipping boys. Washington D.C.: Hemisphere, 1978.

Olweus, D. Stability of aggressive reaction patterns in males: A review. Psychological Bulletin, 1979, 86:252-275.

Olweus, D. Familial and temperamental determinants of aggressive behavior in adolescent boys: A causal analysis. Developmental Psychology, 1980, 16:644-660.

Rule, B. The attributional mediation of human aggression. Paper, presented at the NATO ASI Aggression in children and youth, Maratea, Italy, 1981.

Rule, B.G., Nesdale, A.R. & McAra, M.J. Children's reactions to information about the intention underlying an aggressive act. Child Development, 1974, 45:794-798.

Sarason, I. Social skills and aggressive behavior. Paper, presented at the NATO ASI Aggrression in children and youth, Maratea, Italy, 1981.

Turner, Ch. Classical conditioning processes and aggressive behavior. Paper, presented at the NATO ASI Aggression in children and youth, Maratea, Italy, 1981.

Weiner, B. Theories of motivation. Chicago: Markham, 1972.

II. COGNITIVE AND DEVELOPMENTAL DETERMINANTS OF AGGRESSION

CONTEMPORARY PSYCHOANALYTIC VIEWS OF AGGRESSION

Gian V. Caprara

University of Rome

INTRODUCTION

Aggression is undoubtedly a topic of major importance in psychodynamic theory and, in particular, in psychoanalytic work. However, many issues still remain unresolved with respect to the nature and development of aggression and, generally, to the role it plays in mental functioning.

The difficulty and, in some cases, the impossibility of tracing clear boundaries between behaviors which are only apparently similar or different is one characteristic element of a research strategy which considers as primary objective of investigation not behavior itself but that which determines conduct and gives it significance in the complex experience of the individual.

Furthermore, we must consider the fact that when discussing aggression we refer to a multi-dimensional phenomenon whose analysis implies numerous aspects (emotional, cognitive and behavioral), and relies on different theoretical and empirical approaches even within the same psychodynamic perspective.

For this reason I have decided to limit my discussion to the area of classical psychoanalysis, with particular emphasis on the contributions of Freud and the subsequent development of his ideas by his most faithful students. In particular I believe that three different conceptions of aggression must be taken into consideration: (1) aggression as a primary impulse, not reducible to anything else; (2) aggression as a reaction to frustration; (3) aggression as the extraversion of the death drive. In my opinion, such conceptions are not mutually exclusive, nor can one be reduced to the other; rather, they belong to the different perspectives which are required by the multi-dimensionality of the

88

Kaplan, R.M., Konečni, V.J., Novaco, R.W. (eds.) Aggression in Children and Youth
© 1984, Martinus Nijhoff Publishers, The Hague/Boston/Lancaster
ISBN 90-247-2903-3. Printed in The Netherlands

object of investigation.

These same conceptions we find in the work of Freud correspond to specific problems and research directions which continue to be pertinent to more recent inquiries. According to a developmental perspective, today it seems more possible than ever to reconcile the different points of view and to integrate the different levels of analysis concerning the biological, psychological and social aspects of aggression.

THE CONTRIBUTION OF SIGMUND FREUD

As it has been noted, Freud never reached a definitive ordering of his reflections on the nature, origins, and vicissitudes of aggression, despite the progressively crucial role which this issue played in his work. The last quantity of material produced by Freud in nearly 40 years of observation and writing is at times profound, suggestive, and fragmentary and one of the main difficulties in dealing with such a work lies in the fact that any criteria of order may appear arbitrary.

In analyzing Freud's work as a whole, with particular reference to aggression or aggressiveness, it is not impossible to find examples of different, and often contradictory ideas; over time, different conceptions were formulated, perfected, then substituted to represent psychic functioning and to bridge the gap between clinical experience and theoretical ordering.

According to the line of thought which characterizes a particular period, or is dominant in certain works, it is possible to turn to Freud either for confirmation or refutation of a particular conception.

Perhaps for this reason, several researchers (see for instance Nagera, 1970) thought it wise to attempt to order Freud's work chronologically similar to the approach which led ordering the general theory of drives.

According to this view, it seems possible to distinguish a first phase, ending in 1914, during which aggression figures mainly if not exclusively, as an aspect of the libido or, in any case, in the service of the libido; a second phase, corresponding to the work, Instincts and Their Vicissitudes (1915), in which the previously proposed conception of an aggression independent of the libido, ascribable to the drives of the ego, is more clearly advanced; and, finally, a third phase, beginning in 1920, in which aggression is no longer considered a manifestation of the self-preservation drives, but as extraversion of a newly postulated death drive.

As I stated in two recent works (Caprara, 1978, 1979), I do not believe that this schema faithfully interprets the continuity, and the real progress of Freud's work in which change rarely corresponds to the definitive abandonment of previously advanced ideas, but rather to their integration and further development.

For this reason, I suggested an attentive reading in order to consider, apart from their historical succession, the compatibility and pertinence of the various conceptions of aggression during different periods to indicate different phenomena, and also the same phenomena according to different perspectives or levels of analysis. I am convinced that it is possible to move ahead in this direction with an investigation capable of adapting different levels of analysis such as the biological, psychological and social with the clinical-phenomenological on one side, and with the etiological-causal on the other. In fact, it seems to me that the Freudian investigation moves and constantly.

First indications appear in initial clinical works in relation to the impossibility of neglecting a whole variety of aggressive and destructive phenomena. In Further Remarks on the Neuro-Psychoses of Defense (1896), aggression is associated with sexuality in the genesis of obsessive neuroses. In this work Freud shares the widespread conviction of his time regarding the existence of autonomous drives of an aggressive nature; however it is not clear whether the aggression which is referred to is a subsequent reaction to the sexual seduction the individual has undergone, or rather the expression of some original drive.

Interest in aggression is decidedly greater in The Interpretation of Dreams (1900). There can be no doubt of the importance which fantasies, motives and desires of a hostile nature assume for Freud in the dream.

In particular, the theme of aggression appears in painful counter-wish dreams, in punishment dreams, and in dreams of the death of loved ones.

In painful counter-wish dreams, Freud mentions a masochistic component which originates from the transformation of the aggressive-sadistic component into its opposite (p. 159).

In punishment dreams, Freud hints at a masochistic tendency, independent of any reference to sadistic tendencies and their inversion (pp. 557-558).

The conception of a reactive defensive aggression primarily directed to the satisfaction of other needs, clearly appears when death dreams of loved ones are taken into consideration and when the inherent thematic material, the hostility, ambivalence, and rivalry between parents and children and between siblings, is developed. This thematic material anticipates and, in large part, provides the basis for the subsequent conception of the oedipal conflict.

In these dreams, the death of a loved one corresponds to the individual's leaving a situation in which he carries out a

90

frustrating role; here, to be dead corresponds with being away. In relation to this, the infantile death wishes of the child, with respect to the siblings he is in competition with, as well as the reciprocal death wishes between parents and children are explained as a result of the inherent limitations associated with these relationships.

Thus, we again find different conceptions: first, that of a primary aggression which is translated into sadistic tendencies; second, that of a primary self-destructiveness which is translated into masochistic tendencies; third, that of an aggression understood as reaction to frustration and as manifestation of the ego, directed toward overcoming and leaving behind obstacles and dangers.

However, we are far from a definitive ordering; often it is impossible to distinguish, among different indications and lines of thought, those which have a temporary character and which try to cope with the limits of current language in order to represent certain clinically significant phenomena, and those which already correspond to more solid stands and to outlines of subsequent works.

Again, in the first of the Three Essays on the Theory of Sexuality, when Freud confronts the problem of sexual aberrations in sadism and masochism, he explicitly ascribes an aggressive component to the sexual drive (pp. 158-159). This does not exclude the existence of an aggression which cannot be reduced to simple component of the sexual drive, as this is explicitly referred to in the second essay of the same work (pp. 192-193).

Here, while the reducibility of aggression to a component of the sexual-drive and the existence of an autonomous aggressive drive are discussed, emphasis is placed on the drive for mastery, which may assume aggressive connotations. Also in this essay therefore, we find at least two of the conceptions which I previously mentioned: that of a primary aggressive drive, and that of a reactive aggression, instrumental to both the sexual drive and the drive for mastery.

Both conceptions are found in the essay, Jokes and their Relation to the Unconscious, also from 1905. On one hand, aggression figures as a reaction to the frustration of a libidinal drive (p. 100); on the other, aggression is presented as the manifestation of a primary hostile tendency, largely, subject to the same vicissitudes as the sexual drive (pp. 102-103). The first does not necessarily exclude the second; in fact, the same aggressive-offensive conduct--in this case the same jokes--can represent a means of controlling certain libidinal satisfactions as well as releasing hostile tendencies.

Several years, later, in Analysis of a Phobia in a Five-Year-Old Boy, we again meet both conceptions. In this work Freud alludes to cruel and violent tendencies of human nature, which

91

unfold, still unrestrained, during infantile stages: but he, also mentions hostility as a form of reaction to frustration (pp. 140-141).

With Totem and Taboo (1913), the conception of autonomous aggressive tendencies finds an historical-cultural mooring and a major significance is attributed to aggression in the construction and development of social organization.

However, it is debatable whether the origin of hostile tendencies refers back to innate characteristics of the species, or rather to experiences which have conditioned and progressively shaped the development of individual conduct. It is also uncertain if these tendencies can be traced back to a primary aggression or, rather, to impeded and thus removed, wishes to react aggressively.

Importance is also assigned to aggression in the work, Instincts and their Vicissitudes (1915). More clearly than in the past, in this work aggression figures as a manifestation of the drives of the ego, extended to self-preservation and the control of reality. In particular aggression figures as the typical expression of the drives of the ego in overcoming frustration (p. 138).

In this new perspective, aggression and hatred do not originate from a primary need or wish to cause pain, since the inflicting of pain has nothing to do with the primary orientation of the drive. But rather they originate from the ego's wish to free itself from what constitutes an unpleasurable experience.

The ego hates, abhors and pursues with intent to destroy all objects which are a source of unpleasurable feeling for it... (p. 138).

At the same time, both the conception of a primary aggressive drive and that of a reactive aggression remain valid in the essay, Thoughts for the Times on War and Death (1915). The first, in particular, seems to come into its own and to anticipate the subsequent developments of Beyond the Pleasure Principle, with regard to the theme of death. In confrontation with the war, Freud fouund it impossible to renounce the idea of a primary evil drive which only education and civilization may be able to restrain.

Beyond the Pleasure Principle, which dates from 1920, is certainly one of the most problematic works due to the analysis oscillation between different levels (biological and psychological) and to the questions which explicitly accompany what seems to be a completely hypothetical line of thought. The enigmatic quality which characterizes this work makes it difficult to decide how much it reflects the unease of a generation and of an era, faced with a whole variety of existential questions. Certainly, in this work which states the principle of a general tendency toward the dissolution of living substance, clinical observations on melancholy, masochismn and sadism converge, under the influence of an intellectual involvement with the biology of Weismann and Hering. Furthermore, romantic themes of death are re-evoked with explicit reference to Schopenhauer's philosophy.

As Ellenberger (1970) has observed, there is no doubt that the Freudian concept of the death drive can be even better understood in relation to the interest in the theme of death shared by many of his contemporaries.

As Jones (1953) and Schur (1972) have pointed out, we also must not neglect the fact that the theme of death had been recurring in Freud's fears and reflections over a period of many years; nor must we underestimate the factor of the immanency of death in his daily life.

After the first illusions, the war quickly revealed its violence, its heritage of destruction and misery. This caused Freud's fear for his children who were far away, the loss of economic well-being which had been constructed with great effort, and separation and isolation from colleagues and students. And, aside from the war, we must not neglect the other elements which had brought Freud to reflect on death, i.e., the loss of loved ones (above all the death of his dear friend Anton von Freund and of his daughter, Sophie, only a few days apart), and his awareness of having reached an age when confident plans often turn into resignation.

It is likely that all these factors merged to refine a sensibility which was mainly directed by the necessity to provide a better explanation for a variety of clinical phenomena than that made possible by existing meta-psychology.

The thesis shared by some authors, such as Bibring (1941) or Hartmann, Kriss and Loewenstein (1949) that the theory is primarily biological is not convincing. On the contrary the importance of the new formulation is principally clinical. The problem was, and is, the same as with every form of psychic unease which, from the phenomenological point of view is always experienced as an effort to live and as an opponent to life which must be overcome in order to affirm and restore the desire to live. In a therapeutic context, we have no difficulty in referring to a death drive everything that is opposed to life and which makes life seem undesirable. It is important here to avoid confusing the metaphor, the as if dimension, with essence.

The life-death polarity may well represent the polarity of all clinical work as well as the polarity of every developmental stage.

Lussana (1972) has noted that the new Freudian theory is not a theory of the death drive, but a theory of the fusion of the life drive and the death drive.

Fusion of drives refers back to this polarity, to the constant immanence of death, to our progressive abilities to escape autonomously from that which opposes life and to get used to the idea of death. Since everyone must die, it is clear that what delimits life ultimately prevail.

The experience of this opposition to life varies however, during different developmental stages and conditions of life, and in relation to the supports provided by our biological endowment and to what our organism meets in the environment.

In this perspective it is metaphorically consistent to recognize a death drive in all which, from birth, makes the child's growth difficult and filled with suffering, and which becomes, in old age, the need to free oneself from an overwhelming sense of inadequacy.

Further, it is also plausible to recognize aggression as the extraversion of the death drive, still in the same metaphoric language, to the degree that what opposes life inside of us can provide the model and the motive for opposing life outside.

For the psychic life, as well as for life in general, it is possible to adopt the model of an equilibrium between constructive and destructive processes, substantially determined by the type of exchange the organism has with the environment. This equilibrium is in favor of the constructive processes to the degree to which exchanges are gratifying or, in any case, more frequently sources of satisfaction than of dissatisfaction. Instead, this equilibrium turns in favor of the destructive processes through non-adaptive strategies to the degree to which these exchanges are not gratifying and, too often, sources of frustration.

We must note that the pleasure principle is the inheritor of the experiences of unpleasure connected to states of impotence, dependence, and maximum vulnerability of the infant at birth. These states and the associated feelings determine significantly all later emotional and cognitive development. The child starts to love life if he is nourished, kept clean and warm, attended to, in other words if he feels protected and loved. The child lets himself die, or starts to hate life if the experiences which correspond to his exchanges with the environment are those of privation, refusal, abandonment.

All that the organism experiences as sources of unpleasure can become the motive for growth arrest, or for deformed growth, and at the same time can be the precursor and the prototype of a relationship with reality in which the painful and the destructive components assume the character of the natural and the inevitable. It is from here that not only the plausibility of the concept of extraversion of the death drive derives, but also its mooring in specific experiences, i.e. in specific organism-environment exchanges.

Additionally when parental prohibition becomes internalized, as clarified in The Ego and the Id (1923), it may become a nucleus around which many of those dynamism remaining outside the domain of the ego are linked and whose connotations may be revealed as destructive, both for the type of representations with which they are associated (impediments to the satisfaction of wishes) and for the type of outcome toward which they seem to tend (that of the limitation of the self). Not only the potency of the superego, which can be more or less severe, derives from this, but also the historicity of the superego and of its attributes as enduring expression of the influence and authority of the parents, of specific sanctions and threats, and of specific interpersonal and social relationships.

From all this it can be derived that what opposes life, which is experienced and may be recognized as the expression of destructive drives, belongs to the natural limits of our organism, to the physical characteristics of the environment, and to the sociocultural conditions which determine the internal-external world exchanges. Such exchanges regulate the different developmental processes in providing the requests, satisfactions, frustrations, and models which support first the differentiation of the ego from the id, and then the differentiation of the superego from the ego.

At this point, I wish to emphasize the necessity of bringing about a welding of levels: biological, psychological and social; it becomes clear how psychic functioning initially has its roots in biology (according to what the organism requires) but is then freed from it by leaning toward the social (according to what the environment provides).

The problem of aggression is again proposed in Civilization and its Discontents (1930) with a decidedly psycho-social orientation. In this view, Freud reconsiders the same themes regarding the profoundly conflicting origins of society, which were already anticipated in and Taboo (1913), Current Considerations on War and Death (1915), Psychology of the Masses and Analysis of the Ego (1921) and The Future of an Illusion (1927).

The conflict transcendentally belongs to life itself: to relationships of the species with reality, to characteristics of human society, and to the natural endowment of each individual.

More explicitly, and more decidedly than in the past, in Civilizations and its Discontents, Freud affirms the existence of a primary hostility which continuously threatens to destroy civil society. In this work Freud renounces the doubts which he had held in the past regarding the existence of this primary aggression. However it still remains difficult to understand what type of relationship exists between this presumed aggressive drive, the death drive, and that type of aggression which figures as response to the inhibition of drive satisfaction. In fact, all three conceptions appear in the same work; however, Freud does not hide his perplexity when faced with solutions which evidently are not

95

completely safe from theoretical objections.

In Civilization and its Discontents, the conception of a primary aggression leads Freud to recognize that the principal cause of civilization's unease originates from its necessary repression, experienced individually in feelings of guilt and moral anguish. Primary aggression, directed toward the love object, is repressed to safeguard both the existence of the love object, and of the love relationship. This inhibition with the initial aggression increases already existing hostility; once internalized this hostility becomes a part of the superego and pushes against the ego.

Thus, an important issue becomes that of the nature of the superego and its severity, which can only in part be traced back to the innate constitutional factors. The superego actually becomes the repository of a civilization, through the content which is repressed and the means employed for that repression. In fact, what is internalized and forms the basis of the superego depends largely on the external world, which not only provides the concretely repressing models of authority, but also the model around which the experience of the individual's own needs, as well as external prohibitions, can be organized. In this perspective, the intensity of the aggression refers back on one side, to an internal world made up of needs and fantasies of privation and destruction and, on the other, to an external world made up of prescriptions and sanctions. Whereas it is debatable that aggression is a primary drive, there is little doubt that aggression is a modality of relationship with reality often encouraged, or at least functional, within our civil organization.

In this perspective there is no need to resort to Thanatos to explain that, within our civilization, there are in reality many occasions when aggression can reproduce itself both in our conscious and unconscious, thus becoming a source of unease. On the contrary the discussion is destined to move from nature to civilization, to the mechanisms which assure the reproduction of orders by individuals, and to those which assure the reproduction of relationships of dominion, authority, control, and possession in terms of needs, fears, and fantasies.

THREE RESEARCH DIRECTIONS

Remaining within the framework of classical psychoanalytic tradition, the different orientations which have emerged from the debate on the nature of aggression can be traced back to the three conceptions anticipated by Freud. The conception of a primary aggressive drive, rather similar in its vicissitudes to the libidinal drive, has been taken up and extended, above all in the area of ego psychoanalysis, by Hartmann, Kriss and Loewenstein. The conception of aggression as reaction to the experience of frustration has been clearly reaffirmed by Fenichel. Finally, the conception of the death drive has been taken up and further developed by Melanie Klein.

Beginning with the confrontation between libido and aggression, according to the four characteristics attributed by Freud to each drive (pressure, aim, object, and source), Hartmann, Kriss and Loewenstein (1949) suggest a true parallelism between libido and aggression and recognize in them the two fundamental drives of the psychic apparatus. It appears that the vicissitudes of aggression are so similar to those of the libido as to fully justify the assumption of an aggressive drive as fundamental and primary as the libidinal one.

Starting with the assumption of an undifferentiation phase of the psychic structure during which libidinal and aggressive drives are indistinguishable, the existence of processes of neutralization of aggression is postulated, similar to those of the libido. Such processes contribute significantly toward the consolidation of the ego and the superego as autonomous structures. In particular, with respect to the autonomous functioning of these structures, it would appear that aggression is determining, as it is susceptible to neutralization and, thus, transformation in the service of adaptation and development.

In such a perspective, we come to measure ego strength in terms of the effectiveness of its defences and neutralization processes. These significantly depend on the exchanges, relations and events which determine the organism-environment relationship. Further, whereas emphasis is placed on the concept of neutralization and on the transformations of the primitive drives, the concept of aggression is destined to be extended considerably to include a variety of different manifestations, such as productivity, creativity, assertiveness, etc. However, at the same time, the specificity of the concept is reduced so that it may overlap with the concept of libido or the more general concept of psychic energy.

Fenichel (1945) has traced the different aggressive phenomena back to a reactive type etiology. He has no doubt about the role which aggression plays as source of numerous psychic manifestations which often present impulsive characteristics; however, resorting to a primary aggression seems to Fenichel as debatable as resorting to a death drive to explain the phenomena which seem to share the fact of being reactions or outcomes of reactions to a variety of difficulties.

In such a perspective, aggression figures better as a reaction than as an instinct or drive. Evidently, this reaction may often be inadequate, and its destructiveness is not necessarily intentional and specifically oriented as, for example, in the case of the infant. Directionality and intentionality are further attributes which this reaction may acquire largely on the basis of the evaluation of the adult and in the wake of the organizational function which such an evaluation exercises in the psychic world of the young child.

The awareness and willingness to destroy, i.e., true

97

aggression, figures as a secondary acquisition. Infantile conduct, which the adult interprets as aggressive, in reality demonstrates the child's desire to remove himself from unease; its consolidation into a more or less stable, and more or less autonomous behavior style depends on its proved effectiveness.

Therefore, the problem is not so much that of singling out hypothetical essences as of recognizing. the conditions which determine and consolidate certain modalities both in relating with the environment, and in satisfying one's own needs for security and self-esteem. Along these lines, sadism, masochism, depression, suicide, and destructive aggression do not figure as the expression of an original aggressive drive or of a death drive, but always represent the outcome of failure, privation, or a substantially unsatisfied relationship with reality.

The conception of the death drive was further developed by Melanie Klein (1932, 1948, 1952). With respect to the original Freudian model, in Klein's work the role of the destructive drives during the very first developmental stage is exalted due to their function in the anticipated appearance of the ego and the superego. The precocious emergence of the ego is, in fact, considered necessary in order to contain and direct the original self-destructiveness of the organism toward the exterior, whereas the destructive drives and the anguish which they provoke give rise to the superego and dominate the first stages.

The whole Kleinian metapsychology defers to this very precocious destructiveness from which the organism must protect itself and its objects. In her clinical writings, Klein makes constant reference to archaic fantasies of oral, urethral, and anal sadism, of destruction and annihilation. Frequently her thought seems obscure, daring and desecrating. If Freud removed the last illusions regarding an infantile world extraneous to libido, Klein frontally attacked the conviction of an infantile dimension extraneous to hostility and violence.

To many it seems impossible that during the first few months of life the infant carries these destructive drives which Klein claims she is able to infer from the latent content of games. It seems unbelievable that such a tiny child may have already experienced that ambivalence, anguish, jealousy, those experiences and threats of disintegration, splitting, reconstruction of self and of objects back to which Klein traces the origin of health and illness.

If it already seems difficult to accept the Freudian reality of the Oedipus complex with that charge of aggression which is introduced into the relationship between parents and children, it is even more difficult to accept the fantasies of incorporation, emptiness and penetration which Klein recognizes in the very first relationships of the infant with parts of his parents bodies. However, there can be no doubt about her extraordinary clinical sensibility and the importance of the perspectives she has opened in the psychoanalysis of children. Certainly the sphere of psychosis refers to a primitive world of destruction, persecution, splitting and disintegration.

The primitive reality of the psychic, which emerges from the biological, is constantly tried out by all the demands originating in the internal and external world. The virulence, threat, and destructiveness of the demands and the ways in which they come to be fantasized are only the reflex of the state of dependence and impotence of the child. For Klein as opposed to Freud, the biological mooring is more concretely inherent in the physical nature of the child, in the maturational processes of the organism, in the specific nature of the exchanges of the bodily organism with the external world.

For Klein, as well as for Freud, the death drive corresponds to a metaphor representing everything that renders growth difficult and opposes life, right from the beginning. In particular, the most precocious experiences of satisfaction and frustration are decisive for the development of aggression. Any frustration, whether internal or external, linked to the fragility of our constitution, or rather to the demands of the external environment, may easily correspond to an increase in reactions directed toward escape, or to the destruction of what seems to be the source of painful sensations.

In such a perspective, what we call the death drive is a constitutional fact, to the degree that the effort which life involves and the equipment for life are different for individual constitutions; in this sense, the ability to bear tension and tolerate privations is also a constitutional issue. But the death drive, as well as the ability to bear tension and tolerate privations, is not only a constitutional fact; its outcomes and forms depend precisely on the tensions and privations which the environment imposes on the organism. For this reason, the repeating of experiences in which love prevails over hatred, in which satisfactions definitely prevail over frustrations, is an essential condition for all psychic development.

Countering the total impotence of the infant following the traumatic experience of birth, and all the tensions, demands, and inevitable privations which life and growth entail, the presence, material support, and love of real objects, able to alleviate suffering, unpleasure, fear, destructiveness and a premature sense of guilt seem essential for activating the necessary processes of separation, identification, and reparation.

RECENT CONTRIBUTIONS AND PERSPECTIVES

An examination of the most recent contributions confirms the presence of the three directions discussed here.

Recently, Brenner (1971), Solnit (1972), and Parens (1973)

re-proposed the concept of ego psychoanalysts regarding the validity of a pairing between the libido and aggression, both taken as primary drives.

Stone (1971) and Gillespie (1971), on the other hand, defended the conception of a reactive and instrumental aggression which is more or less functional for the development and adaptation of the individual.

Eissler (1971) and Rosenfeld (1971) further developed the concept of death drive from the clinical point of view, primarily in relation to the theme of narcissism, understood as omnipotent and self-destructive withdrawal of the libidinal cathexes.

These different conceptions are not necessarily alternatives; rather they seem again to refer to different levels of analysis. From a phenomenological point of view, there can be no doubt regarding the impulsive nature of certain aggressive manifestations which may give the impression of being the expression of true death drives. From an etiological point of view, there can be no doubt about the importance of frustration in provoking and consolidating a variety of reactions and aggressive strategies.

Also, it is not rare for investigators to favor more than one conception simultaneously while they seek more precise indications, through research, relative to when and how aggression appears or becomes part of the behavioral repertoire of the subject.

In this same direction, the developmental perspective figures as the most promising; within it, it may be easier to find elements of convergence between the different psychoanalytic orientations and elements of comparison with other disciplines, such as ethology, anthropology, and sociology.

This analysis leads us to consider the bonds of the biological structure in terms of need, resources, time and stages of maturation, while a better understanding is required of how privation, which corresponds with the experience of unpleasure, can favor the development of the aggressive drives or wishes at the expense of the libidinal ones, as recently maintained by A. Freud (1971). But this perspective also leads us to consider the function of aggression within a given social context and the mechanisms and occasions which assure and control its reproduction.

The inclination of the ego toward aggression, and the severity of the superego are actually not only the outcome of a variety of privations and difficulties, but also the outcome of responses which have been selected and encouraged by the social environment which, at the same time, has doled out these difficulties.

The experience of unpleasure organizes itself into desire for retaliation or fear of retaliation, into fantasies or into self-destructive and hetero-destructive conduct in relation to the internalized objects and in relation to the desires, fears, fantasies, conflicts, and conducts of persons on whom the psychological growth of the child depends.

The primitive reactions of annoyance, aversion, opposition, and refusal toward what comes to be experienced as source of unease and disturbance become stabilized and transformed, assume psychological pertinence in terms of intentions, expectations, desires, or fears, according to how they are tolerated, reinforced and labeled by the environment.

Aggression, of which the child is object and spectator before becoming active subject, enters and becomes part of his world in the forms and with the specific connotations of the environment in which he is growing up.

As it has already been noted by anthropologists, sociologists, social and clinical psychologists, these forms vary significantly from culture to culture, from social environment to social environment, and from family to family.

In this perspective aggression can no longer be considered exclusively a personal theme, but figures as such in relation to specific social and interpersonal relationships, from which the conditions of his legitimization and reproduction at the level of structure and modes of functioning of the whole personality derives.

REFERENCES

Bibring, E. (1941). The development and problems of the theory of the instincts. International Journal of Psychoanalysis, 12:102-131.
Brenner, C. (1971). The psychoanalytic concept of aggression. International Journal of Psychoanalysis, 52:137-143.
Caprara, G.V. (1978). Alcune considerazioni per un approfondimento del contributo di S. Freud allo studio dell'aggressività. Giornale storico di Psicologia Dinamica, 4:126-138.
Caprara, G.V. (1979). Personalità e aggressività. I contributi della Teoria Psicoanalitica, Vol. II. Roma: Bulzoni.
Eissler, L. (1971). Death drive, ambivalence and narcissism. The Psychoanalytic Study of the Child, 26:25-78.
Ellenberger, H. (1970). The Discovery of the Unconscious. New York: Basic Books.
Fenichel, O. (1945). The Psychoanalytic Theory of Neurosis. New York: Norton.
Freud, A. (1971). Comments on aggression. International Journal of Psychoanalysis, 53:163-171.
Freud, S. (1962). Further remarks on the neuro-psychoses of defence (1986). The Complete Works of Freud, Standard Edition, 3:162-185. London: Hogarth Press.

Freud, S. (1953). The interpretation of dreams (1900). The Complete Works of Freud, Standard Edition, 4 & 5. London: Hogarth Press.

Freud, S. (1960). Jokes and their relation to the unconscious (1905). The Complete Works of Freud, Standard Edition, 8. London: Hogarth Press.

Freud, S. (1953). Three essays in the theory of sexuality (1905). The Complete Works of Freud, Standard Edition, 7:135-243. London: Hogarth Press.

Freud, S. (1955). Analysis of a phobia in a five-year-old boy (1909). The Complete Works of Freud, Standard Edition, 10:5-149. London:Hogarth Press.

Freud, S. (1953). Totem and taboo (1913). The Complete Works of Freud, Standard Edition, 13:1-161. London: Hogarth Press.

Freud, S. (1957). Instincts and their vicissitudes (1915). The Complete Works of Freud, Standard Edition, 14:117-140. London: Hogarth press.

Freud, S. (1957). Thoughts for the times on war and death (1915). The Complete Works of Freud, Standard Edition, 14:275-300. London: Hogarth Press.

Freud, S. (1955). Beyond the pleasure principle (1920). The Complete Works of Freud, Standard Edition, 18:7-64. London: Hogarth Press.

Freud, S. (1961). The ego and the id (1923). The Complete Works of Freud, Standard Edition, 19:12-59. London: Hogarth Press, 1961.

Freud, S. (1961). Civilization and its discontents (1930). The Complete Works of Freud, Standard Edition, 21:64-145. London: Hogarth Press.

Gillespie, W. (1971). Aggression and instinct theory. International Journal of Psychoanalysis, 52:155-160.

Hartmann, H., Kriss, E. & Loewenstein, R. (1949). Notes on the theory of aggression. The Psychoanalytical Study of the Child, 3/4:9-36. New York: International Universities Press.

Jones, E. (1953-1957). The Life and Work of Sigmund Freud, 3 Vols. New York: Basic Books.

Klein, M. (1932). The Psychoanalysis of Children. London: Hogarth Press.

Klein, M. (1948). On the theory of anxiety and guilt. International Journal of Psychoanalysis, 29.

Klein, M. (1952). The mutual influences in the development of ego and id. The Psychoanalytic Study of the Child, 7.

Lussana, P. (1972). Aggressività e istinto di morte da Freud a M. Klein: teoria e note clinche. Rivista di Psicoanalisi, 18:155-178.

Nagera, H. (1970). Basic Psychoanalytic Concepts on the Theory of Instincts. London: Allen & Unwin.

Parens, H. (1973). Aggression: A reconsideration. Journal of the American Psychoanalytic Association, 12:34-60.

Rosenfeld, H. (1971). A clinical approach to the psycho-analytic theory of the life and death instincts: An investigation into the aggressive aspects of narcissism. International Journal of Psycho-analysis, 52:55-58.

Schur, M. (1972). Freud: Living and Dying. New York:

International Universities Press.

Solnit, J. (1972). Aggression: A view of theory building in psychoanalysis. The Psychoanalytic Quarterly, 40:195-244.

Stone, L. (1971). Reflections on the psychoanalytic concept of aggression. The Psychoanalytic Quarterly, 40:115-244.

STABILITY IN AGGRESSIVE AND WITHDRAWN, INHIBITED BEHAVIOR PATTERNS

Dan Olweus

University of Bergen - Sydnespl. 9, Norway

The present paper gives an overview of research on stability (continuity or longitudinal consistency) in two broad forms of social incompetence or maladjustment and related behavior patterns. One refers to aggressive, disruptive, acting-out behavior, the other to withdrawn, anxious, and inhibited reaction patterns. Different authors have used somewhat different terms to designate these syndromes of disturbance: Unsocialized aggression and over-inhibited behavior (Hewitt & Jenkins, 1946), conduct problems and personality problems (Peterson, 1961), antisocial and neurotic behavior (Rutter, Tizard & Whitmore, 1970), hostility and introversion (Schaefer, 1971), anger-defiance and apathy-withdrawal (Kohn, 1977), undercontrol and ego-brittleness (Block & Block, 1979), externalizing and internalizing syndrome (Achenbach, 1978).

There are probably some real differences between these constructs, due to variation in research purpose and conceptualization, variables, samples and methods of analysis. Not withstanding, it would seem possible to reach considerable agreement on their localization within a two-dimensional model of social-emotional behavior (see Figure 1). Using activity-passivity (or extraversion-introversion) as one reference axis and emotional stability-instability (or good-poor adjustment) as the other, it is obvious that constructs referring to aggressive, acting-out behavior (and such individuals) would be placed in the unstable-active quadrant (unstable extravert, conduct problem). Similarly, concepts reflecting inhibited, anxious and withdrawn reaction patterns (and such individuals) would belong in the unstable-passive quadrant (unstable introvert, personality problem). It appears, however, that withdrawn, internalizing individuals and related constructs as reported in the research literature differ somewhat more among themselves than individuals and concepts of the acting-out type. Accordingly, it is natural to represent the

Kaplan, R.M., Konečni, V.J., Novaco, R.W. (eds.) Aggression in Children and Youth
© 1984, Martinus Nijhoff Publishers, The Hague/Boston/Lancaster
ISBN 90-247-2903-3. Printed in The Netherlands

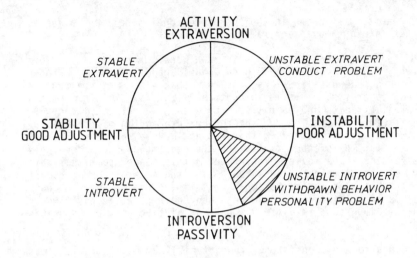

Fig. 1. Two-dimensional model of socio-emotional behavior.

internalizing syndrome in the two-dimensional model by a sector rather than by a point or radius.

Aggressive and anxious, withdrawn behavior patterns, respectively, have generally been considered traits of content (Kohlberg, LaCrosse & Ricks, 1972), that is, motivational or affective traits. This is in contrast with traits of form or temperamental traits and cognitive traits such as intelligence and cognitive style. Though the form or expression of motivational traits may change with age, this has not been a major problem in regard to the present traits for the ages studied. Accordingly, the studies to be reviewed have been mainly concerned with stability or longitudinal consistency in the same or phenotypically similar behavior manifestations, that is, the extent to which individuals in a group have retained their relative positions on similar dimensions in different periods of time (cf. Olweus, 1974, p. 536).

This form of consistency (phenotypic) may be contrasted with consistency as regards underlying processes or dimensions (genotypic consistency) in which orderly developmental transformations are assumed to take place. For such traits or characteristics, there may be little longitudinal consistency with regard to identical or similar forms of reactions. However, considerable continuity or coherence (Block, 1977) may be found if developmental changes and transformations are taken into account. This approach to consistency is particularly typical of stage-sequential theories. These regard an individual's personality development as an orderly sequence of changes where later behaviors, even when phenotypically different, are assumed to be systematically related to the individual's position in earlier developmental stages. Examples of such theories are Kohlberg's conceptualization of moral development (1969) and Loevinger's theory of ego development (1966). Empirical research on consistency from a stage-sequential perspective will not be discussed in the present paper (see Kohlberg, LaCrosse & Ricks, 1972, for an overview).

As evidenced in the terms unstable extraverts and unstable introverts, there is a component of extraversion-introversion in the behavior patterns under consideration. Extraversion-introversion may possibly be called a temperamental trait and is known to have a moderately strong genetic basis (e.g., Eaves & Eysenck, 1975). As shown in Olweus (1980a), the development of aggressive behavior is to some extent affected by individual differences in temperament (active-passive). However, this influence is certainly not strong enough for aggression to be designated as a temperamental trait. Little precise knowledge is available on the role of temperamental and genetic factors in the development of anxious, withdrawn behavior patterns. It would seem, however, that at least some behaviors of the internalizing type are fairly closely related to introversion.

In sum, this paper will focus on longitudinal consistency in two sets of behavior patterns with regard to identical or phenotypically similar behavior manifestations. While a reasonably complete coverage of the research literature (written in English) is attempted for the area of aggression, only a few selected studies of inhibited, withdrawn behavior will be discussed. In no case will research on the stability of self-report data be included. Furthermore, some attention will be paid to follow-up studies of related, but probably more disturbed behavior patterns. I will conclude by briefly discussing some interpretive possibilities and research strategies to be considered if a research project gives evidence of little or no consistency.

I will use the terms stability, longitudinal consistency, and continuity as synonymous expressions in the present context.

STABILITY OF AGGRESSIVE REACTION PATTERNS

My own interest in the stability of aggressive behavior patterns was aroused in the context of a large-scale project on bully/whipping boy behavior (Olweus, 1978). For instance, in one study I found that approximately 80% of boys whom teachers had nominated as marked bullies in grade 6 were again picked out as bullies (marked or less marked) by a different set of teachers one year later. This finding suggested a very high degree of stability over time in aggressive behavior.

In a subsequent study (Olweus, 1977a), 201 boys from 18 classes were rated by their classmates on two occasions, at grade 6 and 9, respectively. The following two dimensions were used for the measurement of aggressive behavior: Start fights ("He starts fights with other boys at school"), and Verbal protest ("When a teacher criticizes him, he tends to answer back and protest").

The main results are presented in Table 1. The stability correlations (product-moment correlations as in the rest of the article) were high, close to .80 for coefficients corrected for measurement error. These findings imply that only rather small changes in the boys' relative positions had occurred in these dimensions during the 3-year period covered. Those boys who were highly aggressive or nonaggressive, respectively, in grade 6 tended to behave in a similar way three years later. Thus, the highly aggressive boys did not in general "outgrow" their aggressive reaction patterns.

TABLE 1

UNCORRECTED AND ATTENUATION-CORRECTED STABILITY CORRELATIONS

FOR A 3-YEAR INTERVAL ($\underline{n}$ = 201)

VARIABLE	UNCORRECTED CORRELATION	CORRECTED CORRELATION
START FIGHTS	.65	.77
VERBAL PROTEST	.70	.81

NOTE: The coefficients reported are product-moment correlations; $\underline{r}$ values of .14 and .18 are significant at the .05 and .01 levels, respectively.

A REVIEW OF STUDIES OF STABILITY IN AGGRESSION

These findings in my own study made me interested in doing a review of other longitudinal investigations of males in the area of aggression (Olweus, 1979). The focus of the review was on studies of aggressive behavior and reaction patterns as observed or inferred by individuals other than the subjects themselves.

It was possible to locate 14 main publications containing 16 independent longitudinal studies (one English sample, two Swedish, and 13 American samples). A total of 24 stability coefficients were available (see Table 2).

Table 2
Longitudinal Studies of Aggression[a]

Study	Method of data collection or integration	N	Reliability at T_1	Reliability at T_2	Age at T_1	Interval in years (T_2-T_1)	Age ratio (T_1/T_2)	Raw correlation (uncorrected)	Correlation corrected for attenuation
Subjects below age 6 at T_1									
Patterson, Littman, & Bricker (1967)	Direct observation	36[b]	.80[e]	.80	3.5	.50	.88	.72	.90
Kohn & Rosman (1972)	Teacher ratings	70[c]	.77	.73	4.0	.50	.89	.56	.74
Jersild & Markey (1935)	Direct observation	24[d]	.80[e]	.80	3.0	.75	.80	.70	.88
Emmerich (1966)	Teacher ratings	53[d]	.85[e]	.85	3.5	.83	.81	.65	.76
Martin (1964)	Direct observation	53[d]	.80[e]	.80	3.5	.83	.81	.52	.65
Block, Block, & Harrington (1974)	Teacher ratings	41	.86	.74	3.5	1.00	.78	.70	.88
Kohn & Rosman (1972)	Teacher ratings	250	.77	.77	4.0	1.00	.80	.53	.69
Kohn & Rosman (1972)	Teacher ratings	250	.77	.83	4.0	1.50	.73	.48	.60
Kohn & Rosman (1973)	Teacher ratings	271	.70	.70[e]	5.0	1.50	.77	.51	.73
Kagan & Moss (1962)	Clinical ratings	36	.70	.90[e]	5.0	18.00	.22	.22	.26
Kagan & Moss (1962)	Clinical ratings	36	.60	.90[e]	2.0	21.00	.09	.29	.36

Table 2
Longitudinal Studies of Aggression[a] (Continued)

Study	Method of data collection or integration	N	Reliability at T_1	Reliability at T_2	Age at T_1	Interval in years (T_2-T_1)	Age ratio (T_1/T_2)	Raw correlation (uncorrected)	Correlation corrected for attenuation
			Subjects above age 6 at T_1						
Wiggins & Winder (1961)	Peer nominations	163	.87	.37	9.0	1.00	.90	.56	.65
Wiggins & Winder (1961)	Peer nominations	176	.81	.31	10.0	1.00	.91	.54	.67
Olweus (1977a)	Peer ratings	85	.81	.31	13.0	1.00	.93	.80	.98
Block (1971)	Clinical ratings	84	.66	.74	12.0	3.00	.80	.54	.69
Olweus (1977a)	Peer ratings	201	.85	.87	13.0	3.00	.81	.68	.79
Farrington (1978)	Teacher ratings	410	.80[e]	.80	9.0	4.00	.69	.51	.64
Eron, Huesmann, Lefko-witz, & Walder (1972)	Peer nominations	71	.90	.82	8.0	5.00	.62	.48	.56
Eron, Huesmann, Lefko-witz, & Walder (1972)	Peer nominations	71	.82	.85	13.0	5.00	.72	.65	.78
Eron, Huesmann, Lefko-witz, & Walder (1972)	Peer nominations	211	.90	.85	8.0	10.00	.44	.38	.44
Kagan & Moss (1962)	Clinical ratings	36	.85	.90[e]	13.0	10.00	.57	.56	.67
Kagan & Moss (1962)	Clinical ratings	36	.85	.90[e]	9.0	14.00	.39	.40	.48
Tuddenham (1959)	Clinical ratings	32	.75	.74	18.0	14.00	.56	.68	.91
Block (1971)	Clinical ratings	84	.74	.78	15.0	18.00	.46	.44	.53

Note. T_1 = time of first measurement; T_2 = time of second measurement.
a SampTes on which stability correlations were based generally included males only, except where indicated by a superscript.
b Subjects were 18 males and 18 females.
c Subjects were male and female.
d Subjects were 29 males and 24 females.
e See Olweus (1977b) for details.

From: Olweus D: Stability of Aggressive Reaction Patterns in Males: A Review. Psychological Bulletin, 86: 854-855.
Copyright 1979 by the American Psychological Association.
Reprinted by permission of the publisher and author.

The age of the subjects at the time of first measurement varied from 2 to 18 years and they were followed for intervals varying from half a year to 21 years. The methods of data collection or integration included direct behavioral observation, peer nominations, peer ratings, teacher ratings, and clinical ratings. The average number of subjects on which the stability coefficients were based amounted to 116--quite a respectable number by usual standards in psychological research. Most theoretical analyses in the review were carried out on attentuation corrected stability coefficients, that is, correlation coefficients corrected for errors of measurement.

An overview can be gained from Figure 2, which presents the stability coefficients as a joint function of the subjects' age at the time of the first measurement (T_1) and the interval between the two times of measurement (T_2-T_1). When the stability correlations were plotted as a function of the interval between the two times of measurement (Figure 3) a relatively regular picture was obtained (see Olweus, 1977b, 1979, for details). As might be expected, the size of the stability coefficient tended to decrease (linearly) as the interval covered increased. For an interval of 1 year the estimated disattenuated stability coefficient was as high as .76, for an interval of 5 years .69.

For several reasons, it was considered of interest to compare the results from the aggressive area with data from the intelligence domain. Thirteen studies on the stability of intelligence test measurements (of Binet type) compiled by Thorndike (1933) were used as a standard of reference. In this case the regression line was based on 36 stability coefficients covering intervals up to 5 years. The subjects were mainly school-age children and the average sample size was 111. The results showed that, although the stability in intelligence was higher than that for aggressive variables, the difference in stability was not great. It could be concluded that there is a substantial degree of stability in aggressive reaction patterns (as well as in intelligence test behavior), often over many years.

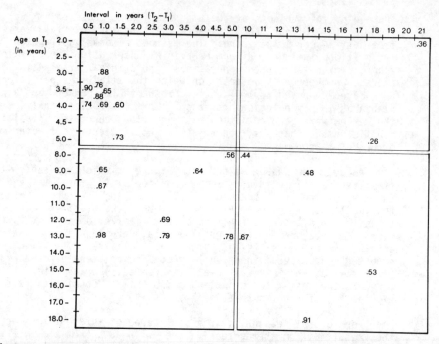

Fig. 2. Summary of disattenuated stability coefficients (correlations) for different intervals in years ($T_2 - T_1$) and different ages at time of first measurement (T_1). Variables studied refer to the area of aggression.

MORE SPECIFIC, DESCRIPTIVE CONCLUSIONS

The substantial degree of regularity manifested in Figure 3 is particularly impressive considering the great variation among the studies in sample composition, definition of variables, research setting, method of data collection and integration, and the researcher's theoretical orientation. There was also a very great range in the ages and intervals studied. After having emphasized the regularity of the data as a general finding, it is appropriate to examine the results more closely for a number of more specific conclusions.

It is obvious that marked individual differences in habitual aggression level manifest themselves early in life (certainly by age 3) and may show (see Figure 2) a high or very high degree of stability for periods of at least 1-1/2 years at this developmental level (in nursery school and school settings). Data from one study (Kagan & Moss, 1962) suggest that ratings of aggression variables that refer to the period from 0 to 3 years may have some predictive value for aggression variables assessed as long as 20 years later. However, to what extent aggressive reaction patterns observable during the preschool years can predict related patterns 10 years later must for the time being remain an open question, since data for such an assessment is not available.

Furthermore, in contrast with the common belief that the method of direct observation gives evidence of much more "behavioral specificity" and less stability than ratings of different kinds, no such tendencies were found in the present material. The average stability correlation for the three studies using direct observation (Jersild & Markey, 1935; Martin, 1964; Patterson et al., 1967) was .81, which can be compared with the average value of .79 for the three comparable studies by Block et al. (1974), Emmerich (1966), and Kohn and Rosman (1972; first study in Table 1) employing teacher ratings (the average stability correlations for the two sets of studies, using uncorrected coefficients, were .65 and .64, respectively). Judging from these studies, there seems to be no difference in degree of stability over relatively limited periods of time (up to a year) for aggression data collected by means of direct behavioral observation and teacher ratings.

Passing on to the school years, it is obvious that aggressive reaction patterns observable at ages 8 or 9 can be substantially correlated with similar patterns observed 10 to 14 years later (some 25% of the variance accounted for). It should also be noted that such patterns can with some success predict certain forms of antisocial violent behavior (violent delinquency; Farrington, 1978) that occur 10 to 12 years later.

Aggressive behavior at ages 12 and 13 may show a high or very high degree of stability for periods of 1 to 5 years (from 50% to more than 90% of the variance accounted for). Also, for periods as long as 10 years the stability is high (some 45% of the

113

Size of correlation
(corrected for attenuation)

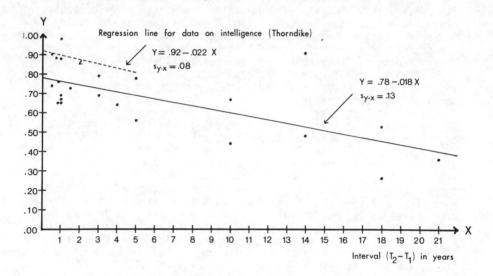

Fig. 3. Regression line showing relationship between attenuation-corrected stability coefficients and time interval ($T_2 - T_1$) in years in the area of aggression (unbroken line). (The regression line is based on 24 stability coefficients [plotted]. For comparison, the regression line for attenuation-corrected stability coefficients in the area of intelligence is shown [broken line]. This regression line is based on 36 stability co-efficients [not plotted]; Thorndike = Thorndike, 1933.)

variance accounted for). Furthermore, aggressive reaction patterns at these ages have considerable predictive capacity for
later antisocial aggression, as evidenced by the studies of Eron
et al. (1972) and Farrington (1978).

Finally, aggressive behavior (chiefly verbal) and reactivity
in the mid-30s are substantially correlated with similar patterns
observed some 15 to 18 years earlier, when the subjects were
teenagers.

In evaluating these results, the general adequacy and validity of the data should also be considered. One should recall
that in several investigations a considerable degree of correspondence was found between the aggression variables studied and
teacher ratings of the same or related behaviors. This was true
for teacher ratings and nominations versus peer ratings (Olweus,
1978; Walder, Abelson, Eron, Banta & Laulicht, 1961; Wiggins &
Winder, 1961) as well as for teacher ratings versus direct
behavioral observation (Jersild & Markey, 1935). If the latter
variables were corrected for attenuation, the correlation between
them very likely would exceed .75, indicating a quite substantial
relationship. In some investigations the aggression variables
studied also manifested relationships of considerable magnitude
with self-report data on similar patterns (Olweus, 1973, 1977b,
1978) and related, but more antisocial forms of behavior (Eron et
al., 1972; Farrington, 1978). In addition, clear associations
were obtained between two of the peer nomination instruments used
in the stability studies and overt aggressive behavior in a con-
trived, naturalistic setting (Winder & Wiggins, 1964) and in a
controlled, experimental situation, respectively (Williams, Meyerson, Eron & Selmer, 1967). Finally, the possible existence of
rater biases and stereotypes was carefully examined in some studies, in particular those by Block (1971) and Olweus (1977a). In
the latter study it was concluded on the basis of several different analyses that "the rating data to an overwhelming degree
reflect characteristics of the boys under study, rather than the
biases and cognitive schemas of the raters irrespective of ratee
characteristics" (Olweus, 1977a, p. 1310).

All in all, the above results derived by different methods
and under a wide variety of conditions constitute strong evidence
of the validity and general adequacy of the aggression data on
which the stability correlations were based. They also attest to
a substantial degree of cross-situational consistency in the sense
that there is a considerable correspondence between aggression
data obtained from independent sources or modes of measurement at
about the same point in time. (The issue of cross-situational
consistency in the area of aggression is not pursued further in
the present article, see Olweus, 1980b).

INTERPRETATION OF THE STABILITY DATA

The descriptive conclusion that there is a substantial degree

115

of stability in aggressive behavior cannot, however, without further analyses be taken as evidence of the corresponding stability of some reaction tendencies or motive systems within individuals. In particular, it might be argued that the observed consistency primarily reflects consistently different conditions for different individuals in the settings studied. Thus, in the first place, the stated conclusion can be said to apply under typical conditions, that is, under a degree of environmental variation (or stability) and pressure for change (or nonchange) typically found in the settings of the subjects for the periods studied (cf. Olweus, 1977a). Accordingly, it is important to examine the conditions characterizing the settings and periods under study, maybe particularly for the highly aggressive individuals, since their relative lack of change is a prerequisite to high stability coefficients.

The issue of environmental stability and change in these studies will not be analyzed here (see Olweus, 1977b, 1979, for a discussion). I will limit myself to stating the conclusion derived from one set of analyses, drawing particularly on the extensive findings regarding a group of highly aggressive school boys, "bullies", selected on the basis of the fact that they often attacked and harassed other children, "whipping boys" (Olweus, 1978). Specifically, the question was considered whether there were particular aversive situations or conditions in the immediate, promixal (i.e., school) environment of the habitually aggressive subjects that might explain their behavior.

Combining several lines of evidence concerning the possible existence of frustrations, failures and rejections in the school as well as other psychological, physical and socioeconomic conditions of the bullies, it was concluded that it is very difficult to explain the behavior of these highly aggressive boys as a consequence of their being exposed to unusually aversive situations or conditions in the school environment. All in all, there was little evidence supporting a view that stable differences in aggression level resulted from consistently different environmental conditions for different individuals in the situation in which the aggressive behavior was studied. (However, there is considerable evidence showing that the conditions in other situations, e.g., within the family, have been and may still at the time of the study be quite different for more and less aggressive boys, see Olweus, 1980a).

GENERAL CONCLUSIONS

On the basis of the results and analyses presented (Olweus, 1979) two general conclusions can be drawn.

1) The degree of stability or continuity in aggressive behavior is much greater than has been recently maintained (e.g., Mischel, 1968, 1969; Kohlberg, LaCrosse & Ricks, 1972, p. 1222). The across-time stability was not, in fact, much lower than that

116

typically found in the intelligence domain. However, to avoid misunderstanding, I want to make clear that when pointing to similarities between results from the intelligence domain and those from the aggression area, I restrict my comparison to the degree of stability over time. I am in no way implying assumptions about similar developmental and operating mechanisms or, for instance, that the degree of genetic influence is the same in the two areas (see Olweus, 1978, chap. 8).

2) The results and analyses strongly suggest that important "determinants" of the observed continuity in aggressive behavior over time are to be found in relatively stable, individual-differentiating reaction tendencies or motive systems, however conceptualized, within individuals (personality variables). These reaction tendencies or motive systems very likely comprise a cognitive component which in highly aggressive individuals may involve a biased perception of the environment. Such perceptions probably affect the likelihood of aggressive reactions from the individual and as a consequence, from his social environment.

The above conclusion should not be taken to imply that situational factors are considered unimportant for the evocation of aggressive behavior (see, e.g., Olweus, 1969, 1973). Nor does it imply that aggressive behavior is independent of rewarding and maintaining conditions in the immediate, proximal environment. However, it is contended here that the explanatory and predictive value of such factors has been exaggerated in the last decade; as concluded above, relatively stable, internal reaction tendencies are important determinants of behavior in the aggressive motive area and they should be given considerably greater weight than has been done recently. (For an overview of how such internal reaction tendencies may develop in the area of aggression, see Olweus, 1978, chap. 8, and 1980a). In line with this argument, it also seems quite reasonable to assume that the inferred, internal reaction tendencies or motive systems within an individual are essential codeterminants of what the individual will perceive as reinforcing. In fact, the analyses presented suggest that highly aggressive individuals to a considerable degree actively select and create the kind of situations in which they are often observed (cf. Bowers, 1973; Wachtel, 1973).

STABILITY OF AGGRESSIVE BEHAVIOR IN FEMALES

It is commonly maintained that there is practically no stability over time for aggressive behavior in females. This generalization is mainly based on the Kagan and Moss 1962 study of 35 girls and 36 boys who were followed from early childhood to adulthood (average age of 24 years). The differential stability in males and females has been interpreted as a function of traditional sex-role standards to the effect that aggressive behavior in a boy is accepted and even positively valued while such behavior is discouraged in girls.

A closer look at the empirical evidence available reveals quite a different picture, as will be evident shortly. As far as I know, there are only three studies (Block, 1971; Kagan & Moss, 1962; Tuddenham, 1959) of the stability of aggressive reaction patterns in females for periods involving adult age. The subject samples of these studies were rather small (Kagan & Moss, 1962; Tuddenham, 1959) or moderate (Block, 1971) and the results conflicting (Block's study which comprised 87 females and 84 males, gave evidence of some stability also in females over an 18-year interval). In consideration of these facts, I will limit myself to studies of subjects up to an age of 19 years.

It has been possible to locate six studies on the stability of aggressive behavior in females, using the same criteria of selection as in the previous review of male studies (Olweus, 1979). These six studies (Block, 1971, 1979; Kohn, 1979; Kohn & Rosman, 1972; Lefkowitz, Eron, Walder & Huesmann, 1972; Bachteman & Magnusson, 1978) also comprised a comparable male sample. The data for the two sexes were thus highly similar in all relevant respects and should enable one to make a meaningful comparison.

A total of 21 stability coefficients were available for each sex. The average age of the subjects was approximately seven years and the subjects were followed for intervals varying from half a year to 10 years. The average interval covered was 2.8 years. The average number of subjects on which the stability coefficients were based amounted to approximately 200. Since the same measuring technique was used on the male and the female samples in each particular study and there was little difference in reliability (where such information was given), the present analysis is carried out on correlation coefficients uncorrected for attenuation.

As evident from Figures 4, 5 and 6, there is a difference in stability of aggressive behavior for males and females. However, though statistically significant and fairly consistent, this difference is not marked. The average r for males is .497 while the corresponding value for females is .439, giving an average difference of .058 correlation points.

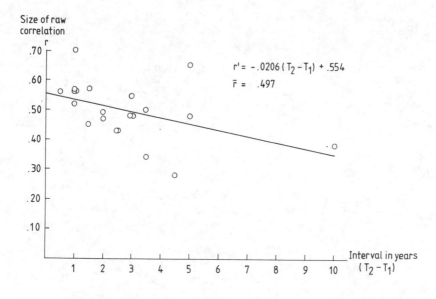

Fig. 4. Regression line showing relationship between uncorrected
stability coefficients in the area of aggression and time
interval ($T_2 - T_1$) in years for males up to age 19 years.
Number of stability coefficients = 21.

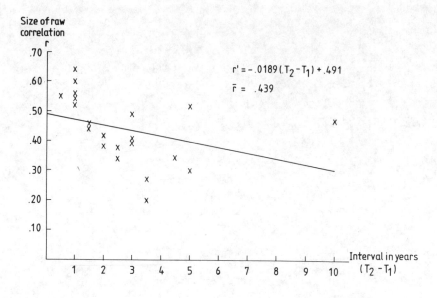

Fig. 5. Regression line showing relationship between uncorrected stability coefficients in the area of aggression and time interval ($T_2 - T_1$): in years for females up to age 19 years. Number of stability coefficients = 21.

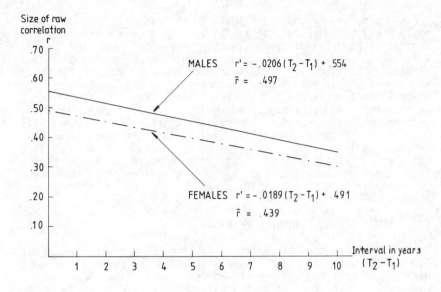

Fig. 6. Regression lines showing relationship between uncorrected
stability coefficients (not plotted) in the area of
aggression and time interval $(T_2 - T_1)$ in years for
females and males up to age 19 years.

It can thus be concluded that, in contrast to what is commonly believed, there is a fairly high degree of stability in aggressive reaction patterns also in females, at least for intervals of 10 years up to age 19. It should be noted that this conclusion is based on six different studies and samples that must be considered relatively large according to usual standards of psychological research. The somewhat lower stability in females as compared with males may partly reflect the fact that, for whatever reason, there are far fewer highly aggressive girls than boys (see e.g., Maccoby & Jacklin, 1974). This will result in lower variability in the female distributions, thereby reducing the size of the correlation coefficient. The difference-in-variability interpretation is supported by the standard deviation data presented in Kohn (1977, Table 6.1).

STABILITY OF CONDUCT PROBLEM BEHAVIOR

The results reported in the literature on the persistence of (probably) more serious conduct problems are in good agreement with the general conclusion derived from studies in the area of aggression. In the Isle of Wight study (Rutter, Tizard & Whitmore, 1970), for example, approximately 60% of the children with conduct disorders at age 10 were classified as having conduct problems 4 years later. Similarly, Robins (1966, 1978) found that the prognosis was quite poor for children referred to a Child Guidance Clinic for antisocial behaviors such as fighting, theft, alcohol abuse, and truancy. When followed up 30 years later, at an average age of 43 years, a considerable portion of them still exhibited serious antisocial problems and 28% were diagnosed as sociopaths. These findings differed radically from the outcome for children referred to the clinic for non-antisocial symptoms and for a control group.

These studies, in particular the ones conducted by Robins, strongly suggest that antisocial behavior in childhood may be an almost necessary but not sufficient condition for later antisocial problems. Thus, nearly all of Robins' adult antisocial subjects had a history of antisocial behavior in childhood (1978). In the Isle of Wight study, it is noteworthy that no children who had exhibited emotional (non-antisocial, neurotic) problems when younger developed into antisocial adolescents (Graham & Rutter, 1973).

In conclusion, aggressive and related acting-out behavior shows a high degree of stability often over long periods of time. The degree of stability seems to vary inversely both with the length of the interval covered and the subjects' age at the time of first assessment.

STABILITY OF INHIBITED, WITHDRAWN BEHAVIOR

I will now pass on to a consideration of the stability of

122

inhibited, withdrawn behavior patterns, located in the lower right quadrant of Figure 1. There seem to be fewer longitudinal studies of such traits than of aggressive behavior patterns. I will limit myself to discussing the results from two research projects which both comprise a male and a female sample and report stability coefficients for a number of intervals. One was conducted by Martin Kohn (1977; the correlation coefficients calculated by sex are not presented in Kohn, 1977, but were obtained in personal communication, 1979), the other by Wanda Bronson in the context of the Berkely Guidance Study (Macfarlane, Allen & Honzik, 1954). Since reliability coefficients were not given in Bronson, only coefficients uncorrected for attenuation will be reported in the following.

The main assessment device in Kohn's study was teacher ratings. On the basis of factor analysis, two broad dimensions of social-emotional functioning were derived, Apathy-Withdrawal vs. Interest-Participation (to be considered here) and Anger-Defiance vs. Cooperation-Compliance (included in the previous comparison of the stability in aggressive behavior for males versus females). The subjects consisted of a 20% random sample of the day care population of New York City. The children were from predominantly lower- and lower-middle-class families, and slightly more than 50% came from broken homes. Different subgroups were followed for different periods of time and, accordingly, the size of the sample on which a stability coefficient was based varied. The average number of subjects was 261 for the boys and 253 for the girls. The periods studied were preschool (at an average age of 4 years) and grades 1 (6 years) through 4 (9 years). The longest interval covered was 5 years, the average interval being 2.4 years.

TABLE 3

STABILITY COEFFICIENTS (r) FROM KOHN'S STUDY

DIMENSION: APATHY-WITHDRAWAL

BOYS

	GR 1	GR 2	GR 3	GR 4	
PRESCHOOL (4y)	.43	.33	.34	.25	
GRADE 1 (6y)		.48	.39	.35	
GRADE 2 (7y)			.43	.43	
GRADE 3 (8y)				.48	r = .391
GRADE 4 (9y)					

GIRLS

	GR 1	GR 2	GR 3	GR 4	
PRESCHOOL (4y)	.28	.37	.31	.30	
GRADE 1 (6y)		.46	.39	.38	
GRADE 2 (7y)			.50	.40	r = .391
GRADE 3 (8y)				.52	

The stability coefficients are given in Table 3 and plotted against the time interval in Figures 7 (for boys; lower part) and 8 (for girls; lower part). In the male as well as the female sample, the average correlation was .391, indicating moderate stability over the average interval of 2.4 years. As expected, the size of the correlation coefficient decreases (linearly) as the interval becomes longer. For each 1-year increase of the interval, the stability coefficient is reduced by approximately .05 correlation points. When the stability coefficients for Apathy-Withdrawal are compared with the corresponding values for the second main dimension in Kohn's study., Anger-Defiance, the latter dimension turns out to be somewhat more stable. The average correlations for boys and girls were .445 for Anger-Defiance and .391 for Apathy-Withdrawal.

Bronson's study comprised 45 boys and 40 girls (roughly representative of the Berkeley population) for whom data were collected yearly between the ages of 5 and 16 years. Information from the mothers, the children, other members of the family, and teachers were condensed into ratings on 5-point scales. In the data analyses, ratings for three consecutive years were grouped together, giving four time periods to be compared: Period A (ages 5, 6 and 7), B (ages 8, 9 and 10), C (ages 11, 12 and 13) and D (ages 14, 15 and 16). The data were reduced to three dimensions, one of which was named Reserved-Somber-Shy/Expressive-Gay-Socially Easy. In all four periods, this dimension had a correlation of approximately .40 with the bipolar scale Anxious-Relaxed.

TABLE 4

STABILITY COEFFICIENTS (r) FROM BRONSON'S STUDY

DIMENSION: RESERVED-SOMBER-SHY/EXPRESSIVE-GAY-SOCIALLY EASY

BOYS

	B	C	D	
PERIOD A (6y)	.73	.60	.69	
PERIOD B (9y)		.80	.79	r = .728
PERIOD C (12y)			.76	
PERIOD D (15y)				

GIRLS

	B	C	D	
PERIOD A (6y)	.72	.51	.47	
PERIOD B (9y)		.82	.66	r = .650
PERIOD C (12y)			72	

The stability coefficients are shown in Table 4 with the periods designated by the average age within each period: 6, 9, 12 and 15 years (the intervals are calculated on the basis of these ages). In the upper part of Figures 7 and 8 the coefficients are plotted as a function of the interval between the ages concerned. The longest interval covered 9 years and the average interval was 5 years.

The average correlation was .728 for the boys and .650 for the girls, indicating a high degree of stability. For the 9-year interval the correlations were .69 and .47, respectively. The stability was generally somewhat lower for girls.

When compared with the results obtained in Kohn's study (in the lower part of Figures 7 and 8), Bronson's data give evidence

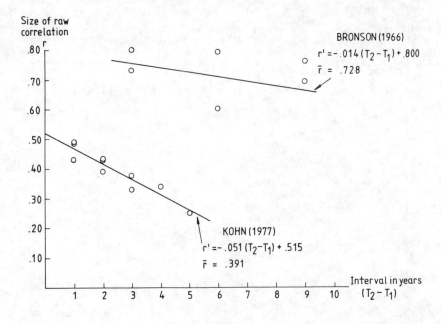

Fig. 7. Regression lines showing relationship between uncorrected
         stability coefficients for withdrawn behavior and time
         interval ($T_2 - T_1$) in years for boys. Data from Bronson
         (1966) and Kohn (1977).

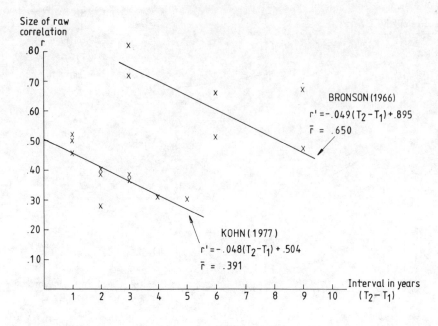

Fig. 8. Regression lines showing relationship between uncorrected
stability coefficients for withdrawn behavior and time
interval ($T_2 - T_1$) in years for girls. Data from Bronson
(1966) and Kohn (1977).

of clearly higher stability. To some extent, the difference in stability is a consequence of the different ages studied (however, the higher stability in Bronson's data is marked also in the period from 6 to 9 years which is included in both studies). Furthermore, there were certain correlation-lowering factors present in the Kohn study (see Olweus, 1977b, p. 46-48) while the coefficients in the Bronson study may have been somewhat inflated (due to "experimental dependence" between ratings for different periods; see Macfarlane et al., 1954, p. 10). On the other hand, the ratings in the latter study were averaged across three con-secutive years for each period, which presumably increased the reliability and generality of the measures to be correlated. Tak-ing these considerations into account, it is probable that the two sets of "true" stability coefficients in these studies are closer to each other than portrayed in Figures 7 and 8. Even so, there is very likely a real difference in stability which may imply that somewhat different behavior patterns have been measured. I will return to this point later.

Summing up so far, behavior patterns of an inhibited, with-drawn nature showed moderate to substantial stability over time as evidenced by the two studies reported on here. The Apathy-Withdrawal dimension in Kohn's study was somewhat less stable than the aggressive dimension, Anger-Defiance.

STABILITY OF PERSONALITY PROBLEM BEHAVIOR

While conduct problem behavior has consistently been found to be fairly or very stable over time, findings have been more con-tradictory with regard to personality problem behavior or neurotic traits. On the one hand, the Robins (1966) study cited before found that children referred to a guidance clinic for emotional problems were not more likely than controls to become adult neu-rotics. Furthermore, she found no clear difference in childhood emotional problems between children who were healthy as adults and those who became neurotic. Similarly, Morris, Soroker and Burrus (1954) found that children referred to a Child Guidance Clinic for withdrawal, fearful and shy behavior were no more likely to be maladjusted as adults than a random sample of the population.

On the other hand, other findings suggest a higher degree of persistence. For instance, Graham and Rutter (1973) recorded that 46% of children with emotional problems at age 10 still showed emotional disturbances 4 years later. While clearly lower than the persistence of conduct disorders (previously cited), this rate was over twice that in the general population.

In a study of a large representative sample of Manhatten children aged 6 to 18 (Gersten, Langner, Eisenberg, Simca-Fagan & McCarthy, 1976) it was found that certain neurotic traits showed fairly low stability over a follow-up period of 5 years. Among these were Repetitive motor behavior, Dependence and Self-destructive tendencies. On the other hand, the factor of

Regressive anxiety (many fears, sleep disturbances, psychosomatic complaints, etc.) which was probably the best indicator of "neurotic symptoms of childhood" displayed a degree of stability that was not much lower than that of the acting-out factors (Fighting, Delinquency, Conflict with parents).

All in all, the above findings suggest that certain neurotic traits such as nail-biting, thumb-sucking, temper tantrums, dependence and repetitive motor behavior show little or no stability over moderate periods of time. These traits or symptoms may primarily reflect somewhat exaggerated reactions to common developmental stresses. However, other symptoms such as severe and pervasive anxiety reactions are likely to manifest more continuity. Anyhow, most authors seem to agree that neurotic or personality problem patterns, even the more persistent ones, are less stable than behavior problems of the acting-out or conduct disorder type.

SHOULD BEHAVIOR PATTERNS OF THE INTERNALIZING TYPE BE DIFFERENTIATED?

In the introductory section, it was pointed out that individuals of the withdrawn, internalizing type (lower right quadrant of Figure 1) were probably more heterogeneous than aggressive, acting-out individuals. This heterogeneity is born out by the above findings on the differential stability of various neurotic behavior patterns.

With regard to the difference in stability between Bronson's and Kohn's data, one may speculate if the behavior patterns measured represent somewhat different dimensions. Bronson's dimension Reserved-Somber-Shy/Expressive-Gay-Socially Easy is reminiscent of Introversion-Extroversion which probably has a moderately strong genetic basis. In addition, this dimension was consistently correlated with a scale of anxiety which can be supposed to show moderate stability, according to the results of Gersten et. al. (1976).

On the other hand, the items defining Kohn's Apathy-Withdrawal factor did not refer to anxiety reactions (Kohn, 1977, Tables 3.1 and 3.2) but seemed rather to reflect apathy, isolation among peers and feelings of sadness. It is thus quite possible that the dimensions in question are somewhat different.

It should be recalled, however, that the customarily persistent acting-out dimension was not much more stable in Kohn's study than Apathy-Withdrawal. Accordingly, the difference in stability in Kohn's and Bronson's studies may also reflect other factors such as population differences as well as the methodological conditions previously cited.

Even if the limited evidence available precludes any strong conclusions with regard to the present studies, it seems safe to assert that too many researchers have been inclined to regard the various behavior patterns of the internalizing type as equivalent with respect to persistence (or lack of persistence). Very likely, such an approach is not warranted. However, more research is obviously needed to make a clearer differentiation between behavior dimensions in this area that are relatively stable and those that are not. Such a differentiation will probably also reveal some differences in antecedent conditions.

DETERMINANTS OF A STABLE AGGRESSIVE BEHAVIOR PATTERN

The present paper has mainly focused on the stability of individual differences rather than on the complementary phenomenon, change. However, for the social sciences, both are equally important to study (as well as other aspects such as changes in level not discussed here). But it should be emphasized that the finding of a high degree of stability or change often only represents a starting point for the identification of factors that account for the particular result obtained.

In this context, it needs to be underlined that a high degree of stability in a behavior pattern is no indicator of a genetic basis for individual differences. With regard to the development of aggressive reaction patterns, for instance, genetic factors very likely play only a weak and indirect role via the child's temperamental make-up. Here the available evidence (see e.g., Olweus, 1980a) clearly points up the importance of environmental conditions such as the basic emotional attitude of the primary caretaker during the preschool years as well as child-rearing factors including permissiveness for aggression and use of power-oriented methods. The nature of the child's peer group and other factors are also of significance.

These and other data suggest that environmental factors affect, in interplay with temperamental characteristics (active-passive), affect the young child's (in particular boys have been studied) cognitive, emotional and behavioral development in such a way that relatively stable reaction tendencies gradually become crystallized. These reaction tendencies are very likely modifiable throughout the whole life cycle but more so in early ages, maybe up to 12-13 years. As previously emphasized, the aggressive reaction tendencies can be considered important determinants of aggressive behavior in a particular situation (Olweus, 1973).

In this context, it is interesting to note that aggressive, acting-out children who are generally exposed to a good deal of environmental pressure for modifying their behavior in more socialized directions change less over time than children of the internalizing, neurotic kind, as previously shown. In general, the latter are subjected to only little or no pressure for change from the environment. Research on the effects of psychotherapy and other remedial measures (e.g., Levitt, 1971; McCord & McCord, 1964; Olweus, 1978) leads to similar conclusions.

INTERPRETATION OF INCONSISTENCY

I will now briefly discuss the problem arising when a zero or low correlation is obtained between measurements of a behavior pattern at two different points in time. How is this to be interpreted?

One fairly frequent way is to regard it as a demonstration of complete inconsistency or discontinuity, implying that the two measures have no systematic variation in common. However, before drawing such a conclusion, it would seem wise to carefully examine the study for possible conceptual methodological weakness. For, as Jack Block has argued (Block, 1977), the easiest way to achieve inconsistency is to do inadequate research. If a study is poorly conceptualized, uses inappropriate assessment techniques and the behavior under consideration is insufficiently sampled, there is no reason to expect consistency over time or across situations.

Elsewhere I have expanded on this theme (Olweus, 1980b), in particular from the perspective of facet analysis and a distinction between one-occasion and multiple-occasion measures. Briefly, if there is poor matching between two (or more) measures in terms of facet elements (such as response forms, interaction partners and settings), there are in general no grounds for expecting much consistency. Conversely, Block and Block (1979) and Epstein (1979) among others have shown that by taking appropriate samples of the behaviors to be intercorrelated, consistency may be substantially increased. Obviously, when adequate research procedures are used, the amount of error variation or "noise" may be considerably reduced.

In addition, acceptance of an inconsistency or discontinuity interpretation as formulated above represents a pessimistic and defeatist position: There is no consistency and we can't tell in what directions the changes to or their causative factors. It is a kind of admission of complete failure: We don't know anything.

But what alternatives are there, if we cannot explain the inconsistency or instability observed by reference to conceptual and methodological weaknesses (and change it into more consistency in a subsequent study)? Obviously, a lack of consistency may come about as a result of systematic changes in different directions which cancel out. However, to be able to detect and replicate such subgroup differences we must have some valid theoretical notions about what variables affect the relationships. We must thus try to make the observed alterations predictable and explicable. Only such systematic changes, in contrast with random variation, are of genuine interest to the developmental psychologist or psychiatrist.

132

THE NEED FOR MORE COMPLEX MODELS

To be able to specify direction and form of possible changes and identify their causative factors, we need more complex and elaborate models. The development of such models may take many directions (e.g., Baltes, Reese & Lipsitt, 1980; Block, 1971; Emmerich, 1977; Foa, 1968; Wohlwill, 1973). In the present context, I will limit myself to a few brief suggestions related to the content of the present chapter.

Referring to Figure 1, the two-dimensional model (with different behavior patterns ordered as a circumplex) might be used to specify probable changes over time. Relying on a principle of proximity (Foa, 1968), we might hypothesize that a behavior pattern at any one location of the circle is more likely to be transformed into proximal rather than remote behavior patterns, if changes occur. Or we might assume that behavioral alterations mainly take place in the horizontal direction, maybe in particular from maladjustment to relative adjustment. Possibly, changes along the Extraversion-Introversion axis are less likely and less marked since this dimension is to some degree genetically determined and exposed to relatively little environment pressure for change. When contemplating such predictions, we might perhaps also come to the conclusion that the model portrayed in Figure 1 is too simple and needs to be replaced by more complex representations of reality.

However, it is certainly not enough to specify the amount, direction and form of possible changes. Of course, it is equally important to identify factors that are responsible for these changes. And here we need more sophisticated theories of the environment and its interaction with biological factors.

The previous discussion may possibly have given the impression that consideration of change and complex models of change become important only when no or little stability or consistency has been found. This is not so, of course. Also in areas where there is a high or fairly high degree of consistency, alterations of behavior are of considerable interest. With regard to aggressive behavior patterns, for example, it is certainly of great significance to find out what direction and form possible changes take and their determining factors. Accordingly, we can conclude by asserting that our basic scientific task is to strive for predictability, that is, to be able to account for both stability and change.

REFERENCES

Achenbach, T.M. (1978). The child behavior profile: I. Boys Aged 6-11. Journal of Consulting and Clinical Psychology, 46:478-488.

Bachteman, G. & Magnusson, D. (1978). Longitudinal stability of personality characteristics. Ratings. Reports from the Department of Psychology, University of Stockholm, No. 537.

Baltes, P.B., Reese, H.W. & Lipsitt, L.P. (1980). Life-span developmental psychology. Annual Review of Psychology, 31:65-110.

Block, J. (1971). Lives through time. Berkeley, CA: Bancroft Books.

Block, J. (1977). Advancing the psychology of personality: Paradigmatic shift or improving the quality of research? In D. Magnusson & N.S. Endler (Eds.), Personality at the crossroads: Current issues in interactional psychology. Hillsdale, NJ: Erlbaum.

Block, J. Personal communication, April 25, 1979.

Block, J.H. & Block J. (1979). The role of ego-control and ego-resiliency in the organization of behavior. In W.A. Collins (Ed.), Minnesota Symposia on Child Psychology, Volume 13. New York: Erlbaum.

Block, J., Block, J.H. & Harrington, D.M. (1974). Some missgivings about the Matching Familiar Figures Test as a measure of reflection-impulsivity. Developmental Psychology, 10:611-632.

Bowers, K.S. (1973). Situationism in psychology: An analysis and a critique. Psychological Review, 80:307-336.

Bronson, W.C. (1966). Central orientations: A study of behavior organization from childhood to adolescence. Child Development, 37:125-155.

Eaves, L. & Eysenck, H.J. (1975). The nature of extraversion: A genetical analysis. Journal of Personality and Social Psychology, 32:102-112.

Emmerich, W. (1966). Continuity and stability in early social development: II. Teacher ratings. Child Development, 37:17-27.

Emmerich, W. (1977). Structure and development of personal-social behaviors in economically disadvantaged preschool children. Genetic Psychology Monographs, 95:191-245.

Epstein, S. (1979). The stability of behavior: I. On predicting most of the people much of the time. Journal of Personality and Social Psychology, 37:1097-1126.

Eron, L.D., Huesmann, L.R., Lefkowitz, M.M. & Walder, L.O. (1972). Does television cause aggression? American Psychologist, 27:253-263.

Farrington, D.P. The family backgrounds of aggressive youths. In L. Hersov, M. Berger & D. Schaffer (Eds.), Aggression and Antisocial Disorder in Children. Oxford, England: Pergamon.

Foa, U.G. (1968). Three kinds of behavioral changes. Psychological Bulletin, 70:460-473.

Gersten, J.C., Langner, T.S., Eisenberg, J.G., Simca-Fagan, O. & McCarthy, E.D. (1976). Stability and change in types of behavioral disturbance of children and adolescents. Journal of Abnormal Child Psychology, 4:111-127.

Graham, P. & Rutter, M. (1973). Psychiatric disorder in the young adolescent: A follow-up study. Proceedings of the Royal Society for Medicine, 66:1226-1229.

Hartup, W.W. (1979). Two social worlds: Family relations and peer relations. In M. Rutter (Ed.), Scientific foundations of developmental psychiatry, London: Heineman.

Hewitt, L.E. & Jenkins, R.L. (1946). Fundamental patterns of maladjustment: The dynamics of their origin. Illinois: D.H. Green.

Jersild, A.T. & Markey, F.V. (1935). Conflicts between preschool children. Child Development Monograph, No. 21.

Kagan, J. & Moss, H.A. (1962). Birth to maturity: A study of psychological development. New York: Wiley.

Kohlberg, L. (1969). Stage and sequence: The cognitive-developmental approach to socialization. In D. Goslin (Ed.), Handbook of Socialization and Theory and Research. Chicago: Rand McNally.

Kohlberg, L., LaCrosse, J. & Ricks, D. (1972). The predictability of adult mental health from childhood behavior. In B. Wolman (Ed.), Manual of Child Psychopathology. New York: McGraw Hill.

Kohn, M. Social competence, symptoms and underachievement in childhood. A longitudinal perspective. Washington, D.C.: Winston & Sons, 1977.

Kohn, M. Personal communication, May 30, 1979.

Kohn, M. & Rosman, B.L. (1972). A social competence scale and symptom checklist for the preschool child: Factor dimensions, their cross-instrumental generality, and longitudinal persistence. Developmental Psychology, 4:430-444.

Kohn, M. & Rosman, B.L. (1973). Cross-situational and longitudinal stability of social-emotional functioning in young children. Child Development, 44:721-727.

Lefkowitz, M.M., Eron, L.D., Walder, L.O. & Huesmann, L.R. (1971). Television violence and child aggression: A follow-up study. In G.A. Comstock & E.A. Rubinstein (Eds.), Television and social behavior (Vol. 3). Washington, D.C.: U.S. Government Printing Office.

Levitt, E.E. (1971). Research on psychotherapy with children. In A.E. Bergin & S.L. Garfield (Eds.), Handbook of psychotherapy and behavior change. New York: Wiley.

Loevinger, J. (1966). The meaning and measurement of ego development. American Psychologist, 21:195-206.

Maccoby, E.E. & Jacklin, C.N. (1974). The psychology of sex differences. Palo Alto: Stanford University Press.

Mcfarlane, J.W., Allen, L. & Honzik, M.P. (1954). A developmental study of the behavior problems of normal children between 21 months and 14 years. Los Angeles: University of California Press.

Martin, W.E. (1964). Singularity and stability of the profiles of social behavior. In C.B. Stendler (Ed.), Readings in child behavior and development. New York: Harcourt, Brace & World.

McCord, W. & McCord, J. (1964). The psychopath: An essay on the criminal mind. New York: Van Nostrand.

Mischel, W. (1968). Personality and assessment. New York: Wiley.

Mischel, W. (1969). Continuity and change in personality. American Psychologist, 24:1012-1018.

Morris, D.P., Soroker, E. & Burrus, G. (1954). Follow-up studies of shy, withdrawn children. I. Evaluation of later adjustment. American Journal of Orthopsychiatry, 24:743-754.

Olweus, D. (1973). Personality and aggression. In J.K. Cole &

D.D. Jensen (Eds.), Nebraska Symposium on Motivation 1972, 261-321. Lincoln: University of Nebraska Press, 1973.

Olweus, D. (1974). Personality factors and aggression: With special reference to violence within the peer group. In J. de Wit & W.W. Hartup (Eds.), Determinants and origins of aggressive behavior. The Hague: Mouton Press.

Olweus, D. (1977a). Aggression and peer acceptance in adolescent boys: Two short-term longitudinal studies of ratings. Child Development, 48:1301-1313.

Olweus, D. (1977b). Longitudinal studies of aggressive reaction patterns in males: A review (Report No. 2). Bergen, Norway: University of Vergen, Institute of Psychology.

Olweus, D. (1978). Aggression in the schools: Bullies and Whipping Boys. Washington, D.C.: Hemisphere.

Olweus, D. (1979). Stability of aggressive reaction patterns in males: A review. Psychological Bulletin, 86:852-875.

Olweus, D. (1980a). Familial and temperamental determinants of aggressive behavior in adolescent boys--a causal analysis. Developmental Psychology, 16:644-660.

Olweus, D. (1980b). The consistency issue in personality psychology revisited--with special reference to aggression. Britism Journal of Social and Clinical Psychology, 19:377-390.

Patterson, G.R., Littman, R.A. & Bricker, W. (1967). Assertive behavior in children: A step toward a theory of aggression. Monographs of the Society for Research in Child Development, 32:(5, Whole No. 113).

Peterson, D.R. (1961). Behavior problems of middle childhood. Journal of Consulting Psychology, 25:205-209.

Robins, L.N. (1966). Deviant children grown up. Baltimore: Williams & Wilkins.

Robins, L.N. (1978). Sturdy childhood predictors of adult antisocial behavior: replication from longitudinal studies. Psychological Medicine, 8:611-622.

Rutter, M., Tizard, J. & Whitmore, K. (1970). Education, health, and behavior. London: Longman.

Schaefer, E.S. (1971). Development of hierarchical, configurational models for parent and child behavior. In J.P. Hill (Ed.), Minnesota symposium on child psychology (Vol. 5). Minneapolis: University of Minnesota Press.

Thorndike, R.L. (1933). The effect of interval between test and retest on the constancy of I.Q. Journal of Educational Psychology, 24:543-549.

Tuddenham, R.D. (1959). The constancy of personality ratings over two decades. Genetic Psychology Monographs, 60:3-29.

Wachtel, P.L. (1973). Psychodynamics, behavior therapy, and the implacable experimentor: An inquiry into the consistency of personality. Journal of Abnormal Psychology, 83:324-334.

Walder, L.O., Abelson, R.P., Eron, L.D., Banta, T.J. & Laulicht, J.H. (1961). Development of a peer-rating measure of aggression. Psychological Reports, 9:497-556 (Monograph).

Wiggins, J.S. & Winder, C.L. (1961). The Peer Nomination Inventory: An empirically derived sociometric measure of adjustment in preadolescent boys. Psychological Reports, 9:643-677.

Williams, J.F., Meyerson, L.J., Eron, L.D. & Selmer, I.J. (1967).
    Peer rated aggression and aggressive responses elicited in an
    experimental situation. Child Development, 38:181-190.
Winder, C.L. & Wiggins, J.S. (1964). Social reputation and social
    behavior: A further validation of the Peer Nomination Inven-
    tory. Journal of Abnormal and Social Psychology, 68:681-684.
Wohlwill, J.F. (1973). The study of behavioral development. New
    York: Academic Press.

DEVELOPMENTAL ISSUES IN ATTRIBUTION, MORAL JUDGEMENT AND
AGGRESSION

Brendan Gail Rule and Tamara J. Ferguson

University of Alberta and The Catholic University
of Nijmegen, Holland

In his examination of developmental changes in the expression
of hostile aggression, Hartup (1974) suggested that the expression
of such aggression presupposes cognitive skills that mediate anger
and its behavioral expression. Despite the observation in
numerous studies that anger influences aggression in young children, there have been few theoretical treatments of the anger-
aggression relationship in the literature. Rather, the role of
anger has been considered only incidentally in current treatments
of children's aggression, whereby attention has focused on how
reinforcement and punishment affect the acquisition and mainte-
nance of aggressive behavior (e.g., Bandura, 1973; Patterson,
Littman & Bricker, 1967). Moreover, when anger has been considered, emphasis has often been placed on its noncognitive and
uncontrolled nature (Berkowitz, 1962). While many instances of
anger may be characterized as uncontrolled and unthinking
responses to harm, there are many occasions in which anger
reflects the perceiver's interpretations of why harm occurred and
whether it was justified. Anger as a thinking and controlled
response is seen in children as well as adults. For example, as
children mature, they express increasingly greater concern for
when and why it is appropriate to express aggression. They also
express shame and guilt according to their own causal responsibility for harm and they evaluate others on the basis of the person's
perceived causal responsibility for harm (e.g., Bandura, 1973;
Camp, 1977; Dodge, 1980; Shantz & Voydanoff, 1973). The purpose
of this paper is to examine the relation of anger and aggression
to cognitive factors, such as attributions and blame, in children
of different ages. In doing this we shall indicate how children's
developing logical reasoning abilities, use of efficient retention

138

Kaplan, R.M., Konečni, V.J., Novaco, R.W. (eds.) Aggression in Children and Youth
© 1984, Martinus Nijhoff Publishers, The Hague/Boston/Lancaster
ISBN 90-247-2903-3. Printed in The Netherlands

and retrieval strategies, as well as perspective taking and empathic abilities contribute to their increasing concern with attributionally and morally relevant considerations in reacting to another's harmful behavior.

The paper is structured in several sections. The first section deals with our model of the relation between causal assignment, blame, anger and aggression. In the second section causal responsibility is defined and the factors that affect causal assignment are discussed. The third section reviews the research on causal assignment, blame, anger and aggression in children.

I. AN ATTRIBUTIONAL PERSPECTIVE ON AGGRESSION

Our examination of the research literature on aggression highlighted the important role that attributions play in influencing anger and retaliation through their effects on blame ascriptions. Hostile aggression, defined as an intentionally committed act designed to interfere with another's psychological or physical welfare, is instigated by anger-inducing stimuli such as insult, attack or frustration (Berkowitz, 1962; Buss, 1961). But the degree of anger and subsequent hostile retaliation in response to these factors depends less on the severity of these types of provocation and more on whether they can be attributed to something about the provocateur's personal characteristics than to characteristics of the situation. More specifically, anger and its subsequent behavioral expression are greater when the provocation is seen as intentional rather than unintentional, foreseeable rather than unforeseeable, or perpetrated for socially unacceptable rather than socially acceptable reasons (e.g., Dyck & Rule, 1978; Greenwell & Dengerink, 1973; Nickel, 1974; Pastore, 1952). Findings such as these prompted us to incorporate attributionally-based constructs in our conceptualization of hostile retaliation.

In a recent paper (Ferguson & Rule, in press) we explicated the factors that affect attributions for harm and indicated how these attributions influence anger and blame ascriptions. Central to our analysis is the proposition that adults become angry in response to harm primarily when they view the actor as behaving in an unacceptable way, that is, in a manner that violates internalized prescriptions or "oughts" regarding behavior (Heider, 1958; Hollingsworth, 1949; Kelley, 1972; Pepitone, 1975). These "oughts" refer to the imperativeness aspect of the obligation to act, think or feel in certain ways. Clearly the infliction of physical or psychological harm itself poses a threat and violates an important "ought" or standard concerning respect for another's welfare. For this reason we would expect some anger in response to any harmful incident regardless of the actor's causal responsibility.

However, the rightness or wrongness of a person's behavior is also judged according to whether the actor's perceived causal responsibility for harm violates or fails to violate internalized oughts concerning proper behavior. The oughts relevant to evaluations of harm embody considerations of causality. The determination of causal responsibility involves attributionally relevant considerations such as whether the actor foresaw the consequences, was actually trying to produce or avoid these consequences, and was trying to achieve a socially acceptable end. The ascribed causal responsibility, in conjunction with perceived oughtness requirements, in turn affects the extent to which the actor is perceived as having behaved improperly, wrongly and unjustifiably, perceptions that are captured in the synonymous terms of blame, moral evaluation and moral culpability. Thus, the perceived discrepancy between the actor's causal responsibility for harm and what the perceiver thinks should have occurred (Kelley's, 1973, "is" versus "ought") influences anger, blame, and the likelihood of retaliation. As the perceived "is-ought" discrepancy increases, the greater anger, blame and desire to retaliate. However, while blame, anger and retaliation are affected by common processes, each may be governed by other processes not common to all of them. Consequently, anger, blame and retaliation may not always be isomorphic to one another.

Our perspective on aggression then is comprised of the following elements. First, the perceiver or recipient of harm appraises the situation to determine the actor's[2] causal responsibility for harm. This judgment entails discerning whether the actor could or actually did foresee the harmful outcome; if foreseen, whether the harmful outcome was intended vs. unintended; and if intended, what the actor's motives were and whether these were malevolent. Based on these assessments, the harmful behavior can be classified as accidental, foreseeable, nonmalevolently intentional or malevolently intentional. Second, ascriptions of blame are based on the perceiver's assessment of what ought to have happened and what actually happened. Assigned moral culpability increases as the actor's causal responsibility for harm deviates from what ought or ought not to have occurred. Finally, anger increases as the degree of assigned blame increases; as anger increases, the likelihood of actual or recommended retaliation increases unless inhibitory factors prevail. With this overview in mind, we will discuss next assignment of causality and how certain factors affect the type of causal responsibility assigned.

II. CAUSAL ASSIGNMENT

A. Definition of Causal Responsibility

In assigning causality the perceiver ascertains whether harm was foreseeable, intended and, if intended, the actor's motives for intending harm. These considerations underlie the different types of causality we distinguish which were based on, but are not identical to, those identified by Heider (1958)[3]. An actor may be linked causally with the harmful consequence of action because the outcome was (1) Accidental, i.e., while it was the actor's behavior that resulted in harm, the actor did not foresee this out

come nor could it have been avoided (2) Foreseeable, i.e., it was
the actor's behavior that caused the harm and the actor either (a)
could have been but was not, or (b) actually was aware of the
potential harmful consequences of action even though these consequences were not the actor's goal, (3) Nonmalevolently intended ,
i.e., the actor produced and wanted to produce the harmful outcome
as a means to obtain or achieve an acceptable end and, (4)
Malevolently intended, i.e., the actor produced, foresaw, and
wanted to produce the harmful outcome either as an end in itself
or as a necessary means to achieve yet another unacceptable end.

Having identified the four types of causal responsibility, we
would like to specify the factors that contribute to whether harm
is assigned to one of these categories. Information from two
sources is believed to affect causal ascriptions. These sources
pertain to causally-relevant personal or stereotypic knowledge of
the actor and causally-relevant information available in the
immediate harmful situation. We shall discuss first how the
perceiver's personal or stereotypic knowledge of the actor affects
causal assignment, after which we shall discuss how information
available directly in the harmful situation affects causal assignment. In each case we will indicate whether children of different
ages appropriately use such causally-relevant information; and, if
not, why we think that they do not. In addition, we will attempt
to specify the developmental processes that underlie the impact of
these factors on causal assignment.

B. Determinants of Causal Assignment

1. Target and category based expectancies. Perceivers are
rarely in a position of feeling that they know nothing about the
actor whose harmful behavior they are observing. Instead, perceivers actively construct knowledge about the actor and derive
from this knowledge an understanding of the actor's causal responsibility for harm. The actor may be categorized on the basis of
the perceiver's perceptions of the actor's attitudes, beliefs,
personal characteristics and typical behavior. From these
categorizations of the actor, the perceiver may form expectations
of when and why the actor would behave aggressively. Such expectations are formed on the basis of knowledge of the actor personally and on the basis of the perceiver's stereotypes about the
group or groups to which the actor belongs. Jones and McGillis
(1976) labelled expectations based on knowledge of the actor personally as target-based expectations and expectations based on
knowledge of group membership as category-based expectations.

Target-based expectations are developed on the basis of multiple and direct interactions with the actor or on the basis of
information provided by credible 'other' people. Based on an
other person's communicated impressions or on the consistency and
distinctiveness (Kelley, 1972) of the actor's past hostile or
nonhostile behavior, the perceiver may conclude that the actor is
characteristically hostile or nonhostile. For example, the perceiver might know an actor (A) who consistently and

nondistinctively derogates others, perhaps in order to make himself or herself look good. The perceiver may know another actor (B) who never behaves in this way; or who would behave in a hostile way only as a last resort to stimulate or encourage others to perform well. When confronted with derogatory behavior by each actor, we think that the expectations of each actor would lead to different causal assignments. Actor A's derogatory behavior would likely lead to a malevolent intent ascription, whereas the same behavior by actor B might lead to a nonmalevolent intent ascription.

Category-based expectations stem from the attitudes, beliefs, personality characteristics and typical behaviors that perceivers ascribe to an actor based on his or her voluntary or involuntary group membership. For example, perceivers may develop different expectations of an actor depending on his or her age, sex, skin color, political or religious affiliation, hobbies and occupation. Perceivers' stereotypes of these groups may specifically incorporate or only imply expectations regarding whether harm was intentional, committed for acceptable reasons, or was unavoidable.

Both types of expectations provide a basis for judging whether harmful behavior is consistent or inconsistent with the actor's perceived attitudes, beliefs, typical behaviors and personality characteristics. The perceived congruency between these characteristics and harmful behavior is then likely to affect inferences about the actor's causal responsibility for harm. Target- and category-based expectations may actually bias perceivers' use of information directly available in the harmful situation to infer whether harm was intended, avoidable or perpetrated for acceptable reasons. The operation of such biases would be inferred when perceivers weigh heavily information that is consistent with their expectations but discount information that is inconsistent with their expectations.

The extent of such expectancy-biased interpretations of causal responsibility probably depends on several factors including the perceiver's existing or anticipated relationship with the actor, the ambiguity of available causally-relevant information, whether the perceiver is a member of the actor's group or a member of an opposing group, and the degree to which harmful behavior challenges the original expectation. Moreover, behavior disconfirming an expectation is likely to lead to uncertainty or skepticism (Jones & McGillis, 1976) about the basis for the harm. Such uncertainty or skepticism either would prompt an active search for information that would disambiguate the actor's causal responsibility or would lead the perceiver to reject the implied causal responsibility. Whether the perceiver engages in an active search or simply denies the implied responsibility may depend on factors such as the seriousness of the implications of assigning a particular type of causality or the anticipated sanctions of the implied causal responsibility.

Although several studies bear on specific aspects of these

142

conjectures, only one study by Rosenfield and Stephan (1977) provides data comparing the impact of target- and category-based expectancies on judgments of causality. Rosenfield and Stephan gave observers information about a verbally aggressive actor's personal characteristics and a group's characteristics. Observers were told that the actor was either a member of his school band and choir or of his school boxing and football teams. Some observers were told also that he was either a kind and considerate person or that he was an emotionally expressive and hostile person. Some observers were also given information about the group's characteristics (the group members either approved or disapproved of open expressions of hostility). When verbal hostility strongly disconfirmed an expectation, it was attributed to causal sources unrelated to the source of the original expectation (e.g., hostility was attributed to situational factors when the actor was kind and considerate and a member of his school band and choir). Moreover, although Rosenfield and Stephan did not measure intent ascription, their personal and situational attributional results were consistent with the idea that perceived intent differences were based on the strength of prior expectations. Finally, target-based expectations were stronger determinants of attribution than were category-based expectations.

Rosenfield and Stephan's data provide evidence that target- and category-based expectancies affect adults' causality judgments about harmful events. But, what evidence is there that children formulate target-based and category-based expectations and how might these affect their causal responsibility assignments? The formulation and use of target-based expectations from multiple direct and indirect observations of the actor presuppose a variety of interrelated skills. These skills include logical and causal reasoning abilities, the use of efficient retention and retrieval strategies, as well as perspective-taking and empathic abilities. For example, given a strong expectation of aggressiveness, the child should be able to discount other causes of aggression as explaining or necessary to explain the observed harm. Or, given a weak expectation of aggressiveness, the child must try to detect causes that would account for the observed harm. In order to understand another's motives or to understand that harm was a reaction perhaps to slighted feelings, the child must be able to view the situation from the actor's perspective. The child must also be able to relate the inference that the actor's behavior reflects something about his or her personal characteristics to an inference regarding the stability and the predictability of similar future behavior. This cause-expectancy inferential relation involves abilities to relate temporally separated events, to conceive of others in terms of inner psychological qualities (such as those embodied by trait attributions of aggressiveness), and to recognize that such trait attributions may be diagnostic of future behavior. These skills obviously require a lot from the perceiver and our review of the relevant developmental literature indicates that there may well be age-related differences in the formulation and use of target-based expectations.

143

Research based on Werner's (1957, 1961) concept of development has shown that children's impressions of others they know well become consistently better differentiated and integrated approximately between seven to 10 years of age. This is the age range within which children consistently manifest less egocentrism and a greater ability to adopt another's perspective and to empathize with the other (e.g., Chandler, 1977; Flavell, 1977; Ford, 1979). In fact, both spatial perspective-taking and social perspective-taking abilities correlate highly with abilities to take account of a person's emotions, motivations, and intentions, as well as to decenter from a reliance on situational cues in resolving social dilemmas (e.g., Cutrona & Feshbach, 1979). Moreover, children older than approximately 10 years of age describe both themselves as well as liked and disliked adults and peers more in terms of abstract or central constructs that refer to inner psychological qualities such as personality traits, general habits, motives, attitudes, and values. Younger children, in contrast, more often describe themselves and others in terms of more peripheral or concrete constructs that refer to observable characteristics such as the actor's physical appearance, sex, body build, identity, kinship relations, occupation, hobbies, and possessions (e.g., Barenboim, 1978; Livesley & Bromley, 1973; Peevers & Secord, 1973; Rosenbach, Crockett & Wapner, 1973; Whiteman, Brook, & Gordon, 1977; Wood, 1978; Yarrow & Campbell, 1963). This descriptive evidence alone suggests that children younger than 10 years of age would be less likely than older children and adults to formulate expectations about an actor's future behavior that are derived from (or that reflect) attributions regarding the actor's behavior in past situations. This conclusion is also consistent with findings indicating that younger children's impressions of others are very "situationally" bound. For example, young children's impressions of a person change with alterations in behavioral valence or appearance, whereas older children's and adult's impressions remain more stable (e.g., Rosenbach, et al., 1973; Rotenberg, 1982).

An experiment by Dodge (1980) more directly assessed when children begin to formulate target-based expectations and when they apply these in interpreting an actor's intentions and motives for action. Children in the 2nd, 4th, and 6th grades evaluated the ambiguously motivated aggressive behaviors of peers who had previously been nominated by children according to whether they tended to "start fights" and "disrupt groups" vs. "cooperate in a group". Children in all grades recommended more retaliation, made stronger predictions of future aggressiveness, and gave lower ratings of trustworthiness regarding the known hostile rather than the known nonhostile peer. Ambiguously motivated aggression was seen as reflecting more about the hostile intentions of the hostile rather than the nonhostile peer, although 2nd graders did not discriminate their attributions of hostile intent to the two actors as much as did 4th and 6th graders. These results suggest that children younger than 10 years of age are beginning to conceive of people in dispositional terms, but that these conceptions may not be reflected consistently in their interpretations or predictions of an actor's behavior (see also Roter

In addition to assessing age-related
children's perceptions of others, some research
related developments in the use of covariation i
passed by Kelly's consistency, distinctiven
attributional criteria. Studies examining abil
information are important to us because we thir
tion of target-based expectations presuppose abi
the causes with which an actor's behavior covaries.
between the ages of five-to-seven years seem to use covariation
information based on the regularity of association between causes
and effects (e.g., Shaklee & Turner, 1979; Shultz & Mendelson,
1975; Smith, 1975). Stable dispositional characteristics are
inferred once attributions based on covariation across time,
modality and person have been made. Nevertheless, there is still
a tendency for children this young to base their judgments more on
the temporal or spatial contiguity between causes and effects than
on the consistency or regularity of association (e.g., Siegler &
Liebert, 1974) unless stimulus presentations are very simplified
and children are explicitly trained to use the available covariation information (see Kassin, 1981). The evidence available
regarding use of distinctiveness information suggests that five
year-olds relative to nine and 13 year-old children do not make
attributions differentiated appropriately according to distinctiveness information (e.g., Shultz, Butkowsky, Pearce & Shanfield,
1975). Considered altogether, these findings seem to suggest that
children younger than about 10 years of age can use covariation
information to infer causality, but that they do not do so in as
reliable a fashion as children older than 10 years of age. If
this conclusion is valid, we should expect children younger than
approximately 10 years of age not to formulate target-based expectations compatible with the attributional implications of Kelly's
covariation criteria.

There is, however, some evidence that appears inconsistent
with our proposition that children younger than 10 years-old cannot formulate target-based expectations or use such expectations
in their causal responsibility assignments. Both DiVitto and
McArthur (1978) and Leahy (1979) report that 1st graders use consistency and distinctiveness information in allocating rewards to
actors or in deciding whether target actors are nicer or meaner
than other actors. For example, actors whose hostile behavior was
low in distinctiveness and high in consistency were rated as
meaner than actors whose hostile behavior was high in distinctiveness and low in consistency (DiVitto & McArthur, 1978). Similarly, nondistinctive and consistent kindness was rewarded more
than distinctive and inconsistent kindness (e.g., Leahy, 1979).
This evidence suggests that even children as young as five-to-six
years of age reliably use covariation as one basis for formulating
target-based expectations which in turn affects their interpretations of actors' behaviors in other situations. Such a conclusion
may be premature, however. Ascriptions of niceness or meanness
need not imply that children perceive actors as dispositionally

145

or mean. This is because trait attributes such as niceness
meanness may be used as descriptors of the quality of
ehaviors, as descriptors of personality attributes of another,
and as indices of the likely quality of the actor's future
behavior. These may be referred to as behavioral, dispositional,
and predictive uses of trait attributes (Wiggins, 1973). We
assume that target-based expectations are being expressed when
trait adjectives are used in dispositional or predictive ways. In
contrast, their use as behavioral descriptors does not express a
target-based expectation. We suggest that children in the DiVitto
and McArthur study could have been using the term "meaner" to convey that one actor had actually behaved meanly on more occasions
than the other. This use need not reflect a dispositional or a
predictive use of the attribute "meanness." Similarly, young
children in Leahy's study could have based their reward alloca-
tions on a behavioral frequency principle, which need not reflect
children's beliefs that one actor was dispositionally nicer or
kinder than another. Because it is not clear in Leahy's or
DiVitto and McArthur's studies how children were using these
adjectives, no definitive conclusions can be drawn about whether
their results reflect target-based expectations differentiated
according to the distinctiveness and consistency of the actor's
behavior.

Interestingly, however, even very young children show evidence of being responsive to category-based information, although
this research has also obscured the different uses of trait attributes. Six-year-old children refer more to immediate and observable characteristics rather than dispositional characteristics in
their explanations for why actors behaved in various ways and
descriptions of what they thought actors were thinking and feeling
(e.g., Wood, 1978). Children as young as four years old evaluate
"white" as positive and "black" as negative (e.g., Dent, 1978) and
show evidence of racial stereotyping (Triandis, 1976). Sex
stereotyping occurs at a very young age (Kleinke & Nicholson,
1979; Williams, Bennett & Best, 1975), especially with regard to
the perception that boys behave more antisocially than girls. For
example, even children as young as three years old view antisocial behavior as more characteristic of boys than girls (e.g.,
Haugh, Hoffman & Cowan, 1980; Kuhn, Nash & Brucken, 1978; Styczynski & Langlois, 1977; Williams et al., 1975). And, preschoolers
expect male but not female intervention in aggressive situations
(e.g., Hardin & Jacob, 1978). Along other lines, actors who have
unpopular relative to popular names or who are ectomorphic rather
than mesomorphic in stature are described less positively and are
seen as behaving in a more antisocial manner (e.g., Lerner, 1969;
Lerner & Korn, 1972; McDavid & Harari, 1966; Staffieri, 1967,
1972; Walker, 1962). Moreover, as with adults, physically unattractive relative to attractive children are described as behaving
more antisocially and are nominated less frequently as friends
(e.g., Dion, 1972; Langlois & Downs, 1979; Styczynski & Langlois,
1977).

Finally, there are age differences in children's memories of

146

social scenarios and in their use of stereotyped expectations to infer the motives of actors in these scenarios. Several studies have shown that younger children's familiarity with the actions and events of a television portrayal influenced their understanding of and memory for the plot (Collins & Wellman, unpublished manuscript; Newcomb & Collins, 1979). For example, seven-year-old children's representations of narratives were incomplete and disorganized relative to older viewers' representations, unless children were familiar with the depicted events. Nevertheless, younger children's ascriptions of motives to the actor were much more stereotyped even when they remembered well the explicitly presented content from which the actual less-stereotyped motives could be inferred. This work suggests that stereotyping based not only on events but also on a person's group membership may bias memory and interpretations of harmful behaviors. Consistent with this idea, Koblinsky, Cruse, and Sugawara (1978) found that fifth graders remembered more sex-stereotype consistent traits suggesting that sex stereotypes serve as an organizational framework for memory. These findings are compatible with those reported for adults (e.g., Cohen & Ebbesen, 1979; Snyder, Tanke & Berscheid, 1977), but the development of stereotypes and their influence on causal responsibility assignments and memory needs further exploration.

2. Characteristics of the observed situation. We have just discussed how causal responsibility assignment may be influenced by expectations based on knowledge of the actor personally or only stereotypically. We would now like to discuss how causal responsibility assignment is influenced by information that is usually available only within the harmful situation itself. Such information may include, for example, the presence or absence of external constraints, the severity of harm, and perceiver involvement.

Observation of the actor's manner of behaving may provide cues about whether he or she intended or could have avoided the harmful outcome. Inferences of intent may be stronger when the actor persists in trying to harm another in spite of repeated obstacles or when, after having caused harm, the actor stops trying to produce a change in the environment. Although there are no data available for children, adults offer higher judgments of intent and foreknowledge when actors exert high relative to low effort in causing harm to another. For example, Joseph, Kane, Gaes & Tedeschi (1976) found that observers ascribed more aggressive intent to a man who drove for 3 1/4 hours rather than for only five minutes to incapacitate another person's car. Similarly, causal responsibility may be inferred from nonverbal behaviors of the actor. Any expression that conveys distress, surprise, or sadness rather than happiness or pleasure about causing harm may be taken as evidence for lacking intent and perhaps even foresight. Consistent with this idea, Savitsky, Czyzewski, Dubord & Kaminsky (1976) found that more punishment was recommended for joyful rather than distressed offenders, suggesting that these differences may, in part, reflect differences in perceived intentionality. Moreover, even children as young as

147

kindergarten age use emotional expression cues to infer whether harmful incidents were intended. For example, it has been found that an actor's happy expression connoted intent to children, whereas an actor's sad expression connoted lack of intent for harmful behavior (Nelson, 1980; Rybash, Roodin & Hallion, 1979).

Many other factors in the situation may reduce adults' perception that the actor had choice to produce harm or that the actor had the necessary ability to avoid harm. For example, extreme stress, provocation, or temporary psychological/physical disability may promote the perception that a negative consequence was less avoidable, even though under other circumstances the actor may have been able and willing to avoid the consequences of action. Although many instances of retaliation in response to provocation will be seen as intentional but justified (Brown & Tedeschi, 1973; Harvey & Rule, 1978), some instances of provoked retaliation may not even be viewed as intentional because the provocation was so extreme that it undermined at least temporarily the actor's ability to control his or her behavior. In such cases, the harm may be seen as foreseeable and perhaps even as accidental. Although he measured only punishment, Leahy's (1979) results are consistent with these ideas. He found that 11-year-old children recommended punishment most for chronic transgressors and those for whom no mitigating circumstance information was known. Provocation, stress, and emotional maladjustment yielded decreasing recommendations of punishment in that order, suggesting that the older children differentiated their perceptions of causal responsibility according to both intent and avoidability. On the other hand, six-year-old children made greater punishment recommendations for stressed and emotionally maladjusted children and reduced punishment recommendations only for non-provoked transgressors compared to provoked transgressors. This suggests that younger children understand that provocation may be an acceptable motive for intentional harm but they do not understand that other factors may reduce the actor's ability to avoid harm.

Whether an actor's behavior has motivational significance for the perceiver also affects adults' inferences of causal responsibility. The concept of hedonic relevance (Jones & Davis, 1965) captures the motivational significance of the actor's behavior for the perceiver, i.e., whether the outcome proves gratifying or disappointing relative to other possible alternatives. Although no research has directly tested this idea, several studies have found either stronger affective or evaluative responses (e.g., Chaiken & Cooper, 1973; Enzle, Harvey & Wright, 1980; Lowe & Goldstein, 1970) or more extreme trait inferences (e.g., Lowe & McConnell, 1976) under conditions of high relative to low hedonic relevance. Given our assumption that the degree of affect experienced by the perceiver is in part a function of how much personal causal responsibility has been inferred and Jones and Davis' proposition that extreme trait inferences will be made only when the behavior is perceived as intended, it may be suggested that adults attributed greater personal causal responsibility to the actor in these studies. However, research with children (e.g., Rosenbach,

148

Crockett & Wapner, 1973) has shown no effects of involvement on their perceptions of others. This evidence, coupled with younger children's failure to grasp avoidability discriminations, leads us to suspect that younger children's perceptions of foreseeability perhaps more so than their perceptions of intent would be unaffected differentially by factors that enhance involvement. We would hasten to qualify this idea, however. We recently found that younger children's moral evaluations of an actor's clearly accidental behavior were affected by a "type" of involvement. When young children role-played a position of responsible authority over an actor and this actor accidentally harmed another, children's moral evaluations were more harsh relative to a "no interaction" condition (Ferguson & Rule, in press). These results tentatively suggest that involvement can affect even younger children's perceptions of foreseeability and intent, although more evidence regarding this suggestion is needed.

Perceptions of foreseeability may also be affected by outcome severity, a factor that has figured prominently in developmental research, and one that promotes hedonic relevance. For example, research with adults has shown that severe compared to mildly harmful outcomes are viewed as more foreseeable, especially when the perceiver is an actual or potential recipient of harm (see Fincham & Jaspars, 1979). While we know of no similar research with children, studies have documented younger children's reliance on consequence severity information as a basis for moral judgment[4] (Collins, Berndt & Hess, 1974; Elkind & Dabek, 1977; Ferguson & Rule, in press; Rule & Duker, 1973). These results may indicate that young children perceive severe compared to mild outcomes as more foreseeable if not more intentional, especially when the actor's casual responsibility is amgibuous. In fact, however, we have recently found that younger children rely on severity information only when other available information (e.g., intentions) does not instantiate a high blame judgment (Rule, Ferguson, Cornell, Hazen & Shockmann-Gates, unpublished manuscript). This evidence suggests that children's use of severity information reflects more their reasoning about what norms to use in moral evaluation than their beliefs regarding whether severe compared to mild outcomes are more foreseeable or intended. Unfortunately, such a conclusion can be made only tentatively pending research including actions that are ambiguous regarding intent and measuring perceived foreseeability and intent.

Any features of the situation providing information about reasons other than malevolent ones for harming should affect the perception that harm was intended but committed for acceptable reasons. Based on Jones and Davis (1965), we assume that perceivers will assume that actors intend to produce the most desirable effects of their actions (e.g., Ajzen, 1971; Lowe & McConnell, 1976). Thus, harmful behavior associated with desireable consequences may be seen as nonmalevolently intended even though the actor's true intentions may have been malevolent. Unacceptable reasons for harmful behavior include harm produced in the service of fulfilling a personally-based or an instrumentally-based motive of the actor. Acceptable reasons for harm include punishing the recipient for poor performance (Fishman, 1965; Gentry, 1970), of redressing a wrong committed against some third party (Rule & Duker, 1973), or saving a child from suffering even greater harm (Darley, Klosson & Zanna, 1978; Ferguson & Rule, 1980). In still other cases, the harm may be considered as perpetrated for acceptable reasons because of other norms, such as the lex talionis, "an eye for an eye, a tooth for a tooth". Retaliation by a provoked person represents such a case (Harvey & Rule, 1978). Consistent with the idea that harm intended for acceptable reasons should reduce responsibility attributions, Fincham and Jaspars (1979) reported that children as young as six years-old view a justifiably motivated harm-doer as less causally responsible than a malevolently motivated harm-doer. No research has considered, however, the various skills that are required to infer from the available information the actor's causal responsibility for harm nor has it assessed perceptions of motive acceptability. These skills are briefly considered here.

Based both on Jones and Davis' (1965) and Kelly's (1972) analyses, we suggest that there are several principles that perceivers apply in interpreting the causal significance of information available in the immediate situation. We believe that principles of temporal and spatial contiguity, causal direction, cause-effect similarity, covariation, discounting, and augmentation (reviewed by Kassin, 1981) are each involved in interpreting another's causal responsibility for harm. Description of only a few of these principles should suffice to indicate the complex task with which perceivers of all ages are confronted in interpreting another's causal responsibility. Children must be able, for example, to compensate for the strength of a known cause by inferring, when necessary, the presence or absence of other causes and their strength. More specifically, an actor who produces harm in spite of the threat of punishment should be seen as intending harm more malevolently than an actor who was not so threatened or who was actually commanded to produce harm. Or, when there are multiple consequences of the actor's harmful behavior, and some of these are positive, the child should be more likely to choose the desirable rather than the harmful effect as intended (Jones & Davis, 1965). Furthermore, as a precondition for intent, the child also needs to assess whether the actor was actually capable of producing harm in the way it was observed, i.e., the child must be able to say with confidence that the actor could successfully inflict the type of harm observed on other occasions. Therefore, the child has to consider the nature of the effect in question in relation to what capabilities would be necessary to achieve that effect.

While but a few examples, they illustrate that inferences regarding causal responsibility presuppose a variety of logical reasoning and social-cognitive skills. These include abilities to discern the presence and strength of causes as well as their inhibitory or facilitory nature; and abilities to conserve or compensate for the facilitory and inhibitory nature of the available causally-relevant information. Use of covariation-based schemata (including use of the augmentation principle) appears during the preoperational period, i.e., in children younger than about seven years. This is also reflected in the research reviewed previously regarding these young children's use of covariation information. For example, even very young children appear to infer greater benevolent intent when kind acts occur despite threatened punishment than in the face of reward (e.g., Suls, Gutkin & Kalle, 1979). Appropriate applications of the multiple sufficient and multiple necessary cause schemata are not observed consistently in children of seven years and younger. In fact, children this young sometimes apply an additive rather than a compensatory or discounting logic in relating causes to effects. For example, Karniol and Ross (1976, 1979) found that young children were more likely to infer that a child who was told to play with a toy wanted to play with the toy more than a child who was not told to play with the toy. In contrast, children older than seven years manifested the opposite choice, thereby showing appropriate use of the multiple sufficient cause schema or discounting principle. These results suggest that children appreciate the conditions necessary to establish malevolent intent at an earlier age than those necessary to establish nonmalevolent intent.

Unfortunately, no research has investigated the conditional relations among these skills nor has it assessed systematically their influence on causal responsibility inferences. We know only that young children appropriately apply the discounting principle when there are socially acceptable goals evident for harm (Rule & Duker, 1973) and sometimes (Leahy, 1979), but not always (Fincham & Jaspars, 1979), when there is prior provocation. Such meager and inconsistent results may reflect differences in the complexity of the stimulus presentation, amount of experience and knowledge with certain situations, and concreteness of the external conditions. Because such matters have not been taken into account systematically in the research, we can draw no conclusions about age differences in use of causal principles and their relation to causal responsibility assignment. Nevertheless, we assume that future research will confirm our expectations about how these various factors affect perceived causal responsibility. With this in mind, we shall now examine more closely the relation between causal assignment and blame ascription.

III. RELATIONSHIP BETWEEN CAUSAL ASSIGNMENT AND BLAME ASCRIPTION.

We assume harm that is avoidable, intentional or perpetrated for unacceptable reasons arouses concerns about the control and prevention of subsequent aggression (Kelly, 1972). Such a concern is expressed in judgments that the actor is morally reprehensible and deserving of punishment. Although causal assignment may be directly related to blame with increasing personal causal responsibility as Heider's analysis suggests, this may not always be the case. Perceivers may differentially weigh the three dimensions (avoidability, intent and acceptability), thereby reducing differences in blame. Consequently, the different types of causal responsibility may not lead to different blame ascriptions. For example, nonmalevolently intended harm is sometimes blamed less than foreseeable harm and as little as accidental harm (e.g., Ferguson & Rule, 1980; Harvey & Rule, 1978). Conversely, actions classified independently as nonmalevolently intended are sometimes blamed as much as malevolently intended harm (e.g., Shaw & Sulzer, 1964). Some studies have demonstrated that younger children may discriminate causal responsibility but nevertheless assign blame to the same extent (Fincham & Jaspars, 1979; Harris, 1977). It is important to examine the possibility that differential weighting of the three dimensions affects blame. Moreover, the criterion for assigning blame may change as a function of the perceiver's level of moral reasoning, or involvement in the situation. For example, a more stringent ought standard may be used by a cognitively naive perceiver.

Many studies have documented differences in the degree of blame ascribed to actions that are portrayed as accidental, foreseeable, nonmalevolently intended, and malevolently intended. With the exception of some of the findings noted previously, the research shows that older children and adults reliably differentiate these types of causality (e.g., Ferguson & Rule, 1980; Fincham & Jaspars, 1979; Harris, 1977). The youngest age at which reliable discriminations are made varies, however, from study to study and depends upon which types of causal responsibility are compared.

For example, even children as young as four-to-five years old reliably differentiate accidental or foreseeable from nonmalevolently and malevolently intended transgressions (see Karniol, 1978; Lickona, 1976; Shantz, 1975; Whiteman, 1979). Such discriminations are most reliable when the unintended vs. intended quality of the outcome is made explicit and the depicted outcome is mild rather than severe. Discriminations between types of causality (e.g., accidental vs. foreseeable, foreseeable vs. nonmalevolently intended, nonmalevolently intended vs. malevolently intended) are less apt to be made by children younger than about 10 years of age (Fincham & Jaspars, 1979; Harris, 1977; Heider, 1958). This is particularly true of the accidental vs. foreseeable comparison, but we must emphasize that studies have operationalized these two types of causality in such a way that not even adults always discriminate them according to the degree of ascribed causality (e.g., Fincham & Jaspars, 1979).

Moreover, while some studies show that children only seven years and older make distinctions between malevolently and nonmalevolently intended actions (e.g., Ferguson & Rule, 1980; Fincham & Jaspars, 1979; Harris, 1977) other studies show that such a distinction is made by children younger than seven years-old (e.g., Rule, Nesdale & McAra, 1974). Several problems make comparisons among these studies difficult. Most notably, the method of operationalizing nonmalevolent intent has varied across the studies. For example, Harris used command to operationalize nonmalevolent intent and it has already been suggested that young children may not reliably view command as a factor that would mitigate an actor's causal responsibility. Rule et al. (1974), on the other hand, explicitly incorporated help to a third party as the socially acceptable motive in an aggressive exchange. Differentiation made between this good motive and the depicted bad motive is consistent with research showing that younger children reliably differentiate scenarios depicting good vs. bad motives as long as these are not confounded with intent or vary in outcome severity (see Karniol, 1978). At the same time, the outcome depicted in Rule et al.'s scenarios was milder than even the mild outcome depicted in Ferguson and Rule's stories, which may account for why children in the latter study did not differentiate nonmalevolent from malevolent intent. Finally, Fincham and Jaspars (1979) employed provoked retaliation as a means of conveying a socially acceptable goal, but the "eye for an eye" norm may not be sufficiently internalized by young children to merit its serving as a justification. This observation is borne out by the tendency of children younger than seven years-old not to appreciate reciprocity-based punishments or explanations of when it is right or wrong to express aggression (see Lickona, 1976).

Age-related developments in the effects of causal responsibility assignment on blame ascription may reflect developmental changes in the standards underlying moral judgment. As children grow older, they begin to reject arbitrary or expiatory punishment and to accept reciprocity-based punishment (see Lickona, 1976). Similarly, children come to rely less on outcome magnitude and more on motives and intentions in morally evaluating both positive and negative outcomes (see Karniol, 1978; Lickona, 1976). Finally, our recent research suggested that age-related differences in moral evaluation reflect neither attentional or memorial factors nor the general cognitive limitations discussed by Piaget. Rather, our results suggested that age differences in moral evaluation reflect what social conventions children think should be applied in making a moral judgment (see also Collins, Berndt & Hess, 1974).

THE RELATION BETWEEN BLAME, ANGER AND AGGRESSION

Violation of social norms presumably instigates anger and the likelihood of retaliation (Pepitone, unpublished manuscript; Weisfeld, 1972). Breaking rules, violating normative values or contracts are considered sufficient to arouse anger even in mere observers of harm (Pepitone, unpublished manuscript). Three sources of data bear on these conjectures. First, Averill (1979) has shown that anger is reported by adults to be greatest in response to intended harm, next to foreseeable harm, and least to justifiable and accidental harm. Second, several studies have shown that attributionally-relevant information affects anger and retaliation (e.g., Dyck & Rule, 1978; Rule, Dyck, McAra & Nesdale, 1975). Third, both children and adults blame and recommend punishment more to a harm-doer whose behavior was intended and unacceptable (see Rule & Nesdale, 1976, for a review of this literature). These results are consistent with our analysis. Unfortunately, however, only one study (Kulik & Brown, 1979) explicitly documents the expected links among blame, anger and aggression, and they did not include all types of causal responsibility, nor are similar studies available with children. In fact, the past seven years have been devoid of such research, leading Masters to his 1981 comment that "the most remarkable aspect of current research on aggression is its general absence" (p. 136).

V. SUMMARY AND IMPLICATIONS

First, several factors lead to assignment to one of the four categories of causal responsibility. With regard to expectancies, younger children are less likely to formulate target and category based expectancies, or to use these in assessing another person's casual responsibility. This reflects, in part, their unreliable use of covariation information. With regard to their response to information in the immediate situation, young children seem to respond to some context factors permitting judgments of intent, avoidability and motive acceptability. Their responsiveness to some but not other conditions seems to reflect their differential ability to apply discounting and augmentation principles. Moreover, younger children perceive attributionally relevant information differently from older children and adults, especially regarding whether causes should be viewed as facilitory or inhibitory. Blame is assigned according to whether harm has been causally classified as intentional vs. unintentional, avoidable vs. unavoidable and acceptable vs. unacceptable. Usually more blame is assigned to malevolently intended aggression, but only children over 10 years of age discriminate reliably among accidental, foreseeable and nonmalevolently intended harm. Although variations in situational conditions may result in different weighting of the intent, avoidability and acceptability dimensions by adults, there are also age differences in the weighting of these dimensions. Such age differences and the lack of parallelism between younger children's cause and blame judgments seem to be based on the younger child's application of different social knowledge and standards of evaluation. Finally, as yet untested in children is the proposition that anger and its subsequent behavioral expression increase as ascribed blame increases. Given this summary, we would like to discuss briefly the implications of our analysis.

From a theoretical perspective, we have specified the link between attribution and aggression by focusing on blame ascriptions. We have also articulated how developmental differences may be implicated in these relations. Our analysis also extends current attributional perspectives to encompass more social attributional considerations, including stereotyping and ingroup-outgroup phenomena. That is, in contrast to past attributional analyses, we have taken into consideration how the perceiver's group affiliation affects the attribution process. At another

154

analyses, we have taken into consideration how the perceiver's group affiliation affects the attribution process. At another level, we have emphasized how children's comprehension of, and memory for, the attributional components of harm affect formation of attitudes and values regarding aggression. Nevertheless, more attention should be given to what children learn from their observations of aggression--in particular, when it is appropriate to aggress, toward whom, in what ways, and with what consequences. Related to the latter point, we wish to emphasize that control of much hostile aggression is achieved through the internalization of moral standards and through the cognitive control of anger.

FOOTNOTES

1. Preparation of this manuscript was facilitated by a research grant to B.G. Rule from the Natural Sciences and Engineering Research Council of Canada.

2. Our terminology accords with that used in the attribution area. The actor is the instigator, the person who harms the recipient. The perceiver may be either the recipient of harm or a more uninvolved observer, both of whom observe, evaluate and possibly react to the actor's behavior. And, of course, it is these perceivers' potential evaluations and behavior in which we are most interested.

3. We have omitted Heider's first type of personal responsibility according to which an actor is merely associated with harm. This stage was omitted because anger and retaliation have not been examined as a function of the association level. Moreover, the reader should note that our responsibility types (3) and (4) are not identical to Heider's descriptions of his last two stages. For example, Heider did not incorporate malevolent and non-malevolent motives in his last two stages of personal responsibility, respectively. Moreover, although we assume that the four levels describe the ways in which the actor is causally associated with an event, we do not adopt Heider's notion that the four types of causality represent a continuum on which there is an increase in personal causation. The levels do, however, describe the different evaluative standards or oughts that could be applied in assigning responsibility as culpability.

4. This relation does not always occur (Ferguson & Rule, 1980; Gottlieb, Taylor & Ruderman, 1977; Immamoglu, 1975; Suls, Gutkin & Kalle, 1979; Surber, 1977; Sedlak, 1979).

REFERENCES

Ajzen, I. Attribution of dispositions to an actor: Effects of perceived decision freedom and behavioral utilities. Journal of Personality and Social Psychology, 1971, 18, 144-156.

Averill, J.R. Anger. In H. Howe & R. Dienstbier (Eds.). Nebraska Symposium on Motivation. 1978. Lincoln: University of Nebraska Press, 1979.

Bandura, A. Aggression: A social learning analysis. Englewood

Cliffs, N.J.: Prentice-hall, 1973.

Barenboim, C. Development of recursive and nonrecursive thinking about persons. Developmental Psychology, 1978, 14, 419-420.

Berkowitz, L. Agression: A social psychological analysis. New York: McGraw-Hill, 1962.

Brown A.H. & Tedeschi, J.T. Determinants of perceived aggression. Journal of Social Psychology, 1976, 100, 77-87.

Buss, A.H. The psychology of aggression, New York: Wiley, 1961.

Camp, B.W. Verbal mediation in young aggressive boys. Journal of Abnormal Psychology, 1977, 86, 145-153.

Chaikin, A.L. & Cooper, J. Evaluation as a function of correspondence and hedonic relevance. Journal of Experimental Social Psychology, 1973, 9, 257-264.

Chandler, M.J. Social cognition: A selective review of current research. In W.F. Overton & J. McCarthy (Eds.), Knowledge and development (Vol. 1). New York: Plenum, 1977.

Cohen, C.E. & Ebbesen, E.B. Observational goals and schema activation: A theoretical framework for behavior perception. Journal of Experimental Social Psychology, 1979, 15, 305-329.

Collins, W.A., Berndt, T.J. & Hess, V.L. Observational learning of motives and consequences for television aggression: A developmental study. Child Development, 1974, 45, 799-802.

Collins, W.A. & Wellman, H.M. Social scripts and the developmental patterns in comprehension of televised narratives. University of Minnesota. Unpublished manuscript, 1981.

Cutrona, C.E. & Feshbach, S. Cognitive and behavioral correlates of children's differential use of social information. Child Development, 1979, 50, 1036-1042.

Darley, J.M., Klosson, E.C. & Zanna, M.P. Intentions and their contexts in the moral judgments of children and adults. Child Development, 1978, 49, 66-74.

Dent, D.M. The salience of prowhite/antiblack bias. Child Development, 1978, 49, 1280-1283.

Dion, K.K. Physical attractiveness and evaluation of children's transgressions. Journal of Personality and Social Psychology, 1972, 24, 207-213.

DiVitto, B. & McArthur, L.Z. Developmental differences in the use of distinctiveness, consensus, and consistency information for making causal attributions. Developmental Psychology, 1978, 14, 474-482.

Dodge, K.A. Social cognition and children's aggressive behavior. Child Development, 1980, 51, 162-170.

Dyck, R.J. & Rule, B.G. Effect of retaliation of causal attributions concerning attack. Journal of Personality and Social Psychology, 1978, 36, 521-529.

Elkind, D. & Dabek, R.F. Personal injury and property damage in the moral judgment of children. Child Development, 1977, 48, 518-522.

Enzle, M.E., Harvey, M.D. & Wright, E.F. Personalism and Distinctiveness. Journal of Personality and Social Psychology, 1980, 39, 542-552.

Ferguson, T.J. & Rule, B.G. Effects of inferential set, outcome severity, and basis for responsibility on children's evaluations of aggressive acts. Developmental Psychology, 1980,

16, 141-146.

Ferguson, T.J. & Rule, B.G. The influence of inferential set, outcome intent and outcome severity on children's moral judgments. Developmental Psychology, in press.

Fincham, F. & Jaspars, J. Attribution of responsibility to the self and other in children and adults. Journal of Personality and Social Pscyhology, 1979, 37, 1589-1602.

Fishman, C.G. Need for approval and the expression of aggression under varying conditions of frustration. Personality and Social Psychology, 1965, 2, 809-816.

Flavell, J.H. Cognitive development. New Jersey: Prentice-Hall, 1977.

Ford, M.E. The construct validity of egocentrism. Psychological Bulletin, 1979, 86, 1169-1188.

Gentry, W.D. Effects of frustration, attack, and prior aggressive training on overt aggression and vascular processes. Journal of Personality and Social Psychology, 1970, 16, 718-725.

Gottlieb, D.E., Taylor, S.E. & Ruderman, A. Cognitive bases of children's moral judgments. Developmental Psychology, 1977, 13, 547-556.

Greenwell, J. & Dengerink, H.A. The role of perceived versus actual attack in human physical aggression. Journal of Personality and Social Psychology, 1973, 26, 66-71.

Harden, R.R. & Jacob, S.H. Differences in young children's expectations of women's and men's intervention in aggression. Perceptual and Motor Skills, 1978, 46, 1303-1309.

Harris, B. Developmental differences in the attribution of responsibility. Developmental Psychology, 1977, 13, 257-265.

Hartup, W.W. Aggression in childhood: Developmental perspectives. American Psychologist, 1974, 29, 336-341.

Harvey, M.D. & Rule, B.G. Moral evaluations and judgments of responsibility. Personality and Social Psychology Bulletin, 1978, 4, 583-588.

Haugh, S.S., Hoffman, C.D. & Cowan, G. The eye of the very young beholder: Sex typing of infants by young children. Child Development, 1980, 51, 598-600.

Heider, F. The psychology of interpersonal relations. New York: Wiley, 1958.

Hollingsworth, H.L. Psychology and ethics: a study of the sense of obligation. New York: Ronald, 1949.

Imamoglu, E.O. Children's awareness and usage of intention cues. Child Development, 1975, 46, 39-45.

Jones, E.E. & Davis, K.E. From acts to dispositions: The attribution process in person perception. In L. Berkowitz (Ed.), Advances in Experimental Social Psychology, (Vol. 2). New York: Academic Press, 1965.

Jones, E.E. & McGillis, D. Correspondent inferences and the attribution cube: A comparative reappraisal. In J.H. Harvey, W.J. Ickes & R.F. Kidd (Eds.), New Directions in Attribution Research, (Vol. 1). Hillsdale, N.J.: Lawrence Earlbaum, 1976.

Joseph, J.M., Kane, T.R., Gaes, G.G. & Tedeschi, J.T. Effects of effort on attributed intent and perceived aggressiveness. Perceptual and Motor Skills, 1976, 42, 706.

Karniol, R.   Children's use of intention cues in evaluating behavior. Psychological Bulletin, 1978, 85, 76-85.

Karniol, R. & Ross, M. The development of causal attributions in social perception. Journal of Personality and Social Psychology, 1976, 34, 455-464.

Karniol, R. & Ross, M. Children's use of a causal attribution schema and the inference of manipulative intentions. Child Development, 1979, 50, 463-468.

Kassin, S. From laychild to "layman": Developmental causal attribution. In S. Brehm, S. Kassin, F. Gibbons (Eds.), Developmental Social Psychology Theory and Research. New York: Oxford Press, 1981.

Kelley, H.H. Causal Schemata and the Attribution Process. New York: General Learning Press, 1972.

Kelley, H.H. The process of causal attribution. American Psychologist, 1973, 28, 107-128.

Kleinke, C.L. & Nicholson, T.A. Black and white children's awareness of de facto race and sex differences. Developmental Psychology, 1979, 15, 84-86.

Koblinsky, S.G., Cruse, D.F. & Sugawara, A.I. Sex role stereotypes and children's memory for story content. Child Development, 1978, 49, 452-458.

Kuhn, D., Nash, S.C. & Brucken, L. Sex role concepts of two- and three-year-olds. Child Development, 1978, 49, 445-451.

Kulik, J.A. & Brown, R. Frustration, attribution of blame and aggression. Journal of Experimental Social Psychology, 1979, 15, 183-194.

Langlois, J.H. & Downs, A.C. Peer relations as a function of physical attractiveness: The eye of the beholder or behavioral reality? Child Development, 1979, 409-418.

Leahy, R.L. Development of conceptions of prosocial behavior: Information affecting rewards given for altruism and kindness. Developmental Psychology, 1979, 15, 34-37.

Lerner, R.M. The development of stereotyped expectancies of body build-behavior relations. Child Development, 1969, 40, 137-141.

Lerner, R.M. & Korn, S. The development of body build stereotypes in males. Child Development, 1972, 43, 908-920.

Lickona, T. (Ed.) Moral development and behavior. New York: Holt, Rinehart & Winston, 1976.

Livesley, W.J. & Bromley, D.B. Person perception in childhood and adolescence. London: Wiley, 1973.

Lowe, C.A. & Goldstein, J.W. Reciprocal liking and attributions of ability: Mediating effects of perceived intent and personal involvement. Journal of Personality and Social Psychology, 1970, 16, 291-297.

Lowe, C.A. & McConnell, H.K. Intent, dispositional attribution, and correspondent inferences. Paper presented at American Psychological Association, 1976.

Masters, J.C. Developmental Psychology. Annual Review of Psychology, 1981, 32, 117-151.

McDavid, J.W. & Harari, H. Stereotyping of names and popularity in grade school children. Child Development, 1966, 37, 453-459.

Nelson, S.A. Factors influencing young children's use of motives and outcomes as moral criteria. Child Development, 1980, 51, 823-829.

Newcomb, A.F. & Collins, W.A. Children's comprehension of family role portrayals in televised dramas: Effects of socioeconomic status, ethnicity, and age. Developmental Psychology, 1979, 15, 417-423.

Nickel, T.W. The attribution of intention as a critical factor in the relation between frustration and aggression. Journal of Personality, 1974, 42, 482-492.

Pastore, N. The role of arbitrariness in the frustration-aggression hypothesis. Journal of Abnormal and Social Psychology, 1952, 47, 728-731.

Patterson, G.R., Littman, R.A. & Bricker, W. Assertive behavior in children: A step toward a theory of aggression. Monographs of the Society for Research in Child Development, 1967, 86, 145-153.

Peevers, B. & Secord, P.F. Developmental changes in attribution of descriptive concepts to persons. Journal of Personality and Social Psychology, 1973, 27, 120-128.

Pepitone, A. Social psychological perspectives on crime and punishment. Journal of Social Issues, 1975, 31, 197-216.

Pepitone, A. Preliminary notes on the role of values in human aggression. University of Pennsylvania, unpublished manuscript, 1974.

Piaget, J. The moral judgment of the child (M. Gabain, Trans.). New York: Free Press, 1965.

Rosenfield, D. & Stephan, W.G. When discounting fails: An unexpected finding. Memory & Cognition, 1977, 5, 97-102.

Rosenbach, D., Crockett, W.H. & Wapner, S. Developmental level, emotional involvement, and the resolution of inconsistency in impression formation. Developmental Psychology, 1973, 8, 120-130.

Rotenberg, K.J. Children's use of intentionality in judgments, character and disposition. Child Development, 1980, 51, 282.

Rotenberg, K.J. Development of character constancy of self and other. Child Development, 1982, 53, 505-515.

Rule, B.G. & Duker, P. The effects of intentions and consequence on children's evaluations of aggression. Journal of Personality and Social Psychology, 1973, 27, 184-189.

Rule, B.G., Dyck, R., McAra, M. & Nesdale, A.R. Aggression serving personal versus prosocial purposes. Social Behavior and Personality: A International Journal, 1975, 3, 55-63.

Rule, B.G., Ferguson, T.J., Cornell, E., Schokman-Gates, K. & Hazen, L. Salience of intent, consequence severity, and attractiveness information in children's similarity and moral judgments. Unpublished manuscript, University of Alberta.

Rule, B.G. & Nesdale, A.R. Moral judgment of aggression. In R. Geen & E. O'Neal (Eds.). Perspectives on Aggression. New York: Academic Press, 1976.

Rule, B.G., Nesdale, A. & McNamara, M.J. Children's reactions and information about the intentions underlying an aggressive act. Child Development, 1974, 45, 794.

Rybash, J.M., Roodin, P.A. & Hallion, K. The role of affect in children's attribution of intentionality and dispensation of punishment. Child Development, 1979, 50, 1227-1230.

Savitsky, J.C., Czyzewski, D., Dubord, D. & Kaminsky S. Age and emotion of an offender as determinants of adult punitive reaction. Journal of Personality, 1976, 44, 311-320.

Sedlak, A.J. Developmental differences in understanding plans and evaluating actors. Child Development, 1979, 50, 536-560.

Shakelee, H. & Turner, D. Cognitive bases of development in inferences of ability. Child Development, 1979, 50, 904-907.

Shantz, C.U. The development of social cognition. In E.M. Hetherington (Ed.), Review of Child Development Research. Chicago: University of Chicago Press, 1975.

Shantz, D.W., Voydanoff, D.A. Situational effect on retaliatory aggression at the age levels. Child Development, 1977, 44, 149-153.

Shaw, M.E. & Sulzer, J.L. An empirical test of Heider's levels in attribution of responsibility. Journal of Abnormal Social Psychology, 1964, 69, 39-46.

Shultz, T.R., Butkowsky, I., Pearce, J.W. & Shanfield, H. Development of schemes for the attribution of multiple psychological causes. Developmental Psychology, 1975, 11, 502-510.

Shultz, T.R. & Mendelson, R. The use of covariation as a principle of causal analysis. Child Development, 1975, 46, 394-399.

Siegler, R.S. & Liebert, R.M. Effects of contiguity, regularity and age on children's causal inferences. Developmental Psychology, 1974, 10, 574-579.

Smith, M.C. Children's use of the multiple sufficient cause scheme in social perception. Journal of Personality and Social Psychology, 1975, 32, 737-747.

Snyder, M., Tanke, E.D. & Berscheid, E. Social perception and interpersonal behavior: On the self-fulfilling nature of social stereotypes. Journal of Personality & Social Psychology, 1977, 35, 656-666.

Staffieri, J.R. A study of social stereotypes of body image in children. Journal of Personality and Social Psychology, 1967, 7, 101-104.

Staffieri, J.R. Body build and behavioral expectancies in young females. Developmental Psychology, 1972, 6, 125-127.

Styczynski, L.E. & Langlois, J.H. The effects of familiarity on behavioral stereotypes associated with physical attractiveness in young children. Child Development, 1977, 48, 1137-1141.

Suls, J., Gutkin, D. & Kalle, R.J. The role of intentions, damage, and social consequences in the moral judgments of children. Child Development, 1979, 50, 874-877.

Surber, C.F. Developmental processes in social inference: Averaging of intentions and consequences in moral judgment. Developmental Psychology, 1977, 13, 654-665.

Triandis, H. (Ed.) Variations in black and white perceptions of the social environment. Champaign: University of Illinois Press, 1976.

Walker, R.N. Body build and behavior in young children: II. Body build and nursery school teachers ratings. Monographs of the Society for Research in Child Development, 1962, 27, (3, Serial No. 84).

Weisfeld, G. Violations of social norms as inducers of aggression. International Journal of Group Tensions, 1972, 2, 53-70.

Werner, H. The concept of development from a comparative and organismic point of view. In D.B. Harris (Ed.), The concept of development. Minneapolis: University of Minnesota Press, 1957.

Werner, H. Comparative psychology of mental development. New York: Science Editions, 1961.

Whiteman, M., Brook, J.S. & Gordon, A.S. Perceived intention and behavioral incongruity. Child Development, 1977, 48, 1133-1136.

Whiteman, M. The role of intention in subjective and objective responsibility. In M. Bortner (Ed.), Cognitive Growth and Development: Essays in Memory of Herbert G. Birch. New York: Bruneo Mazel, 1979.

Wiggins, J.S. In defense of traits. Unpublished manuscript. Seminar presentation at the Institute of Personality Assessment of Research, Berkeley, November, 1973.

Williams, J.E., Bennett, S.M. & Best, D.L. Awareness and expression of sex stereotypes in young children. Developmental Psychology, 1975, 11, 635-642.

Wood, M.E. Children's developing understanding of other people's motives for behavior. Developmental Psychology, 1978, 14, 561-562.

Yarrow, M.R. & Campbell, J.D. Person perception in children. Merrill-Palmer Quarterly, 1963, 9, 57-72.

THE ANTECEDENTS OF ANGER: A DEVELOPMENTAL APPROACH

Seymour Feshbach, Norma D. Feshbach,
Robin S. Cohen & Michael Hoffman

University of California, Los Angeles

The present paper is addressed to the antecedents of anger and to the developmental changes that occur in these antecedents in children during their early and middle elementary school years. The data on which this report is based were obtained in the context of the investigation of developmental changes in the antecedents of the major affects (N. Feshbach & Hoffman, 1978). The goals of this present investigation of anger are both descriptive and theoretical. There is surprisingly little data available on the situations that evoke anger in children, and basic descriptive information concerning developmental changes and constancies in the nature of these situations are clearly needed. Secondly, an analysis of developmental shifts in anger eliciting stimuli, and how these changes vary with sex and social class, could augment our understanding of both the processes mediating the affect of anger, and the developmental tasks and challenges that confront the child during this age period.

In recent years, there has been a renewal of theoretical interest in the properties of emotions and an increased amount of research activity on this topic. This theoretical and empirical effort, ranging from social psychological studies of the role of attributions in the determination of affects to psychophysiological studies of facial indicators of affects, has included a good deal of attention directed toward the processes mediating the arousal and reduction of anger. Nevertheless, very little attention has been given to the study of anger in children. In a relatively recent volume devoted to the development of affect, there are only four references to anger (Lewis & Rosenblum, 1978). In two of these references, anger appears as simply one word in an enumeration of affects along with happiness, surprise, fear and

162

Kaplan, R.M., Konečni, V.J., Novaco, R.W. (eds.) Aggression in Children and Youth
© 1984, Martinus Nijhoff Publishers, The Hague/Boston/Lancaster
ISBN 90-247-2903-3. Printed in The Netherlands

sadness. In a third reference, anger is listed along with fear and surprise in a sentence indicating that these three affects "became prominent in development only during the latter half of the first year" (p. 145). The fourth reference is more extensive and entails a brief but relevant paragraph in which Izard (1978, p. 398) notes that "the emergence of anger marks the transition of the baby from one who deals with troubles and frustrations primarily through the use of the distress cry to obtain help from others to one who may add to a distress-anger cry a determined effort to remove or change the frustrating condition. Between 4 and 6 months, the infant is capable of experiencing and expressing anger, and the anger experience motivates efforts to deal with frustrating restraints and barriers. Thus anger increases the infant's opportunities to sense self-as-casual agent and hence to experience self as separate, distinct and capable" (pp. 398-399).

We shall consider subsequently some of the interesting ideas contained in this brief summary on the development of anger. It is noteworthy that even this paragraph is based upon a very limited set of observations. It is clear that a great many questions regarding the origins and antecedents of anger and developmental changes in its manifestations and functions have not yet been empirically examined. For example, although six-month-old infants have been shown to display anger-like reactions in situations in which they are thwarted, there is little information concerning the variability with infants and between infants of the anger-eliciting property of these situations, or of factors influencing this variability. Is the anger reaction of young infants' response to the frustration of learned expectations--such as the removal of a bottle after a few minutes' sucking--similar or equivalent to the frustration of a relatively new behavior sequence--such as the infant's falling when attempting to raise itself? Are interpersonal elements particularly relevant to the anger response? Does it make a difference if the frustrating agent is the child's mother? Do anger responses during the infant's first year occur primarily in connection with frustrations in the feeding situation.

In addition to these questions concerning the antecedents of the anger response are many other important issues regarding the consequences of anger and the relationship of the anger response to other competencies and behaviors of the organism. What degree and type of cognitive organization accompanies the expression of anger? What developmental changes occur in the expression of anger? Presumably temper tantrums are indicative of disorganized and primitive behaviors. What are the developmental antecedents of the temper tantrum? What factors determine modifications in this form of anger expression and the development of more integrated response patterns in the expression of anger? And we have not yet traced how the response of parents, siblings and peers to manifestations of anger influence the frequency and mode of its occurrence. Nor do we have any data bearing upon the conditions under which anger becomes integrated with instrumental aggresive behaviors. This enumeration of questions related to the

163

antecedents, manifestation, consequences, and "fate" of anger is by no means exhaustive. However, it does serve to illustrate the paucity of knowledge regarding developmental questions pertaining to anger in humans.

There is an obvious relationship between anger in humans and anger in infrahumans, so that one can expect some similarity in their respective biological antecedents and, as Darwin proposed, in their respective biological functions (Ekman, 1973). One is often struck by the similarity in anger expression between primates and humans. Both human and ape anger are characterized by a direct gaze and clenched jaws with lips compressed (or a partly open mouth with lips retracted vertically). But there are also differences between human and primate anger expressions, especially when signs of anger in young children are considered. Thus, Watson described anger in the young infant as characterized by a stiffening of the body, striking or slashing movements of hands and arms, holding of the breath, a flushed face, and crying escalating gradually into screaming.

When do the direct gaze and clenched jaw that characterize anger in adults develop? Descriptions of anger outbursts during the toddler period as well as infancy do not correspond to the vestigial anger expressions that presumably characterize the adult. Charlesworth writes "It is safe to conclude that anger, as inferred from gross behaviors as well as from crying and screaming is well-developed in infants under 6 months of age. Temper tantrums (which usually involve kicking, scratching and rolling on the floor) are not usually evident until the beginning of the second year (Bridges, 1932; in Charlesworth & Kreutzer, 1973, p. 114). Goodenough's (1931) description of the varied behaviors characterizing anger in the older preschool child leads one to question whether the entire pattern can be considered a simple biological expression of affect. The behavioral elements as noted by Goodenough include "kicking, stamping, jumping up and down, striking, making the body limp, refusing to move, struggling and running for help", facial expressions involving closing of the mouth firmly (in contrast, we might note, with the open mouth of the angry ape), frowning, making faces, panting and sulking.

The differences between the expressions of anger in young children and its expression in primates necessitate caution in assuming that equivalent biological mechanisms are involved. And there are undoubtedly profound differences in social and cognitive mechanisms. As Goodenough has pointed out, anger comes under increasing instrumental control of the child as the child matures, and is expressed in a more integrated, less diffuse manner. The antecedents of anger in humans undergo a profound change as a function of the child's psychological and social development. The few studies tracing developmental changes in the antecedents of anger have beeen restricted to observations of children from upper socioeconomic strata and, in addition, have given insufficient attention to sex differences (Gesell & Ilg, 1949; Goodenough, 1931; Zeligs, 1945). The present project, in addition to taking

164

these variables into account, applies a systematic and comprehensive scheme to the analysis of situational antecedents of affect. The data yielded, in addition to being of descriptive interest, should also contribute to our understanding of changes in the child's social development during the period being assessed.

METHOD

The initial approach to the determination of developmental changes in the antecedents of anger was exploratory. Children at different age levels were interviewed to determine those events that caused the greatest anger, and it is these data that will be reported upon here. The interview sample consisted of 192 children, 96 boys and 96 girls attending kindergarten, second, third, fourth and sixth grades in four elementary schools located in lower and middle class neighborhoods. There were approximately equivalent numbers of children from Anglo, Black, Chicano, and Asian-American backgrounds.

The children were individually interviewed. During the interview, the child was simply asked to recount a personal experience that strongly elicited a specific emotion. For example, in regard to anger, the interviewer requested the child to state something that made him or her "very, very angry." In addition, they were also asked to indicate a hypothetical situation that would make one very angry. The results from the responses to the hypothetical and the actual inquiry were generally similar, and the data to be presented are based on the child's reports of actual events that evoked anger.

It should be noted that each child was asked to indicate only one situation. While this procedure yields less information than might be gained if the child were asked to enumerate all the kinds of situations that lead to anger, it does have several methodological advantages. First, it equates the response contributions of each participant. Second, it focuses the children on those situations that are the most prepotent elicitors of anger.

RESULTS

The development of a scheme that would incorporate the relevant dimensions of the situation for content analysis poses an important methodological and conceptual challenge. Comparable kinds of issues arise in the dimensional structures of story content formulated by experimental psychologists in their studies of memory of complex thematic material. The dimensional structure employed in the analysis of the antecedents of anger was formulated as a general model for the analysis of affect eliciting situations (N. Feshbach & Hoffman, 1978). In essence, the method stems from the observation that the children's descriptions of emotionally arousing situations took the form of a "story in a sentence." In relating a situation, the child would spontaneously

165

tell a complete story replete with actor, plot, and context, often in a single sentence. The prototypical story sentence dealt with a transaction between an agent and a subject over a resource. For example, "My friend, Robert, made me angry when he hit me because I wouldn't let him ride my new bike." The resource could simply be the child's personal well-being--e.g., "My brother made me angry when he hurt me." These transactions take place in a social context which usually consists of the subject and agent but may include other figures that are present at the interaction. And the physical environment, when indicated, is still another contextual variable. The specification of the resource that is at issue in the anger interaction ordinarily is indicative of the subject's need that is being violated or frustrated. However, resources may serve different needs, and inferences regarding the need involved, although much more subjective than the scoring of the resource, can enrich and deepen our understanding of the reasons for the child's anger. However, for the age groups studied, the analysis of needs yielded findings similar to the analysis of resources, and therefore will not be separately presented.

Still other dimensions of the child's report were scored that failed to provide much variance in the children's responses, such as the intentionality of the agent. Finally, the protocols were analyzed for the action taken by the agent, and these data bear on the relationship between anger and instrumental aggression.

TABLE 1

Developmental Variations in Primary Agents Provoking Anger

Agents	Grade				
	K	2	4	6	Total
Parents	7	8	10	20	45 (23%)
Siblings	15	13	17	12	57 (30%)
Peers	13	19	9	12	53 (28%)
Self/Others	13	8	12	4	37 (19%)

166

Agent

We turn first to an analysis of the social figures that are the primary agent provoking the child's anger (Table 1). The three primary sources of children's anger are siblings, peers and parents, with the self being cited as a fourth source. While the differences in the totals for siblings, peers and parents are small, there are significant developmental differences and changes in their relative importance (X^2=19.99; p<.02). The percentages for siblings and peers remain relatively constant across age groups, one possible exception being the drop from 40% for peers in 2nd grade to 19% in 4th grade; however, this percentage rises to 25% for 6th graders.

In comparison, the increment that occurs between kindergarten and 6th grade in the frequency with which parents assume the role of primary agent (from 15% to 42%) is developmentally consistent and highly significant (p<.01). One observes the same trend regardless of social class and ethnic group. Boys and girls display a similar increase in the tendency to perceive parents as the principal source of evoking anger as they approach adolescence, except that the shift is greater for girls than for boys (from 12% in kindergarten to 54% in 6th grade for girls, the corresponding figures for boys being 17% and 29%). This possible sex difference in relationship to parents as the child becomes older is of interest, and warrants replication. It is of note that while parents increase as the source of anger as girls increase in age, girls maintain a similar frequency of references to parents as the agents of happy events, regardless of the girls' ages. In contrast, boys are less likely to see parents as the source of positive affect or happiness as they grow older. Still another sex difference that merits replication is the greater frequency (36%) with which girls cite sibs as sources of anger as compared to boys (23%). This latter difference (p<.05) corresponds to one observed between middle and lower income children with 45% of the former vs. 30% of the latter citing sibs. In comparison, anger at peers is higher in low SES children, 37% of this group and 18% of the middle SES children citing peers as the primary source of anger.

Social Context

Social context refers to the social figures present in the affective situation. In the case of situations evoking happiness or pride, it was not uncommon for parents and peers to appear as participants without being the specific agent. However, in the case of anger, the findings for context were very similar to those obtained for agents. The principal exception was the significantly greater frequency with which girls, as compared to boys, cited anger events involving self, parents, and another child in a triangular relationship. It is of interest to speculate here whether boys' sibling rivalries reflect power and control struggles while girls' sibling rivalries are more likely to reflect competition for parental support and attention.

167

Resource, Psychological Need

The occasion for anger typically entails frustration or a noxious experience. While there is undoubtedly some relationship between the agent and the type of frustration and psychological need that is blocked, one finds, for each agent, considerable variation in the needs that are blocked and considerable overlap between agents. As Table 2 indicates, the marginal percentages for each of the psychological needs or resources are very similar. However, there are important, although not unexpected developmental shifts in the frustrated needs or resources that become salient at different ages.

TABLE 2

Developmental Variations in Principal Psychological

Needs and Resources Implicated in Anger Provoking Situations

	Grade				
Need Resource	K	2	4	6	Total
Physical Well Being	21	16	10	6	53 (28%)
Objects	12	14	17	6	49 (26%)
Self-Esteem	6	10	12	21	49 (26%)
Entertain/Pic. Social Partic.	4	8	9	13	34 (18%)
Uncoded	5	0	0	2	7 (3%)

There is a marked decline in physical threats and physical pain inflictions as a source of anger with increasing age of the child, from 44% in kindergarten to 12% in 6th grade (p<.01). This decline is accompanied by a comparable increase in the importance of situations involving self-esteem, from 12% in kindergarten to 44% in 6th grade (p<.01). Loss or destruction of material objects--toys, records, and other possessions, is an important occasion for anger throughout most of the age span--25% citing some kind of physical resource in kindergarten and 35% in 4th grade, but declines sharply in 6th grade to 12% (p<.01). This decline primarily occurs among the girls, the number citing a physical object in the 6th grade being 0, while the percentage for the 6th grade boys is still 25%. Overall, boys are more likely to cite threats to loss of material objects than are girls--33% to 18% (p.<.10). Self-esteem injuries tend to be cited more often by females than males, but the difference is not significant--30% to 21%. The sex difference becomes most marked in the 6th grade--29% vs. 15%, but given the other variations that can occur in these percentages, the difference requires replication before one can assert that self-esteem injury becomes more important to females than to males as puberty is approached.

The overall developmental shifts that have been noted--the decline in physical attacks or threats and the increase in the importance of self-esteem as the child matures, and the decline in the importance of threats to material objects in 6th graders, holds for the two socioeconomic groups and for the different ethnic groups, but the shades of emphasis do vary in some instances. Thus, physical harm is cited more often by children from low as compared to middle socioeconomic groups--35% to 18% (X^2=6.3; p<.05). Other incidental social class findings regarding the antecedent situations evoking anger are of interest. About 60% of the time, the children failed to indicate the environmental context--home, parks, etc., where the anger situation occurred. However, when the environment was specified, lower-class children cited both home and school--59% at home and 41% at school, while the middle-class children predominantly cited the home (93% at home and 7% at school). The fact that school is a much more frequent occasion for anger for lower-class than for middle SES children is not surprising but does serve to underline the profound difference in socialization experiences that social class occasions.

In addition to assessing the need that was frustrated and the context in which the anger provocation occurred, an effort was made to assess the cognitive attributes of the situation evoking anger. Not much of interest was elicited in this regard. Most of the children, including the kindergarteners, maintained that the provocation was intentional. There is an increase with age in the attribution of intentionality--from 75% in kindergarten to 89% in 6th grade (p<.05). While this shift is in accord with cognitive developmental changes, the high frequency with which intent is cited by the five-year-olds in kindergarten raises questions concerning the Piagetian view regarding developmental changes in apprehending the importance of the intentionality of a deviant act versus the injurious consequences of the act. It may be that five-year-olds attribute more importance to consequences than to motivation in judging morality of an action. However, they clearly are capable of perceiving intentionality, and the attribution of intentionality to a provoking agent is a common component of the phenomenology of an anger-inducing even for these young children.

169

Response to Provocation

In most of their situational descriptions, the children indicated the action they took in response to their anger and provocation. About half the kindergarten age children, 47%, respond with
physical aggression. The proportion gradually drops off with
increasing age, to 11% in 6th grade (p<.01). The decline in the
use of physical aggression corresponds to an increase in the use
of verbal responses and non-physical punishment with increasing
age of the child. Thus, teasing increased from 9% in kindergarten
to 17% in 6th grade. Blaming and accusation increased from 0 in
kindergarten to 4% in 4th grade to 17% in 6th grade, and embar-
rassing and rejecting the provocateur increased from 7% to 26%
over this six-year period. It is somewhat surprising that there
is no difference in reported use of physical aggression between
males and females (28% males to 31% females). In fact, sex
differences in reported responses to provocation are minor. Thus,
teasing tends to be greater in females, but not significantly so,
while males display a stronger tendency to retaliate by destroying
or misusing objects or property--30% for males to 15% for females
(p<.05).

There were, however, substantial social class differences in
the use of physical aggression in response to anger-provocation--
35% for LSES children to 18% for middle SES childred (p<.05). The
middle SES children were more likely to deny some satisfaction or
insist on an obligation ("I won't play with her until she gives me
another book like the one she tore up") than the low SES
children--29% SES to 15% Low SES (p<.05). These social class
differences are consistent with other data indicating that lower-
class families are more likely to make use of shame and physical
modes of punishment.

It is important to recognize that the action taken by the
subject which he or she sees as a response to provocation can be
perceived by the agent as a provocation. The roles of subject and
agent can rapidly change, and the distinction between provocation
and punishment can become blurred or, at the very least, is dependent upon the different perceptions of the subject and agent.
Nevertheless, it is an important distinction to maintain, even if
not always readily discernible.

SUMMARY AND CONCLUSIONS

The analysis of the antecedents of anger in children has
yielded a number of findings that bear not only on developmental
changes in factors eliciting anger but also upon broader processes
and issues of socialization. The principal findings may be summarized as follows:

1. Siblings, peers and parents are the primary agents or
instigators of children's anger between the ages of 5 and 12. The
role of siblings and parents is relatively constant across age

groups while a substantial increase takes place between kindergarten and 6th grade in the extent to which parents are perceived as the primary source of anger.

2. Girls are more likely than boys to cite siblings as agents of anger; girls, when older, also are more likely to cite parents. The contextual setting in which provocation of anger takes place also suggests that girls, more than boys, are engaged in struggles with siblings for parental approval and attention.

3. Physical threats and pain infliction show a substantial decline between kindergarten and 6th grade as antecedents of anger while threats to self-esteem increase in importance over this age span.

4. Anger provoking events are seen as intentional (and also unjustified) as early as kindergarten age.

5. Physical aggression as a response to anger provocation declines between kindergarten and 6th grade while verbal aggression and non-physical punishments increase over this age span.

6. Other sex differences include a sharper decline among 6th grade girls as compared to 6th grade boys in the percentage citing loss of destruction of a material object as the occasion for anger, a tendency for self-esteem threats to become more important to girls relative to the increase for boys with increasing age, and a stronger tendency for males as compared to females to retaliate to anger-provocation by destroying or misusing material objects. In contrast, the similarity of boys and girls in reported use of physical aggression and other responses to provocation is notable.

7. In general, the developmental changes reported held for the different ethnic and socioeconomic groups that were sampled. However, some SES differences in the reported antecedents of and response to anger provocation were observed. Middle SES children are more likely than low SES children to cite siblings as a source of anger while the latter are more likely to cite peers. Physical threats and physical harm are mentioned more often by lower SES than middle SES children as antecedents of anger, and provocative situations are much more likely to occur at school for the low SES as compared to the middle SES child. Also, lower SES children report greater use of physical aggression than middle SES children while the latter are more likely to deny some satisfaction or favor restitution as a response to anger provocation.

The observed social class differences are consistent with other data regarding social class differences in aggression and in punishment practices (Feshbach, 1970). Unanticipated, although not surprising, is the greater frequency with which lower SES children cite peers and the lesser frequency with which they cite sibs as compared to middle SES children. These data suggest the possibility that sibling rivalry and related familial struggles

171

may be markedly affected by the child's peer group experiences and social contextual dimension.

The data on sex differences also suggest important differences in the dynamics of anger and in developmental changes that may arise from social variables. In the case of sex differences, there is, of course, the possibility that biological factors may be the major determinant of sex differences in the antecedents of anger. However, at this point in our state of knowledge, it is more important to establish and confirm the nature of these sex differences. Is it the case, as the data suggest, that girls are more concerned than boys with obtaining parental support and approval, and that sibling rivalries in girls are mediated by different needs than those in boys? These admittedly speculative questions are nonetheless intriguing possibilities that merit further exploration. It suggests the utility of studying in detail the antecedents of anger in boys and girls in the context of the family and in their interactions with peers. While the differences between boys and girls in the reported antecedents of anger are consistent with the conceptions of boys as more "instrumental" and girls as more "affiliative," more specific analyses and observations are required to give meaning to these generalized descriptions.

At the same time, in drawing inferences from the data, it must be recognized that the data are dependent on self-reports. In addition, the children report those anger incidents that are the most salient for them. Consequently, the anger incidents that have been reported are not exhaustive of the range of events that may evoke anger in these age groups. The reports of the children may also be affected by defensiveness concerning certain antecedents, by variations in insight and possibly by normative stereotypes. However, the method despite its limitations, constitutes one useful approach to the study of developmental changes in the antecedents of anger. The data point to important regularities and developmental changes in anger antecedents. The absence of certain potential antecedents--e.g., "territoriality" is also noteworthy.

The decline in physical attacks and conflicts over material objects and the increase in the significance of humiliation, somewhat stronger for females than males, but central for both, as they approach adolescence, constitutes a profound difference between humans and infrahumans in the dynamics of anger. Humiliation or "loss of face," and related psychological conditions are complex, acquired motivational-affective systems. There is no simple counterpart to which one can point and study in infrahumans. Moreover, threats to self-esteem are not inherent properties of stimulus situations. These threats, unlike physical pain, depend as much upon the psychological characteristics of the subject as they do upon the actions of the agent. Children and adults who are very secure and firm about their self-concept may be relatively unaffected by humiliation efforts. An analogous situation is that of the therapist, who, secure in his or her self-evaluation, can attribute derogatory remarks made by a client to the client's problems and difficulties. And, there is the converse situation of the insecurity of the individual who has internalized a negative self-evaluation such that humiliation attacks are perceived as confirmation of rather than threats to the self-concept.

It is of interest that "territoriality" does not appear as a major antecedent of anger. Material possessions could be considered as a form of territoriality but, as already noted, their significance as an antecedent of anger sharply declines by the time the child reaches the age of 11 or 12. We know that a form of "territoriality" is important as a source of conflict for certain groups of urban adolescents. It should be emphasized, however, that the territorial behavior of adolescent gangs is far from universal and is displayed by a minority of adolescents-- probably, a small minority. What appears to have happened for these adolescents is that territories have become related to self-concept. This relationship is probably fundamentally no different in kind than the process by which the fate of athletic teams, devaluation of one's school, neighborhood, city, perhaps nationality as well, became threats to one's self-concept and antecedents of anger.

Anger in humans is not a simple clenching of the jaw, or baring of the teeth, or gesticulation of the limbs. It is a complex set of behaviors, with cognitive components, that undergoes changes that have yet to be assessed. As the data reported here indicate, the antecedents of anger undergo substantial developmental shifts that are significantly affected by social variables. And the response to anger also appears to be a malleable behavior. Cross-cultural studies of the antecedents, expression and response to anger are very much in order. And, from a clinical as well as scientific perspective, we need to know more about the physiological consequences of the different modes of expressing and responding to anger. In regard to these and related issues of the antecedents and response to anger, a developmental approach employing observation along with the kinds of interview procedures utilized in the present study would appear to be promising.

REFERENCES

Charlesworth, W.R. & Kreutzer, M.A. Facial expressions of infants and children. In P. Ekman (Ed.), Darwin and facial expression; a century of research in review. New York: Academic Press, 1973, pp. 91-168.
Ekman, Paul (Ed.). Darwin and facial expression; a century of research in review. New York: Academic Press, 1973.
Feshbach, N.D. & Hoffman, M.A. Sex differences in children's reports of emotion-arousing situations. In Symposium on sex differences: Comotion, motion, or emotion (Diane McGuines, Chair). Western Psychological Association Meeting, San

Francisco, April, 1978.

Feshbach, S. Aggression. In P.H. Mussen (Ed.), Carmichael's manual of child psychology. New York: Wiley, 1970.

Gesell, A. & Ilg, F.L. Child development: An introduction to the study of human growth. Vol. II, The child from 5 to 10. New York: Harper & Brothers, 1949.

Goodenough, F. Anger in young children. Minneapolis: University of Minnesota Press, 1931.

Izard, C.E. On the ontogenesis of emotions and emotion-cognition relationships in infancy. In M. Lewis & L.A. Rosenblum (Eds.), The development of affect. New York: Plenum Press, 1978, pp. 389-413.

Lewis, M. & Rosenblum, L.A. (Eds.). The development of affect. New York: Plenum Press, 1978.

Zeligs, R. Social factors annoying to children. J. of Applied Psychol. 29:75-82, 1945.

III. REGULATION OF ANGER AND AGGRESSION

SOCIAL AND COGNITIVE SKILLS TRAINING: AN ANTIDOTE FOR ADOLESCENT ACTING OUT

Irwin G. Sarason and Barbara R. Sarason

University of Washington

Aggression, delinquency, and other forms of acting-out are examples of maladaptive behavior that seem particularly interpretable as failures in information-processing. Such behavior occurs when the individual's skills in interpreting and responding to situational demands, constraints, and opportunities are not commensurate with calls for action. Calls for action are challenges with which the individual feels it is necessary to deal. They vary in urgency and become stressful when they lead to such cognitions as "I'm on the spot" and "I've got to do something," and when success is not certain.

Because of deficits in the areas of social and problem-solving skills, many people make mistakes in searching the environment for relevant cues, selecting cues that play roles in effective thought and action, integrating new information with old, and identifying behavioral options. Children are likely to make these mistakes because they have not yet had adequate opportunities to acquire the cognitive and social skills required for successful adaptation to the community. The demands in adolescence for new social and cognitive behaviors may be considerable, and they also represent a dramatic change from the situational and self-initiated demands of earlier years. During this period, both self-expectations and the expectations of society about what behavior is appropriate may not only be altered but may be subject to continued change.

Adolescents may lack needed social and cognitive skills to meet the special calls for action posed by approaching adulthood. The interaction between these lacks (person variables) and the novel challenges of this period of life (developmental and environmental variables) accounts for much of the inappropriate

175

Kaplan, R.M., Konečni, V.J., Novaco, R.W. (eds.) Aggression in Children and Youth
© 1984, Martinus Nijhoff Publishers, The Hague/Boston/Lancaster
ISBN 90-247-2903-3. Printed in The Netherlands

and acting-out behavior seen in adolescents. The increase in aggression, crime, and other forms of acting-out behavior typical of some young people may be seen as products of the unmet demands from person-situation interactions. A promising recent development that may be of use in dealing with acting out adolescents has been research on a skills training approach to social and cognitive deficits. While the behavioral deficits in adolescence or other periods can come about for a variety of reasons, their end products are not only difficulties for all concerned, but even more important, they are limitations on the personal growth and successful adaptation of the individual.

A number of skills training programs have been devised to strengthen effective human functioning in a variety of target groups. Examples of successful clinical applications of the skills training paradigm include efforts to improve the functioning of chronic psychiatric patients (Goldsmith & McFall, 1975; Goldstein, Sprafkin, Gershaw & Klein, 1980; Hersen & Bellack, 1976), severely retarded persons (Matson & Martin, 1979), and impulsive and hyperactive children (Douglas, Parry, Marton & Garson, 1976; Kendall & Wilcox, 1980). While the skills on which the programs focus vary, the programs are usually multifaceted, including the elements of modeling, behavioral rehearsal (practiced role playing), feedback, and social reinforcement. Three additional features of these programs are their applicality to groups of people rather than individuals; the fact that they can be targeted to specific behaviors; and their efficiency--work on the targeted behavior is usually time limited and requires a relatively small number of hours. One of the most promising recent developments has been a focus on specific cognitive skills and the self-control of behavior. Programs concerned with this topic are aimed at improving how people think and solve problems (Goldstein et al., 1980; Kendall & Hollon, 1979; Meichenbaum, 1977; Sarason, Johnson, Berberich & Siegel, 1979; Snyder & White, 1979).

Several researchers have used social skills training programs in the rehabilitation of juvenile delinquents. A primary ingredient of these programs is the modeling of socially appropriate ways of achieving desired ends and coping with stress (Freedman, Donahoe, Rosenthal, Schlundt & McFall, 1978; Ollendick & Hersen, 1979; Prentice, 1972; Sarason & Ganzer, 1973). For example, Ollendick and Hersen (1979) developed a training program for incarcerated juvenile delinquents that consisted of instruction, feedback, modeling, behavior rehearsal, social reinforcement, and graduated homework assignments. The subjects were assessed using self-reports, role-playing, and behavioral techniques before and after participation in the program. Ollendick and Hersen found that the program was successful in strengthening interpersonal skills, reducing anxiety, increasing the subjects' internal locus of control, and improving the behavioral adjustment.

Social skills training programs for delinquents have been evaluated in a variety of ways, with follow-up investigations of program effectiveness varying widely. In some cases the programs

176

seem to be effective over the short term; in others, positive results have persisted over time. In an investigation reporting positive long-term effects over a five-year period, Sarason (1978) studied institutionalized boys between the ages of 15 and 18 who had committed serious offenses.

A SKILLS TRAINING PROGRAM FOR DELINQUENT JUVENILES

The program to be reported here (Sarason, 1968, 1978; Sarason & Ganzer, 1973) consisted of 16 one-hour group sessions in which models demonstrated specific behaviors (resisting peer pressure, asking for help, dealing with authority figures); then the boys rehearsed the scenes that the models had enacted.

Each modeling session had a particular theme; for example, how to apply for a job, how to resist temptations by peers to engage in antisocial acts, how to take problems to a teacher or parole counselor, and how to pass up immediate gratification in order to lay the groundwork for achieving more significant goals in the future. In each situation, emphasis was placed on the generality of the appropriate behaviors being modeled and their potential usefulness in a variety of situations.

In the first-day orientation for each new group, the boys were told: "We think that small groups working together can learn a lot about appropriate ways of doing things by playing different roles and watching others play roles. By role we mean the particular part a person acts or plays in a particular situation, kind of like the parts actors play in a movie scene, only this will be more realistic. These roles will be based on actual situations that many young people have trouble with, like how to control your anger or resist being pressured into doing destructive things by friends. Some roles are directly related to fellows like yourselves who have been in an institution...this is like acting, only it is realistic because it involves situations in which you might really find yourselves...".

Following the first day's orientation, which included a short example scene, each subsequent meeting adhered to this format: one of the models began the session by introducing and describing the particular scene to be enacted that day. These introductions served the purpose of orienting the boys to the group's work for the day and to afford them a rationale for the particular scene. The models role-played the particular scene for the day while the boys observed. Following this enactment, one boy was called upon to summarize and explain the content and outcome of what had just been observed. After a short break, the boys took turns enacting the situation that had been modeled. Each meeting ended with final summaries and comments concerning the scene, its most salient aspects, and its generalizability. The Handling Anger Scene illustrates the approach taken in the modeling portions of the sessions.

Handling Anger Scene

The group leader introduced the scene in the following way:

One thing that gets some of you guys in trouble is losing your temper. When some of you get mad at another fellow, you get in fights. When you get mad at a teacher or a boss, you tell him or her off and get tossed out of class or off a job. You get smart with a police officer or a cottage supervisor and get thrown in the pokey.

Others of you don't get mad in the same way. You kind of say "to hell with them" and refuse to cooperate any more. No matter what they ask you do to when you're mad, you turn them off. The result is usually the same--you get thrown off the job or out of class or end up in the pokey.

Others of you may just walk off and leave the boss or teacher flat--quitting school or your job. The result is again that you've lost something--education or a paycheck--because you won't take the static. It's harder to "take it" when you know you're right and the teacher or the boss is wrong in bugging you. So we're going to play a scene in which there is no good reason for the other person to bug you.

Here is the first scene. This scene takes place in a gas station. Bill is working on a car in the lube room. The boss comes in looking and acting real angry. He is not mad at Bill but probably at some personal problem. In this situation, the boss is wrong, but Bill will have to control his own temper. Bill has a reason to get mad, but if he does, the chances are that he'll be fired. This is a two-part scene. First, the boss chews Bill out; then, two hours later, Bill has to go back and talk to the boss again.

Then the two group leaders roleplayed the following interchange:

Boss: What do you think you're doing?

Bill: I'm servicing this Chev--lube, oil, and filter.

Boss: I thought I told you that I wanted the lube room cleaned and the shipment of oil put away before anything else was done.

Bill: Not me--maybe you told Sam. I figured I'd better get on this right away. The service sheet says that the guy wants it in an hour.

Boss: Don't tell me I didn't tell you. I remember I did. Now get that car off the rack and do what you're told.

Bill: But the guy will be back for his car before I can get the

178

lube room done.

Boss: Look, I'm running this business. You do what you're told. NOW! I don't want any more arguments from you. I don't have to take any static from you. I did a pretty good turn for you by hiring you even though I knew you had a record. Not many guys would stick their necks out for a kid like you.

Bill: Okay.

Boss: (turns and stalks out)

Then one group leader continued the presentation by saying:

Now the hard part comes. You're mad at the boss, but you have to keep acting as if nothing has happened. We don't mean that you crawl. You don't tell the boss he's right or get extra friendly. You just forget it and act as if nothing happened. This is really important at work or at school. You can often avoid some guys your own age who bug you by walking away from them, but you can't leave the classroom or the job...you have to stick with it and that's what is tough. This scene takes place in the same gas station approximately two hours later. The required work is done. In the meantime, the customer has come in to find his car has not been serviced. Bill enters the office.

The two group leaders continued the roleplay with this script:

Bill: The lube room is clean and the oil's put away.

Boss: It's about time. You're going to have to move a little faster around here if you want to keep your job.

Bill: Yes, sir. Can I go now? I'm a little overtime.

Boss: Hell no...you've got to finish that Chev. That guy was just in here yelling at me because it wasn't done.

Bill: Well, you know I wanted to leave on time. I told you this morning I had a date.

Boss: That's your problem. I told you that you're going to finish the Chev, so you'd better get at it. That's all.

Bill: Okay...well...I'm going to call my girl first and tell her I'll be late.

Boss: Yeah, but hurry it up.

After the role play, the two group leaders led a structured discussion about the modeling scenario just completed. The discussion covered the following points:

1. It's okay to get angry. What you do with your anger is what is important.

2. Did Bill stand up for his rights? Describe exactly what happened.

3. What are the steps to take when you feel yourself getting angry? First, recognize it. Then decide what is the most profitable thing to do. Remember that too many people just react without thinking, which often makes things worse. Keep in mind the idea that the point is not whether you are wrong or right; it's what might happen to you as a result of what you do.

4. The two role play situations are different, but the boy reacts in the same way. In these situations, he sometimes won't risk expressing anger even though he knows he is right, because blowing up doesn't have the best payoff for him.

In this study, follow-up data on those boys in the modeling and role-playing program were compared with data on boys in a Discussion condition whose content was similar to the Modeling sessions and also with that of an untreated Control group. In addition to significant short-term effects (staff ratings, self-reports, and behavioral variables), the recidivism rate was significantly lower for the modeling-rehearsal group than for a comparable control group. The group in which the same content had been dealt with using a discussion format also yielded a significant reduction in recidivism. Five years after participating in the special rehabilitation program, both groups of experimental subjects showed a 50% reduction in recidivism compared to the control group.

Another type of follow-up data was derived from an analysis of the recollections of a sample of experimental subjects 3 years after participation in the experiment. The interviewer first asked each subject to recall and describe what he could remember about the procedure, content, and described purpose of the group in which he had participated while at the institution. Subjects' recall of each of these three aspects of their group participation was rated as good or adequate or poor. The proportions of subjects falling into these categories for each of the two ratings are summarized in Table 1. A greater proportion of Modeling group subjects recalled the content and purpose of the groups than did subjects who had participated in the Discussion groups. While it was expected that recall of the contents would be superior for Modeling group boys because of the greater specificity and repetition involved in the imitative procedures, their better recall of the purposes of the groups might not have been anticipated, since approximately the same amount of time was taken by models or leaders in describing this aspect of the group sessions.

Table 1

Interviewees' Recall of Group Participation

Category	Group	Rating Adequate-Good	Poor
Recall of group procedures	Modeling	15	4
	Discussion	10	3
Recall of content	Modeling	15	4
	Discussion	5	8
Recall of purpose	Modeling	13	6
	Discussion	7	6

A SKILLS TRAINING PROGRAM FOR HIGH SCHOOL STUDENTS

If a skills training approach is useful in the rehabilitation of institutionalized juvenile delinquents, might it play a useful role in a school setting? In an attempt to answer this question, an experiment was carried out in an inner-city high school (Sarason & Sarason, 1981). A relatively small proportion of the school's graduates go on to further education. A substantial number of members of the student body could be described as dropout and delinquency prone; that is, they were low in academic skills and scholastic achievement, had poor school attendance records, and were likely to come to the attention of school authorities for disciplinary infractions. Family income levels were relatively low, and many of the families had a wide variety of psychosocial problems.

The research was carried out in class sessions as part of a regular course. The basic experimental procedure involved using modeling to demonstrate social and cognitive skills, followed by rehearsal of the modeled behavior. One group of subjects saw live demonstrations, another saw the same models on videotape, and a control group received no special treatment. The program that was developed differed from the program for institutionalized delinquents primarily in that it dealt with problem-solving skills at both the cognitive and behavioral levels. That is, the subjects saw demonstrations of both effective overt responses (e.g., how to ask a teacher a question) and the cognitive antecedents of effective behavior (e.g., deciding between alternative courses of action). Repeated emphasis was placed on the links between thought and action.

Based on pilot studies that were carried out, the experimental program included emphasis on the following specific areas: (a) the consequences of an action; (b) the alternatives available in a particular situation; (c) the effect of the individual's behavior on others and the importance of understanding others' points of view in a situation; (d) the development of communication skills (particularly communication with non-peers).

The first step in the project was an effort to specify the kinds of skills these students might lack and what they and those who work with them saw as the problem areas in their behavior. To secure this information, extensive interviewing was done. A cross-section of students attending the school, former students who had dropped out and were now attending a special evening program, teachers and counselors, and employers who often hired students from this school were all questioned about what they saw as the most common problems that contributed to low grades, dropping out, and unemployment among students.

From these interviews a consistent picture emerged. All groups thought the students lacked such social skills as how to present themselves to employers and teachers. Many students remarked that they avoided contacts with non-peers because they

182

did not know how to approach them, and lacked the skills to present themselves in a pleasantly assertive manner. The students believed little in the school curriculum to be of relevance to their present or future lives. They also appeared to have little concern about any consequences of their present behavior on any aspect of their future life.

Both the school personnel and the employers stressed the students' inability to tolerate frustrations if the solution to a problem was not immediately available. They focused on the need the students had for immediate rewards and their lack of problem-solving skills. They saw the students as lacking awareness of their effect on others and others' points of view. The students' limited future orientation and their lack of perception of cause and effect relationships in their behavior toward others were also emphasized.

With these points in mind and with the use of interview data about specific problem areas, role play scripts were written for the following situations:

1. a job interview
2. resisting peer pressure in school or on the job
3. asking for help in school
4. asking questions in class
5. getting along with the boss
6. dealing with frustration on the job
7. cutting class
8. asking for help at work
9. getting along with parents

The role play modules differed from those used in the institutional study in that not only behavior, but also cognitions, were modeled. An example of a script including this cognitive modeling follows.

Cutting Class Scene

Tom: Hey, Jim, you want to go down to Green Lake fourth period?

Jim: What are you gonna do down at Green Lake?

Tom: A bunch of us are gonna take the afternoon off and party it up.

Jim: I don't think I can go. Sixth period Mr. Smith is reviewing for the algebra exam.

Tom: What about coming over and staying until sixth?

Jim: Well, I kind of like Mr. Jones's class. Besides, it's too hard to get to Green Lake and back in an hour and forty minutes. I could come after school.

Tom: You know Lydia is going to be there.

Jim: (noticeable interest) She is?

Tom: Yeah. And by the time school is over, who knows if the party will still be there. We might go over to someone's house.

Jim's cognitions: Gee, I really want to go to the party. Maybe I can get up the nerve to ask Lydia out. But I should stay for that algebra review, at least. The test will be hard enough without missing the review.

Tom: You know, it is Friday afternoon and a beautiful day.

Jim's cognitions: I wish Tom would let me make my own decision. This isn't easy. Maybe I could study hard during the weekend. Then I don't need to go to the review. But will I really study on Saturday?

Tom: Well, are you going to come?

Jim: I don't know, Tom. I'll have to think about it some more. Maybe I'll see you there fourth. If not, I'll probably come later.

Tom: Okay, I hope you come.

In addition to the specific topic portrayed by each script, each script itself and the leader's comments about it also stressed the concepts of assessing a problem from another's viewpoint, the importance of considering probable consequences or an action, and the advantage of thinking of several alternatives before acting in a challenging situation. Skills in relating to non-peers (parents, teachers, and employers) were also emphasized. In some cases two scripts were written on a topic because pilot work showed that students became bored with repeated role plays of the same situation.

The models in the live and video conditions were students from the school who represented several racial/ethnic groups-- Western European, Mexican-American, Filipino, and Black. Many of the students were recruited from the school drama class, others were recommended through the vocational counselor, and still others were recommended by their peers who had already been recruited. The student models were paid nominal wages for their participation and were excused from their classes to put on the live modeling sessions. The two psychology graduate students who administered the course also served as models in the role plays. They filled roles of teacher, employer, and parent in the modeling presentations. Both were male, one of European descent and one Black.

The experimental program was evaluated using both short- and long-term dependent measures. A Means-Ends Problem Solving (MEPS) type of test was administered at the conclusion of the experiment, as was a specially devised alternatives test. The MEPS-type measure and the alternatives task were employed as indices of cognitive functioning. The MEPS required the subject to think through problems and establish a link between the beginning and end of a story. The means-ends problem solving approach has been studied intensively by Spivack et al. (1976). Research with adolescents (Platt, Scura & Hannon, 1973; Platt, Spivack, Altman, Altman & Peizer, 1974) has shown that those who are behaviorally maladjusted on a number of criteria show some deficiency in means-ends cognitions, as compared with equivalent groups who do not show such maladjustments.

In this study, means-end stories of the same type as MEPS stories were used. The stories were created to deal with situations that were particularly relevant for this population. For each, the initial problem situation and the outcome were described. The task for the subject was to supply the behavioral steps that led to the outcome. The three story-situations were:

1. You noticed that your friends seemed to be avoiding you. But you wanted to have friends and be well liked. The story ends with your friends liking you again. Begin where you first noticed your friends avoiding you.

2. You are having trouble getting along with the foreman on your job. You are very unhappy about this. The story ends with your foreman liking you. Begin the story where you aren't getting along with your foreman.

3. You want to apply for a summer job that pays well. You are worried, though, because several of your friends have already been turned down for the job. The story ends with you getting the job.

The research of Spivack and his co-workers has also emphasized the importance of the generation of alternatives as a problem-solving skill. Competent individuals produce more relevant alternatives than do less competent persons when they are asked to generate solutions to interpersonal problems (Platt & Spivack, 1972; Shure & Spivack, 1972). To the extent that changes in cognitive effectiveness are correlated with behavioral effectiveness, positive results for the cognitive measures would reflect favorably on the modeling-rehearsal intervention.

The alternatives measure consisted of two problem situations. For each situation, the subjects were asked to list all the alternative solutions they could. The problem situations used were as follows:

1. You want to watch a TV special, but your brother is watching his favorite program. What could you do?

2. Your score on your first History test is the lowest in
    the class, and the teacher says it is a failing grade. You
    want to pass the course. What could you do?

The alternatives given were each scored for adaptiveness by
independent raters. Scores were given for the number of alternatives mentioned, the sum of the ratings of all alternatives mentioned, and the value of the highest rated alternative.

    Another, more behavioral measure was the opportunity given to
students to sign up for a job interview several months after the
experimental sessions. The job interview situation seemed especially relevant to the present experiment because the modeling-
rehearsal program emphasized self-presentation in job interviews
as well as dealing with authority figures and co-worders when one
has a job. Two modules were devoted to job interview role plays.
Every effort was made to achieve a real-life quality in publiciz-
ing and conducting the job interviews. There was no evidence that
students saw any connection between the job interviews and the
experimental program. In the interview, subjects' self-
presentational skills, ability to maintain eye contact with the
interviewer, and ability to express interest in the job were
assessed.

    Finally, counts were made of the incidence of tardiness and
behavioral referrals during a one-year period following the experimental program. This variety of dependent measures was used to
gain information about the different ways in which a social skills
program might influence participants.

    The major results of the experiment concerned the relation-
ship between the experimental treatments and cognitive skills, on
the one hand, and overt behavior, on the other. Subjects who participated in the social and cognitive skills course gave better
solutions to the problem situation stories on the MEPS measure.
In addition, they were able to think of more, and often better,
alternatives to problematic situations than were control subjects.
They also handled themselves better in a job interview situation
than did controls. For example, Table 2 presents the results for
an analysis of eye contact as a function of conditions. The live
modeling group showed significantly more eye contact than did the
video modeling or control group. The video modeling group showed
significantly more eye contact than did the control group.

Table 2

Ratings of Subjects' Eye Contact in Interviews[1]

Group	M
Live Modeling	6.33
Video Modeling	4.00
Control	2.00

[1]Rated on scale of 1 (avoids) to 7 (constant).

The interview study occurred a few months after subjects' participation in the experiment. Since the goal of the project was long-term behavior change, data on the students' absences, tardiness, and behavior referrals during the year subsequent to conduct of the experiment were collected. Table 3 presents the means for occurrences of absences, tardiness, and behavioral referrals during the one-year period following the experiment. The three conditions differed significantly for each of these dependent measures.

Table 3

Mean Occurrences of Absences, Tardiness, and Behavior Referrals

Group	Absences	Tardiness	Behavior Referrals
Live Modeling	2.72	.55	.28
Video Modeling	3.61	.87	.30
Control	3.92	1.73	.72

The factor of video as well as live enactments of modeled responses was included in this experiment because of the potential benefits (standardization, efficiency) of videotaped materials. Though some of the results would seem to favor live modeling enactments, the differences between the two experimental groups were usually not striking.

The results of this study are encouraging. Both social and cognitive skills of low-achieving high school students seem amenable to change through the behavioral methods of modeling and role playing. The small number of contact hours necessary to produce a behavioral change that is maintained for at least a year following the intervention suggests that many individuals, even those who do not initially seek out behavior change for themselves, may profit from cognitive modeling programs that deal with topics they see as relevant. The follow-up data also suggests that there may be generalized results of the program in preventing maladaptive behavior. An advantage of the present program is that its format, with its use of videotaped discussion, lends itself to classroom administration by interested teachers who do not have specific psychological background or extensive training in the use of this program.

CONCLUSIONS

It seems clear, not just from observation but from a wide variety of research data, that interpersonal skills are associated with adjustment throughout life. A varied literature in both problem solving and role taking suggests that these skills are associated primarily with such adjustment and are not necessarily highly related to intellectual ability. Many behavior disorders can be analyzed in terms of cognitive and social skills deficits (Kendall & Finch, 1979; Meichenbaum & Asarnow, 1979; Rathjen, Rathjen & Hiniker, 1978). Experimental data also indicate that social skills and certain behavioral characteristics such as impulsiveness are related to adjustment (B. Sarason, 1981).

It would be a mistake to see social and cognitive skills training as a complete cure or preventive for maladaptive behavior, in general or aggression or acting out in particular. Other factors also play roles, for example, the realities the person must confront and the extent to which social supports are available for helping the person to cope with stress. Acting out in delinquent or aggressive ways is often triggered by personally salient problematic situations. Lack of cognitive skills in accurately appraising situations and planning response strategies, together with poor social skills, increases the likelihood of self-defeating, socially undesirable, and aggressive behavior under such circumstances.

Modeling, coaching, role playing, and practice can contribute significantly to the acquisition of valuable social and cognitive skills. Strengthening response competencies increases the individual's sense of self-efficacy and optimism about the possibility of solving the problems of day-to-day living. There is growing reason to believe that widening the range of people's social skills increases their effectiveness in handling difficult situations (Argyle, 1980; Goldstein, 1981). The advantage of training for cognitive skills as well is the enhanced generalizability of the skills acquired. A skills training approach may be particularly helpful in strengthening communication, relationship-building, and assertiveness skills that can be used in effectively meeting the developmental challenges associated with the transition from childhood status to adulthood.

Further research is needed in order to identify the contributions of a variety of factors to the effectiveness of a skills training approach. They include the personal characteristics of both the model and the observer, the medium in which modeled information is presented, the role of incentives in performance, and transfer and generalization effects. The content areas most amenable to skills training also must be specified, e.g., listening and speaking to others; getting information and help; planning, problem-solving and trouble-shooting; asserting oneself; and expressing warmth to others.

It is generally recognized that one of the most effective procedures for helping people overcome some forms of maladaptive behavior, for example phobias, is exposure to the problematic situation (Wilson & O'Leary, 1980). In the case of most phobias, the individual is potentially capable of making the non-phobic response (e.g., touching the snake, boarding an airplane). It seems reasonable to hypothesize that such exposure will be most effective when the person has the competencies needed to overcome problems, frustrations, and challenges. In the kinds of situations many adolescents face, such skills are often lacking. The lack of skills is made more important because the demands of the situations that confront adolescents may be relatively novel to them. This age period is one in which there are both many demands for new behaviors and many expectations about new possibilities in the areas of social, school, and work-related behaviors. Because of these personal and environmental changes during adolescence, skills training, especially interpersonal skills training, may be particularly helpful. A skills training approach may be valuable either by itself or in conjunction with other techniques in forestalling inappropriate or aggressive behavior by providing practice in effective alternative ways of dealing with challenge.

FOOTNOTE

1. The research reported in this chapter was supported in part by the National Institute of Mental Health, Grant No. MN 24823, and the Office of Naval Research, Contract No. N00014-80-C-0522, NR 170-908.

REFERENCES

Argyle, M. Interaction skills and social competence. In P. Feldman & J. Orford (Eds.), The social psychology of psychological problems. Chichester, England: John Wiley, 1980.

Douglas, V.I., Parry, P., Marton, P. & Garson, C. Assessment of a cognitive training program for hyperactive chilren. Journal of Abnormal Child Psychology, 1976, 4, 389-410.

Freedman, B.J., Donahoe, C.P., Jr., Rosenthal, L., Schlundt, D.G. & McFall, R.M. A social-behavioral analysis of skill deficits in delinquent and nondelinquent adolescent boys. Journal of Consulting and Clinical Psychology, 1978, 46, 1448-1462.

Goldsmith, J.B. & McFall, R.M. Development and evaluation of an interpersonal skill-training program for psychiatric inpatients. Journal of Abnormal Psychology, 1975, 84, 51-58.

Goldstein, A.P. Social skill training. In A.P. Goldstein, E.G. Carr, W.S. Davidson II & P. Wehr (Eds.), In response to aggression. New York: Pergamon Press, 1981.

Goldstein, A.P., Sprafkin, R.P., Gershaw, N.J. & Klein, P. The adolescent: Social skills training through structured learning. In G. Cargledge & J.F. Milburn (Eds.), Teaching social skills to children: Innovative approaches. New York: Pergamon Press, 1980.

Hersen, M. & Bellack, A.S. Social skills training for chronic psychiatric patients: Rationale, research findings, and future directions. Comprehensive Psychiatry, 1976, 17, 559-580.

Kendall, P.C. & Finch, A.J., Jr. Developing non-impulsive behavior in children: Cognitive-behavioral strategies for self-control. In P.C. Kendall & S.D. Hollon (Eds.), Cognitive-behavioral interventions: Theory, research, and procedures. New York: Academic Press, 1979.

Kendall, P.C. & Hollon, S.D. (Eds.). Cognitive-behavioral interventions: Theory, research, and procedures. New York: Academic Press, 1979.

Kendall, P.C. & Wilcox, L.E. Cognitive-behavioral treatment for impulsivity: Concrete versus conceptual training in non-self-controlled problem children. Journal of Consulting and Clinical Psychology, 1980, 48, 80-91.

Matson, J.L. & Martin, J.E. A social learning approach to vocational training of the severely retarted. Journal of Mental Deficiency Research, 1979, 23, 9-16.

Meichenbaum, D. Cognitive-behavior modification: An integrative approach. New York: Plenum Press, 1977.

Meichenbaum, D. & Asarnow, J. Cognitive-behavior modification and metacognitive development: Implications for the classroom. In P.C. Kendall & S.D. Hollon (Eds.), Cognitive behavioral interventions: Theory, research, and procedures. New York: Academic Press, 1979.

Ollendick, T.H. & Hersen, M. Social skills training for juvenile delinquents. Behavior Research and Therapy, 1979, 17, 547-554.

Platt, J.J., Scura, W.C. & Hannon, J.R. Problem-solving thinking of youthful incarcerated heroin addicts. Journal of Community Psychology, 1973, 1, 278-281.

Platt, J.J. & Spivack, G. Problem-solving thinking of psychiatric patients. Journal of Consulting and Clinical Psychology, 1972, 39, 148-151.

Platt, J.J., Spivack, G., Altman, N., Altman, D. & Peizer, S.B. Adolescent problem-solving thinking. Journal of Consulting and Clinical Psychology, 1974, 42, 787-793.

Prentice, N.M. The influence of live and symbolic modeling on promoting moral judgment of adolescent delinquents. Journal of Abnormal Psychology, 1972, 80, 157-161.

Rathjen, D.P., Rathjen, E.D. & Hiniker, A. A cognitive analysis of social performance: Implications for assessment and treatment. In J.P. Foreyt & D.P. Rathjen (Eds.), Cognitive behavior therapy: Research and application. New York: Plenum Press, 1978.

Sarason, B.R. Improving the social competence of the low achieving high school student. In J.D. Wine & M.D. Smye (Eds.), Social competence. New York: Guilford Press, 1981.

Sarason, I.G. Verbal learning, modeling, and juvenile delinquency. American Psychologist, 1968, 23, 254-266.

Sarason, I.G. A cognitive social learning approach to juvenile delinquency. In R. Hare & D. Schalling (Eds.), Psychopathic behavior: Approaches to research. London: John Wiley, 1978.

Sarason, I.G. & Ganzer, V.J. Modeling and group discussion in the rehabilitation of juvenile delinquents. Journal of counseling psychology, 1973, 20, 442-449.

Sarason, I.G., Johnson, J.H., Berberich, J.P. & Siegel, J.M. Helping police officers to cope with stress: A cognitive-behavioral approach. American Journal of Community Psychology, 1979, 7, 593-603.

Sarason, I.G. & Sarason, B.R. Teaching cognitive and social skills to high school students. Journal of Consulting and Clinical Psychology, 1981, 49, 908-918.

Shure, M.B. & Spivack, G. Means-ends thinking, adjustment, and social class among elementary school-aged children. Journal of Consulting and Clinical Psychology, 1972, 38, 348-353.

Snyder, J.L. & White, M.J. The use of cognitive self-instruction in the treatment of behaviorally disturbed adolescents. Behavior Therapy, 1979, 10, 227-235.

Spivack, G., Platt, J.J. & Shure, M.B. The problem solving approach to adjustment. San Francisco: Jossey-Bass, 1976.

Wilson, G.T. & O'Leary, K.D. Principles of behavior therapy. Englewood Cliffs, NJ: Prentice Hall, 1980.

EMPATHY, EMPATHY TRAINING AND THE REGULATION OF AGGRESSION IN ELEMENTARY SCHOOL CHILDREN

Norma Deitch Feshbach

University of California, Los Angeles

INTRODUCTION

The rationale to develop a psychoeducational program to train aggressive children in empathic skills for the purpose of regulating aggressive behavior and promoting positive social behavior grew out of a long-standing research interest and program concerned with the structure and functions of empathy (N. Feshbach & Roe, 1968; N. Feshbach, 1975, 1978, 1982). The Empathy Training Program, the main focus of this presentation, was designed in conjunction with a series of field studies carried out in a number of elementary schools in Los Angeles (Feshbach & Feshbach, 1977; N. Feshbach, 1980).

Manifestations of aggressive behavior in the context of the classroom, including minor infractions as well as more severe forms of violence, are a major burden for all members of the classroom (Halatyn, 1981; U.S. Department of Health, Education and Welfare, 1978). It distracts the teacher from the major task of education and increases the already considerable job stress associated with teaching (N. Feshbach & Campbell, 1978). Aggression, violence, and delinquency also make teachers afraid. And while fear of aggression in schools is disproportionately greater than the number of reported incidents, the fear itself is personally and professionally disabling (U.S. Department of Health, Education and Welfare, 1978).

Classroom disruptions associated with aggressive incidents pose problems for all the students, including those not directly involved in the aggressive altercations. At the very least the teacher is distracted from meeting the major educational objectives of the lesson at hand and also must spend a disproportionate amount of time on the precipitating event. Moreover, the climate

192

Kaplan, R.M., Konečni, V.J., Novaco, R.W. (eds.) Aggression in Children and Youth
© 1984, Martinus Nijhoff Publishers, The Hague/Boston/Lancaster
ISBN 90-247-2903-3. Printed in The Netherlands

of a classroom characterized by frequent aggressive incidents, incidents that inevitably evoke retaliation, tension, and discipline, is not an ideal atmosphere for learning (S. Feshbach, Adelman & Fuller, 1977).

The misbehaving aggressive child who is hitting, kicking or verbally assaulting peers or teachers fares the worst. Aggressive behaviors in classrooms, as elsewhere, are usually maladaptive and dysfunctional. Aversive aggressive actions by a pupil inevitably stimulate a counter-reaction chain of punishment, rejection, and alienation to that pupil, reactions that exaggerate the very conditions of anger, frustration, and depression that initially stimulated the aggressive behavior. The aggressive child is a child in trouble, a child encumbered by psychological problems, and yet not equipped with well-developed cognitive, problem-solving, and social skills to effectively cope with these problems (Bandura, 1973; Rathjen & Foreyt, 1980; Spivak, Platt & Shure, 1976).

In earlier papers we have posited that aggressive, acting-out children may either have limited empathic skills or alternatively may have empathic skills which they do not use in a wide range of situations. Data supporting this assumption have been found by a number of investigators. In an early study carried out by Seymour Feshbach and myself, we found that six- and seven-year-old boys low in empathy manifested more aggression, as compared to children with higher empathy scores (Feshbach & Feshbach, 1969). Since that time a number of investigators have replicated the findings relating high aggression to low empathy (Huckabay, 1972; Mehrabian & Epstein, 1972). Other studies have reflected relationships between aspects of empathy, such as role and perspective taking and aggressive, acting-out, disruptive behavior (Burka & Glenwick, 1975; Kurdek, 1978). Also, an early training study of perspective-taking skills resulted in an initial significant increase in perspective taking and a subsequent decrease in delinquency (Chandler, 1973). As with the initial Feshbach & Feshbach study the relationship between empathic skills and aggressiveness is not universally obtained across all ages and for each sex (Shantz, in press). However, the overall consistent findings relating empathy and aggression suggest that empathy may play a particularly significant role in the control of aggression.

EMPATHY AND THE CONTROL OF AGGRESSION

An inquiry into the role that empathy training might play in the regulation of aggression requires an examination of the properties and functions of the empathy construct. There are a number of different views of the meaning and functions of empathy, with corresponding differences in its assessment. The approach that has guided our laboratory research in this area as well as our joint field research efforts on empathy training is derived from a three-component model of empathy (N. Feshbach, 1975, 1978; N. Feshbach & Roe, 1968; Feshbach & Feshbach, 1972). The

193

affective empathic experience in an observer perceiving another person's emotional reaction is conceptualized as a shared emotional response that represents the resultant outcome of three interactive elements. The first is the capacity to discriminate an emotional state in another. For a child or adult to react empathetically to another individual's sadness or joy or anger, the child or adult must be able to identify the relevant affective cues that discriminate these emotional states from each other and from a neutral affective state. But empathy requires more than the ability to identify feelings. It also entails a more sophisticated cognitive skill--the ability to assume the perspective and role of another person. It is as though the observer can view the situation determining the emotion in a similar way as the individual who is actually experiencing the event. It is possible for an observer to share another's perspective and to identify accurately that person's feelings without experiencing an empathic response. What may be lacking is the ability to respond affectively, an ability posited to be the third required component of empathy. This component may be lacking in individuals who are highly repressed and constricted.

This three-component model does not purport to be a complete description of the very complex social-emotional dimension of empathy. It is clear from the data yielded by studies carried out by ourselves and others that the nature of the affect involved-- whether joyous or dysphoric--has a bearing upon the functional implications or an empathic response (N. Feshbach, 1980, 1982). Also, other factors such as the level of cognitive competence and degree of affective reaction of an individual may contribute to qualitative differences in the meaning and significance of an empathic response. Thus, it requires greater cognitive sophistication and emotional sensitivity and responsiveness to respond empathically to the masked distress of someone in a subtle conflict situation than it does to respond with equal empathy to the perception of an individual in obvious pain. There are additional factors that affect the significance and meaning of an empathetic reaction such as similarity and familiarity (N. Feshbach, 1978). However, the three-component model provides a structure that can incorporate these factors and offers an initial basis for determining the theoretical relationship between empathy and other social behaviors such as aggression.

How can empathy influence emotional aggression or anger, instrumental aggression, aggressive drive? With regard to emotional aggression, empathy would be expected to affect the antecedents of anger such as feelings of frustration, rejection and unfairness. The empathic person, by virtue of understanding the other point of view, is less likely to become angered through misinterpreting the other person's behavior as arbitrary or unfair. On the other hand, one would not expect empathy to affect the intensity with which anger is experienced. In fact, empathic children, because of their emotional responsiveness, may experience greater anger than children low in empathy. Elsewhere is reported evidence that a subgroup of empathic boys displayed behaviors indicative of emotional lability (N. Feshbach, 1980, 1982). However, in general, the overall data suggest that when there are adequate emotional controls, empathic children manifest less anger in social interactions.

The role that empathy plays in the regulation of instrumental and hostile aggression is less subtle than was the case for emotional aggression. There are both empirical and theoretical reasons to expect empathy to modulate children's aggression. There is a research literature that indicates that empathy facilitates behaviors that are incompatible with aggression. In a number of investigations of prosocial behaviors such as altruism, sharing and generosity, empathy is postulated to be a key mediating mechanism (Hoffman, 1978; Staub, 1971). At a theoretical level empathy should be an inhibitor of aggression. Aggressive behavior causes pain and distress. The observation of these pain and distress cues should elicit distress responses in an empathic child even if that child is the initiator of the aggressive act. Thus, the vicarious affective response of empathy can function as an inhibitor of an individual's aggressive inclinations, thereby contributing to an inverse relationship between empathy and aggression.

These considerations regarding the relationship between empathy and aggression provided the theoretical rationale for the development of the Empathy Training Project. The project reflected an integration of two long-standing research interests-- one, in the theoretical properties of the development of empathy and its measurement, and the other in the dynamics and regulation of aggression (S. Feshbach, 1970). The project also reflects a shared concern with the social problems posed by aggression and violence in our homes, schools, and in society at large (Feshbach & Feshbach, 1976; Feshbach and Fraczek, 1979). As indicated earlier of the basic assumptions of the Empathy Training Project, supported by some empirical data, was that aggressive, acting-out children have limited empathic skills. It was further assumed that the components of empathy could be trained through prescribed intervention procedures that were derived from the conceptual model of empathy that has been described here.

THE EMPATHY TRAINING PROGRAM

The Empathy Training Program was part of a broader training program co-directed by Seymour Feshbach and myself in which training procedures and curricula were developed for use with children in the middle elementary grades. The major purpose of the training procedures and the project was to foster personal growth in children while enhancing the development of positive social behaviors. We had three specific objectives for our training project: Firstly, to develop empathy and training procedures to be used with preadolescents in a variety of settings, especially public schools, for the purpose of reducing aggression and antisocial behaviors and fostering prosocial values and behaviors; secondly, to further our theoretical understanding of the psychological properties of empathy, particularly in regard to its role in the regulation of aggressive behaviors and the mediation of positive, prosocial values and actions; thirdly, to develop specific curricula to be used in schools and other settings to implement affective educational goals related to the regulation of aggression and other social actions (Feshbach & Feshbach, 1977).

A major theoretical and social question is how to reduce, modify, or regulate aggressive and violent behaviors in children--whether they occur in the home, school, or community--without incurring adverse side effects in the process. In view of our general orientation toward the use of positive socialization practices in child training, including the regulation of aggression, it is not surprising that we selected empathy as a major intervention strategy (Feshbach & Feshbach, 1978).

FUNCTIONS OF EMPATHY

While the basis for the construction of the curriculum and training strategies derives from the question of what empathy is, the question of what empathy does provides the rationale, theory, and empirical basis for the project itself. The question of what empathy does raises a different set of issues and changes the focus from the components of empathy to the functions of empathy. An analysis of the functions of empathy, especially in children, suggests a broad network of possible mediating effects which might include increased self-awareness, social understanding, greater emotional competence, heightened compassion, caring and related behaviors, enhanced communication skills, and greater cohesion between the cognitive, affective and interpersonal aspects of the child's behaviors--this later function being the main focus of this paper and the current field project. While the literature relative to each of the possible developmental effects of empathy has not been extensive and the findings in some cases are ambiguous, the research, in general, indicates that empathy is likely to have a positive effect on the child's personal and social adjustment (N. Feshbach, 1975, 1976; Shantz, in press).

Although the goal of our study was to modify and possibly eliminate aggressive behavior, our plan to accomplish this did not focus on aggression per se, but on the enhancement of a child's empathic skills. In the initial phase of the project which lasted almost a year, we developed sets of training procedures and measures. During the second phase we carried out a pilot experiment. The pilot study was actually a fully designed study. It was designated as a pilot because we carried it out in one school, and because we had decided a priori to use the obtained data as a basis for refining the training procedures. And, indeed, on the basis of the findings, which incidentally were significant and consistent with the experimental hypotheses, changes were made in the experimental procedures. The third phase of the project, the study proper, was carried out in two schools in the Los Angeles area.

196

TRAINING EXERCISES

One of the first major tasks was the conceptual articulation and production of the curriculum for the empathy training programs and for a problem solving control training program. Two sets of materials, each set consisting of 30 hours of exercises and activities, were devised. These exercises were designed for elementary school children in grades three to five, for use in small groups of four to six children. Each activity lasts from 20 to 50 minutes. Efforts were made to include a variety of tasks and to have the materials presented in an interesting and engaging manner. Activities included problem-solving games, story telling, listening to and making tape recordings, simple written exercises, group discussion, and more active tasks such as acting out words, phrases, and stories. Several exercises involve videotaping children's enactments and replaying them for discussion.

For the Empathy Training Condition, activities were derived from the three-component model of empathy described above (Feshbach, Feshbach, Fauvre & Ballard-Campbell, in press). The model states that a truly empathic response to another human being requires identifying the other's emotional state (affect identification), understanding the situation in which the other person is involved from that person's point of view (perspective taking), and experiencing in oneself the emotions felt by the other person (emotional responsiveness). To increase skill in affect identification, children were asked to identify the emotions conveyed in photographs of facial expressions, tape recordings of affect-laden conversations, and videotaped pantomimes of emotional situations. In addition, the children themselves role played in a wide range of games and situations in which they acted out and guessed feelings. To foster children's ability to assume the perspective of another person, training exercises include a variety of games and activities that become progressively more difficult as training proceeds. Early in the training program, the children were asked to experience and imagine various visual perspectives ("What would the world look like to you if you were as tall as Wilt Chamberlain--or as small as a cat?"). They were asked to imagine the preferences and behavior of different kinds of people ("What birthday present would make each member of your family happiest?" "What would your teacher (your older brother, your best friend, a policeman) do if he found a lost child in a department store?"). Children listened to stories, then recounted them from the point of view of each character in the story. Numerous later sessions were devoted to role playing. In these role-playing sessions children were given the opportunity to play a part in a scene, then to switch roles and play the parts of other characters, thus experiencing several perspectives on the same interaction. For other activities children viewed videotapes of their enactments to enable them to gain an outside perspective of themselves and the situations enacted. Discussions followed role-playing sessions and included identification of the feelings experienced by the characters enacted.

197

While exercises designed for empathy training can be characterized as having a general focus on the experience and expression of emotions, exercises designed for the problem solving control training focused on the improvement of students' problem-solving skills in nonsocial settings. A large portion of these exercises focused on discovery learning through science experiments involving interesting chemical reactions and work with solutions of different density and solubility. A number of the exercises are games of logic, using attribute blocks and other commercial games. Spatial relations and physical perspective-taking skills are developed through graphing activities and mapping projects. Wherever possible, these control exercises are very similar to the experimental group exercises in format, with only the content varying. For instance, if the empathy training groups played the game "Concentration" and matched facial expressions (happy to happy, angry to angry, etc.) of the various individuals portrayed on the game cards, the control group played "Concentration" but matched shapes printed on the same cards.

All of our experimental and control exercises have an objective both in terms of the specific component of empathy addressed as well as the specific skill intended to be engendered in the child. The procedure for each exercise is spelled out so that a group leader, teacher, graduate student, or any designated trainer could carry it out by following the instructions. The exercises were revised many times, the most significant modifications introduced as a result of the pilot study. The modifications were made on the basis of information provided by all the participants: group leaders, observers, research staff, and the children. As a result of this evaluation, efforts were made to make the activities more effective and more involving by eliminating and by changing the exercises and their sequence.

MEASURES

The project entailed a series of different measures. One set was designed to assess the dynamics of the training process itself and involved the continuous monitoring of each child at each training session on a variety of aggressive, prosocial, and attentional scales by highly trained but naive observers. Another set of measures was included to assess the effects or outcome of the training program on the children's level of aggression, prosocial behavior, and achievement skills. A third set of measures was developed in connection with this project to provide information on the effects of the training on the mediating processes of empathy and social understanding. This latter set of measures includes an Affective Matching Test, an Emotional Responsiveness Measure, an Audio-Video Empathy Measure, and a Role Taking Measure. Each of these four new measures corresponds to the conceptual model of Empathic Behavior that has guided the study and the curriculum.

In order to provide appropriate affective stimuli for the

measures, stimuli that would be age-, sex-, and ethnic-group-appropriate, we conducted a study to determine situations that have emotional impact for children. A survey of situations having emotional impact for children from five to eleven years of age was undertaken. A total of 240 children including boys and girls from kindergarten, second, third, fourth, and sixth grades, from five schools, were interviewed over a period of several months. The children were questioned about situations which respectively aroused each of the following eight emotions: sadness, anger, fear, happiness, pride, embarrassment, surprise, disgust. Responses that were normative across sex and ethnicity and the ages we were working with were then used in developing the Empathy Measures (N. Feshbach & Hoffman, 1978; Hoffman & N. Feshbach, 1979; Feshbach, Feshbach, Cohen & Hoffman, in press).

For both the pilot and study proper the measures administered before and after the ten-week experimental period included: teacher ratings of aggressive and prosocial behaviors (Adelman & Feshbach, 1973), student self-ratings of aggression and prosocial behaviors (Adelman & Feshbach, 1973), spatial perspective taking (Phinney, 1977) (this measure yields an "Other Perspective"--correct response--and "Ego Perspective" score), WISC Vocabulary and Comprehension (Wechsler, 1974), Wide Range Ready Achievement (WRAT) (Jastak, Jastak & Bijou, 1965), three TAT-type cards, a role-taking measure (Walker, 1977), and a Use of Social Information measure (Cutrona & S. Feshbach, 1979). In adition, the children in both studies were rated by their teachers for two days each week during the course of the ten-week period. Also, behavior observations were obtained for each child in the training groups during each training session.

THE PILOT EXPERIMENT

The pilot experiment was conducted at an elementary school consisting of Black, Chicano, and Anglo children in third, fourth, and fifth grades, of which 30 were girls and 30 were boys. The children were selected for participation in the study on the basis of teacher ratings of their aggressive behavior. Two-thirds of the sample selected were from the group identified as High Aggressives, while the rest were from the Medium and Low groups. Each group in the study had six children and was composed of four High Aggressive children, was mixed racially, and included three boys and three girls.

In addition to these participating subjects, there was an additional sample of 24 nonparticipating controls who were pre- and post-tested but did not take part in any other activities. Subjects were assigned at random to experimental and control conditions, with the constraints regarding level of aggression, sex, and ethnicity noted above. Each experimental and control group met with a trained "Instructor" or group leader for an hour at a time, three times a week, for a ten-week period. The project had been assigned a regular classroom in the school, which was used for the duration of the study. To control for Instructor effects, every group met with three different Instructors, and each Instructor worked with three or four different groups.

Perhaps the most striking and encouraging finding of the pilot data was the pattern of change scores for the teacher's ratings of aggression (N. Feshbach, 1979). The greatest decrement in aggression was manifested by the Affective-Cognitive group while the least difference was manifested by the Non-Participating Controls, this difference being statistically significant. When an individual analysis was carried out on those subjects who displayed the most positive changes in behavior after empathy training, we found that half of the subjects in the experimental groups showed considerable change on both the aggressive prosocial measures, while only one subject in the control groups showed a marked improvement on both of these dependent measures. A finding that lent support to our notions linking cognition and affect was the impressive performance changes on the cognitive tasks among subjects who showed the greatest improvement in aggressive and prosocial behavior. Of the eight experimental subjects who showed the greatest positive behavior change, six improved dramatically on spatial perspective taking, particularly in their lowered tendency to make egocentric responses. Four subjects showed marked improvement in their ability to assume the social role of another person. Perhaps more surprising, two subjects showed improvement on the WISC-R Vocabulary subtest of more than two standard deviations.

THE EMPATHY TRAINING STUDY

The participants in the empathy training study proper were 98 third and fourth graders. These children attended two middle-class elementary schools in the Los Angeles City Unified School District. A third of our sample (and the school itself) was made up of minority children. After the pilot study a number of measures, including a teacher rating of social behavior in the classroom (the Social Interaction Inventory) and a modified peer evaluation of interpersonal functioning (the Class Play) (Walker, 1977). The sample of children selected received the battery of tests that was used in the pilot study, as well as modifications of the Sear's Self Concept measure and the Rothenberg measure of social sensitivity (Rothenberg, 1970), and the new tasks created to assess the components of empathy.

Following the pretest period, the children were randomly assigned to six-member treatment groups, four children in each group having scores above the mean of both criterion measures of aggression and two children having scores below the mean. Four of the members were boys and the other two were girls. Apart from these restrictions, random assignment to the groups was carried out. Of the twelve groups, eight received training in empathy skills and four received control exercises designed to enhance problem-solving skills. The remaining 24 children in the sample were the nonparticipating controls.

The children who had been assigned to groups met for 45-minutes thrice weekly. The training phase lasted for approximately 10 weeks and was followed by a period of post-testing.

The results of the study proper, while not spectacular, reflected systematic and statistically significant positive changes in children who participated in the empathy training activities. Following the empathy training experience, children reflected a more positive self-concept and displayed greater social sensitivity to feelings than children in the two control conditions. As in the pilot experiment, the children in the empathy training groups declined in aggression relative to the nonparticipating controls, but the problem solving control activity groups also displayed a decline in aggressive behaviors. Apparently, taking these children out of the classroom and providing them with positive small group experiences facilitated a reduction in aggression, whether or not the training experience focused on empathy or on interesting academic content.

However, empathy training proved to be critical in regard to positive shifts in prosocial behaviors. Children in the empathy training condition significantly differed from both control conditions in the increase of incidents of such prosocial behaviors as cooperation, helping, and generosity. In the case of prosocial behaviors, merely taking the children out of the classroom was not sufficient. These behaviors were facilitated by specific training in affect identification and understanding, role playing, and emotional expressiveness.

In general, both the pilot and major field studies have yielded findings consonant with the theoretical expectations that led to the implementation of the empathy training program. The results indicate that empathy training helps bring about more positive social behaviors and a more positive self-evaluation in aggressive and in nonaggressive children.

IMPLICATIONS

What inferences are we to draw from these findings? What policy implications do they have? How do they relate to the increasingly pervasive climate of violence to which reference was made at the beginning of this presentation? The response to these questions is not a simple one. It entails a deeper consideration of the properties of empathy and of the social context in which empathy training and related intervention programs are implemented.

The philosophy behind the idea of training empathy was based on a nonjudgmental premise. We did not attempt to encourage or reinforce a particular social behavior such as cooperation, generosity or the inhibition of aggression. The training effort was directed toward the development and enhancement of particular affective and cognitive skills. The empathy training program is not devoid of a value statement, since one major goal is the regulation and reduction of aggression. However, the training content does not focus on discouraging aggressive behaviors, nor does it attempt to reward manifestations of empathy. What are valued, trained and reinforced, are the child's ability to perceive situations from the perspective of other people, to discriminate and identify feelings, and to express feelings that he or she may be experiencing. Through the training of these skills, the child's range of alternative behaviors should be expanded, and possibilities other than aggressive and egocentric reactions should become available in the child's behavioral repertoire.

Other skill-oriented training programs share this non-judgmental character. The Spivak and Shure (1974) means-end program is designed to get children to think in terms of alternative solutions to problem situations, and the possible consequences to which different actions might lead. The training entails reinforcing young children for thinking of different ideas in response to the posing of a particular problem question--for example, how to get to play with a toy another child has. The children are rewarded for the variety of solutions they verbalize, not for offering any particular solution, even if it be the socially desirable one. A very different kind of approach, but one that has similar non-judgmental features, is represented by Aronson's jigsaw technique (Aronson, Blaney, Stephan, Silva & Snopp, 1978). The goal of this technique is to foster cooperative behaviors. The procedure involves dividing the classroom into small groups with about five to six members. The lesson material to be learned is then divided into as many parts as there are group members. Each group member is responsible for teaching his or her part to the other members of the groups. The group members are thus dependent upon each other for mastery of the material, and only through cooperation with each other can effective learning of all the material take place.

The jigsaw techniques and the means-end problem solving technique, like empathy training, have been evaluated in experimentally controlled field studies and have been shown to enhance prosocial behaviors. In addition, all of these procedures can be readily incorporated into the regular classroom. One of our objectives in formulating the empathy training program was to develop training exercises that could be used in the standard elementary classroom. While the experimental evaluation that I described was based on a training program conducted with small groups, many of the exercises have already been implemented in a large classroom setting. In particular, there are naturally occurring events in the classroom--the arrival of a new child, reactions to a physically handicapped youngster, a conflict between two children--that provide special opportunities for the introduction of a pertinent empathy training exercise. The direct relevance of the exercise to the problem situation addressed by the class can only serve to enhance its effectiveness.

The development of empathy training exercises for use in regular classrooms was an especially important feature of the project. For a program to have a potential social impact, it must be economically feasible and structurally flexible to allow its implementation on a large scale. We believe that the empathy training program has these attributes as do the means-end, jigsaw and related training programs. It seems to us that the public schools, which function as major socializing and change agents, are the appropriate context for the implementation of these programs. An important feature of these intervention programs is their positive effect on cognitive skills as well as social behaviors.

The usefulness of psychoeducational programs that foster empathy, cooperation, and social problem solving does not mean that they will be inevitably adopted by elementary schools. There is a wide gap between availability and social utilization. To bridge this gap, we have to assume the role of community psychologists and function as change agents. Key gatekeepers in the educational structure must be contacted; the cooperation of community forces must be engaged; and a network of individuals and groups concerned with bringing about curriculum changes directed toward the enhancement of social understanding and empathy must be established.

At the same time, we recognize that affective and socially oriented curricula cannot, by themselves, bring about significant changes in societal aggression. As Seymour Sarason (1972) has reminded us, one cannot anticipate changes in a major social problem through isolated intervention programs. The phenomena of crime and violence, like other expressions of social pathology associated with poverty, discrimination, isolation, and powerlessness are supported by a matrix of forces operating in the larger community. These forces can overwhelm any modest change accomplishment by an empathy training program in elementary schools.

However, it does not follow from the modest role that school curriculum changes can play in the reduction of aggression and violence that we should dispense with efforts to introduce such changes. We cannot use the behavioral assessment of the effects of these training programs as the only criterion by which we evaluate their utility. Empathy curricula, directed toward children, also can raise a community's consciousness of the meaning and significance of empathic feelings and understanding. Education would profit if teachers and school administrators developed stronger and more consistent empathic attitudes. Similarly, many parents, in their relationships with each other, with their own children, and with other children, can profit from greater awareness of an empathic orientation. Adults who engage in child abuse display a clear lack of empathy, and individuals who engage in spouse abuse are equally lacking in their ability to relate empathically. We think it a reasonable hypothesis that the violence that these and other individuals display, no less than the aggression of children, would be modified by the development of stronger empathic attitudes.

We do not view empathy as a panacea for the aggression and violence in our midst, nor do we believe that empathic attitudes are easily developed, sustained and generalized. What we are proposing is that efforts to foster empathy in children can contribute to greater consciousness on the part of members of the society at large of the potential role that empathy can play in the regulation of aggression and the development of positive forms of social interaction. We have provided a partial answer to the question that stimulated this paper--namely, the relevance of empathy training for children to the problem of crime and violence that has beset American society. We concur with the view espoused by various behavioral scientists and social commentators, that empathy is a key ingredient in the development and sustenance of positive social relationships. And we see empathy training as one of a number of approaches that should be taken to foster and enhance empathic attitudes and interactions. It is almost a social psychological truism, reinforced by the experience of psychotherapists, that the greater our understanding of a fellow human being, the more we can enter into another's frame of reference and share his experiences and feelings, the less likely we are to feel hostile to and condemn that person. We may still condemn antisocial, destructive actions on the part of that individual, but through the empathic process, we are able to understand and identify with his humanity.

There is an interesting and important relationship between empathy and attachment--the experience of a positive bond between ourself and another person. Although there is little research data bearing on this relationship, experience suggests that the stronger one's attachment to a person, the easier it is to empathize with that individual. Empathy, in turn, through the shared emotional experience it entails, should help sustain and contribute to the social bond or attachment to that other person. In addition, the perception by that individual of your empathic response increases his attachment to you. Thus, there appears to be a reciprocal and mutually sustaining interaction between empathy and attachment.

This reciprocal interaction process suggests that a classroom program designed to enhance children's empathy should contribute to positive attachments among the children, and between the children and teacher. There is an obvious incompatibility between attachments and aggressive interactions. Intense positive relationships can become the occasion for anger and even hatred when the other partner threatens that relationship. However, in general, one is less likely to aggress against someone whom one likes than against a person whom one dislikes.

The fostering of empathy would seem to be such a natural step to take in any long-term approach to the problem of interpersonal violence that one may wonder why this apparent partial solution is not readily and widely adopted. The fact of the matter is that there is much about empathy that we do not yet understand. Research in this area is relatively recent, and we do not have a substantial body of knowledge regarding the development of empathy and its dynamics. We know that similarity between observer and a stimulus person facilitates empathy, but much more precise data are required regardiang the particular dimensions of similarity that are relevant to an empathic response (N. Feshbach, 1978). We also need to know a great deal more about the factors that block empathy and interfere with the understanding and sharing of another's perspective and experience.

Still, we must begin somewhere. It appears to us that the training of empathy in children offers a useful approach, both from a scientific and societal standpoint. As we implement and evaluate empathy training programs, knowledge will be acquired regarding the variables relevant to the development and its manifestation in social situations. With regard to social utility, we have already alluded to the positive changes in social cognition and social interaction that are brought about by the training of empathy in children. Given the evidence of significant continuity between the level of aggression displayed in the elementary-school-age years and the level of aggression manifested during adolescence, the implementation of programs designed to reinforce and stabilize the effects of empathy training would appear to be a productive avenue to pursue.

We are currently undergoing a period in which the behavioral sciences are under severe attack. Resources that will help us cope with the mental health, developmental and socioeconomic antecedents of crime and violence are being diminished rather than being increased. In this atmosphere, it will be difficult to find funding to help implement alternatives to an escalation of punishment as the primary method for controlling violence. However, we believe this situation will be quite temporary. The persistence and severity of the social problems that confront this society make it imperative that various long-term and short-term approaches to the regulation and reduction of violence are explored, refined, and implemented. And while empathy training has definite limitations in regard to its impact on aggression, we have hardly begun to explore its potential.

REFERENCES

Adelman, H. & Feshbach, S. Early identification of educational and mental health problems. Presented at American Psychological Association, Montreal, August, 1973.
Aronson, E., Blaney, N., Stephan, C., Silva, J. & Snopp, M. The jigsaw classroom. Beverly Hills, CA: Sage Publications, 1978.
Bandura, A. Aggression: A social learning analysis. Englewood Cliffs, NJ: Prentice Hall, 1973.
Burka, A.A. & Glenwick, D.S. Egocentrism and classroom

adjustment. Paper presented at the Jean Piaget Society Meeting, Philadelphia, 1975.

Chandler, M.J. Egocentrism and antisocial behavior: The assessment and training of social perspective-taking skills. Developmental Psychology, 1973, 9, 326-332.

Cutrona, C. & Feshbach, S. Cognitive and behavioral correlates of children's differential use of social information. Child Development, 1979, 50, 1036-1042.

Feshbach, N. Empathy in children: Some theoretical and empirical considerations. The Counseling Psychologist, 1975, 5 (2), 25-30.

Feshbach, N. Empathy and the Regulation of Aggression in Children, Abstract Guide. XXI International Congress of Psychology, July 1976, p. 55.

Feshbach, N. Studies of empathic behavior in children. In B.A. Maher (Ed.), Progress in experimental personality research, Vol. 8. New York: Academic Press, 1978.

Feshbach, N. Empathy training: A field study in affective education. In S. Feshbach and A. Fraczek (Eds.), Aggression and behavior change: Biological and social processes. New York: Praeger, 1979, pp. 235-249.

Feshbach, N. The psychology of empathy and empathy of psychology. Presidential Address, presented at the 60th Annual Meeting of the Western Psychological Association, Honolulu, May 5-9, 1980.

Feshbach, N. Sex differences in empathy and social behavior in children. In N. Eisenberg-Berg (Ed.), The development of prosocial behavior. New York: Academic Press, Ind., 1982.

Feshbach, N. & Campbell, M. Teacher stress and disciplinary practices in schools: A preliminary report. Paper presented at the American Orthopsychiatric Association Meetings, San Francisco, March 27-31, 1978. ERIC #162-228.

Feshbach, N. & Feshbach, S. The relationship between empathy and aggression in two age groups. Developmental Psychology, 1969, 1, 102-107.

Feshbach, N. & Feshbach, S. Cognitive processes in the self-regulation of children's aggression. Invited paper presented at the Conference on Developmental Aspects of Self-Regulation, La Jolla, CA, February 1972.

Feshbach, N., Feshbach, S., Fauvre, M. & Campbell, M. Affective communication skills. Santa Monica, CA: Scott, Foresman and Company, in press.

Feshbach, N. & Hoffman, M. Sex differences in children's reports of emotion-arousing situations. Paper presented in Diane McGuiness (Chair), Sex differences: Commotion, motion or emotion: Psychological gender differences. Symposium presented at Western Psychological Association Meetings, San Francisco, April 19-22, 1978.

Feshbach, N. & Roe, K. Empathy in six and seven year olds. Child Development, 1968, 39, 133-145.

Feshbach, S. Aggression. Chapter in P. Mussen (Ed.), revision of Carmichael's manual of child psychology, Vol. II. New York: John Wiley & Sons, 1970, 159-259.

Feshbach, S., Adelman, H. & Fuller W. The prediction of reading and related academic problems. Journal of Educational Psychology, 1977, 69 (4), 299-308.

Feshbach, S. & Feshbach, N. Children's aggression. In B. Wolman (Ed.), The International Encyclopedia of Neurology, Psychiatry, Psychoanalysis and Psychology, 1976, 364-377.

Feshbach, S. & Feshbach, N. Effects of fantasy and empathy training on aggression. National Science Foundation Grant No. BNS76-01261 (University of California, Los Angeles), 1977.

Feshbach, S., Feshbach, N., Cohen, R.S. & Hoffman, M. The antecedents of anger: A developmental approach. In Kaplan, R.M., Konecni, V.J. & Novoco, R. (Eds.), Aggression in children and youth. Sijthoff/Noordhoff International Publisher. Alphen den Rijn: The Netherlands, 1982.

Feshbach, S. & Fraczek, A. (Eds.), Aggression and behavior change: Biological and social processes. New York: Praeger, 1979.

Halatyn, T.V. Preliminary results of the statewide SB-72 survey of school crime and associated programs and strategies. Presentation prepared for the Educational Leadership Seminar at San Jose, CA on March 23-24, 1981.

Hoffman, M. Empathy: Its development and prosocial implications. In C.B. Keasey (Ed.), The Nebraska symposium on motivation, 1977: Social cognitive development. Lincoln: University of Nebraska Press, 1978.

Hoffman, M. & Feshbach, N. The ontogeny of sadness in elementary school children. Paper presented at the 59th Annual Meeting of the Western Psychological Association, San Diego, April 5-8, 1979.

Huckabay, L.M. A developmental study of the relationship of negative moral-social behaviors to empathy to positive social behaviors and to cognitive moral judgment. Science and direct patient care II, 5th Annual Nurse Scientist Conference Proceedings, Denver, CO, 1972.

Jastak, J., Jastak, S. & Bijou, S. Wide Range Achievement Test. Delaware: Guidance Corp., 1965.

Kurdek, L.A. Relationship between cognitive perspective-taking and teachers' ratings of children's classroom behavior in grades one through four. Journal of Genetic Psychology, 1978, 132, 21-27.

Mehrabian, A. & Epstein, N. A measure of emotional empathy. Journal of Personality, 1972, 40 (4), 525-543.

Phinney, J. Developmental changes in perspective taking. Paper presented at the American Psychological Association, San Francisco, August 1977.

Rathjen, D.P. & Foreyt, J.P. (Eds.), Social competence: Interventions for children and adults. New York: Pergamon Press, 1980.

Rothenberg, B.B. Child's social sensitivity and the relationship to interpersonal competence, intrapersonal comfort and intellectual level. Developmental Psychology, 1970, 2 (3), 335-350.

Sarason, S.B., Grossman, F.K. & Zitnay, G. The creation of a community setting. Syracuse, New York: Syracuse University Press, 1972.

Shantz, C.U. Social Cognition. To appear in J.H. Flavell & E.M.

207

Markman (Eds.), Cognitive Development, volume in P.H. Mussen
(Ed.), Carmichael's Manual of Child Psychology, 4th edition.
New York: Wiley, in press.

Spivak, G., Platt, J.J. & Shure, M.B. The problem solving
approach to adjustment: A guide to research and intervention. San Francisco: Jossey-Bass, 1976.

Spivak, G. & Shure, M.B. Social adjustment of young children: A
cognitive approach to solving real-life problems. San Francisco: Jossey-Bass, 1974.

Staub, E. The use of role-playing and induction in children's
learning of helping and sharing behavior. Child Development,
1971, 42, 805-816.

U.S. Department of Health, Education and Welfare. Violent
schools-safe schools: The Safe School Study report to
Congress. Washington, D.C.: U.S. Government Printing Office,
1978.

Walker, A. Social competence in middle childhood: Conceptions
and characteristics. Unpublished doctoral dissertation,
UCLA, 1977.

Wechsler, D. Manual for the Wechsler Intelligence Scale for
Children--Revised. New York: Psychological Corp., 1974.

ANGER AND AGGRESSION AMONG MILITARY PERSONNEL

Raymond W. Novaco and Gregory L. Robinson

University of California, Irvine

The nature of the military, with regard to both its organizational mission and its training procedure, inherently involves the occurrence of anger and aggression. Although
this point is obvious, there is no existing delineation of
the forms that these phenomena take in military organizations, and there is little systematic work on the environmental determinants of anger and aggression among military
personnel outside of combat. Yet, various conditions of the
training regimens, role strain, and interpersonal conflict
within an authoritarian organizational structure can induce
strong emotions and result in either direct or displaced
hostility.

It is important to recognize that the military is a
highly significant institution of socialization and education. Nearly 30 million men living in the United States
today are veterans--a sizeable proportion of the adult male
population. At any given time, the vast majority of those
in the Armed Services are young men in their late teens, who
undergo a major socialization experience. They are trained
to be highly disciplined in their personal activities, to
work hard, to persevere on difficult tasks, to respect authority, to control their emotions, to function effectively
as a member of a team, and to develop and maintain high standards of performance and achievement. The military also has
an educational role that is becoming increasingly important,
as technically advanced weaponry requires greater verbal and
quantitative abilities. Recruits who have inadequate educational backgrounds must improve their basic scholastic skills
in order to profit from the technical training afforded by the
military. In this regard, some have claimed that the military
has been more effective than the public school system in handling those with educational deficiencies (Barber, 1972).
Moreover, continuing education is an integral part of career
development among commissioned and non-commissioned officers.

209

Kaplan, R.M., Konečni, V.J., Novaco, R.W. (eds.) Aggression in Children and Youth
© 1984, Martinus Nijhoff Publishers, The Hague/Boston/Lancaster
ISBN 90-247-2903-3. Printed in The Netherlands

The principal function of military training is to organize and indoctrinate young enlistees to insure that the military remains capable of meeting its prescribed mission. Society clearly does not provide the experiences and training necessary for survival in situations where the military might be deployed. However, it is useful to bear in mind the distinction made by Merton (1968) regarding manifest and latent functions. Manifest functions refer to intended objective consequences, whereas latent functions refer to unintended, unrecognized, but nevertheless identifiable consequences that result from a standardized practice. In this regard, military training performs a collateral or latent function of providing education, employment, and opportunity otherwise not available to a segment of the adolescent population. This is particularly so for racial minorities and other disadvantaged youths in the peacetime military. There are also sub-groups within society having distinctive needs and desires (e.g., adventure seekers, risk takers) that are unsatisfied by established institutions. Military training thus provides alternative channels of social mobility for those otherwise excluded from the more traditional civilian avenues for personal and social advancement. Additionally, military experience provides an opportunity for many to overcome a history of failure and maladjustment.

ANGER AND AGGRESSION: THEORETICAL FRAMEWORK

Outside of combat, episodes of anger and aggression have been and continue to be problems for military organizations. We will describe and classify the various manifestations of anger and aggression in military contexts, but, before doing so, some brief clarification of concepts is needed, particularly as problems of anger and aggression relate to conditions of human stress. The relevance of the stress framework is that stressful circumstances of the physical and social environment can engender anger/aggression problems that can be viewed as maladaptive attempts at coping.

Provocation to anger has salient manifestations. Anger arousal is marked by physiological activation in the cardiovascular and endocrine systems, tension in the skeletal musculature, antagonistic thought patterns, and, at times, aggressive behavior. The view of anger taken here is that it is an emotional state defined by the presence of physiological arousal and cognitive labeling. The cognitive label need not be precisely that of "anger" but may be something semantically proximate, such as "annoyed," "irritated," "enraged," "provoked," etc. The cognitive labeling dimension may be otherwise viewed as the "subjective affect" dimension of emotional state. Implicit in the cognitive labeling is some impulse to action. That is, the cognitive labeling process inherently involves an inclination on the part of the person to act in an antagonistic or confrontative manner towards the

210

source of provocation. These action impulses in part define the emotional state and are incorporated in the cognitive labeling process.

The general model of anger is that of a cognitively mediated emotional state that is reciprocally related to cognitions and to behavior. The theoretical foundation of this model and its relationship to a larger conceptual framework for human stress have been previously developed (Novaco, 1979). A central proposition is that there is no direct relationship between external events and anger. The arousal of anger is a cognitively mediated process. Expectations and appraisals are designated as the principal classes of cognitions that determine the occurrence of anger.

Another proposition is that anger is neither necessary nor sufficient for aggression, yet it is a significant antecedent of aggression and has a reciprocal relationship with aggression. This bidirectional causality postulate (Konecni, 1975) means that the level of anger influences the level of aggression and vice-versa. Whether or not aggression occurs following provocation is thought to be a function of various social learning factors other than anger, such as reinforcement contingencies, expected outcomes, and modeling influences. These same social learning factors can also influence the occurrence of aggression independent of anger arousal. Thus, it is possible for someone to aggress without becoming angry, as when the infliction of injury or damage is expected to produce personal gain or when the aggressive act is a well-learned behavior.

In the present theoretical model, anger is viewed as an affective stress reaction (Novaco, 1979). That is, anger arousal is one kind of response that occurs in conjunction with exposure to environmental demands. Stress is understood as a hypothetical state defined by the functional relationships between environmental demands (stressors) and adverse health and behavior consequences (stress reactions). The demands or stressors are elements of various environmental fields (i.e., physical, biological, psychological, social) which exert pressure on the organism to adapt. The routine exposure to environmental demands in the absence of commensurate coping resources induces stress reactions that represent impairments to psychological functioning and physical health.

Anger is incorporated into the larger theoretical framework of human stress for several reasons. First, one defining property of anger is physiological arousal, and it is unquestionably the case that arousal is activated by exposure to stressors, such as noise, heat, traffic congestion, crowding, difficult tasks, and high pressure job environments. The importance of this is that acute and prolonged exposure to such conditions may induce arousal that is experienced by the

211

individual in conjunction with other events that pull for the cognitive label "anger". Exposure to certain stressors may produce arousal or excitation that decays slowly, leaving a residual excitation that can subsequently transfer to other experiences (Zillman, 1971). This residual excitation then adds in a non-trivial way to the arousal induced by subsequent events appraised in terms of anger. Thus, anger should be understood in terms of contextual conditions as well as the more immediate and identifiable provoking events. The stress framework provides theoretical guidelines for the disaggregation and analysis of contextual factors (environmental demands and moderators) that may act as determinants of anger and aggression.

As an emotional state, anger has adaptive as well as maladaptive functions. It may energize coping activity, act as a discriminative cue for problem-solving efforts, or serve as a vehicle for communicating negative sentiment. On the other hand, it can disrupt information processing, defeat the opportunity for self-scrutiny, and instigate aggressive behavior. Analysis of the functional properties of anger (Novaco, 1976) indicates that it should not automatically be viewed as a negative or undesirable condition of the organism. The determination of anger as a clinical problem is a matter to be evaluated in terms of various response parameters (frequency, intensity, duration, and mode of expression) by which we can gauge the severity of anger reactions with regard to effects on performance, health, and personal relationships. Concepts of stress and adaptation can be useful for understanding the enduring or long-term effects of anger. To the extent that anger is associated with impairments to health and psychological functioning, stress research can inform us about the extended and unanticipated costs of anger proneness.

Thus, the stress framework can improve our identification of the range of circumstances that engender anger and the varied impacts that anger can have on well-being. Furthermore, it is here suggested that among persons who are prone to provocation the anger response represents a learned coping style. That is, chronic anger reactions can be understood as a way of coping with life demands. To the extent that military training and organizational functioning fosters aggressive response patterns, the individual might thereby become more inclined to respond to problem situations in a forceful, angry manner. On the other hand, efficient performance on tasks and in situations relevant to combat requires that disruptive emotions be minimized and managed, hence military training also has emotion regulating objectives which can attenuate the tendency to respond with anger or aggression.

MANIFESTATIONS OF ANGER AND AGGRESSION IN THE MILITARY

We are concerned with anger and aggression from the standpoint of individual behavior, as opposed to the study of intergroup conflict. Toward understanding the types of anger/ aggression phenomena that can be found in military settings, we discuss their mainfestation with regard to combat itself, combat-induced stress reactions and aftereffects, organizational and interpersonal conflict, and basic training. The latter context has been the arena for our own research, which has been concerned with both recruits and training personnel. While we have conducted extensive observations and analyses in that setting, much has been written with regard to other contexts in which anger and aggression emerge.

Combat

The business of war is the destruction of the enemy and their will to fight. Technological advances have not only increased the destructive capacity of weapons, they have modified the extent to which the soldier must mobilize aggressive energies to carry out the destructive act. In fact, some weapon systems only require a mechanical routine to attack a distant and unseen target, as with various types of missiles and heavy artillery. Nevertheless, contemporary forms of warfare still entail energized aggressive activity (Janowitz, 1960). Certain sophisticated weapons, such as supersonic aircraft with computerized, radar-guided missile systems, rely upon the combative nature of their operating personnel to be effective. For example, the heroic efforts of pilots in strafing runs, aerial dogfights, and attacking naval vessels played a pivotal role in the war between Britain and Argentina over the Falkland Islands. Reflecting on the importance of the "fighter spirit" Janowitz (1960) stated:

"...no military system can base its expectation of victory on the initial exchange of fire power--whatever form that initial exchange may take. Military planners must assume that there will be subsequent exchanges which will involve military personnel--again, regardless of the armaments--who must be prepared to carry on the struggle as soldiers. That is, they must be prepared to subject themselves to military authority and to continue to fight, regardless of their own preferences" (pp. 33-34).

Technological proficiency is certainly an asset in a military campaign, but the conduct of the war can ultimately be determined by the aggressive spirit of the fighting forces. Military experts have recently taken note of this ultimate dependence on the will to fight and perseverance of combat forces, as was demonstrated in the Falkland conflict in the South Atlantic, in the war between Iraq and Iran in the Middle East, and in the Vietnam war.

These revelations of recent wars echo observations made during the Second World War. In a highly regarded analysis of military behavior, Marshall (1947) found that less than one-fourth of the men in combat fired their weapons. Marshall

213

concluded that the cohesiveness of primary groups enables the soldier to fight, and he emphasized the importance of individual intitiative in characterizing the effective fighter. This point made about initiative is further supported by the discoveries in World War II and in the Korean War that less than one percent of Air Force pilots became aces (i.e., achieved five air battle victories), but these few pilots accounted for 30 to 40 percent of the downed enemy aircraft (Janowitz, 1959). Going back to the American Civil War Battle of Gettysburg, over 18,000 muskets that unmistakably had not been fired were found on the battle field. The evidence was that 12,000 had two charges, both undischarged, rammed down the barrel; and another 6,000 had three to ten packed charges. It was concluded that the men had panicked and were loading the weapons purposelessly or that they deliberately wanted to appear as though they were firing (Karsten, 1978).

In building motivation for combat, the military indoctrinates soldiers to despise the enemy who are labeled by assorted derogatory characterizations. It is as if the soldier must come to believe that those whom he is fighting are less than human. However, Grinker and Spiegel (1945) stated that:

"It is erroneous to consider that hatred of the enemy is necessary for a good fighting morale, for hatred and sadistic gratification from killing are sources of guilt to the hater and are not the best motivation for objective and successful combat" (p. 40).

They maintained that until one is personally injured by the enemy, or has experienced the loss of close friends, it is hard to escape the inner revulsion associated with killing the enemy. Furthermore, the teamwork and coordination necessary in battle precludes giving vent to uncontrolled aggressive inclinations.

The notion that combat provides a socially approved opportunity for giving vent to aggressive, destructive impulses has been exaggerated. Extensive studies during the Second World War clearly make this point. Ginzberg (1959), in a major investigation of personality and performance, concluded that for all but a few, combat was experienced as acutely stressful. And, although a small percentage of individuals do find release on the battle field, being responsible for the death of others later induces guilt and apprehension.

Whatever the place of valor and heroism, warfare is invariably ugly. Aggression takes on an ignominious character when fighting degenerates to wanton destructiveness and atrocities perpetrated upon civilians and/or prisoners. Early writings in military psychiatry, such as Grinker and Spiegel (1945), interpreted excessive aggression in battle as an overcompensating defense against anxiety. Their analysis of

214

motivation for combat emphasized group identification, emotional ties to comrades, family traditions, and competitive spirit. They minimized the importance of factors that are associated with Freudian death instinct interpretations:

"There is another facet to motivation for battle, which has sometimes been overemphasized. That is the respectable, socially approved release of aggressive and destructive impulses provided by combat. Few Americans anticipate pleasure from destruction or killing, and, although some chronically hostile, aggressive individuals may be fascinated by the prospect of getting all the fighting they want, they frequently find it impossible to adapt their habitually irascible personalities to the controlled environment of teamwork and coordination necessary in battle" (Grinker & Spiegel, 1945, p. 43).

Other writers have taken a more sour and condemning attitude toward the psychological make-up of the combatant, especially as particular atrocities during the Vietnam war prompted many to look harshly upon military activity in general. One particularly caustic analysis is that of Barnes (1972) who characterizes the soldier as having been shaped to have a Janus-like personality:

"On the one hand, he must be meek, obedient, and agreeable towards his superiors; on the other, he must be aggressive, cruel, and bloodthirsty towards the designated enemy. He must, in other words, play the roles of both nigger and killer. As one GI rather graphically put it, 'We're supposed to have no balls or four balls, but never just two!'...Ironically the killer role is often easier to assume than the servile role, especially after the soldier gets used to it. It affords at long last, an opportunity to release pent-up aggression and to establish a claim to a type of manhood. The pressures on the soldier's personal identity are removed, as are the restraints of civilized society. Those dark and violent urges that seem to run through all men are uncorked and even glorified" (Barnes, 1972, pp. 89 and 91).

These characterizations, exaggerated and dramatized as they are, reflect the discontent and disillusionment that resulted from revelations of atrocities during the Indochina war. Quite in contrast to Grinker and Spiegel (1945) who wrote about our World War II troops as noble warriors who feel revulsion about killing--"Ruthless killing and disregard for individual life and integrity have been too foreign to our training" (p. 43)--our news media carried stories of heinous acts by American combat personnel. Colonel George Walton's (1973) incredible account of the attack on the My Lai village on March 16, 1968, in which over seven hundred defenseless villagers, a great many of whom were women and children were

215

massacred, poignantly depicts the nadir of American dishonor during this war. Yet, as Walton indicates, the My Lai massacre was not the first of its kind in U.S. Army history. Sadly, there were a number of parallel occurrences during the wars with the American Indians, as cavalry and militia slaughtered hundreds of Cheyenne and Sioux in their villages.

While the My Lai massacre was horribly unique in its proportions, it nevertheless bears resemblance to a range of activities that were prevalent in Vietnam (e.g., "free fire zones," "area prepping," chemical defoliation, and depersonalization of the enemy). In this regard, it would be a mistake to view such atrocities as extreme acts of aggression performed by individual actors. "The American tradition is to locate the source of evil deeds in evil men. We have yet to learn that the greatest evils occur when social systems give average men the task of routinizing evil" (Opton & Sanford, 1971, p. 106).

Summarizing our discussion of aggression vis-a-vis combat, we have pointed to the fact that energized aggressive behavior remains an intrinsic part of warfare, despite technological advances in weapon systems. The fighting spirit of individual soldiers and combat units continues to play a pivotal role in the outcomes of war. We have also noted that certain viewpoints have exaggerated the role of combat as an opportunity for giving vent to destructive impulses. It is a cynical and insensitive over-simplification to view soldiers as being gratified by the expression of pent-up aggressive urges. On the other hand, abberations indeed have occurred where aggression in combat has taken senseless and appalling forms. While one might be inclined to view war atrocities as the products of defective personalities, it is always wise to consider the social and organizational context of the behavior of individual actors.

Stress Reactions and Combat Aftereffects

We have just discussed aggression as an intrinsic part of war against an enemy. However, anger, hostility, and aggressive acts not directed toward the enemy can occur during wartime as a result of the stress of combat. The stress associated with exposure to the extreme environments of warfare has been studied extensively. Among the most notable works are those of Grinker and Spiegel (1945) on air combat units, Kardiner and Spiegel (1947) regarding traumatic neuroses, Bourne (1969; 1970) on psychological and physiological stress reactions in Vietnam, and Figley (1978a) on combat-related stress disorders among Vietnam veterans.

Combat environments entail multiple sources of stress which have cumulative effects. Stress is engendered, in part, by exposure to elements of environmental fields that require an adaptive response from the organism or system (Novaco, 1979). Harsh physical circumstances that affect tissue needs are one category of stressors that are prevalent in warfare. This includes (a) deprivation of food, sleep, or oxygen, (b) extreme stimulation involving aversive temperatures and noise, (c) disease-engendering conditions linked to inadequacies in hygiene, diet, and medical care, and (d) wounds and injuries which induce trauma and confirm the soldier's most basic fear.

These harsh physical conditions are only one dimension of the stress-inducing circumstances of warfare. The more pervasive dimension is the threatening psychological ambiance of combat. This has several components: the continuous threat of death and injury, the loss of friends, and the recognition of one's own destructive capacity. Along with the harsh physical conditions of war, these psychological sources of strain summate over time to increase risk of psychological impairment. All wars involve immersion in a hostile atmosphere. The soldier is enveloped by the sights, sounds, and smells of destruction. The clandestine nature of the fighting in Indochina exacerbated the psychological strain of the combat ambiance. American troops developed "a sense of helplessness at not being able to confront the enemy in set piece battles. The spectre of being shot at and having friends killed and maimed by virtually unseen forces generated considerable rage which came to be displaced on anyone or anything available" (DeFazio, 1978, p. 30). An elaboration of these stress conditions associated with warfare can be found in Novaco, Cook, and Sarason (1982).

Exposure to this multiple stressor context involving the most catastrophic of risks gives rise to stress which is manifested as anger, hostility, and aggression. In the earliest work on psychopathology resulting from combat, Kardiner and Speigel (1947) wrote about the tendency to aggression and violence as being

"...one of the most common complaints of traumatic neuroses. Most patients have complete insight into this characteristic, are troubled by it, and want relief from it. It is, of course, intimately related to the irritability and hypertoxicity of the entire muscular system. The aggression may show itself in the tendency to 'tempers.' Easily aroused to anger, these patients are very prone to motor expression. They either break or tear objects in these fits of temper, or strike the people who happen to be around them. This symptom is subject to wide variations. If the outburst is accompanied by loss of consciousness, the patient is usually dangerous; assault in this state is not uncommon. Often these patients injure themselves unintentionally... The aggressiveness of the traumatic neurotic is not deliberate

217

or premeditated. His aggression is always impulsive...
The sadomasochistic complex is related to the irritability, the incapacity to analyze stimuli in the environment" (pp.212-213).

Explosive irritability and unwarranted rage were identified
by Kardiner and Spiegel as a stage in the progressive development of incapacitating breakdowns, which begin with poor ap-
petite and carelessness, then involve irritability and exaggerated reactions of rage, and culminate in freezing, sleep
disturbances, and being terrified of one's own artillery.
This conceptualization of the traumatic neuroses as progressive disorders is based upon observations during the first
and second World Wars. "Shell shock" and "combat fatigue"
were considered to be time-determined phenomena. It has been
learned in subsequent wars, particularly Vietnam, that combat
stress reactions are not necessarily progressive disorders
but are more dynamic (Bourne, 1970). Our focus here is not
on the nature of combat stress reactions, about which there
is a considerable literature, but on the anger/aggression
aspects of the traumatic disorders.

Variations in the contextual conditions of war have
produced variations in the prevalent manifestations of anger,
aggression, and hostility as components of combat stress.
The combat environment of World War I was particularly harsh,
as soldiers spent lengthy periods on the front lines, enduring extremes of discomfort and danger. Kardiner's experiences
with chronic cases during that war and his collaborative work
with Spiegel regarding the Second World War led to the above
cited account. But at least three factors came into play
between World War I and Vietnam to influence the nature of
combat stress reactions: (1) the physical conditions of warfare, (2) the socio-political climate, and (3) the practice
of military psychiatry itself.

With regard to the latter, important changes in mental
health care occurred as a function of experience in succeeding wars. By 1918 it was learned that prolonged exposure to
front line danger and deprivation produced very disabling
syndromes and also that when soldiers were evacuated to distant hospital zones their symptoms did not remit. Consequently, what were otherwise transient stress reactions became
chronic conditions. Some military psychiatrists thus began
to provide for treatment close to the front lines--this
removed the instrumentality of the symptoms, maintained identification with the fighting unit, minimized guilt about
desertion, and provided for some sense of efficacy, as opposed
to reinforcing beliefs about one's inability to cope. During
the Second World War, it was recognized that this treatment
strategy (which later became the foundation of crisis intervention work) was the most advantageous approach to combat
fatigue, however, it was not until the Korean war that the

218

U.S. military had an effective program. Psychiatrists and psychologists then began to work in conjunction with field units (which was a predecessor of the practice of community psychology). For the Vietnam war, explicit policies were established that limited the tour of duty, as soldiers served for 12 months (13 for Marines) in Vietnam.

Yet more changed across these wars than the practice of military psychiatry and the policies it influenced. Most pertinent to the anger/aggression components of stress reactions, the Vietnam conflict was very different in its physical and socio-political dimensions. The combat iself varied markedly from previous wars and the identity of the enemy was often unclear. While there were occasional intense battles, fighting was more typically sporadic against an enemy that came out of the shadows. The inability to distinguish friend from foe, the necessary mistrust of villagers, the emphasis on body counts, and the political tensions of the war created an atmosphere where indiscriminate killing occurred and dehumanizing conditions prevailed.

The psychological ambience of combat associated with the Vietnam war had a particular negative effect on veterans who began to manifest "delayed stress responses" (Horowitz & Solomon, 1975). The common themes of the post-combat syndrome are guilt and self-punishment, feeling scapegoated, indiscriminate rage, "psychic numbing," alienation, and doubt about one's ability to love and trust others (Shatan, 1978). The delayed stress syndrome is a multifaceted condition involving recurrent intrusive thoughts, images, and nightmares, intense emotional re-experiences, depersonalization and denial, impaired self-concept, reactive rage, and fear of losing control over destructive impulses. Pertinent to our focus, occurrences of frustration, anger, aggression, and hostility are a prominent part of the symptomatology. Often, it is the experience of rage and the fear of one's own destructive impulses that prompt the individual to seek treatment.

Horowitz and Solomon (1975) describe the typical case of delayed stress syndrome as someone who has been back from Vietnam for about a year and a half, having done ostensibly well in this period, during which he has secured a job and has married. Typically, he has been reluctant to discuss combat experiences. At some point he begins to have sleep disturbances and recurrent images of war atrocities, whether or not he was involved in their occurrence. He is typically suspicious, easily frustrated, and feels as though he will lose control over his hostile impulses. Thoughts of doing severe violence to others are found to be pleasurable, although such thoughts generate guilt and worry about going crazy. "There may be startle reactions, psychosomatic syndromes, anxiety attacks, loss of motivation, and depression. The person often turns to drugs such as heroin or sedatives because they temporarily relieve the depressive, anxious, fearful, and hostile mood states. Interpersonal difficulties may (arise) because of the person's continued and uncontrollable suspicions, moodiness, surly behavior, or excessive demands..." (Horowitz & Solomon, 1975, p. 71). These authors point out that unlike obsessional neurotics, the recurrent intrusive thoughts of the combat veteran are based on historical reality, not fantasy.

In his review of research of the psychosocial adjustment of Vietnam-era veterans, Figley (1978b) concluded that there is considerable evidence that Vietnam service impaired adjustment. His own research had shown that combatants, compared to noncombatants, got into more verbal fights, more frequently had violent fantasies and dreams, and had fewer close friends (Figley & Eisenhart, 1975). DeFazio, Rustin and Diamond (1975), studying a college sample of Vietnam veterans who had been out of service an average of five years, found that 67% had nightmares and 41% felt themselves to be short-tempered or hotheads. Importantly, it may well be that these personality disturbances were a product of the unique aspect of the Vietnam conflict. In a study that compared American (Vietnam) and Israeli (Yom Kippur) soldiers who were psychiatric patients, Merbaum and Hefez (1976) found that the American psychiatric sample was distinguished by significant elevations in the MMPI Psychopathic Deviate and Hypomania scales, suggesting impulsivity, aggression, and poorly controlled behavior. Personality disorders were virtually absent diagnostically from the Israeli psychatric group. Since these samples had very different pre-war personal histories, it is difficult to attribute psychiatric outcome to the war context per se, but it is clear that the anger/aggression dimensions of the delayed stress syndrome are not a necessary outcome of extreme war stress.

The Horowitz and Solomon (1975) model has been influential for treatment approaches to the problems of Vietnam veterans (cf. Figley, 1978a). However, neither of the chapters concerning treatment strategies present much about therapeutic interventions for anger and aggression. In fact, they say incredibly little, given the importance of this dimension in the delayed stress syndrome. Horowitz and Solomon describe a role playing technique ("using the therapist as an introject") and a response substitution technique (substituting a response lower on a hierarchy of aggressive acts). Other authors have reported the use of hypnotherapy (Balson & Dempster, 1980; Brende & Benedict, 1980), however, there is no published psychotherapeutic outcome study on Vietnam veterans that is experimental in nature.

In this section we have portrayed the centrality of anger and aggression to traumatic disorders associated with exposure to warfare. Irritability and explosive rage have always been observed among the psychiatric casualities of combat, and with regard to the delayed stress syndromes associated with the Vietnam war, problems of anger and aggression are particularly salient. The occurrence of these phenomena illustrate the role of environmental, contextual factors as determinants of anger and aggressive behavior, particularly as cumulative exposure to harsh ambient conditions predisposes the person to experience anger or to act aggressively. Secondly, the involvement of this emotion-behavior complex in clinical syndromes indicates that their significance is considerably more than that of transient psychological states. The value of the stress theoretic framework is well-illustrated here.

In the next section, we will turn to manifestations of anger and aggression under the more ordinary circumstances of organizational life.

Organizational and Interpersonal Conflict

With regard to organizational conflict and aggression, our analysis might begin at the level of institutions, dealing with the conflict between military and civilian organizations in various political and national contexts. These topics are addressed by sociological analyses of civil-military relations (cf. Andreski, 1968; Janowitz, 1975; Lang, 1972; Perlmutter, 1977). However, these are matters of intergroup conflict, which at this broad level of analysis are beyond the scope of our presentation.

We do want to note that little empirical research has been done to link conceptualizations of civil-military relations to the affective and behavioral responses of individuals. There is always the potential for friction in contacts between men in uniform and members of the host community where military personnel are garrisoned. Yet, investigations in this area typically are limited to the specific causes of particular incidents (Lang, 1972). One must also look to broadly-based societal attitudes for relevant contextual factors. Feld (1971) has observed:

"To begin with, the existence of any particular group within the general society--from the family on upwards-- poses problems of conflict. The conventional democratic attitude seems to be that these can almost always be resolved with mutual benefit...Between armed forces and a society considering itself democratic, on the other hand, this assumption is considered to be somewhat shaky. A widely spread sentiment holds that armed forces are at least a necessary evil and at worst a social menace" (p. 269).

221

This at best ambivalent attitude toward the military prevailing throughout large segments of society creates a backdrop of tension for military personnel. Members of the armed forces are beset with economic frustrations due to military pay scales, a relatively low social status that provides no tradeoff for these economic shortcomings, and the fact that their distinct appearance makes them easy targets for the expression of negative public sentiment. These conditions of the social fabric can predispose military personnel to feel anger and resentment towards civilians and society at large.

This was never more prevalent than during the Vietnam period when American combat soldiers became bitter and enraged toward particular subgroups who opposed the war and to American institutions in general.

"Vietnam veterans are frequently described as being a very angry group. It is not really sufficient to say that some of these men are or were merely angry. Their words and the tone of their words are saturated with vindictiveness...In a combat situation the vindictiveness is often experienced as a righteous wrath, while in peacetime it is felt as a smouldering resentment directed at institutions and individuals in authority" (DeFazio, 1978, p. 32).

In many ways, the Vietnam veterans carried the burden of the war's unpopularity, and their rage followed from their belief that they had been manipulated and betrayed (Bourne, 1970; Shatan, 1978). In his field trips to Vietnam, Moskos (1970) reported that he "repeatedly heard combat troops--almost to a man--vehemently denounce peace demonstrators back in the United States" (p. 162). Their resentment, which is in a way ironic, stemmed from the perception that the peace demonstrations were directed against the soldier himself, as if the war was his responsibility. The antagonism was also an outgrowth of class hostility, because the demonstrators were seen as privileged college students who escaped their military obligations through loopholes in the draft designed to benefit the socially advantaged. This polarization was heightened by antagonisms across American college campuses aimed at Reserve Officer Training Corps (ROTC) programs. Considerable pressure from students and faculty resulted in the withdrawal of academic credit for military science courses and the eventual abandonment of ROTC altogether (Scott, 1971). In addition, the peace demonstrators were seen to be undercutting the sacrifices of American troops, who would have "died for nothing" (Moskos, 1970). These sentiments associated with unpopular wars are not unique to American soldiers. To take another example from warfare in Indochina, French officers who had spent much of their time after World War II in Indochina began to resent the French people for their lack of

222

sacrifice and support. Their anger grew particularly sharp as they weighed the total effort expended by the Viet Minh in contrast to what they perceived as irresponsible criticism in the French press and the "unpatriotic" indifference of their countrymen (Hauser, 1973).

While these illustrations of institutional level conflict bear mention, our concern with anger and aggression continues to be at the level of individual behavior. In this regard, macrolevel analyses of institutional conflict need to be supplemented by studies of intraorganizational conflict. At times, reference is made to the military as though it is an homogenous entity, perhaps due to its singular authoritarian structure or to its social insulation from the rest of society. Yet, there is considerable diversity in the military organization. As Perlmutter (1977) has observed, it is by no means the case that the military is a cohesive, coherent, monolithic group, as there are many divisions and disputes between and within military ranks and hierarchies. To facilitate the identification of the organizational conditions which can engender anger and aggression, we again turn to the stress framework. Stress has become a popular topic in the field of organizational behavior, yet the study of occupational stress per se (cf, Cooper & Payne, 1978; 1980) is much too broad given our present focus. We will concentrate, therefore, on several specific organizational demands that can elicit strong affective reactions. Anger and aggressive behavior may result from task-generated stress, role-based stress, and stress arising from interpersonal relations.

Task-generated stress. Tasks, by their very nature, represent demands for action directed toward some goal or the resolution of some problem. Organizational goals are operationalized by assigning tasks to persons to perform. When task demands exceed the person's resources, stress occurs, as our model stipulates, and it is in the interest of work organizations to minimize the probability of stress by arranging for a fit or match between job and worker. One way that task stress might occur is when particular task demands are beyond the person's capabilities. Various formal and informal selection mechanisms are utilized to assure that tasks can be done by those hired to do them. Yet there is another way that task-generated stress arises, which would seem to be more common. This is when the worker must deal with a multiplicity of tasks and when the workload is exacerbated by fatigue or debilitating emotional states linked to the sequence of task demands.

In this latter form of task-generated stress, the demands of any given task are within the person's capabilites, but, on some particular occasion or in the overall job context of workload and responsibility, stress results from a depletion of resources. Anger and aggression occur under

223

these circumstances for a number of reasons: (1) the person becomes frustrated by various constraints that impede goal attainment, (2) physiological activation induced by heavy workload increases the probability of anger, (3) cognitive flexibility is reduced by stress, increasing the probability of antagonistic appraisals or threat perception, and (4) anger and aggression have instrumental value in controlling one's environment.

As we have indicated, it is beyond our purpose here to deal in any thorough way with occupational stress topics. Since the concept of task stress is connected to the topics of job content and job satisfaction there is a broad literature in organizational psychology that is relevant. Regarding anger and aggression, one could link task stress and job design to problems of morale and satisfaction (Gross, 1970; Lawler, 1973). Workers who are dissatisfied with job content or design express annoyance in the form of complaints, hostile jokes, or even the destruction of company property. This is as prevalent in military organizations as anywhere else, perhaps more so. However, apart from matters of morale and satisfaction, we would like to give an example from our own research of task-generated stress that has anger-inducing consequences. This concerns drill instructors in the United States Marine Corps. Our research is ongoing and is being conducted in collaboration with Dr. Irwin G. Sarason of the University of Washington, who has also contributed to this volume.

The Marine Corps drill instructor is responsible for the basic training of recruits over an 11 week cycle. During the training cycle, the drill instructor must cope with the strain imposed by (1) a rigorous training schedule in which activities are programmed to the minute, (2) extremely long working hours (allowing an average of five hours sleep per night) over extended periods (having less than seven non-working days during the entire cycle is common), (3) the myriad difficulties of managing the behavior of 60-90 eighteen-year-olds, (4) family conflicts linked to the heavy workload, (5) the presence of constant supervision and evaluative scrutiny, and (6) competitive pressures among peers.

In longitudinal studies (Novaco, Sarason, Robinson, & Cunningham, 1982) we have found stress levels to significantly escalate as a function of length of time as a drill instructor. Our assessments were made just prior to the start of duty, after three months, and after one year. Self-report, physiological, and performance assessments converge to confirm the stress increases. Among our results, we have found highly significant increases in measures of anger that are associated with job stress. Using the Novaco Provocation Inventory (described in a later section with regard to our research on recruits), we found significant correlations at the one-year

224

point between anger and a summary index of perceived job stress (r = .47, N = 60, p < .001), and a significant inverse relationship between anger and job performance evaluations (r = -.32, N = 59, p < .006). We also measured Type A (coronary proneness) behavior patterns using the Jenkins Activity Survey and found JAS Factor A scores at our three month assessment to be predictive of the anger measures at one year (r = .34, N = 59, p < .004). Moreover, we have found that the speed/impatience component of the Type A pattern to have highly significant increases (one standard deviation) over the longitudinal period and that the JAS items contributing most strongly to this increase in Factor S are those pertaining to temper and irritability. We are currently engaged with Irwin Sarason in a project designed to remediate conditions of stress among drill instructors.

Role-based stress. This organizational condition contributes significantly to anger provocation in the peace-time military and, in extreme cases, has provoked homicidal aggression against superior officers in combat settings. Kahn, Wolfe, Snoek and Rosenthal (1964) found that five out of six men in a national sample of the labor force reported experiencing some form of role based tension. Fully one half of these reports were found to involve conflict with organizational superiors. While role conflicts are clearly not exclusive to the military, problems stemming from differences in rank and concomitant superior-subordinate relationships can be exacerbated in the military because its authoritarian disciplinary methods clash with the more or less liberal social philosophy of advanced industrialized society. This essential disparity is amplified by an organizational structure which tends to emphasize the status differential between officers and the enlisted ranks. Van Doorn (1975) traces the historical development of this split to the aristocratic heritage of early military leadership. A common social origin in the upper classes and the accompanying sense of belonging to an elite affirmed the exclusiveness and the solidarity of the officer corps in this era. The high social status of the officer thus contributed to his sharp division from the enlisted ranks who were, prior to and within the nineteenth century "chiefly of proletarian elements often crimped or even--in the navy--pressed into service, or reared in traditional submission to the bearers of authority" (p. 38). The rise of democratic principles in contemporary society has had little impact toward the reform of this traditional caste system.

"Officer privilege has been the subject of rank-and-file hostility for many years. Despite widespread public criticism, however, the anachronistic social distinctions of military life remain intact: enlisted men and officers have separate mess halls, separate clubs, and separate latrines; commanders live in luxurious homes,

225

while GIs and NCOs live in row houses or family apartments; officers may not perform manual labor; they are "gentlemen" and their wives are "ladies"; etc." (Cortright, 1975, p. 231).

A cartoon described by Charles Moskos, in his analysis of the American enlisted man (1970), illustrates the pervasiveness and depth of the distinction between officers and enlisted men with biting effectiveness. Here, "two officers are looking at a scenic sunset. One turns to the other and says: 'Beautiful view. Is there one for enlisted men?'" (p.6). In a more quantitative vein, the enlisted man's bitterness toward officers and the formal system of the military was well documented in the volumes of The American Soldier by Stouffer and his associates. Summarizing these voluminous findings Moskos (1970) notes:

> "Indeed, it appears that resentment toward the "caste" system of the Army and the differential treatment of officers and enlisted men generated the strongest feelings about army life. In table after table, the data show wide discrepancies between officer and enlisted attitudes...The tenor of the gripes indicated in these findings was succinctly typified by one of the interviewees: 'What's the matter with us enlisted men, are we dogs?'" (p. 7).

While hostility between the enlisted and officer ranks is one variant of this role conflict, officers in command but otherwise socially distant from their men may have an easier time than their noncommissioned officers. The non-com or NCO is placed between the incompatible expectations of his superiors and his subordinates. Like his industrial analogue the foreman, he is too close to the lower layer to be independent from his men, and too clearly enmeshed in the hierarchy to bend the rules.

> "...In many ways the animosity between lower-ranking enlisted men and NCOs has come to override the traditional enlisted hostility toward officers. For in most cases, it is an NCO rather than an officer who directly supervises an enlisted man on the job. Owing to this close working association within an authoritarian and hierarchical setting, the potentiality for personality conflict is correspondingly heightened. Moreover, in the company area where the troops reside, it is the NCO who must oversee unpleasant housekeeping details. Indeed, except for periodic inspections, soldiers rarely see an officer in the barracks" (Moskos, 1970, p. 71).

The hierarchical structure of military authority is predicated on the ultimate need to direct troops in battle. Orders emanating from higher echelons are presumed to reflect superior

226

information and strategic ability. However, this structure of hierarchical roles and authoritarian discipline has been criticized as deriving from an era when men had to be forced into open fire in mass infantry maneuvers. Contemporary analysts observe that this tradition serves to impede the individual responsibility required in many modern military occupations. Emphasizing the requirement for individual initiative in combat encounters, it is thought that, "the more an army relies on spontaneous motivation in place of harsh discipline, the more unified and efficient it will be" (Cortright, 1975, p. 227).

Nowhere is between-role conflict more strongly linked to anger and aggression than in combat. Grinker and Spiegel (1945) note that many combat veterans become far more aggressive and hostile after the fighting has ended. The object of their animosity, however, is not the enemy but the veteran's own army and leaders. They ascribe such hostility to failures in leadership or group morale which, by instigating feelings of parental rejection, result in displaced aggression in the combatant. Elegant psychodynamic interpretations need not be made of the practice of "fragging" which became commonplace in the Vietnam war. The term stems from the use of fragmentation grenades by enlisted personnel to assault officers and NCOs. Walton (1973) notes that the killing of unpopular officers by their own troops was not unique to the Vietnamese war. Colonial soldiers in the American Revolution fighting in Pennsylvania are said to have killed their captain, and in the American Civil War General Jesse Reno was killed by his own men. Army records indicated that by 1972, incidents involving assaults with explosive devices in Vietnam numbered 551, with 86 soldiers dead and over 700 injured. Over 80% of those killed were officers or NCOs (Cortright, 1975). These figures undoubtedly underestimate the true number of incidents in that shootings with firearms are not included. Here, between-role conflict reached a zenith of hostility. The majority of enlisted men in Vietnam during these years wished only to return home safely. A platoon sergeant quoted by Walton (1973) summed up the prevalent attitude: "The object is to spend your year without getting shot at, or if you do, to get the fewest people hurt. We don't try to frustrate the captain's attempt to kill gooks, but we don't put our heart in it. I put the welfare of the men first" (p. 234). Perusing accounts of these events, it is easily understood why the ardent young junior officer eager to engage the enemy and push his unit to heroic victories was considered a doomed figure.

Role conflicts in the military context assume other forms with less dramatic links to anger and violence as well. Another type of role-based stress can arise when a set of role demands contain internally contradictory expectations.

For example, such stress may be elicited by a tension between military obedience and professional competence or ethics.

Another form of role-based conflict may be called inter-role conflict. A typical form involves the conflicting demands of one's occupational role and family life. Military assignments are frequently rotated between installations, and the paternal role may conflict with the disruptions necessitated by such moves. Units consistently under alert or under strenuous training assignments may impose significant disruptions on family routines. While such conflicts may be identified as pertaining to the allocation of time and energy (to job or family), situations of conflict between two or more work roles are present in the military context as well. This type of inter-role conflict is ascribed a causal role in the decline of ROTC enrollment. The student electing to participate in the Reserve Officer Training Corps in a university setting must resolve the tension between the discordant values, structures of authority, and style of the military program and the academic tradition of humanism in the host institution (Scott, 1971). His simultaneous roles as university student and military officer trainee were thus potentially opposed. This inter-role conflict was certainly amplified by the violent protest of his colleagues against the military presence in an academic milieu, which we have alluded to above.

Stress arising from interpersonal relations. While a variety of structural differences distinguish the armed forces from the societies they serve, military organizations are essentially microcosms of the larger social order. In this regard, interpersonal strain stemming from racism, sexism, and class conflict is as likely to exist in the military context as in society at large. Conflict of this nature is particularly problematic within military institutions since it is group cohesion rather than ideological commitment that makes effective fighting men (Shils and Janowitz, 1948). Bobrow (1971) notes that:

"Military personnel are drawn from major ethnic, racial, and religious groups in the civil society. Military organization assumes that men from different groups do not regard each other as enemies. This is the case even though the group members in the military are drawn from the young male segment of the national population most likely to express group enmity directly" (p. 305).

In recent history, interpersonal conflict based upon race, gender and social class within military organizations has provided a severe test of this assumption.

The majority of recorded incidents of racial conflict have involved strife between blacks and whites, although the

228

discord has extended to Puerto Ricans and Chicanos. Blacks have fought in each of this country's wars, including the struggle for independence, the War of 1812, the Civil War, the Spanish-American War, both World Wars, the Korean Conflict, and the Vietnam War. Never before World War II, however, was the number of blacks in the military proportionate to their number in the total population. The role of the black soldier was typically limited to non-combat services, and as late as the early fifties he was likely to serve in a segregated unit. Although President Truman issued an executive order in 1948 providing for equal treatment regardless of race, color, religion or national origin, it remained for the Korean War to sound the death knell on a segregated army. The enlistee of today would have difficulty recognizing that some three decades ago, the military was one of America's most segregated institutions:

"...Today, color barriers at the formal level are absent throughout the military establishment. Equal treatment regardless of race is official policy in such nonduty facilities as swimming pools, chapels, barbershops, Post Exchanges, movie theaters, snack bars, and dependents' housing as well as in the more strictly military endeavors involved in the assignment, promotion, and living conditions of members of the armed services. Moreover, white personnel are often commanded by black superiors, a situation rarely obtaining in civilian life" (Moskos, 1970, p. 121).

In spite of the fact that formal military desegregation antedated both the civil rights movement of the late 1950's and the Black Power movement of the 1960's equal treatment in the military context has yet to be fully realized.

Unequal job placement is a principle complaint of minority servicemen. Blacks are disproportionately assigned to low-skill military occupations and to frontline combat duty. While black servicemen constituted 12.1 percent of all enlisted people in 1971, many infantry units in Vietnam were more than twenty percent black, and blacks held few technical positions--e.g., only 4.9 percent of the jobs in the electronics equipment field (Cortright, 1975). Although a large measure of the placement decision is determined by written test scores, such instruments have been criticized as inherently discriminatory in that they measure academic training and understanding of majority cultural norms rather than native intelligence. An obvious consequence of the overassignment of blacks to combat units is the higher casuality rate. From 1961 to 1966, blacks constituted 10.6 percent of military personnel in Southeast Asia while accounting for 16.0 percent of those killed in action (Moskos, 1970). In the area of promotions, advancement opportunities come slower to minority troops. Blacks are today under-represented in the officer ranks. Moreover, they continue to suffer discrimination that official orders can not eradicate. In this regard, discrimination in housing is a major grievance. Civilian landlords, both in the United States and abroad, have racist policies which compel blacks to accept inferior housing far from their duty stations (Glick, 1971), despite programmatic interventions implemented to combat this tendency.

Discrimination also has been observed in the formal system of military justice. Article 15 punishments, administered at the commanding officer's discretion, have been issued to blacks at double the rate for caucasians for confrontation or status-type offenses, such as disrespect (Cortright, 1975). Punitive discharges and pre-trial confinement are also disproportionately meted out to black servicemen. Cortright (1975) suggests that the prominence of white southerners in the military command hierarchy may be partially responsible for such institutional discrimination. Whatever the locus of responsibility, black servicemen in the late 1960's and early 1970's organized to challenge discrimination and the ossified practices of military justice during this era. The resulting incidents, protest demonstrations, and backlash reactions were replete with anger and aggression. Particularly violent were the conflicts in European garrisons. While it would take us too far afield to provide specific descriptions of these incidents, it should be noted that racial conflicts on military installations and ships at sea involved individual beatings, riots, destruction of property, and in one extreme case, the detonation of a fragmentation grenade in a crowded mess hall in Germany.

While these acts of aggression are here construed as manifestations of stress arising from interpersonal relations, their elements do meet Konecni's (1977) criteria for intergroup conflict. However, we are not compelled to broaden our level of analysis, for as Konecni has argued:

"...a situation involving only two people could be considered...an instance of conflict that is just as intergroup as is a battle involving all adult members of two tribes. Indeed, at the behavioral level, many cases of intergroup conflict consist principally of one-on-one confrontations between members of the groups in question..." (p. 11).

Our perspective on racially-based antagonisms in the military is consonant with Konecni's emphasis upon the analysis of individual behavior and on a class of events (having aversiveness in common) as a precursor of conflict. Thus, we are led to consider the structure of the military itself which places extraordinary discretionary authority in the hands of individual officers.

"By allowing commanders virtually arbitrary power over judicial and disciplinary proceedings, the services invite widespread abuse and, in effect, license discriminatory practices. Many officers retain deeply rooted prejudices, which, through excessive command influence, result in serious injury to minority servicemen" (Cortright, 1975, p. 209).

Interpersonal conflict based upon differences in economic class or social standing and upon gender are further sources of organizational stress. While these are less dramatically linked to aggression in the military context, each has been observed to provoke anger. Karsten (1978) notes that sensitivity to class seems to have been voiced more frequently by the wealthy than by the poor serviceman. He provides historical examples stemming from the distress some aristocratic southerners felt upon finding themselves subordinate to "vulgarians" during the Civil War. Typical here are refusals by upper class privates to obey orders on the grounds that the officer issuing the command was not a gentleman:

"It is galling for a gentleman to be absolutely and entirely subject to the orders of men who in private life were so far his inferiors, and who when they met him felt rather like taking off their hats to him than giving him law and gospel" (Karsten, 1978, p. 135).

A more contemporary account of the resentment of military life by lower-ranking soldiers from middle class backgrounds (especially draftees with college educations) is provided by Moskos (1970). Although this hostility is typically articulated as an indictment of the authoritarian character of the military system, it is his perception that these men actually resent having to compete on a relatively equal basis with servicemen from lower class backgrounds, many of whom are also not caucasian. Moskos notes that the scapegoating of NCOs by those from higher social classes is rarely accompanied by similar denigration of officers, who, as he points out, are likely to have similar social backgrounds. This analysis is consistent with the findings of Stouffer (1949) who identified tensions during World War II between better educated draftees and less well educated regular army NCOs. He found that frustration resulting from not climbing the status ladder faster was much more characteristic of the better educated selectee than other servicemen. It appears that much of the hostility toward military life and his immediate superiors harbored by the better educated enlisted man is based upon his occupancy of a subordinate position rather than essential disagreement with the hierarchical structure of the military.

Interpersonal conflict related to gender has become a more salient source of stress as the number of women in the military has escalated in recent years, and as these women

231

have been assigned to a growing number of duties. Similar to racial minorities and parallel to conditions in society at large, service women perceives discrimination reflected by their exclusion from positions of authority and disproportionate assignment to low skill, service occupations. Cortright (1975) cites a House Armed Services subcommittee report indicating that although women score higher on aptitude tests and are more likely to be high school graduates than men, they are promoted at lower rates than men and are highly likely (70%) to serve in secretarial or clerical occupations. The reactions of servicewomen to these circumstances have resulted in litigation, and, as their numbers grow, more confrontative and hostile reactions may ensue.

Basic Training

In this section we will draw upon some of our research concerning recruit training in the United States Marine Corps which also has been conducted in collaboration with Irwin G. Sarason. Before describing aspects of this project relevant to anger and aggression, we will discuss some general points about basic training in the military, continuing to portray as we have their connections to the stress framework.

One perspective on recruit training is to view it in terms of a transition from the civilian to the military culture. Boot camp has been conceptualized as a process of personal conversion:

"The process is fundamentally one of acculturation in which the recruit is subjected to a forced change of reference group, and the skills he learns are basically those necessary for survival and successful adaptation under these circumstances" (Bourne, 1967, p. 187).

"The objective of basic training is to shape the total person into being a disciplined cog within the military machine. Ultimately, basic training is where the most profound changes must be made; it functions as the military's agency for primary socialization" (Arkin and Dobrofsky, 1978, p. 158).

"Training is seen as the intentional disruption of civilian patterns of adjustment, replacement of individual gratifications with group goals, inculcation of unquestioning acceptance of authority and development of conformity to official attitudes and conduct" (Yarmolinsky, 1975, p. 158).

In the conversion process, stress has an intrinsic function, which is to promote socialization to military norms. From this perspective, stress is not merely a result of recruit training but also is an intentional component engineered to facilitate training objectives. In Education Under Duress, O'Neill and Demos (1971) describe how stress can operate to effect an ideological conversion. First, in the recruit training environment, the individual rapidly becomes aware that excellence is rarely rewarded overtly and that punishment and negative reinforcement, the cessation or avoidance of an aversive consequence, are the preeminent contingencies in effect. Therefore, stressors such as yelling and "incentive training" (rigorous calisthenics) have an operant role in shaping behavior.

Second, stress contributes to the tendency toward perceptual "tunnel vision" and cognitive rigidity. Lazarus (1966) noted the constriction of the perceptual field under stress and argued from existing research that anxiety resulting from stress interferes with learning and performance by narrowing the range of attention and by limiting perceptual cue utilization. Thus, stress in training can be thought to reduce the capacity for critical thinking and for intellectual reflection about the recruit's experience.

Third, stress may also heighten suggestibility and thereby increase receptivity to institutional influences. O'Neill and Demos make this point as a generalization of Pavlov's principle of transmarginal inhibition. Pavlov discovered that deviation from previously established response tendencies (the "inhibition" of conditioned behavior) resulted whenever the stimulus situation was sufficient to exceed the "margin" for effective response.

"Pavlov discovered that dogs, even previously conditioned to respond in a given manner, could be "unconditioned" as a result of acute emotional provocation if subjected to severe stress. Such unlearning appeared to be basically a function of the active inhibition of such previous learning and seemed likely to occur only when the animal had been stimulated "transmarginally" (O'Neill and Demos, 1971, p. 79).

Several of the conditions noted by Pavlov (1928) that can generate this phenomenon are: a prolongation of anticipation under stress (e.g., an abnormal delay between behavior and anticipated reward), the introduction of significant confusion or inconsistency into the conditions necessary for effective response, and fatigue in the responding subject. These conditions are unmistakably part of the training process. Thus, stress may function primarily to "decondition" previously established response tendencies (civilian behavior).

Another perspective on basic training is to view it as an arena for developing stress coping skills (Novaco et al., 1982). In this regard, boot camp may be understood as analogous to a stress inoculation procedure (Meichenbaum, 1975; Novaco, 1977). Viewed from this perspective, recruit training occurs in an intentionally aversive environment designed to prepare personnel to function effectively under the conditions of overstimulation found in combat.

Stress inoculation therapy is a cognitive-behavioral method of increasing one's capacity to deal effectively with problem situations by minimizing disruptive thoughts and emotions. The treatment procedure aims to facilitate behavioral adaptation to environmental demands which previously diminished one's task orientation. The treatment phases of stress inoculation therapy (cognitive preparation, skill acquisition, and application training) are analogous to progress through the initial period of socialization, classroom experience with weapons and other military apparatus, and subsequent phases of recruit training which involve field maneuvers under live fire. Recruit training cultivates the tendency to respond quickly to orders without deliberation through continuous practice in an environment filled with yelling, airplane noise, and the din created by adjacent platoons. Responding reflexively and single-mindedly to orders (remaining task oriented) despite stressful circumstances has potential survival value for the individual combatant and is essential if military objectives are to be achieved. Stressors of high intensity in recruit training provide an opportunity to cultivate such a task focus in an environment in which the consequences of failure are less catastrophic than in warfare.

There are a number of accounts of stress in recruit training to be found in the popular media, but there is also an ample scientific literature. The intense demands of the training environment have been found to be associated with both adverse health reactions and psychoendocrine effects. Voors, Stewart, Gutekunst, Modlow, and Jenkins (1968) identified stress as a precipitant of respiratory infection among Marine recruits. Stress has been similarly conceptualized as a determinant of 17-hydroxycorticosteroid excretion in recruits undergoing basic training for the National Guard, a related but indubitably less intense environment (Poe, Rose & Mason, 1970). Bourne (1967), in an analysis of Marine Corps recruit training, cites research indicating that during the period of induction, the psychological stress imposed is most dramatically reflected by 17-hydroxycorticosteroid levels which are comparable to those of schizophrenic patients measured during incipient psychosis.

Our investigation of anger in military recruit training was conducted in conjunction with a larger investigation of the psychological and organizational factors pertaining to

234

attrition from recruit training in the United States Marine Corps (Novaco, Sarason, Cook, Robinson, & Cunningham, 1979; Sarason, Novaco, Robinson, & Cook, 1981). Guided by conceptualizations of psychological stress, our general hypothesis was that cognitive and affective factors related to stress proneness would distinguish recruits who perform well in training from those who perform poorly. In this regard, we expected that attriters from training (particularly those whose failure was attributed to psychological or behavioral reasons) would be characterized by different patterns of reported anger than successful recruits. While it can be shown that anger has energizing functions so as to augment performance in particular circumstances of challenge, high levels of anger more typically impair performance by interfering with attention, information processing, and coordinated response sequences (Novaco, 1976).

A key assumption is that the experience of anger (psychological stress) detracts from a task orientation necessary for recruits to execute commands rapidly and efficiently. High levels of experienced stress tend to result in performance deficits. Performance failures, in turn, elicit aversive reactions from training supervisors (and at times, from other recruits), which can heighten stress responses. Unless the recruit develops effective coping skills, this deficit-amplifying cycle may culminate in training setback or attrition. Our finding that the majority of psychological/behavioral attrition from Marine Corps recruit training occurs during the first two weeks of the process suggests that recruits who are deficient in coping abilities are identified rapidly.

Quite obviously, all stress resulting from exposure to training demands does not result in anger. The form of stress responses will vary according to individual predispositions and contextual conditions. In addition, with regard to anger manifestations, Funkenstein, King, and Drolette (1957) found that stress can produce anger directed outward or anger directed inward. Therefore, particularly low levels of anger in response to conditions of high environmental demand may be psychologically significant. Moreover, the role of cognitive structures and appraisal processes are central to the experience of stress and anger. What may leave one person unmoved may enrage another. The experience of anger is, in large part, linked with perceptions of threat and personal thwarting. Anger often occurs as a response to situations which the person perceives as devaluations of the self. Consonant with the themes we have developed earlier, the tendency to become angry, as a dispositional state, is a product of perceptual sensitivities and the inclination to interpret events as provocations based on their ego-threat properties.

When high anger is consistently reported in response to a particular class of provocation events, inferences can be

235

made about cognitive structures, as well as about coping responses. Individual differences in anger reported in response to distinct categories of provocation events might also contribute to the prediction of person-environment fit in highly stressful settings, such as recruit training, which are distinguished by particular types of demands.

Assessing Anger Reactions. A number of self-report measures of anger are reported in the psychological literature. Perhaps the most widely known is the Buss and Durkee "Hostility Inventory" (Buss & Durkee, 1957). However, items on this inventory involve what people do when angry rather than the kinds of things which provoke anger. Endler and Hunt (1968), in a framework similar to that of their work with anxiousness, developed the "S-R Inventory of Hostility". Their results show that persons, situations, modes of response, and their interactions all contribute to test score variance, but their sampling of situations (14 items) was quite limited. An instrument developed by the first author, the Novaco Provocation Inventory (NPI) offered the broadest sample of events. The NPI was developed to investigate the kinds of things that provoke anger rather than what people do when angered. It consists of 80 items describing situations of provocation for which the respondent rates anger on a five-point scale. The total NPI instrument score (a sum of the individual item ratings) is considered to be an index of the general disposition to experience anger and has been used in psychotherapy research for pre- and post-treatment measures of subjects' anger reactions (Novaco, 1975). A review of anger self-report instruments can be found in Biaggio (1980).

The Novaco Provocation Inventory was used to assess levels of reported anger in recruit training which were then examined for their relationship to performance and adjustment measures taken during training and after graduation in a longitudinal analysis. The NPI was administered to a cohort sample of Marine Corps recruits on the the first day of processing at the training base in San Diego, California.

Participants were escorted to the testing area by training personnel, who then left for the duration of the testing session. Subjects were informed that individual scoring information was not accessible to training personnel, nor would it become part of any military record. The voluntary nature of participation was emphasized, and recruits who elected to participate (approximately 93%) signed a consent form. A total of 392 completed the anger inventory.

Pursuing our ideas about anger determinants, we proceeded to group or categorize the provocation events which comprise the NPI, sorting items on an a priori basis into classes of events. Seven such categories were identified: (1) Irritating, Annoying, Inconsiderate or Rude Behavior of Others (25 items); (2) Humiliation or Verbal Insult (11 items); (3) Personal Injustice or Unfairness (12 items); (4) Social Injustice (8 items); (5) Frustration (12 items); (6) Personal Clumsiness (6 items); and (7) Physical Assault to one's self or property (6 items). Both authors independently sorted items into these categories resulting in a 93.75% rate of agreement concerning scale membership.

In addition to the seven scales created by sorting items a priori into categories, the NPI data was factor analyzed. Principal axis factoring resulted in the selection of five factors for rotation to a terminal solution, employing a normalized varimax criterion of simple structure. Our strategy here was to view the structures identified by this procedure as merely heuristic (Kim & Mueller, 1978) such that specific factor score coefficients were ignored. The factor-based subscales were constructed by summing Z-scores for items with loading coefficients greater than .35 on the first two factors, which accounted for 40% of the variance in the instrument. The first factor converged closely with the a priori category of Physical Assault, plus other items describing tangible or operant obstruction. The second factor consisted of ten of the eleven items sorted a priori into the Humiliation or Verbal Insult category and an additional item. Taken together, these items pertain to social or interpersonal devaluation.

In addition to the NPI and several psychological protocols related to stress and cognition, the recruits' home town size, level of education, race, birth order, family background, and ratings of the quality of home life and school experience were obtained. Performance data consisting of rifle marksmanship score, physical fitness test, and oral and written tests of military knowledge were obtained from regimental archives according to platoon rosters. Also, ratings were performed by each senior drill instructor for all recruits in his platoon on the dimensions of motivation, cooperation, intelligence, and overall performance at the time of recruit graduation. In addition, as part of a longitudinal study with this recruit cohort, follow-up performance ratings were obtained from commanding officers two and one-half years after graduation.

NPI Subscale Scores and Demographic/Background Variables. To assess pretraining differences in reported anger based upon the demographic characteristics of the recruit sample, analyses of variance and product-moment correlations were computed. Correlational analyses were conducted for the recruit's age, weight, height, and assessments of the quality of home life and school experience. Analyses of variance were computed on the basis of categorical variables denoting high school graduation status, contact sports experience, parental caretaker, race, birth order, and the size of the recruit's home town.

237

The correlational analyses revealed few significant relationships. Age was found to have a low magnitude, inverse association (-.09 to -.23) across subscales. No significant relationships emerged between NPI subscales and the recruits' height, weight, and ratings of the quality of home life and school experiences. The analyses of variance indicated that anger scores were unrelated to contact sports experience or to birth order. However, a consistent pattern of significant differences emerged according to race. Across each category of provocation events, black recruits were found to report the least anger, while the highest level of anger was reported by the "other" racial category (including Orientals and American Indians, but predominantly Chicano recruits in this sample). The mean level of anger reported by caucasian recruits was intermediate to these other racial groupings. This effect was statistically significant ($p < .05$) on virtually all NPI subscales, except for Physical Assault. It was also found that individuals raised by their fathers or a relative other than their mothers had higher anger scores than those raised by either both parents or by their mothers.

NPI Subscale Scores and Recruit Attrition. Training outcome for this sample was categorized according to whether the recruits graduated (N=330), attrited for psychological/behavioral reasons (N=22), attrited for medical reasons (N=24), or for other reasons (N=8). For level of anger at the start of training, graduates and psychological/behavioral attriters did not differ significantly across subscales, although the anger scores were higher for the latter group on each scale except "physical assault". Recruits discharged for medical reasons, however, obtained significantly lower scores than graduates on the subscales of "frustration," "personal clumsiness," "physical assault to self or property," and on the factor based scale of physical provocations (p's < .03).

Pursuing the anger differences reported for race, we then conducted two-way analyses of variance with training outcome category and race (Caucasian, Black, Other) as grouping factors. A statistically significant interaction effect was obtained for these factors on each NPI subscale, although low cell sizes for the "Black" and "Other" racial groups in both the medical and psychological attrition categories limited these analyses. For each subscale, however, the interaction effect was found to be attributable to extremely low levels of anger reported by black medical attriters. The mean subscale scores in this cell were uniformly greater than one standard deviation below the mean for the entire sample. Furthermore, when the means for black graduating recruits were contrasted with the means for black medical attriters, highly significant differences were obtained, F's (1,77) from 4.5 to 16.6, p's < .037 to .0001. No significant differences in levels of reported anger were found to distinguish caucasian medical attriters from graduates.

238

These findings are reminiscent of the research by Harburg and his associates concerning the relationship between one's style of coping with anger and blood pressure. In their Detroit Area project, they found that black men in high stress areas who were characterized by suppressed hostility (keeping their anger in when provoked and feeling guilty if their anger was expressed) had the highest average blood pressures and the highest percentage of hypertensives (95+ mm diastolic) in the sample (Harburg, Erfurt, Hauenstein, Chape, Schull & Schork, 1973). The Harburg et al., data indicate that approximately 10-20% of their subjects reported a suppressed hostility response to hypothetical provocations, which is consistent with the ratio of recruits in our sample reporting very low anger to those with NPI scores closer to the mean. Whether other similarities exist between these findings will be clarified by future research. Certainly the relationship between anger, racial extraction, and health outcomes merits further attention in the military context. It may in fact be a matter of special significance for drill instructors, about whom we are currently conducting longitudinal studies of stress.

NPI Subscale Scores and Performance. Correlations of the anger subscales with training performance measures for graduating recruits resulted in a few significant but low magnitude inverse coefficients (.-11 to -.17) with physical fitness test scores and with drill instructor ratings of recruits. Higher anger scores on several scales (with the exception of anger toward physical provocation) were associated with lower performance, particularly with regard to ratings of recruit motivation. No significant interactions resulted when race was introduced as an additional factor.

The most intriguing findings were obtained in the longitudinal follow-up of graduating recruits. Here, commanding officers provided evaluative ratings of those in our sample still on active duty two and one-half years after graduation. We have achieved a 70% return rate for these mailed questionnaires. In order to assess the relationship of individual differences in anger on the first day of training to the longitudinal follow-up measure, median splits were made on each NPI subscale distribution. This created a grouping factor of high versus low anger levels that was used to analyze the variance in commanding officer ratings, as well as the subject's self report data. The principal finding is that those recruits who, based on pre-training response, were classified as high in anger for Physical Assault provocations received higher performance evaluations in the follow-up. Those scoring high in anger on this subscale were rated by their commanding officers as more desirable members of their units ($p < .001$), and as superior in military proficiency ($p < .001$), conduct ($p < .008$), and physical fitness ($p < .01$). Similarly, these men were rated as significantly better than low anger Marines on the dimensions of motivation, leadership,

239

and overall performance (all p's < .03). Marines who rated physical assault events as highly anger inducing also rated recruit training retrospectively as a more valuable experience and indicated more satisfaction with and liking for life in the Marine Corps (all p's < .02) High anger Marines also characterized themselves as more cheerful (p < .005), and less sad (p < .001) and were more optimistic about the future of the United States of America (p < .002) than Marines with low scores on the physical assault subscale.

These findings strongly suggest that those who are highly aroused to anger by physical assault provocations attain a greater degree of fit with the Marine Corps organization. In view of these results, we then examined whether changes in anger over the course of recruit training were linked with training unit conditions that we had previously found to be associated with the performance of training personnel (drill instructors).

Anger Change in Recruit Training. We have conceptualized recruit training as a process of exposure to military demands while learning the skills necessary to perform effectively under the stressful conditions associated with attaining military combat objectives. However, the stress in training has at least two sources: (1) the standards of the Marine Corps and (2) the manner in which the drill instructor team implements the training regimen to achieve these standards. Extensive analyses (Novaco et al., 1979; Sarason et al., 1981) clearly indicate that platoon attrition rates are a valid index of the effectiveness of the drill instructor team--low attrition reflecting better performance. Further analyses of recruit adjustment confirms that low attrition platoons are superior social settings for the development of personal abilities and stress coping proficiencies.

In view of the follow-up results and to learn more about the social environments of platoons distinguished by different rates of attrition, changes in anger level across the span of training were monitored in high and low attrition training units. Low attrition platoons were found to be characterized by increases in the level of anger (overall NPI score), while recruits in high attrition platoons varied little in reported anger across training. The decomposition of this effect by race revealed similar mean anger gains for black and caucasian recruits in low attrition platoons (approximately 1/2 standard deviation), and no appreciable change for either black or caucasian recruits in high attrition training units.

Thus, although recruit training is frequently thought to amplify the level of anger among recruits, it appears as though this effect occurs differentially with respect to characteristics of the platoon environment. The specification of the characteristics of the drill instructor team which are

associated with anger gains and the elucidation of the relationship between this phenomenon and the platoon rate of attrition are tasks for future research.

SUMMARY AND CONCLUSIONS

In this chapter we have established the role of anger in
the larger theoretical framework of human stress. Describing
anger as an affective response to stress, we illustrated the
utility of the stress framework to identify the range of circumstances that engender anger in a military context. With
regard to combat, we noted that despite technically advanced
weapons, individual initiative and energized aggressive behavior are prerequisite to successful action. While anger
indeed has a salient role in warfare, the effective combatant
is motivated less by the opportunity to express pent-up hostility than by group identification and emotional ties to his
comrades. We noted that variations in the context of warfare
in recent history have produced concomitant variation in the
anger and aggression components of combat stress. Delayed
responses to the stress of conflict in Vietnam have frequently
involved anger ranging from states of chronic irritability to
incidents of explosive rage. We next examined the stress
inducing organizational conditions linked to the elicitation
of anger and aggression in the military outside of combat.
In this regard, we identified task based, role-based, and
interpersonal conflict sources of stress. Finally, we presented some of the results from our empirical research in
the recruit training setting.

Psychological formulations of stress emphasize the role
of the perceived environment. In this regard, the arousal of
anger is mediated by expectations and cognitive appraisal
processes. Thus, there is no direct relationship between
external events and anger. When stressful circumstances of
the physical or social environment engender anger or aggression, these responses may be viewed as maladaptive attempts
at coping. We have emphasized that anger must be understood
in terms of contextual conditions. Long term exposure to
many of the stressful conditions intrinsic to the military
setting which we have outlined in this chapter may contribute
to arousal, thus potentiating the appraisal of more immediate
and identifiable provoking events in terms of anger. The
stress framework is indispensible here to provide theoretical
guidelines for the analysis of contextual factors and to
identify predisposing characteristics of the individual which
interact to comprise determinants of anger and aggression.
We are presently engaged in empirical work of this nature and
with the development of interventions designed to amplify the
coping proficiencies of U.S. Marine Corps recruits and training personnel. Clearly, additional research is also necessary
to establish empirically the links between organizational

241

characteristics and individual affective responses. Such research has specific relevance to the well-being of military personnel and to organizational functioning. This point has particular salience with regard to the relationship between anger and aggression and psychologically related health disturbances such as cardiovascular disorders. In addition, the occurrence of anger and aggression associated with interpersonal conflict among military personnel and between them and civilians has implications for performance and career success. Interventions designed to impart coping proficiencies and anger control are important to those in demanding duty assignments (e.g., drill instructors) who may tend to displace pent-up frustrations and hostilities onto family members, leading to domestic problems. The military organization is one in which decision making processes can frustrate those who must implement policies that they feel powerless to change. Those who feel highly constrained may cope with their frustrations similarly by displacing anger toward "safe" targets.

Our concern with interventions has lead us to scrutinize the very fabric of Marine Corps training. One of the primary purposes is to provide the recruit with the skills needed to confront and defeat an armed opponent. The recruit is trained to acquire the physical skills and the confidence to engage in a hostile situation and to win. While discipline and self-control are emphasized, attention in this regard is focused on observable response patterns rather than on internal processes. Virtually no attention is given to the self-regulation of internal states of arousal and emotion. However, high levels of activation and aggressive response patterns are clearly instrumental for achieving certain goals in the military. It may thus be particularly important that the person effectively discriminate the circumstances in which energized, aggressive responses are adaptive from those where alternative problem-solving strategies are advisable. Instances of spouse abuse, child abuse, and brawling could be viewed as resulting from an overgeneralized use of confrontative, coercive tactics.

The theoretical section of this chapter presented anger as a coping response. In particular, persons who are prone to provocation can be viewed as relying on anger as a way of coping with stress. Anger becomes a way of exerting control over environmental circumstances that are experienced as thwarting, constraining, annoying, or debilitating. In the military organization, considerable emphasis is placed upon responsibility and accountability on the part of unit leaders. Those in leadership roles can in fact become preoccupied with maintaining a firm control over unit members and activities. Given the "aggressive ambience" present in the Marine Corps in legitimized, functional forms, the question arises as to whether the prepotent anger/aggressive responses are activated by some leaders as a way of exercising control and if so, at

242

what cost to unit and organizational performance? While
leaders are unlikely to physically assault those under their
command, they do have the capacity to administer punishment
in a variety of forms. The use of punitive strategies to
regulate the behavior of unit members may be related to anger
arising from the perceived threat of "loss of control" (e.g.,
"Sir, this son-of-a-bitch deserves to have the book thrown at
him. I can't handle him any longer;" or "Sir, if you don't
do something to teach him a lesson, I'm afraid of what I
might do."). The leader's degree of reliance on anger/aggres-
sive strategies for achieving control may be related to various unit performance indices, rates of desertion or unauthor-
ized absences, and rates of attrition from the organization.

REFERENCES

Andreski, S. Military organization and society. Los Angeles:
    University of California Press, 1968.
Arkin, W., & Dobrofsky, L.R. Military socialization and
    masculinity. Journal of Social Issues, 1978, 34, 151-
    168.
Balson, P.M., & Dempster, C.R. Treatment of war neuroses
    from Vietnam. Comprehensive Psychiatry, 1980, 21,
    167-175.
Barber, J.A. The social effects of military service. In S.E.
    Ambrose & J.A. Barber (Eds.), The military and American
    society: Essays and readings. New York: The Free
    Press, 1972.
Barnes, P. Pawns: The plight of the citizen-soldier. New
    York: Alfred A. Knopf, 1972.
Biaggio, M.K. Assessment of anger arousal. Journal of
    Personality Assessment, 1980, 44, 289-298.
Bobrow, D.B. Adaptive politics, social learning, and military
    institution. In M.R. Van Gils (Ed.), The perceived role
    of the military. Rotterdam: Rotterdam University Press,
    1971.
Bourne, P.G. Some observations on the psychosocial phenomena
    seen in basic training. Psychiatry, 1967, 30, 187-196.
Bourne, P.G. The psychology and physiology of stress. New
    York: Academic Press, 1969.
Bourne, P.G. Men, stress, and Vietnam. Boston: Little,
    Brown, & Company, 1970.
Brende, J.O., & Benedict, B.D. The Vietnam combat delayed
    stress response syndrome: Hypnotherapy of "dissociative
    symptoms". The American Journal of Clinical Hypnosis,
    1980, 23, 34-40.
Buss, A.H., & Durkee, A. An inventory for assessing different
    kinds of hostility. Journal of Consulting Psychology,
    1957, 21, 344-349.

Cooper, C.L., & Payne, R. (Eds.). Stress at work. New York: John Wiley & Sons, 1978.

Cooper, C.L., & Payne, R. (Eds.). Current concerns in occupational stress. New York: John Wiley & Sons, 1980.

Cortright, D. Soldiers in revolt: The American military today. Garden City: Anchor Press/Doubleday, 1975.

DeFazio, V.J. Dynamic perspectives on the nature and effects of combat stress. In C.R. Figley (Ed.), Stress disorders among Vietnam veterans: Theory, research and treatment. New York: Brunner/Mazel, 1978.

DeFazio, V.J., Rustin, S., & Diamond, A. Symptom development in Vietnam era veterans. American Journal of Orthopsychiatry, 1975, 45, 158-163.

Endler, N.S., & Hunt, J.M. S-R inventories of hostility and comparisons of the proportions of variance from persons, responses, and situations for hostility and anxiousness. Journal of Personality and Social Psychology, 1968, 9, 309-315.

Feld, M.D. Professionalism and politicalization: Notes on the military and civilian control. In M.R. Van Gils (Ed.), The perceived role of the military. Rotterdam: Rotterdam University Press, 1971.

Figley, C.R. (Ed.), Stress disorders among Vietnam veterans: Theory, research and treatment. New York: Brunner/Mazel, 1978. (a)

Figley, C.R. Psychosocial adjustment among Vietnam veterans: An overview of the research. In C.R. Figley (Ed.), Stress disorders among Vietnam veterans: Theory, research and treatment. New York: Brunner/Mazel, 1978. (b)

Figley, C.R. Symptoms of delayed combat stress among a college sample of Vietnam veterans. Military Medicine, 1978, 143, 107-110. (c)

Figley, C.R., & Eisenhart, W. Contrasts between combat/noncombat Vietnam veterans regarding selected indices of interpersonal adjustment. Paper presented at the annual meeting of the American Sociological Association. San Francisco, 1975.

Funkenstein, D.H., King, S.H., & Drolette, M.E. Mastery of stress. Cambridge: Harvard University Press, 1957.

Ginzberg, E. The lost divisions. New York: Columbia University Press, 1959.

Glick, E.B. Soldiers, scholars, and society: The social impact of the American military. Pacific Palisades, CA: Goodyear Publishing Company, Inc., 1971.

Grinker, R.R., & Spiegel, J.P. Men under stress. Philadelphia: Blakiston, 1945.

Gross, E. Work, organization, and stress. In S. Levine & N.A. Scotch (Eds.), Social stress. Chicago: Aldine Publishing Company, 1970.

Harburg, E., Erfurt, J.C., Hauenstien, L.S., Chape, C.,
    Schull, W.J., & Schork, N.A. Socio-ecological stress,
    suppressed hostility, skin color, and black-white blood
    pressure: Detroit. Psychosomatic Medicine, 1973, 35,
    276-296.
Hauser, W.L. America's army in crisis: A study in civil-
    military relations. Baltimore: The Johns Hopkins
    University Press, 1973.
Horowitz, M.J., & Solomon, G.F. A prediction of delayed
    stress response syndromes in Vietnam veterans. Journal
    of Social Issues, 1975, 31, 67-80.
Janowitz, M. Sociology and the military establishment. New
    York: Russell Sage Foundation, 1959.
Janowitz, M. The professional soldier: A social and political
    portrait. Glencoe, IL: The Free Press, 1960.
Janowitz, M. Military conflict: Essays in the institutional
    analysis of war and peace. Beverly Hills: Sage Publica-
    tions, 1975.
Kahn, R.L., Wolfe, D.M., Snoek, J.E., & Rosenthal, R.A.
    Organizational stress: Studies in role conflict and
    ambiguity. New York: Wiley, 1964.
Kardiner, A., & Spiegel, H. War stress and neurotic illness.
    New York: Paul B. Hoeber, Inc., 1947.
Karsten, P. Soldiers and society: The effects of military
    service and war on American life. Westport: Greenwood
    Press, 1978.
Kim, J., & Mueller, C.W. Introduction to factor analysis.
    Beverly Hills: Sage Publications, 1978, 13.
Konecni, V.J. Annoyance, type and duration of postannoyance
    activity, and aggression: The "Cathartic Effect."
    Journal of Experimental Psychology, 1975, 104, 76-102.
Konecni, V.J. The role of aversive events in the development
    of intergroup conflict. In W.G. Austin and S. Worchel
    (Eds.), The psychology of intergroup relations. Monterey:
    Brooks/Cole, 1977.
Lang, K. Military institutions and the sociology of war:
    A review of the literature with annotated bibliography.
    Beverly Hills: Sage Publications, 1972.
Lawler, E.E. Motivation in work organizations. Monterey:
    Brooks/Cole Publishing Company, 1973.
Lazarus, R.S. Psychological stress and the coping process.
    New York: McGraw-Hill, 1966.
Marshall, S.L.A. Men against fire. New York: William Morrow
    and Co., 1947.
Meichenbaum, D. A self-instructional approach to stress
    management: A proposal for stress inoculation training.
    In C. Speilberger and I. Sarason (Eds.), Stress and
    anxiety (Vol. 2). New York: Wiley, 1975.
Merbaum, M., & Hefez, A. Some personality characteristics
    of soldiers exposed to extreme war stress. Journal of
    Consulting and Clinical Psychology, 1976, 44, 1-6.
Merton, R.K. Social theory and social structure. New York:
    Free Press, 1968.

Moskos, C.C. The American enlisted man: The rank and file in today's military. New York: Russell Sage Foundation, 1970.

Novaco, R.W. Anger control: The development and evaluation of an experimental treatment. Lexington: D.C. Heath, Levington Books, 1975.

Novaco, R.W. The function and regulation of the arousal of anger. American Journal of Psychiatry, 1976, 133, 1124-1128.

Novaco, R.W. Stress inoculation: A cognitive therapy for anger and its application to a case of depression. Journal of Consulting and Clinical Psychology, 1977, 45, 600-608.

Novaco, R.W. The cognitive regulation of anger and stress. In P. Kendall and S. Hollon (Eds.), Cognitive behavioral interventions. New York: Academic Press, 1979.

Novaco, R.W., Cook, T.M., & Sarason, I.G. Military recruit training: An arena for stress coping skills. In D. Meichenbaum & M. Jaremko (Eds.), Stress reduction and prevention. New York: Plenum Press, 1982.

Novaco, R.W., Sarason, I.G., Cook, T.M., Robinson, G.L., & Cunningham, F.J. Psychological and organizational factors related to attrition and performance in Marine Corps recruit training (AR-001). Seattle: University of Washington, November, 1979.

Novaco, R.W., Sarason, I.G., Robinson, G.L., & Cunningham, F.J. Longitudinal analysis of stress and performance among Marine Corps drill instructors (AR-ONR-007). Seattle: University of Washington, April, 1982.

O'Neill, W.F., & Demos, G.D. Education under duress. Los Angeles: LDI Books, 1971.

Opton, F.M., & Sanford, N. Lessons of My Lai. In M. Oppenheimer (Ed.), The American military. Chicago: Aldine Publishing Company, 1971.

Pavlov, I.P. Lectures on conditional reflexes: The higher nervous activity (behavior of animals) (Vol. 1). London: Lawrence and Winshart, 1928.

Perlmutter, A. The military and politics in modern times: On professionals, praetorians, and revolutionary soldiers. New Haven: Yale University Press, 1977.

Poe, R.O., Rose, R.M., & Mason, J.W. Multiple determinants of 17-hydroxycorticosteroid excretion in recruits during basic training. Psychosomatic Medicine, 1970, 32, 369-378.

Sarason, I.G., Novaco, R.W., Robinson, G.L., and Cook. T.M. Recruit attrition and the training unit environment (AR-004). Washington: University of Washington, April, 1981.

Scott, J.W. ROTC retreat. In M. Oppenheimer (Ed.), The American military. Chicago: Aldine Publishing Company, 1971.

Shatan, C.F. Stress disorders among Vietnam veterans:
    The emotional content of combat continues. In C.R.
    Figley (Ed.), Stress disorders among Vietnam veterans:
    Theory, research and treatment. New York: Brunner/
    Mazel, 1978.
Shils, E.A., & Janowitz, M. Cohesion and disintegration in
    the Wehrmacht in World War II. Public Opinion Quarterly,
    1948, 12, 280-315.
Stouffer, S.A., et al. The American soldier (Vol. 1).
    Combat and its aftermath (Vol. 2). Princeton: Princeton
    University Press, 1949.
Van Doorn, J. The soldier and social change: Comparative
    studies in the history and sociology of the military.
    Beverly Hills: Sage Publications, 1975.
Voors, A.W., Stewart, G.T., Gutenkunst, R.R., Moldow, C.F., &
    Jenkins, C.D. Respiratory infection in Marine recruits.
    American Review of Respiratory Disease, 1968, 98, 801-809.
Walton, G. The tarnished shield: A report on today's army.
    New York: Dodd, Mead & Company, 1973.
Yarmolinsky, A. The military establishment. New York:
    Harper and Row, 1971.
Zillman, D. Excitation transfer in communication-mediated
    aggressive behavior. Journal of Experimental Social
    Psychology, 1971, 7, 419-434.

IV. MASS MEDIA EFFECTS AND EPIDEMIOLOGICAL APPROACHES

TOWARDS A RENEWED PARADIGM IN MOVIE VIOLENCE RESEARCH*

J.-P. Leyens, G. Herman and M. Dunand

Universite Catholique De Louvain, Belgium

...The way in which communication is transmitted in various types of social structure is an obvious example where the individual and the group are interdependent.

C. Hovland, 1951

The interest in aggressive behavioral effects of filmed violence started with two great American researchers. We all know them: Bandura and Berkowitz. However, neither were interested, at least in the beginning, in the effects of filmed violence per se. Bandura was studying imitation, especially aggressive imita-tion; and the use of a videotaped model was a more economical and methodologically sound solution than a "live" model. Because there was no difference of effect between these two kinds of model, a new paradigm for studying the influence of filmed violence was created. As it arose within the framework of "social learning theory", it is no surprise that all the variables which have subsequently been investigated have concerned learning (rein-forcements, generalizations, etc.). Berkowitz, on the other hand, was revising the old frustration-aggression hypothesis. He insisted on the presence of stimuli associated with violence; and aggressive films were precisely such stimuli. Again, it is not surprising that the factors studied in this tradition were con-cerned with their power to elicit more or less aggression (the

---

* Abridged version of a chapter published in P. Stringer (Ed.), Confronting Social Issues: Applications of Social Psychology. London: Academic Press, 1981. Copyright 1981 by Academic Press. Reprinted by permission of the publisher.

248

Kaplan, R.M., Konečni, V.J., Novaco, R.W. (eds.) Aggression in Children and Youth
© 1984, Martinus Nijhoff Publishers, The Hague/Boston/Lancaster
ISBN 90-247-2903-3. Printed in The Netherlands

meaning of the films, the moral justification, the anxiety provoked by the films, etc.).

Both the researchers and their followers immediately saw the
implications of their experiments for the mass media violence
problem. Data were accumulated which showed that, under given
conditions, aggressive films enhance, rather than decrease or fail
to modify, the aggressive behaviors of viewers. But criticisms
emerged, mainly from people in the television industry and in
departments of communication. In general these criticisms were
directed at: (1) the use of artificial films, (2) the unnatural
setting of the laboratory and (3) the dubious validity of the
means of measuring aggression.

At a time when relevance was fashionable if not compulsory in
the American universities, experimenters answered these criticisms
in the following way. They went to the field, to natural life
settings, and showed regular commercial movies or television programs to subjects--mainly children and adolescents--whose aggressive behaviors were observed in various ways. One study (Feshbach
and Singer, 1971) found a decrease in aggression for some subjects
in the violent treatment. [1]Another one (Milgram and Shotland,
1973) did not find any effect[1]. While the results of yet other
field experiments (Goldstein et al., 1975; Leyens et al., 1975;
Parke et al., 1977; Stein & Friedrich, 1972; Steuer et al., 1971)
were, in general, identical to those found in the laboratory:
violent films or television programs increased the aggressive
behaviors of the viewers, especially of those who were usually
aggressive.

The conclusion of this stream of research seemed self-
evident: because ofthe results obtained in the laboratory and in
the field coverage, the problem is exhausted. Why not look at
another problem? And indeed one notices that during the past few
years there have been scarcely any papers on the topic in major
social psychological journals. But we do not accept that conclusion. On the contrary we think that many aspects of the effects
of mass media violence still need to be investigated. We know
that such violence can have an effect upon viewers. Sometimes,
researchers have found how this effect comes about, at a psychological level. But they have scarcely ever tried to answer the
"how" question in terms of social variable.

This neglect has its origin in the theoretical issues (social
learning and frustration-aggression) which led to the studies and
to the experimental paradigms used in the laboratory: a single
subject confronting a given film and just one confederate and/or
experimenter whose behavior is carefully programmed. Going into
the field did not reverse the perspective. Actually, when experimenters left the laboratory for the field, they did not change
their approach very much. They merely made slight modifications
to the independent and dependent variable. Overall the paradigm
was borrowed from the laboratory. The films are still considered
as the only source of influence, individuals are taken as the unit

of analysis and, if they are distinguished, it is done according to their base-line aggressive behavior. This last variable also reflects the laboratory situation in which subjects are made angry or not. Such an approach neglects the fact that individuals exposed to different treatments belong to particular groups which have their own dynamics. These dynamics may have an effect on their reaction to the films. Moreover, within the groups, members are not equivalent and they do interact while the independent and dependent variables are taking place. These two factors may also influence reactions to the treatment[2]. The wholesale transference of the approach from the laboratory to the field seems to us an obvious demonstration that researchers were holding firmly on to their basic assumption that all subjects are directly and immediately, rather than indirectly and in a mediated fashion, influenced by the violent films to which they have just been exposed. Among other things, such an assumption implies that each individual becomes a duplicate of any other individual and that the total audience is reduced to the sum of separate and equivalent units.

As long as the research was concerned with imitation (as a special case of social learning) and with the frustration-aggression hypothesis per se, that assumption of direct and immediate influence may indeed have been a useful one. But when studies are concerned with the effects of filmed violence as such, it seems to us that this assumption is actually harmful. Viewing a film or a television program does not occur in a social vacuum. We rarely go to a cinema alone; we very seldomly watch television without companions (Maccoby, 1951). We belong to reference groups (Riley & Riley, 1951), we read newspapers, we sometimes discuss a program beforehand, while it is on or afterwards (Codol, 1967); we see and hear the reactions of other viewers during a screening (Rabbie, 1978); and so on. Why not now systematically study the impact of such social factors, which make the social context of viewing and which may elucidate the real dynamics of influence? Why not take the example of Katz and Lazarsfeld (1955) who did not restrict their study to the mere characteristics of senders, receivers and messages, but investigated the interrelationship between the three in real-life settings and discovered the multi-steps flow of communication?

These ideas occurred to us at the completion of our own field study (Leyens et al., 1975). We were looking at the effects of repeated exposure to filmed violence upon the behaviors of secondary school boys who were institutionalized because of inadequate home care or behavioral problems. These boys belonged to four rather autonomous cottages. Observations about their aggressive, active and interactive behaviors lasted for three weeks: a pre-film week, a film week (every evening members of two cottages saw a violent commercial film, while the others viewed comedies) and a post-film week. They were made during the midday and evening reactional periods while the members of each cottage interacted with their group. Additional individual and group measures were taken: cohesion and dominance conflicts in the cottages, status of dominance, popularity and usual aggressiveness of individuals within each cottage. Overall the violent films had an effect upon the viewers' aggressive behavior; but some groups (cottages) were more influenced than others. Why? Some subgroups within a cottage (the most aggressive, dominant and popular) were more affected by the filmed violence than others. Why? All subgroups did not react at the same time. Why? As Parke et al. (1977) wrote in the conclusion to this study and other similar ones conducted in the United States: "It is not only the stimulus side that needs more attention. The contexts in which our behavioral measures are obtained need careful study as well if we are not only to predict but even to understand the effects of movie violence in naturalistic settings".

We therefore suggest that a renewed paradigm[3] to investigate such effects should encompass the study of the social context of viewing. Nothing, however, can be more general than this proposal. How should one proceed? Given the seminal work of Lazarsfeld, Berelson, Merton and others, an obvious solution would be to follow the example of sociologists. However, they do not seem to be better off than social psychologists. In the 1951 autumn issue of the "Public Opinion Quarterly", the Rileys wrote:
"It is our conviction that sociological theory is now far enough developed to throw a great deal of light on the selection of media and programs, the interpretation of media messages, and the nature and extent of media influence. At the same time, however, operational techniques have lagged far behind this theoretical development."
The same claim is rephrased in 1953 by Freidson:
"Relatively little research has centered on the relation of social setting to the reception of mass communications."
Twenty-five years have passed since then, but it seems that the problem remains; according to the Edgars (1971),
"Perhaps the most serious of these gaps is the omission of the wider social context in which viewing takes place. The child watching a violent program is usually considered a completely privatized being, isolated before a staring eye that provides dangerous stimuli. Data on the number of hours spent watching television are not modified by considering who watches with the child, what discussion follows, whether the child ignores or rejects values and behavior not reinforced in his normal circles of interaction, and so on. What appears needed is an integration of mass media research with sound sociological theory."
Assuredly, it would be a Promethean task to take into account the whole social context at once. Therefore the rest of this chapter will be devoted to several lines of research which our laboratory has been developing in recent years.

DECENTRATION AND FOCUS ON AESTHETIC QUALITIES

According to Koriat et al. (1972) involvement is the most natural reaction immediately available to the spectators of a film. The social context, however, can alter that spontaneous involvement. Individuals may be trained to look at special features of the film, rather than to restrict themselves to the raw story. A newspaper report may guide their attention towards specific characteristics of the film, and so on. We refer to that phenomenon as decentration. By that we mean a process whereby the spectator of a particular film distances himself from the immediately available content of the film, and changes the probability of occurrence of the usual modal responses by altering the traditionally controlling variables. The focus is still on the film, but on the "mediate" rather than on the exclusively "immediate" content. Decentrated viewers are not asked to neglect the film which they are watching, nor to perform another task completely apart from the film. The induction of decentration simply changes the usual context of viewing, giving the viewers another frame of reference from which to evaluate what they see. For example, spectators may be induced to enlarge their attention from the development of the plot and the film's characters (the usual centration on the immediate content) to other aspects which previously were not always taken into account (decentration) such as the aesthetic value of the film, technical qualities, the Weltanschauung of the director, and so on.

Depending upon the type of decentration and the nature of the stimulus-film, it is assumed that not only the viewers' overt behavior (e.g., aggression) after the film be modified, but so also will such mediating variables as the meaning of the film stimuli, the arousal of the spectators and their identification with the hero.

To control the variables as closely as possible in the first series of experiments, we restricted the operationalization of the decentration process to a focus on aesthetic qualities which might be attributed to aggressive slides.

Cisneros et al. (1974) were particularly interested in the change of meaning of the stimuli. According to Gestalt principles, we expected that decentration would influence the immediate or usual meaning of the filmed stimuli. Indirect support for such a hypothesis is found in studies of coping processes conducted by Lazarus and his colleagues. Lazarus and Alfert (1964), for instance, showed their subjects a film depicting ritual ceremony of very painful subincisions of the penis in an aborginal tribe. While the film was usually interpreted as anxiety-provoking, an orienting commentary denying the depicted suffering (e.g., "Think of the joyful experience of the adolescents who are being initiated into manhood") changed the meaning of the film accordingly. In the Cisneros et al. (1974) study, 44 Belgian military recruits were exposed to either aggressive or neutral slides. About half of these soldiers had been trained to look at the aesthetic qualities of the slides, while the remainder received no training or special instructions.

The hypothesis was validated. The semantic differential questionnaire which was administered immediately after the projection showed a change in the meaning of the aggressive slides. Compared to the others, subjects who had been submitted to the decentration training rated the weapons as significantly slower, weaker, better, less violent, less aggressive, less wicked and more familiar.

In a subsequent study, special attention was paid to aggressive reactions after the projection (Leyens et al., 1976). Forty-eight Belgian French-speaking military recruits participated in the experiment, 12 in each of the four experimental conditions. Two of these groups were shown, either aggressive or neutral slides without special instructions. The third group saw only aggressive slides, under decentration instructions (focus on the aesthetic quality of the slides), while the subjects in the fourth condition had to accomplish a subsidiary task (to give associations to the objects depicted on the slides). This last condition was a control for the effect of the intellectual task implied by the decentration; but, for the subsidiary task, attention was focused only on the immediate content. After the projection, all subjects were insulted by a partner and had to decide on the intensity (from 0 to 100) of electric shocks which they wanted to give him.

As can be seen in Fig. 1, the results were clear-cut. First, the "weapons effect" (Leyens & Parke, 1975) was replicated in the no-decentration aggressive slides condition. Secondly, decentrated subjects were no more violent than those who saw neutral slides. Apparently, this result cannot be attributed to the effect of an additional "intellectual" task upon aggressive behavior, because the reactions in the subsidiary task condition did not differ from those in the no-decentration aggressive slides condition.

Obviously many practical questions are raised by the process of decentration. Although decentration did not reduce aggression in the experiment just mentioned, this may not always be the case. What are the exact characteristics of decentration which can elicit a decrease or an increase in aggressive meaning and behavior? Does decentration training have long-term effects; is it transferrable from one film to another (whether similar or dissimilar); is it restricted to some individuals or is everyone capable of being decentrated; and so on?

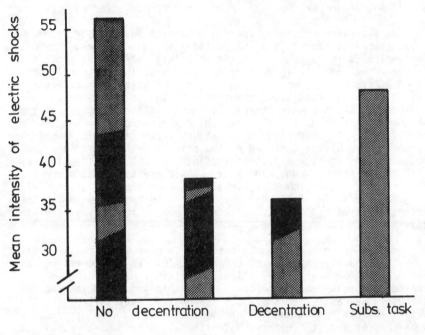

Certainly all these questions are important, especially in the light of potential applications of experimental social psychology. Unfortunately our population in the Army and at the University became so familiar with our topic of research that we had temporarily to interrupt the program. As our next population, we chose very young children in the hope--fulfilled until now-- that they would remain naive. Because Moscovici (1970) once wrote that the selection of psychological problems to be studied should not be foreign to the characteristics of the social environment, we also altered our subject of concern somewhat. The new program still dealt with social decentration but, this time, the meaning of the term corresponded more precisely to the one coined by Piaget[4].

In one of the very few experiments which took the social context into account, Hicks (1968) showed that public disapproval by adults of filmed violence diminishes the aggressive reactions of children. Similar results have been obtained recently by Horton and Santogrossi (1978). What if, instead of disapproving, the adult were to focus the children's attention on the aggressor's malevolent act, on the consequences for the victim or on alternate courses of action? We assume that this induction of social decentration should increase the empathy of the young viewers and, consequently, should decrease their violent reactions. Other variables, such as their cognitive and moral development, are also being investigated to verify their links with empathy when embedded in the aggressive context. This new line of research has just started, with the collaboration of our colleague in Developmental Psychology, Mrs. Christiane Vandenplas-Holper. At present our hopes for this project are inversely proportional to the amount of data gathered.

PASSIVE AUDIENCE AND SOCIAL DOMINANCE

In the two preceding lines of research, the social context, or the audience, can be considered as very active. On the one hand, the experimenter, acting as a socialization agent, clearly instigated the focus upon aesthetic qualities and, on the other hand, the children trained towards decentration reacted in groups which were heterogenous from the point of view of chronological age and level of moral development. What about the role of a more passive audience?

A few studies (e.g., Balance et al., 1972) have reported that the mere presence of a co-spectator can alter the impact of the message. However, as suggested by the experiment of Leyens et al. (1975), the investigation of the quality of the audience seems a more promising avenue of research[5]. In that field study, the individuals of the cottage most influenced by the violent treatment reacted very differentially. It appeared that the most dominant adolescents reacted more extremely and more rapidly at the beginning of the aggressive-film week than the least dominant ones, who showed a slight increase of aggression only at the end

255

of the film treatment. Our investigation was not aimed at explaining these differences, but several explanations are possible (Parke, 1974). Is it because submissive persons need a greater quantity of aggressive stimuli to provoke a reaction? Is it because the dominant members who "benefitted" from the aggressive films served as secondary models for their submissive partners? Is it because the dominant became such obnoxious boys, as a result of their viewing the aggressive films, that their victims had no other alternative than to retaliate?

Despite its lack of a definite answer, that anecdotal observation enlightened us about the role of the dynamics in the audience upon the one of the influence. As Doob and Macdonald (1979) have shown, the use of television is not indifferent to whether one lives in a peaceful community or in a high-risk section of town. Moreover, the implicit learning from television will be different. Consumers of violent television programs in a dangerous environment will be more afraid of being themselves victimized than will other heavy consumers of television violence who have the luck to live in quiet and peaceful areas.

To study the role of the audience (the most obvious immediate surrounding) we followed the line suggested by the Leyens et al. study. We decided to study the reactions of very young children (4 to 6 years old) who were classified either as very dominant or clearly submissive. The first step of the program included three phases:

(i) To study the differential reactions of dominant and submissive children when tested alone. In order to test systematically the effects of the social context of viewing, it is necessary to control as many as possible of the variables which are involved. Therefore, before investigating the effects of an interaction between dominant and submissive children on the reactions to filmed violence, one should know the reactions of these two categories of spectators when tested alone.

(ii) To study the differential reactions of boys when tested with a companion of the same or different status. Here a distinction is introduced between the mere presence--where a difference of status should not matter--and the specific attributes of the companion--where these same differences are of paramount importance.

(iii) To explain the potential differences noticed in (ii), in ways other than through the independent variables investigated up to now.

In the first study of this series (Leyens et al., in preparation), 4- to 6-year-old boys, elected by their teacher as really dominant or submissive, were viewed alone with a female experimenter on one of the three nine-minute films that we produced for our purposes.

256

(a) <u>real aggression</u>: a dominant boy treats a submissive one badly

(b) <u>neutral aggression</u>: a dominant boy treats a submissive one gently

(c) <u>play aggression</u>: two boys of about the same status play aggressive games

After the projection, all subjects were frustrated by a fictitious partner who did not want them to watch cartoons on his television set. The reaction available to the provoked child was to darken his companion's set by$_6$ pushing one of five buttons (i.e., from clear to completely dark)[6].

Manipulation checks showed that the operationalization of the variables was adequate. More importantly, the three films led to different levels of aggression, the real aggression film inducing the highest level and the neutral one the lowest. This result is particularly marked for the submissive children.   As might be expected, when the film is neutral or when it depicts play aggression, dominant children tend to be more aggressive than submissive children.   However, they do not react very much to the real aggression film. This may be due to a ceiling effect, the most obnoxious button being No. 5 which produces a dark screen for the frustrating peer.

A second experiment attempted to replicate the first set of findings, except that only boys in the third year of pre-school were used and the play aggression film was omitted.

Figure 2 shows the results for the third year pre-school boys in the two experiments.   One can see that the parallelism is excellent. No effect of period is found by analysis of variance; but there is a main effect for the films (F[1.56]=14.8; P<0.001) and one for the status (F[1.56]=13.8; P<0.001), as well as a significant interaction between these two factors (F[1.56]=4.62; P <0.05). As might be expected, the aggressive film leads to more violence than the neutral one and the dominant boys are, in general more aggressive than the submissive ones. Finally, the significant interaction indirectly shows that <u>submissive children do not necessarily need a great amount of aggressive stimulation in order to react violently.</u>   In these two experiments, they were very$_7$sensitive to the aggressive film, even more than the dominant ones[7].

Now, what about the effects of the audience? A third experiment confronted either a pair of submissive-submissive five-year-old boys or a pair of submissive-dominant ones with an invisible and frustrating partner (in the same procedure as before) after they had watched an aggressive or a neutral film.   Several hypotheses are available to account for the reactions of the submissive boy who was to be the first to attack the annoying partner (i.e., before the independently obtained reactions of his submissive or dominant companion)[8].

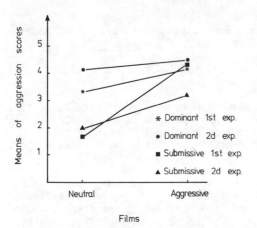

Films

One hypothesis is derived from Zajonc's (1965) social facilitation theory. According to his formulation, the mere presence of
an observer should increase the probability of occurrence of dominant responses. In our context, and on the basis of the first
experiment and of its replication, aggressive and non-aggressive
responses can be considered as the dominant reactions of a submissive child after a violent and peaceful film, respectively. Thus
in terms of Zajonc's hypothesis, lone submissive boys should be
less aggressive than pairs after the neutral film, while they
should be more aggressive after the violent film. In either case,
the status of the co-spectator should have no influence.

In recent years, however, Zajonc's theory has come under
severe criticisms (e.g., Cottrell, 1972). Other hypotheses
predict a differential effect according to the quality of the
audience. One such hypothesis concerns social inhibition. The
presence of a superior peer could diminish the self-concept of a
submissive child who could then inhibit or restrain his spontaneous aggressive reactions. No such process should occur when the
two boys have the same low status, as compared with when they are
viewing alone.

The lack of empirical and theoretical evidence allows a third
hypothesis to be drawn up, exactly opposite to the preceeding one,
i.e., one referring to social disinhibition. The first experiment
and its replication have already shown that, in the presence of a
prestigious and encouraging experimenter, submissive subjects
reacted strongly to the aggressive film. Why could not the submissive child take as his own norm the aggression he perceives to
be present in his dominant peer? After all, there are two of them
(one of them a boss in the class) to counter-attack the unknown
annoying partner. Of course, when the film is neutral, this auda-
city should be lessened: no particular instigation is present.
The same lack of instigation should preside over the conditions
where the two boys are submissive.

258

In other words, the last two hypotheses concerning the quality of the audience predict the same results for the pairs of submissive boys. But the inhibition hypothesis suggests a dimunition of aggression after the violent film on the part of a lone submissive boy accompanied by a more dominant one, while disinhibition hypothesis predicts just the opposite.

The absence of theoretical background and of previous research evidence in the area prevents us from drawing up unequivocal hypotheses. What then are the empirical results?

Zajonc's mere exposure theory is definitely not confirmed. For all analyses, the mere (submissive or dominant) presence of a companion does not modify the aggressive behavior of the submissive subjects.

The picture is strikingly different when one considers the quality of the audience (see Fig. 3). When the film is violent, the companion makes a great difference: the submissive subject accompanied by a dominant peer is significantly more aggressive than one escorted by another submissive subject (for the interaction between films and type of companion, F[1.47]=3.65; P<0.058). In other words, the most instigating condition (in Berkowitz's terms) or the most disinhibitory one (in Bandura's terms) leads to a differential reaction on the part of our submissive subjects which depends upon their comparison.

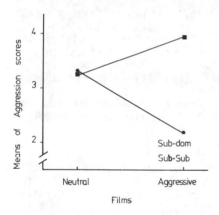

How may one explain these data? How is there such a difference when the film is aggressive and the submissive child has a dominant partner? Is there an illustration of the Marxist statement: a given society's culture is the culture of its dominant class? In other words, do the norms of the dominant boy become also those of the submissive one? Explanations in terms of ideology, disinhibition of instigation seem poor to us; they are par excellence the "deus ex machina". Faithful to Gestalt principles, we would like to use the Q-sort technique recommended recently by Bem and Funder (1978), in order to have an idea of what are the processes followed by the different members in the various situations. Is it not plausible that to have a dominant rather than a submissive companion changes the whole meaning of the setting, the films, the frustrating partner, the punishment, and so on?

In the absence of a grand theory which could encompass all these problems, we are forced to proceed by small steps. Perhaps we do not use a sufficiently large range of small steps in experimental social psychology. This might have some pointers for applied social psychology.

FOOTNOTES

1. Possible methodological deficiencies in the Feshbach and Singer study have been so thoroughly examined elsewhere (e.g., Liebert et al., 1972) that it would be pointless to open the discussion again. On the other hand, the Milgram and Shotland studies probably constitute the best recipe available in the literature on how not to find an effect. Indeed, with the financial aid of a major television company, these authors chose the weakest instigating stimuli they could find and expected these to induce a real delinquent act.

2. The criticisms do not apply to the Milgram and Shotland and the Goldstein et al. studies. Their audiences were constituted by individuals who did not belong to a single existing group.

3. By paradigm, we mean an established way of asking questions and testing hypotheses in a given field. In this sense one speaks of the passive avoidance paradigm, the learned helplessness paradigm, etc. Compared to other possible meanings, this is assuredly a weak one. But let us hope that someday we will be able to write another chapter, entitled: Towards a new paradigmatic theory of movie violence research.

4. For a more detailed account of the notion of decentration and its implications for social development, see Vanderplas-Holper (1979).

5. Borden agrees with us when he writes: "With respect to aggressive behavior (...) the effect of an observer's presence is apparently more a function of who is watching than simply whether or not anyone is watching" (1975, p. 572).

6. The complete report concerning this new "aggression machine" will be presented elsewhere. Let us just say that its validity as an aggression measure is perfectly reliable. We are very grateful to Richard Robert, Paul Thibaut and Bernard Paris who constructed the apparatus.

7. To explain the reaction of the dominant children, we have already suggested a ceiling effect. Another explanation would be that the dominant boys are not accustomed to being annoyed by a peer. Because they resented such frustration so much, the films, aggressive or neutral, may have lost any impact upon them.

8. The data for the second attackers go well beyond our aims in this chapter. We prefer to present them later on in their global context in a paper of a more traditional format.

REFERENCES

Balance, W.D., Coughlin, D. and Bringmann, W.G. (1972). Examination of social context effects upon affective responses to "hot" and "cool" communications media. Psychol. Rep. 31, 793-794.

Borden, R.J. (1975). Witnessed aggression: influence of an observer's sex and values on aggressive responding. J. Pers. Soc. Psychol. 31, 567-573.

Cisneros, T., Camino, L. & Leyens, J.-P. (1974). La décentration: auto-contrôle de l'influence de la violence filmée. Revue de Psychologie et des Sciences de l'Education 2, 301-316.

Codol, J.P. (1976). Une étude expérimentale sur l'influence de la critique cinématographique. Cahiers de Psychologie 10, 83-98.

Cottrell, N.B. (1972). Social facilitation. In "Experimental Social Psychology" (C.G. McClintock, ed.). Holt, Rinehart and Winston, NY.

Doob, A.N. & Macdonald, F.E. (1979). Television viewing and fear of victimization: Is the relationship causal? J. Pers. Soc. Psychol. 37, 170-179.

Edgar, P.M. & Edgar, D.E. (1971). Television violence and socialization theory. Public Opinion Quart. 35, 608-612.

Feshbach, S. & Singer, R.D. (1971). "Television and Aggression: an Experimmental Field Study". Jossey-Bass, San Francisco.

Freidson, F. (1953). The relation of the social situation of contact to the media in mass communication. Public Opinion Quart. 17, 230-238.

Goldstein, J.H., Rosnow, R.L., Raday, T., Silverman, I. & Gaskell, G.D. (1975). Punitiveness in response to films varying in content: a cross-national field study of aggression. Eur. J. Soc. Psychol. 5, 149-166.

Hicks, D.J. (1968). Effects of co-observer's sanctions and adult presence on imitative aggression. Child Devel. 38, 303-309.

Horton, R.W. & Santogrossi, D.A. (1978). The effect of adult commentary on reducing the influence of televised violence. Pers. Soc. Psychol. Bull. 4, 337-340.

Hovland, C. (1951). In "Reader in Public Opinion and Communication" (Berelson & Janowitz, eds0. Glencoe, IL.

Katz, E. & Lazarsfeld, P.F. (1955). "Personal Influence". Free Press, Glencoe, IL.

Koriat, A., Melkman, R., Averill, J.R. & Lazarus, R.S. (1972). The self-control of emotional reactions to a stressful film. J. Person. 40, 601-619.

Lazarus, R.S. & Alfred, E. (1964). The short-circuiting of threat by experimentally altering cognitive appraisal. J. Abnorm. Soc. Psychol. 69, 195-205.

Leyens, J.-P. & Parke, R.D. (1975). Aggressive slides can induce a weapons effect. Eur. J. Soc. Psychol. 5, 229-236.

Leyens, J.-P., Camino, L., Parke, R.D. & Berkowitz, L. (1975). The effects of movie violence on aggression in a field setting as a function of group dominance and cohesion. J. Person. Soc. Psychol. 32, 346-360.

Leyens, J.-P., Cisneros, T. & Hossay, J.F. (1976). Decentration as a means for reducing aggression after exposure to violent stimuli. Eur. J. Soc. Psychol. 6, 459-473.

Leyens, J.-P., Herman, G., Dunand, M., Ghysselynckx, A. & Delfosse, M. (1981). "The Social Context of Viewing Filmed Violence. I". The differential reactions of dominant and submissive preschool boys when tested alone (in preparation).

Parke, R.D. (1974). A field experimental approach to children's aggression: some methodological problems and some future trends. In "Determinants and Origins of Aggressive Behavior" (J. De Wit & W.W. Hartup, eds.). Mouton, The Hague and Paris.

Parke, R.D., Berkowitz, L., Leyens, J.-P., West, S. & Sebastian, R.J. (1977). Some effects of violent and nonviolent movies on the behavior of juvenile delinquents. In "Advances in Experimental Social Psychology" (L. Berkowitz, ed.), Vol. 10. Academic Press, NY.

Rabbie, J.M. (1978). Minicrowds, an experimental study of audience behavior. Paper presented to the General Meeting of the European Association of Experimental Social Psychology, Weimar, D.D.R., March 28-April 1.

Riley, M.W. & Riley, J.W. (1951). A sociological approach to communications research. Public Opinion Quart. 15, 445-460.

Liebert, R.M., Sobol, M.D. & Davidson, E.S. (1972). Catharsis of aggression among institutionalized boys: fact or artifact. In "Television and Social Behavior. Vol. 5. Television effects: Further explorations" (G.A. Comstock, E.A. Rubinstein & J.P. Murray, eds.), pp. 351-359. Government Printing Office, Washington, DC.

Maccoby, E. (1951). Television: its impact on school children. Public Opinion Quart. 15, 421-444.

Milgram, S. & Shotland, R.L. (1973). "Television and Antisocial Behavior". Academic Press, NY.

Moscovici, S. (1970). Préface. In "Psychologie Sociale, une discipline en mouvement" (D. Jodelet, J. Viet and P. Besnard, eds.). Mouton, Paris, La Haye.

Stein, A.H. & Friedrich, L.K. (1972). Television content and young children's behavior. In "Television and Social Behavior. Vol. 2. Television and Social Learning" (J.P. Murray, E.A. Rubinstein & G.A. Comstock, eds.), pp. 202-317. Government Printing Office, Washington, DC.

Steuer, F.B., Applefield, J.M. & Smith, R. (1971). Television aggression and the interpersonal aggression of preschool children. J. Exp. Child Psychol. 11, 422-447.

Vandenplas-Holper, C. (1979). "Education et développement social de l'enfant". P.U.F., Paris.

Zajonc, R.B. (1965). Social Facilitation. Science 149, 259-274.

THE FUNCTION OF TELEVISION IN CHILDHOOD AGGRESSION

Robert D. Singer

University of California at Riverside

INTRODUCTION TO THE ISSUE

Considerable focus has been placed on the issue of whether television programs in general, and specifically programs with a high content of violent behavior, play a causal role in the aggressive and violent behavior of children and adolescents. Put most simply, the issue has been: "Does T.V. cause aggression and violence?" For those who were convinced that T.V. causes aggression and/or violence, the next issue became delineating the psychological mechanisms which accounted for the assumed causal link. Modeling, disinhibition, imitation, vicarious reinforcement, activation, and habituation, were invoked in various combinations by different theoreticians (Bogart, 1980).

Despite the inability of a number of studies to find a causal link between T.V. viewing of violent programming and aggression in children or adolescents, another set of studies claims to have found such a link. Although the amount of variance in aggressive behavior accounted for in such studies seems to hover around five percent, the investigators consider the purported phenomenon to be important given the size of the T.V. viewing population and the amount of hours viewed (Comstock, 1980; Rubinstein, 1980).

The perhaps important but modest results of those obtaining positive results suggests to some that T.V. may be mildly implicated in the aggressive behavior of some children but not in those of others. Indeed, the literature shows that a variety of variables are involved in both how much and what is watched on T.V. and the extent to which a relationship exists between T.V. viewing and aggression. Such variables include sex, age, social class, ethnic group, intelligence level, recreational patterns, social adjustments, psychopathology and a variety of parental child rearing practices (Dorr & Kovanick, 1980). When looked at in this fashion, the role of T.V. in aggression seems to be that of one of a set of interacting variables. The sole or unique role of

263

Kaplan, R.M., Konečni, V.J., Novaco, R.W. (eds.) Aggression in Children and Youth
© 1984, Martinus Nijhoff Publishers, The Hague/Boston/Lancaster
ISBN 90-247-2903-3. Printed in The Netherlands

T.V., in aggression or violence, if any, or its causal role becomes impossible to ascertain from current information. A number of variables interact in complex ways to produce aggression and part of this complex, for some children and adolescents, may include the heavy viewing of T.V. and particularly of aggressive programs. The hypothesis of bidirectionality, that such viewing is partly caused by correlates of aggressive behavior and is also implicated with other variables in causing aggression is also tenable. So is the uni-, directional hypothesis that for some children their real life aggression leads to watching aggressive programs on T.V. (Kaplan & Singer, 1976). That T.V. alone would lead to heightened aggression without the contribution of other variables seems less tenable. It is the view of this paper that the most tenable view, given current data, is that for some children and adolescents T.V. viewing is part of a complex of interacting variables which together codetermine the level of aggression observed. In addition, the direction of the effects seems to be, at least partly, bidirectional. To oversimplify, a variety of variables including the child's aggression may lead to viewing aggressive television programs and such viewing, together with other variables, may contribute to aggression and violence.

To understand the possible role of violence on T.V. in childhood and adolescent aggression one has to comprehend the functional role of T.V. Why do some children watch a large amount of television in general and/or a large amount of violent programs on T.V.? In particular, what does such T.V. viewing do for highly aggressive children and adolescents? Finally, how is the functional significance of violent T.V. and/or heavy T.V. viewing linked to aggression? Such questions have received scant attention since Feshbach and Singer in their book Television and Aggression raised it in 1971:

> "Since the fantasy aggression which results from viewing these programs precedes recorded history and since individuals persist in their desire to consume such fantasies through the mass media, certainly fantasy serves some function. People not only persist in dreaming, daydreaming, and telling stories, but also read comics, buy novels, watch television and go to movies. One may postulate a relatively constant need for fantasy activity since the time people spend in it seems fairly constant, regardless of the media involved. If television is unavailable, there is more comic book reading and greater movie attendance. If television is readily available, then the consumption of the other fantasy media declines.... Thus, we can assume that fantasies do something for people; otherwise they would not engage in them... What, however, are the specific effects of engaging in

264

fantasy activities? Why are these activities reinforcing? Do they satisfy aesthetic, emotional, and
cognitive needs exclusively or do they also relate
to overt behavior?" (Feshbach & Singer, 1971).

ANALYSIS OF AGGRESSION AND VIOLENCE

Before turning to a functional analysis, however, it is
important to develop a careful analysis of aggression and
violence. Most of the literature on television and aggression
suffers from the lack of such an analysis. There is seldom
any differentiation of degrees of aggression or a meaningful
definition of violence. One important recent study involves,
among other analyses, a comparison of high and low aggressive
3 and 4 year olds in terms of their T.V. viewing habits, including amount of viewing of violent shows (Singer & Singer,
1981). The mean of the low aggressive children was about 1.5
and of the high aggressive children about 2.0. This was on a
5 point scale, with the sample quite skewed to the nonaggressive end, with the high aggressive group averaging only 2 on
the 5 point scale. A 2 represents: "Child is restless and
moves about the room carelessly bumping into others' toys,
occasionally disrupting others' games or play space." A 3 on
the scale is: "The child shows at least one incidence of
banging or wrecking own toys or those of others or kicks an
object in anger or frustration." No direct attacks on other
children are scored here, however. (A 4 would include a
physical attack or several attacks on property, and a 5, two
attacks on others.) Although the authors, in one sentence,
point out that a so-called high aggressive child in this
study is a rather peaceful one, this is soon lost sight of in
all sorts of comparisons concerning the high and low aggressive groups.

In other studies aggression consists of striking a toy
specifically constructed for the purpose of being struck,
such as a Bobo doll or in pushing a button that activates a
mechanism which strikes a doll. Although these may or may
not be legitimate predictors of real life aggression and/or
accurate predictors of other sorts of aggressive activity,
clearly the equating of high aggressive groups of children
based on such measures with high aggressive groups based on
incidences of fistfights among themselves or on commission of
violent crimes, is inadvisable (Kaplan & Singer, 1976).

Equally troubling is the general lack of understanding
shown about the nature of aggression in the literature on
television and aggression. Aggression is viewed as an evil
to be eliminated. Its origins are not discussed except for
statements that it is a learned behavior and its existence is
usually seen as an unfortunate outcome of its succeeding and
thus becoming reinforced. Completely ignored, usually, is

265

the fact that aggression exists not only in almost every
culture and member of the human species and in all nonhuman
primates, in fact, in all known mammals, not to mention
avians, arachnids, and other assorted creatures, including
the jelly fish (Vale, 1980). Clearly, aggression has been
generally selected for in evolution. The development of
aggression in a variety of species has enhanced and not
impeded their species survival. Unless and until humans blow
themselves into oblivion with atomic or other weapons, one
has to face the fact that so far, even with major wars,
aggression has not impeded human survival as a species.
Indeed there are more of us around than one cares to think
about. As we shall see, this does not necessarily make
aggression desirable, however.

The advantages conferred by intraspecies aggression in
non-human species is clear. In some species the aggressiveness of organisms towards members of their own kind results
in their remaining further apart than they might otherwise.
This makes for a more efficient utilization of existing
resources. Another function of aggression is related to
reproduction. In many species much of the breeding is done
by the strongest or most dominant. This ensures that in each
generation the best equipped behaviorally to reproduce will
do so, and thus the reproductive vigor required for success
will continue. A third function of aggression in nonhuman
animals is to aid in the selection of those most capable of
defending infant offspring, youth, the less dominant and the
weaker in their groups against predators. Aggression as a
proximate factor in terms of family and extended group defense
becomes altruism and can be the basis for ritualized behavior,
redirected activities and social bonds. Spacing, rivalry and
the achievement of dominance and status are the outcomes of
aggression, however, subtly or grossly expressed, and all
contribute to the ultimate factor of fitness (Vale, 1980).

For humans, as cultural animals, gestures, postures, and
language can convey aggressive meaning symbolically without
our having to resort to, or even see, actual overt physical
aggression. Ceremonies and rituals, diplomatic activity,
conferences, interviews, arguments, all serve as activities
in which humans engage in threats, displays, and gestures,
often leading to victories, defeats or compromises, with the
possibility of threat of overt violence and destruction playing an important role (Vale, 1980).

Many social and behavioral scientists sensitive to the
suffering caused by aggression strongly believe aggression to
be entirely undesirable. Whatever can be accomplished by
violence, they contend, can be equally accomplished by other
means, which do not involve insult, pain, injury, and death.
Violence is not a desirable way, in their view, to decide who
gets what, where and when. Indeed some argue that aggression

266

is immoral, an unfortunate biological legacy of an evolutionary history in which it was advantageous for survival. Now,
ironically, they say, it may threaten survival and must be
eliminated.

Evolution, however, is not a moral force. It is what is
and not what someone believes it ought to be. As has been
pointed out about the evolution of aggression: "It is a name
given to a series of related events in nature, which are in
the long run quite efficient although in a given instance
usually seem opportunistic and expedient. The relevant fact
is that aggression works" (Vale, 1980). Since it works the
issue becomes not so much how to account for aggression but
how to control it, including seeing to it that it works as
seldom as possible for those to whom it is repugnant. Aggression is least likely to occur when resources are abundant
and/or when organisms have effective alternatives to aggression for promoting their wants. Aggression is, at least to a
significant extent, an evolutionary extension of competition
(Bigalow, 1972; Marler, 1976).

Aggression is quite complex behaviorally and probably
neurologically and biochemically. Biologists list eight kinds
of aggressive behavior which some feel are governed by partly
separate but overlapping neuronal circuits open to various
types of facilitation and inhibition: (1) predatory; (2)
intermale; (3) fear-induced; (4) irritable; (5) territorial;
(6) maternal; (7) instrumental; and (8) sex related. In
humans, aggression has sometimes been classified into two
major categories, instrumental or affective, according to
whether it is used as a means of gaining some goal object or
is pursued for the primary purpose of causing injury. Aggression in humans has also been classified into a more differentiated set of functional categories, such as (1) coercion;
(2) punishment and revenge; (3) specific goal attainment; (4)
self defense; and (5) attention seeking (Moyer, 1971, 1976).

Most psychologists consider aggression to be learned
(Bandura, 1973). To the extent that this is true, it is
highly trivial. It seems impossible not to learn aggression,
which cannot be said for calculus or the flying of jet
aircraft. Aggression appears in some form in all cultures
and in most species. The fundamentals of aggression are the
use of the body to cause injury, such as kicking, biting,
striking, scratching, and secondarily thrusting or throwing
objects. It is questionable whether learning plays more than
a trivial role in the appearance of such fundamental, almost
maturational behaviors or in the appearance of anger and
rage. In fact, cultures all spend time teaching children
where not to be aggressive and whom not to attack. The issue
of whether aggression is innate or learned is not meaningful.
What is clear is that it will appear and that no special pains
have to be taken to teach it. The issue with aggression is
how to limit its performance.

267

What is learned about aggression are: (1) appropriate
targets and (2) specific complex aggressive skills. One
learns when to attack and sometimes complicated ways of doing
it. The actual performance of aggression depends largely on:
(1) specific social rules about how, when and where aggression
may be expressed and what type of aggression is permissible
under what circumstances, and (2) the consequences of aggression, including actual experienced enforcement and lack there-
of of the social rules. The repeated performance of aggression depends largely on its consequences (Bandura, 1973).

VIOLENCE AS OPPOSED TO MILD AGGRESSION

Given the previous analysis, violent programming on T.V.
may be thought to contribute to aggression in a number of
ways: (1) the learning of specific aggressive skills such as
how to load a gun and aim it, how to make a bomb, or to hijack
an airplane using force. Television networks in the United
States as policy are very careful, however, not to show precise sequences that could lead to successful complex learning
in these regards; (2) the learning of specific targets, such
as in the repeated portrayal of certain groups as justified
targets of aggression or as the perpetrators of aggression
and thus deserving punishment; (3) the interpretation of
social norms and their consequences. To the extent that
television-portrayed norms influence expectations about real
life outcomes, T.V. can be seen as possibly contributing to
real life behavior; and (4) television may convey expectations
about the consequences of aggression.

The attention paid to learning and activation variables
in the T.V. and aggression literature may have led to the
relative neglect of the role which television may play in the
development of cognitive skills and internal control mechanisms, which, among other functions, are involved in the regulation of aggression. The real issue with humans is the
regulation of aggression, the inhibition of aggressive performance, and the finding of successful alternatives to aggression. This, particularly the development of nonaggressive
coping skills which enable the child to get what he or she
needs without aggression, demands cognitive abilities for
which, as we shall see, television may be a less than successful substitute and a poor teacher. In this analysis television is viewed not as a direct instigator of aggression but
as a factor interfering with the development of skills the
child needs to avoid aggression.

The definition of violence adopted by the National
Commission on the Causes and Prevention of Violence is:
"Overtly threatened or overtly accomplished application of
force which results in the injury or destruction of persons
or property." The current legal definition of violence sees

268

it as equivalent to dangerousness, which in turn is based on whether or not there is a high probability of substantial injury. Dangerous or violent acts are those: "acts characterized by the application of overt threat of force which is likely to result in injury to people." Injury is taken to mean physical injury. The term includes such acts as homicide, mayhem, aggravated assault, forcible rape, battery, robbery, arson, and extortion, killing in self defense or shooting a fleeing felon (Report of the National Commission on the Causes and Prevention of Violence, 1974). These examples and definitions are given in order to underline how far most studies of television and aggression are from dealing with the effect of television on real violence. Only a very few studies actually include measures of real life violent behavior. The rest mainly include measures of aggression of a milder sort, ranging from so-called aggressive play through verbal aggression such as swearing or shouting and physical aggression such as shoving, pushing, or occasional fist-fighting or roughhouse wrestling.

The assumption is made by some that milder forms of aggression are predictive of both current and later violent behavior. Mild or average forms of aggressive behavior in children seem relatively predictive of future aggression at similar levels (Bandura, 1973; Eron, et al., 1972). Not much is known about whether present mild aggression tends to escalate into later violence. Some studies do seem to indicate that it is from the ranks of the high aggressive children that often the truly violent adults come (Belson, 1978). We also know of the killer and even mass killer who was passive as a child. Clearly most so-called high aggressive children do not become violent adults and it would be useful to know what variables determine the outcome. It would also be useful to know in what way and to what extent, if any, television contributes to violence as opposed to milder forms of aggression. One assumes that the main concern of those who worry about the violence shown on television is that it may lead to serious violence and not that it will account for 5 percent of the variance in taking someone else's toy or in shoving, swearing or quarreling. At least one major study does suggest that high viewing of T.V. violence is associated in a causal manner with serious violent behavior (Belson, 1978). That is the focal point of concern.

FUNCTIONAL ANALYSIS OF TELEVISION AND AGGRESSION

Having dealt with the nature of aggression, its relation to learning, and the differentiation between mild aggression and violence, it is now possible to turn to a functional analysis of television and aggression. The mystery of aggression and violence, despite impressions gained from the news reports, is not why there is so much but why there is not even more. Aggression is basically a way of getting what you want and of punishing others. Our desires to punish others, however, are often prompted by the other not doing what we want or keeping us from obtaining what we want.

What keeps aggression and violence usually within levels allowing for species survival and relative calm for humans is adhering to social norms based ultimately on the reality of direct or indirect retaliation and the availability of successful non-aggressive modes of gratification. Weaker animals tend not to aggress against the stronger, one does not attack three, and easy availability of food over a wide territory leads to non-contact foraging behavior rather than fighting to take away another animal's food (Vale, 1980). In humans social codes concerning rules about aggression and violence are taught and backed to varying degrees by actual sanctions for transgression. Forms of cooperation, assertion, peaceful achievement and nonviolent competition are taught along with compromise negotiation and other social skills as forms of behavior very often or most often to be preferred to aggressive and violent forms of conduct.

The role of imitation and the effects of reward and punishment on aggressive performance have been amply addressed in the literature. The role of disinhibition as a function of observing unpunished and/or successful aggressive models has also been demonstrated. The same is true for activation (Bandura, 1973). The concern here is with how television may be implicated in the development or lack of development of cognitive mechanisms or modes of behavior generally antithetical to aggression.

Feshbach and Singer as well as Jerome Singer have outlined the role of fantasy as a cognitive coping mechanism (Feshbach and Singer, 1971; Singer, 1973). The ability to engage in fantasies is seen as an adaptive function which helps the human organism to cope with the long periods during which external reinforcements may not be available. For instance, the child who is frustrated but has a vivid fantasy life is more able to cope than a frustrated child who does not have this ability. The former child is not driven to inappropriate disturbing behaviors, while the other child is likely to engage in such behaviors as social withdrawal and disorganized thinking. Connections have been found between the ability to fantasize and irritable, overly motoric, and hyperactive behavior. The ability to fantasize can be taught and leads to a diminution of restlessness and increased ability to pay attention (Feshbach and Singer, 1971).

Fantasy, the making up of stories in a variety of internal forms, is cognitive activity and is related to problem solving and planning. Although fantasy is not bound by the constraints of realistic probability it requires producing mental contents, placing them in sequence, manipulating symbols, and producing imagined outcomes. Play is often fantasy, and is the work of children which is a form of cognitive learning to cope with life and not only the senseless fun it seems to many. Imaginative play, which includes fantasy, is a method through which children can develop their symbolic capacities. It consists of transforming the immediate environment and practicing new kinds of cognitive structures (Feshbach and Singer, 1971; Singer, 1973).

Although television clearly stimulates imaginative play by providing ready made themes and contents, as do books, it tends, by being both visual and auditory, and usually explicit and simple, to leave much less to the child's imagination. Since many hours are spent in front of the television with one show following another, there is less opportunity for the child to fantasize or play imaginatively than if the parent read to the child for half an hour per day, or if, when able to read, the child read for an hour or so. Television may both preempt the child's free playtime and provide ever available, externally produced simplistic fantasies, which may serve some regulatory function but interfere with the child's ability to develop self-produced controls. Television may be linked to a relative lack of internal resources and a dependence on externally generated events. Television lends itself to assimilation and does not require very much accommodation. As such it may retard rather than encourage the differentiation and development of cognitive structures (Singer, 1980).

Fantasy, imaginative play, and eventually planning and problem solving are seen, in this view, as standing as a protection between the internally aroused individual and the need to engage in possibly damaging external behavior. Since part of fantasy is cognitive, children who are more cognitively differentiated are better able to utilize fantasy in constructive ways than less cognitively differentiated children. Consequently variables like higher intelligence, upper middle class family background, provision of books, and time alone are productive of the ability to develop cognitive skills and to use fantasy constructively (Singer, 1971, 1980). Television may be a provider of readily understood fantasies which do not contribute much to cognitive differentiation and which do not encourage internal transformation.

CORRELATES OF T.V. AND AGGRESSION

The ability to fantasize, to play imaginatively, and to differentiate cognitively are effected by a variety of variables of which television is only one. The ability to develop alternate strategies to obtain desired outcomes, without

271

resorting to aggression, also depends on a variety of variables. We would, therefore, expect the relationship between television and aggression to be moderate or low, and to hold for some children and not others, depending on the degree of presence or absence of the other pertinent life experiences.

The main point to be presented here is as follows. Television may be part of a complex of variables which interferes with cognitive differentiation, the development of non-aggressive and social skills, coping skills, and the development of empathy which tends to inhibit aggression. In turn, television is a source of satisfaction for those who cannot relate well to others, are often rejected, or have trouble succeeding in school or other spheres of life. Television can be a nondemanding refuge and source of escape for those who do not derive sufficient rewards from other people, school, or work (Stein & Friedrich, 1972; Schramm, et al., 1961). Such excessive dependence on an externally produced fantasy medium may further lower the ability to produce appropriate behavior and lead to above average levels of aggression. Of course, a large variety of variables influence aggressive performance, and it would be unlikely if other than a moderate causal relationship could be found for television viewing, even for susceptible groups of children.

A recent study of 3 and 4 year olds, including data on television and aggression, found that children who watch many aggressive programs show more aggression than those who do not. Further, such high aggressive television content viewing children are lower in I.Q. and come from families lower in socioeconomic status. The homes of such children are somewhat disorganized, there are fewer toys, and they have fewer books, fewer records, and fewer musical instruments. They are allowed to stay up late at night and to wake up late in the morning. The whole family watches a lot of television, even when they are eating. There is a lack of regular bedtime routine and little or no storytelling at bedtime. The cultural interests of the families of the high violent T.V. watching-higher aggressive child are few. The child mainly gets taken grocery shopping and more often than other children to the movies. They are very seldom taken to parks, picnics, museums, or other activities. The parents tend to be superficially religious and to display sex role stereotypes (Singer & Singer, 1981).

This is a type of lifestyle which discourages imagination and thinking and which also inhibits flexible coping skills while encouraging rigidity. The viewing of television and particular types of television content is clearly not an isolated event but a part and parcel of a specific lifestyle. Although television seems to be contributing to the higher aggressive levels in these children (the levels of aggression are generally moderate or low) it is only one, as we have

272

just reviewed, of a complex set of interacting variables. If television, including the violent programs, were not available to these children, it is hard to predict what the effect would be on the level of their aggressive behavior if the other variables were not also altered.

The so-called high aggressive children not only watched more violent programs but were more likely to be punished by spanking and less likely to be rewarded by praise. In addition, they tended to have high activity levels (Singer & Singer, 1981). These variables tend to be independently associated with higher aggression levels in the general child development literature. These children are also less socially cooperative and less likely to show specific talents. A reasonable supposition is that watching a lot of television, particularly violent shows, is an externally produced fantasy outlet and refuge for less intellectually and socially capable children. In turn, the high violence viewing level interferes further with the development of non-aggressive cognitive-behavioral skills for obtaining life rewards.

One investigator has concluded that the relationships between violence viewing and aggression is mediated by intellectual deprivation (Thomas, 1972). Two other studies find that more intelligent children watch less television (Chaffee & McLeod, 1972; Stein & Friedrich, 1972). The contention has also been made that children with few interests are more likely to imitate television models. Still another study found a relationship between lowered intellectual functioning, early psychopathology and absence of desirable life events and high T.V. viewing, high violent show viewing, and higher aggression five years later, and another study has found that lowered popularity is associated with greater amounts of television viewing and another that deficit in intellectual functioning is a precursor to television viewing (Lefkowitz & Huesmann, 1980). The conclusion of reviewers of the literature is that children try to obtain vicarious rewards and stimulation from television after they encounter difficulties in obtaining these rewards in other ways (Lefkowitz & Huesmann, 1980). It is the contention here that, unfortunately, heavy television viewing makes it even more likely that the needed coping skills will not be developed. This in turn increases the probability of aggressive tactics to cope with life problems.

Studies clearly show that lower class youth and their parents report viewing more violent T.V. programming than is true of the middle class. Only one study including social class has not reported this finding, and even this study found that working class children watch more television overall. There are indications in the literature that in children 9 to 15 years old, nonwhites may watch more television violence than do whites (Lefkowitz & Huesmann, 1980). It is

273

possible, therefore, that children from groups which tend to do less well in school also watch more television, including more violent shows. Such heavy viewing is not helpful in relation to classroom performance or cognitive differentiation. A cycle of failure and lowered self esteem may lead to enhanced aggressive behavior which may lead to at least some sort of satisfaction.

THE DIRECTIONALITY OF T.V. AND VIOLENCE

A large scale survey study done in London, England, relying on self reports of minor and serious violence finds a possibly causal relationship between heavy exposure to violence on television and seriously violent behavior. The general finding is that high viewing of violent programs is associated with unskilled, spontaneous, unplanned acts of violence of the type that call for little or no cognitive activity. The association between T.V. viewing in general or high viewing of aggressive programs and delinquency and socially undesirable or pathological behavior has been shown in a number of other studies. However, in all these cases the hypothesis that delinquent, aggressive, or disturbed children use T.V., including violent programming, as an escape, substitute and refuge, is about as supported by the data as the possibility that T.V. causes violence in these more violent youth. The London study purports to show that it is, indeed, T.V. that leads to violence and not the other way around. The data, of course, are correlational (Belson, 1978).

Where there have been attempts at assessing the direction of causality from correlational data, that is whether T.V. watching causes aggression or aggression causes T.V. viewing, the findings have not tended to be clear cut. One causal side or the other has received varying degrees of support (Singer & Kaplan, 1976). Part of the answer may be that an interactive, rather than a simple form of causation is operative, as this paper contends.

We still know little about the relationship of violent programming on T.V. to the commission of seriously violent acts, nor about the magnitude of such a relationship, if any. One writer in this area notes that television addicts who are deeply involved in viewing of violent shows may be affected by it, but that one would still have to investigate why some people become television addicts. More important, he believes, is that fact that T.V. addiction is more prevalent among low income viewers, the very people for whom crime and violence are more likely to be personally relevant. It is they who live in high crime districts or, as a function of little economic hope, may become the perpetrators of crime. He raises the question of whether the increase in actual crime and violence over the last decade and the even larger

274

rise in the fear of crime may explain a good deal of the popularity of television violence. People who are afraid after having been victimized by crime, he speculates, may enjoy watching T.V. shows in which criminals are eventually punished, and often violently. And, he adds, precisely because they at least seem to be seldom so punished in the real world. He sees violent T.V. programming to be a latent dysfunction of an increasingly violent culture, rather than a significant cause of violence (Gans, 1980).

An accurate assessment of television, in terms of its possible contribution to childhood violence, is quite difficult but possible. Any such assessment must depend on correlational methods and despite modern correlational techniques which purport to lead to causal statements, they depend, as any analysis, on what goes into the analyses. For instance, the study of 3 to 4 year olds which finds a purportedly causal relationship between television and aggression, also reports elsewhere in the writeup that the parents of high television-high aggression children take their children to the movies frequently and are higher in their use of physical punishment. Perhaps it is one or both of these variables correlated with high viewing of violent T.V. programming which may be the cause of aggression. Or perhaps all three contribute to aggression, or only in some combinations, or together with altogether unmeasured variables. Nevertheless, modern techniques of causal analysis based on nonexperimental data do allow us to tackle such problems. It is surprising that there have been relatively few attempts to apply causal analysis in this research area.

DOES T.V. CAUSE VIOLENCE?

There are those who do not believe that there is any significant link between television and real violence. To quote one such scholar, who is referring to the last ten years of research on T.V. and aggression:

> If there is, however, no significant causal relationship between television and real violence—as I believe the case—then the researchers were being used to support a spurious solution to a real social problem. Moreover, at the time it seemed like an easily achievable solution, and one that would not require having to deal with the inequities in the economy and the criminal justice system. The researchers themselves may not have shared any of these values and perhaps were not even aware of them. They could do the research because they were personally opposed to television violence. In addition, they may have wanted to eliminate television violence as a first step in upgrading television fare generally.

I do not mean to suggest conspiracies, to the contrary, I think the basic impulse behind much of the
television research on violence and other topics is
more prosaic and much less political. Some researchers, I think, would like to upgrade television fare
for themselves, using research here instead of
market power, because researchers--and academics
generally--are too small a population to be profitable to televisions' advertisers. But there is
another aim which is equally latent and lies behind
a good deal of research on topics other than mass
communications: To reduce the differences between
intellectuals and nonintellectuals and between experts and laypersons--or, to put it more simply,
to remake the American public to be more like us.

These are only hunches, to be sure, and I put them
on paper mainly to raise the question of the role
of television research in television itself; to ask
what television researchers want to do for the
audience, and for the larger society, intentionally
or otherwise. The next questions, then, are: What
can television research actually do to and for the
audience and what should it do, assuming it ever
obtained the power to do anything significant (Gans,
1980).

Despite the studies which fail to find the link, and
despite the difficulties in showing that the link is causal,
the literature certainly makes the proposition that television
contributes to childhood and adolescent aggression a possible
one. This paper has attempted to explicate psychological
mechanisms which would account for such a possible or probable
causal link. It seems, however, quite true that television
may not be the place to start if one wanted to seriously
reduce human aggression. The links between unemployment and
aggression, a 1 percent rise in unemployment is associated
with a 5 percent rise in crime, and between being a battered
child and then later a violent adult, are much clearer. Nevertheless, certain events following specific types of exposure
over T.V. are cause for concern. The showing of a movie
portraying "Russian roulette" with a revolver on T.V. was
followed by a dozen or more reported deaths from playing
"Russian roulette." Of course, no one knows what the annual
"Russian roulette" death rate is, nor whether these were
essentially suicides who wouuld have killed themselves anyway
without benefit of T.V., in some more prosaic fashion. The
movie had been shown first in movie theaters and was a critical
as well as a popular success. Publicity given to airplane
hijacking or terrorist hostage holding on T.V. seems to be
followed by several more attempts or acts of a somewhat similar vein. Some have claimed a "contagion effect" prompted by
T.V. publicity, usually on news shows. Surely this is serious
cause for concern.

THE REGULATION OF TELEVISION

It is difficult to evaluate some of the above claims and even more perplexing is to know what to suggest if they are true. I personally suspect they are true in some cases. Censorship of the news or news management is abhorrent to many as would be allowing some films to be shown widely in movie theaters in every city, but not on television. The danger that children or, more likely, adolescents may imitate violent acts seen on television may be a real one, particularly for certain predisposed subgroups. Self restraint by television broadcasters seems a reasonable request.

When the nature of a possible danger is really unknown, as it is with T.V. and violence, the question to raise is what would be lost in erring on the side of the most stringent regulation? That is, what would be lost if children and adolescents did not have available to them a continual parade of violent cartoons, detective shows, terror, and horror films on T.V.? The answer seems to be, not much. For those children and adolescents needing aggressive and violent fantasy stimulation there would still remain some on T.V. plus the movies and comic books as well as paperback detective and spy stories, science fiction and westerns. Books, it seems, may actually be the most helpful fantasy providing stimuli since they are most likely to help develop the ability to produce one's own fantasies and more likely to lead to cognitive differentiation. T.V. industry or governmental regulation, if safeguarding civil and political liberties, seems not really overly objectionable to me in this area.

CONCLUDING STATEMENT

As for my own values, I have come to the conclusion that my wishes are to lessen the distance between the intellectual and the rest of society. My quarrel is that almost all of television in the United States is mindless, tasteless entertainment requiring nothing and adding nothing. I do not object to children seeing aggression or violence on T.V. if they are seeing Little Red Ridinghood, Jack and the Beanstalk, Hansel and Gretel, Hamlet, Romeo and Juliet or Macbeth, or for that matter Star Trek, the Charge of the Light Brigade, Casablanca, or one of my all time favorites, I Was a Teenage Werewolf. It is certainly possible to produce programs or to show films on television which have considerable aggressive or violent content, but within a meaningful context conveying matters of importance about the human condition in a manner which elevates rather than diminishes us, whether children, adolescents, or adults.

I hold out little hope, however, for such developments. Those in the United States crusading the hardest to eliminate aggression and also sex from the T.V. screen are not particularly pushing for quality, nor do they seemed concerned about civil or political liberty. Their approval list of television programs consists of those with the least violence and sexuality. They are, however, in my view, almost all shows which are aesthetically and intellectually inferior, although certainly antiseptic. Junk is okay as long as it isn't tough or sexy with those crusading groups. A genuine concern for children and adolescents should center about creating conditions which would help them develop their capacities as human beings to an optimal extent, rather than about saving them from particular contents such as aggression or sexuality. If quality became the standard, then gratuitous, senseless, attention grabbing violence for its own sake would fade from the T.V. screen in any case. However, between the obsessions of the moral majority crusaders, and the drive for profits of the major networks, there is little reason to expect excellence in public free television entertainment. The only reasonable possibility for improvement in the current situation is control by parents over what their children are exposed to and the availability of better programs over cable and pay T.V. Alas, the parents of the high violence viewing, high "so-called" aggressive children report that it is their 3 and 4 year old children who control what is usually watched on the T.V. set. I suspect they are not telling the truth, and that may be perhaps even sadder. Cable and pay T.V. may not prove much better than free T.V., but this remains to be seen.

In closing I wish to leave with you my view that the television and aggression literature of the past 10 or 15 years should be a great cause for humility. This literature clearly demonstrates the limitations of social science research in attacking complex, real life issues and lays open the striking way in which investigator values and motivations can bias both research and the conclusions drawn from research. If these lessons are taken to heart, the greatest contributions of this literature may be to improvements in research methodology and improvements in both the honesty and quality of attempts to prescribe policy in future areas of investigation.

REFERENCES

Bandura, A. Aggression: A social learning analysis.
   Englewood Cliffs, NJ: Prentice-Hall, 1973. .
Belson, W. Television violence and the adolescent boy.
   New York: Saxon House, 1978.
Bigelow, R. The evolution of cooperation, aggression and
   self-control. In J. Cole & D. Jensen (Eds.), Nebraska
   Symposium on Motivation, 20: University of Nebraska
   Press, 1972.
Bogart, L. After the Surgeon General's report: Another look
   backward. In R. Abeles (Ed.), Television and social
   behavior. Hillsdale, NJ: Lawrence Erlbaum, 1980.
Chaffee, S., & McLeod, J. Adolescent television use in the
   family context. In E. Comstock & E. Rubinstein (Eds.),
   Television and social behavior, 3: U.S. Government
   Printing Office, 1972.
Comstock, G. New emphasis in research on the effects of
   television and film violence. In E. Palmer & A. Dorr
   (Eds.), Children and the faces of television. New
   York: Academic Press, 1980.
Dorr, A., & Kovaric, P. Some of the people some of the time--
   but which people? Television violence and its effects.
   In E. Palmer & A. Dorr (Eds.), Children and the faces of
   television. New York: Academic Press, 1980.
Eron, L., Huesmann, L., Lefkowitz, M., & Walder, L. Does
   television violence cause aggression? American
   Psychologist, 1972, 27, 253-263.
Feshbach, S., & Singer, R. Television and aggression.
   San Francisco: Jossey-Bass, 1971.
Gans, H. The audience for television - and in television
   research. In S. Witney & R. Abeles, Television and
   social behavior. Hillsdale, NJ: Lawrence Erlbaum, 1980.
Kaplan, R., & Singer, R. Television violence and viewer
   aggression: A reexamination of the evidence. In R.
   Singer & R. Kaplan (Eds.), Television and Social Behavior,
   Journal of Social Issues, 1976, 32, No. 4.
Lefkowitz, M., & Huesmann, L. Concomitants of television
   violence in children. In E. Palmer & A. Dorr (Eds.),
   Children and the faces of television. New York:
   Academic Press, 1980.
Marler, P. On animal aggression: The role of strangeness
   and familiarity. American Psychologist, 1976, 31,
   239-246.
Moyer, K. The physiology of aggression and the implications
   for aggression control. In J. L. Singer (Ed.), The
   control of aggression and violence. New York: Academic
   Press, 1971.
Moyer, K. The psychobiology of aggression. San Francisco, CA:
   Harper and Row, 1976.
Report of the National Commission on the Causes and Prevention
   of Violence. Washington, D.C., 1974.

Rubinstein, E. Television violence: A historical perspective. In E. Palmer & A. Dorr (Eds.), Children and the faces of television. New York: Academic Press, 1980.

Schramm, W., Lyle, J., & Parker, E. Television in the lives of our children. Stanford, CA: Stanford University Press, 1961.

Singer, J. The child's world of make-believe. New York: Academic Press, 1971.

Singer, J. The power and limitations of television. In P. Tannenbaum (Ed.), Television and entertainment. Hillsdale, NJ: Lawrence Earlbaum, 1980.

Singer J., & Singer, R. Television, imagination, and aggression. Hillsdale, NJ: Lawrence Earlbaum, 1981.

Singer, R., & Kaplan, R. Television and social behavior. Journal of Social Issues, 1976, 32, No. 4.

Stein, A., & Freidrich, L. Television content and young children's behavior. In J. Murray, et al. (Eds.), Television and social behavior, 2. Washington, D.C.: U.S. Government Printing Office, 1972.

Thomas, S. Violent content in television: The effect of cognitive style and age in mediating children's aggressive responses. APA Proceedings, 7, 97-98, 1972.

Vale, J. Genes, environment and behavior. San Francisco, CA: Harper and Row, 1980.

THE MASS MEDIA, INDIVIDUAL CHARACTERISTICS, AND AGGRESSION AGAINST WOMEN

Neil M. Malamuth

University of Manitoba, Winnipeg, Canada
and
University of California, Los Angeles

INTRODUCTION

Varied sources of data suggest that male aggression against females occurs with considerable frequency among young people. For example, Giarusso, Johnson, Goodchilds, and Zellman (1979) reported that over 50% of the large sample of male high school students interviewed believed that it was acceptable "...for a guy to hold a girl down and force her to have sexual intercourse" in various situations, such as when "she gets him sexually excited" or "she says she's going to have sex with him and then changes her mind." Similarly, Kanin and his associates (Kanin, 1957, 1965, 1967; Kanin & Parcell, 1977) found that over half of the female college students interviewed reported experiencing offensive male sexual aggression during the previous year. Furthermore, FBI Crime Statistics (1978, 1979, 1980) indicate consistently that the most frequent age of arrest for rape is 18 years. Consequently, the topic of aggression against women is certainly relevant to the primary focus of this book--aggression in children and adolescents.

Over the past several years we have conducted a research program designed to analyze the role of cultural factors and individual characteristics (as well as the interaction between these variables) in causing aggression against females. Our primary focus has been on aggression in the general population rather than in individuals who were arrested for crimes such as rape. We anticipate, however, that the findings will shed some light on the roots of aggressive acts that come to the attention of the law.

One of the ways we have attempted to study the role of cultural factors is by focusing on the mass media. According to numerous writers (e.g., Brown, 1981; Goffman, 1979), the media both reflect and shape cultural images, values, social scripts, etc. At the same time, our research on individual characteristics has been geared, as a first step, to identify

281

Kaplan, R.M., Konečni, V.J., Novaco, R.W. (eds.) Aggression in Children and Youth
© 1984, Martinus Nijhoff Publishers, The Hague/Boston/Lancaster
ISBN 90-247-2903-3. Printed in The Netherlands

males within the general population who show greater inclinations to aggress against females. It is our expectation that once we have succeeded in distinguishing among those with different inclinations to aggress against women, we can proceed to investigate the background characteristics responsible for these differences.

In this paper, I will first give examples of the findings we have obtained to date in these two areas--the effects of the mass media on aggression against females and research designed to identify men with relatively higher propensity to aggress against women. Next, I will give an example of work focusing on the interaction between the effects of the mass media and individual characteristics. Finally, some recent developments that are intended to provide a framework for further research in this area will be described.

EFFECTS OF THE MASS MEDIA

Our research concerning the effects of the mass media on aggression against women has been designed to use a variety of stimuli, settings, and dependent measures. We have utilized unedited feature length films (e.g., Malamuth & Check, 1981b), magazines (e.g., Malamuth, Reisin, & Spinner, 1979), books (e.g., Ceniti & Malamuth, in preparation) and audiotapes (e.g., Malamuth & Check, 1980a). Subjects have been exposed to the stimuli in movie theatres (Malamuth & Check, 1981b), in "adult" book stores (Malamuth, Feshbach, Fera, & Kunath, 1978), their homes (Ceniti & Malamuth, in preparation) and the laboratory (e.g., Malamuth & Check, 1980a). Dependent measures included self-reported (e.g., Malamuth & Check, 1980b), and penile tumescence (e.g., Malamuth & Check, 1980a), measures of sexual arousal, self-reported fantasies (e.g., Malamuth, 1981a), perceptions (e.g., Malamuth & Check, 1980a) attitudes (e.g., Malamuth & Check, 1981b), negative and positive affect (e.g., Malamuth, Heim, & Feshback, 1980), and aggression (e.g., Malamuth, 1978). A related series of studies focusing on laboratory aggression has been conducted by Ed Donnerstein and associates at the University of Wisconsin-Madison (e.g., Donnerstein, 1980; Donnerstein & Berkowitz, 1981).

A review of the findings of this research program was recently presented elsewhere (Malamuth & Donnerstein, in press). While there is some variability in the data, the overall conclusion emerging consistently from this research suggests that mass media exposure can facilitate the acceptance of aggression against women. I would like to illustrate more fully the nature of these findings by describing in greater detail one of our recent studies.

In this experiment (Malamuth & Check, 1981b), two hundred and seventy-one male and female university students served as subjects. Some had agreed to participate in a study ostensibly focusing on movie ratings. They watched on two different evenings either (1) the movies Swept Away and The Getaway, films that show women as victims of aggression within erotic as well as non-erotic incidents or (2) neutral feature-length movies. These movies were viewed in theatres on campus and some of the films (i.e., one experimental and one control movie) were being shown by the university as part of the campus film program. Members of the classes from which subjects had been recruited but who had not signed up for the experiment were also used as a comparison group. The dependent measures were scales assessing acceptance of interpersonal violence (AIV) against women, rape myth acceptance (RMA), and beliefs in adversarial sexual relations (ASB) (Burt, 1980). These measures were embedded within many other items in a Sexual Attitude Survey administered to all students in classes several days after some of them (i.e., those who had signed up for the experiment) had been exposed to the movies. Subjects were not aware that there was any relationship between this survey and the movies.

Results indicated that exposure to films portraying aggressive sexuality as having "positive" consequences increased males' but not females' acceptance of interpersonal violence against women and tended to increase males' acceptance of rape myths. These data demonstrated in a non-laboratory setting, not vulnerable to criticisms of laboratory artificiality and "demand characteristics", that movies that portray sexual violence can have significant attitudinal effects.

This study raises questions regarding the type of aggressive-sexual stimuli in the mass media most likely to cause antisocial effects. The undesirable effects occurred following exposure to movies that have been shown on national television and were clearly not X-rated pornography. Moreover, the primary theme of the films was not aggressive sexuality. It may be that a film that is explicitly pornographic is perceived as highly unrealistic and stimulates subjects' defenses against accepting the information conveyed uncritically. In contrast, the type of films used in this study may communicate more subtly false information about women's reactions to sexual aggression and consequently may have more potent effects since viewers are not "forewarned" (Freedman & Sears, 1965) by the label "X-rated" or "pornographic."

With respect to pornography, however, our research does indicate that certain types of pornographic portrayals can affect reactions to rape (e.g., Malamuth & Check, 1980a). These findings were recently extended in an experiment by Zillmann & Bryant (in press) who found that exposure to "massive" amounts of pornography over a period of about nine weeks resulted in more callous attitudes towards rape and a

283

general trivialization of this crime. This effect was found
several weeks following the exposure phase of the research.

ETHICAL CONSIDERATIONS

Some concerns have recently been raised regarding the
ethicality of research that exposes subjects to media portrayals of aggression against women, particularly to certain
types of aggressive pornography (e.g., Sherif, 1980). These
concerns have prompted investigators to attempt to assess the
effectiveness of debriefing procedures presented following
research participation (Malamuth & Check, in press; Donnerstein & Berkowitz, 1981; Check & Malamuth, in press). Such
debriefings have been designed to dispel rape myths by presenting more accurate information. Assessment of the effectiveness of these debriefings have been conducted as long as
four months following research participation (Donnerstein &
Berkowitz, 1981) as well as without subjects' awareness that
the assessment is related to their earlier research participation (Malamuth & Check, in press; Check & Malamuth, in press).

The findings of these studies show consistently that the
overall impact of research participation (including the debriefings) is to reduce subjects' acceptance of rape myths.
While the data indicate that the information contained within
the debriefings may be sufficient for some attitude change,
the combination of exposure to violent pornography that
portrays rape myths and the presentation of a debriefing that
specifically addresses these myths appears to be most effective in reducing rape myth acceptance (Check & Malamuth, in
press). These data have important implications for researchers focusing on the possible detrimental effects of violence
in pornography since the possibility of adversity affecting
participants could be a serious inhibitor to future research.
Knowledge that a debriefing may result in the total research
experience having a beneficial impact is likely to encourage
future work in this area. These data, however, should not be
taken as a carte blanche to justify any pornography exposure-
debriefing procedures. It is important that researchers in
this area design debriefing procedures which are appropriate
for their specific materials and assess their effectiveness
whenever possible (Sherif, 1980).

INDIVIDUAL CHARACTERISTICS

As indicated earlier, an important initial step in our
goal of studying individual characteristics that make certain
men more inclined to aggress against women has been to identify those men within the general population who show a relatively higher propensity to aggress against women. We believe
that we have been somewhat successful in this goal. This

284

research is presented in detail elsewhere (Malamuth, 1981b) and will be summarized here.

In studying individual characteristics and aggression against women, we have chosen to focus on rape. The following four steps were undertaken in order to determine whether a procedure could be developed to identify men with greater inclinations to rape and to obtain some assessment of the construct validity (Cronbach & Meehl, 1955) of such a procedure.

1) Developing a procedure of identifying males with a relative propensity to rape.

2) Finding dimensions that discriminate between rapists and non-rapists.

3) Determining whether men identified in Step 1 as having a relative propensity to rape are more similar to rapists on the relevant dimensions identified in step 2.

4) Assessing whether men identified as having a relative propensity to rape will actually be more aggressive against women.

The following discussion will present more information regarding the procedures used in each of these steps and the data obtained.

1.   Identifying Individuals with a Propensity to Rape

In an attempt to identify individuals who may show relatively stronger inclinations to aggress against women, males (mostly college students) were asked in a series of studies (Malamuth, 1981a; Malamuth, Haber & Feshbach, 1980; Malamuth & Check, 1980a, 1981a; Malamuth et al., 1979; Tieger, 1981) to indicate the likelihood that they personally would rape if they could be assured of not being caught and punished. The samples were derived from varied parts of North America including the Los Angeles and Stanford areas in California and the Winnipeg area in Canada. Typically, they were asked to indicate their responses on a five-point scale ranging from (1) not at all likely to (5) very likely. This question was asked under a variety of conditions, such as after viewing a videotaped interview with an actual rape victim, following the reading of a pornographic description of rape, and without any prior "exposure treatment" at all. While, as might be expected, there was some variability in the distribution of responses across studies, in general there was a great deal of consistency showing that a sizeable percentage of the respondents indicated some likelihood of raping (i.e., the LR report). Across these studies, an average of about 35% of males indicated any likelihood at all of raping (i.e., a 2 or

285

above on the scale) and an average of about 20% reported a 3 or above.

In order to determine the utility of LR reports as one means of distinguishing among men with differing inclinations to rape, we now turn to the second step of the research program--finding some general dimensions that characterize the responses of convicted rapists.

2. Finding Dimensions that Discriminate Between Rapists and Non-Rapists

Investigators have attempted to identify differences between convicted rapists and control groups on a variety of general measures. For example, comparisons have been made on the Rorschach Inkblot Test: (e.g., Perdue & Lester, 1972), the MMPI (e.g., Carroll & Fuller, 1971), the Edwards Personal Preference Schedule (Fisher & Rivlin, 1971), the Buss-Durkee Hostility Inventory (Buss & Durkee, 1957; Rada, Laws, & Kellner, 1976) and intelligence scales (Rada, 1978). As discussed by Rada (1978), these studies have failed to provide reliable differences between rapists and non-rapists.

There have been, however, two types of responses that appear to discriminate between rapists and the general population. Not surprisingly, these responses seem to be more directly linked to acts of rape. It has been found that rapists are more likely than other males (1) to hold callous attitudes about rape and to believe in rape myths, and (2) to show relatively high levels of sexual arousal to depictions of rape (see Malamuth, 1981b for a more detailed description of these differences in attitudes and sexual arousal).

3. Likelihood of Raping Reports and Dimensions Characterizing Rapists

LR and Rape Myths. It has been found consistently that individuals with higher LR reports hold more callous attitudes towards rape and believe in rape myths to a greater degree than those with lower LR scores (Malamuth et al., 1980a; Malamuth & Check, 1980a; Tieger, 1981; Malamuth et al., 1979). For example, higher LR scores have been shown to be related to the belief that other men would rape if they knew they could avoid being caught, to identification with rapists in depictions of rape, to perceptions that rape victims cause such assaults and derive pleasure from them (in fictionalized portrayals and in an actual interview with a rape victim), and with the belief that women in general secretly desire and enjoy such victimization. The conclusion that LR scores are strongly associated with callous attitudes towards rape and with beliefs in rape myths thus seems well supported. The magnitude of the differences between High vs. Low LR subjects is illustrated in data presented later in this chapter.

LR and Sexual Arousal. LR ratings have been found to be positively correlated with sexual arousal to rape but not with arousal to consenting depictions (Malamuth et al., 1980b; Malamuth & Check, 1980a, 1981a). This has been particularly true of self-reported sexual arousal, although similar results have been obtained recently with tumescence measures (Malamuth & Check, 1980a, 1981a). Sexual arousal patterns to rape and consenting-sex portrayals of High LR subjects have consistently been found to be much more similar to those of rapists (e.g., Abel, Barlow, Blanchard & Guild, 1977) than the responses of Low LR subjects (Malamuth, 1981b).

4. Likelihood of Raping and Aggressive Behaviour

The data reviewed above indicate that LR scores are associated with rape myth acceptance and callous attitudes about rape as well as with sexual arousal to rape in a theoretically expected manner. However, it remains to be demonstrated that LR reports can predict aggressive acts. Obviously, it is impossible to examine rape within an experimental setting. An alternative is to determine whether LR ratings predict acts of aggression that can be studied within a research context. While it is not suggested that such aggression constitutes an actual analogue to the crime of rape, it is suggested that rape is an act of violence related to other acts of aggression against women (Burt, 1980; Clark & Lewis, 1977). Therefore, measures assessing rape propensity should predict other acts of aggression against women. In determining whether LR ratings are associated with aggression we have examined subjects' own self-reported acts of aggression in dating interactions, as well as a more "objective" measure-- aggressive behaviour in the laboratory.

Date Aggression. A significant association has been found consistently between LR ratings and subjects' reports that they have personally used force against females in sexual relations and may do so again in the future. This association was obtained both when subjects reported such "data aggression" on items embedded within other questions on a lengthy questionnaire (e.g., Malamuth & Check, 1981a) and using a scale developed by Koss and Oros (1982) to measure the incidence of sexual aggression (Check & Malamuth, 1982a).

Laboratory Aggression. Within the context of research designed to determine whether certain measures predict aggressive behaviour against women (Malamuth, in press), 42 male college students were asked how likely they would be to rape if they could not be caught (i.e., the LR). Days later, the same subjects participated in what was ostensibly a totally different experiment; it was actually the second phase of the research. Post-experimental questionnaires verified that subjects believed they were participating in two completely unrelated experiments. In this second phase of the research, subjects were mildly rejected and insulted by a woman (confederate of the experimenter). The study used a "Buss paradigm." Subjects were allowed to choose among different levels of aversive noise (i.e., the measure of behavioural aggression), that they could (ostensibly) administer to the confederate as punishment for incorrect responses. In addition, subjects reported how angry they felt towards the woman and to what extent they had wanted to hurt her. LR reports were correlated with anger, r (40) = 0.36, p < .02, behavioural aggression, r (40) = 0.32, p < .05, and a reported desire to hurt the woman, r (40) = 0.37, p < .02. These data suggest that LR reports are related to male aggression against women.

MASS MEDIA EFFECTS AND INDIVIDUAL CHARACTERISTICS

The data presented heretofore have indicated that 1) the mass media can affect responses related to aggressive acts against women and 2) that meaningful distinctions can be empirically made among men in the general population vis-a-vis their propensity to aggress against females. We now turn to an example of our research designed to relate these two lines of investigation by analyzing whether individual characteristics of men mediate the impact of media stimuli.

In this experiment (Malamuth & Check, 1981a) male undergraduates were classified as Low vs. High LR on the basis of their responses to a questionnaire administered in a preliminary session. A laboratory session was also held at a later date. In this laboratory session, subjects were randomly assigned to listen to audio-tapes that were systematically manipulated in their content along the dimensions of Consent (woman's consent vs. non-consent) and Outcome (woman's arousal vs. disgust). Later, subjects completed a questionnaire that queried about their beliefs regarding the percentage of women, if any, that would derive some pleasure from being raped. While ethical questions may be raised concerning such questions, the fact that much research shows that such a myth is believed by many individuals (e.g., Burt, 1980; Malamuth et al., 1980a) and the use of a debriefing shown to be effective at counteracting such false beliefs (see earlier discussion) may justify these inquiries within a research context.

The results indicated a main effect of Likelihood of Raping reports, with High LR subjects estimating much higher percentages of women enjoying being raped in comparison with Low LR subjects (M = 24.7% and M = 6.63%, respectively, p < .0001). In addition, an interaction effect was obtained between the Consent and Outcome content manipulations. Whereas the manipulation of Outcome (i.e., woman's arousal vs. woman's disgust) within the consenting portrayals had no impact on subjects' perceptions of women's reactions to rape, manipulations of the Outcome dimension within non-consenting (i.e., rape) depictions did affect subjects' perceptions. However, further analyses indicated that this Outcome by Consent interaction primarily occurred in the High LR group: High LR subjects who had earlier been exposed to the "rape-woman's arousal" depiction believed that more women would enjoy being raped (mean of 36.9%) than High LR subjects presented with the "rape-woman's disgust" depiction (M = 20.0%, p < .008). As noted, manipulation of the Outcome dimension within the consenting-sex depictions had no impact on subjects' estimation of victims' reactions to rape for either High LR subjects (M = 21.4%) or Low LR subjects (M = 6.4%). For Low LR subjects, the manipulation of Outcome within the rape depictions did not have a significant effect either, although the pattern of the means (10.6% for the arousal vs. 3.8% for the disgust depiction) was in the same direction as the significant differences obtained for High LR subjects. These data suggest that men who already are accepting of rape myths to a relatively high degree may be particularly susceptible to the influence of media depictions of such myths.

RECENT DEVELOPMENTS

In this section, I will describe some of the recent developments intended to extend the earlier work described in this chapter and to provide a framework for further research in this area. The two developments that will be discussed concern individual differences among subjects and the validity of the measures used in the research.

Individual Differences

The individual differences variable described above was based on subjects' self-reported likelihood of raping. In light of the support obtained for the utility of this dimension, we have been attempting to develop a more rigorous measure of inclinations to aggress against women. As a first step in this process, in addition to asking males how likely they would be to rape, we have also asked them to indicate how likely, if at all, they would be to force a female to participate in sexual acts "she really didn't want to" if they could be assured that they would not be caught. Of the 356 male participants in a study using both the reported likelihood of raping and likelihood of forcing items (Briere & Malamuth, 1981), 99 indicated some likelihood of both raping and forcing (R+F+), 6 indicated some likelihood of raping but not forcing (R+F-), 108 indicated a likelihood of forcing but not raping (R-F+) and 143 indicated no likelihood of raping or forcing (R-F-). Given the small size of the R+F- group, these subjects were excluded from the analysis.

While in the research reported earlier comparable findings were found if reported likelihood of raping is treated as a continuous variable or if it is dichotomized (i.e., no likelihood vs. any likelihood), Briere and Malamuth (1981) sought to determine whether dividing the sample into three subgroups as described above may be preferable to dichotomizing the sample. Subjects were administered various scales designed to measure rape-supportive attitudes (e.g., rape myths). Such attitudes have been consistently found, as noted earlier, to be associated with reported likelihood of raping. Polynomial analyses revealed highly significant linear relationships between levels of willingness to rape or force and degree of rape-supportive attitudes (with R-F- group being the lowest, then the R-F+ group, and the R+F+ group the highest). These data suggest that dividing samples into the three subgroups described may provide even better discrimination than a dichotomous separation.

Validity of Measures

Three types of measures have been employed in the research program described in this chapter. These are measures of attitudes about aggression, sexual arousal to rape, and aggressive behaviour in the laboratory. The attitude and sexual arousal measures concern "real world" aggression such as rape and wife-battering. In a recent experiment, Malamuth (in press) reasoned that if measures designed to assess factors contributing to "real world" aggression against women were found to predict successfully aggression within a laboratory setting, this would provide support for the construct validity of a nomological network (Cronbach & Meehl, 1955) composed of 1) the theory underlying the development of the predictive measures, 2) the measures designed to predict rape and other acts of aggression against women, and 3) the methodology of assessing such aggression within an experimental context as a basis for testing theory in the area, futher refining the predictive measures and for drawing implications to non-experimental settings.

The research by Malamuth (in press) was conducted in two phases. In the first phase, two factors theorized to cause rape and related acts of aggression against women were assessed. The subjects were males from the general population, mostly college students. The first factor was labelled "Sexual Arousal to Rape," which was measured by the "rape index" developed by Abel et al., (1977) (i.e., sexual arousal to rape relative to arousal to consenting depictions). Two separate measurements of this index were taken several weeks apart using different rape and consenting depictions. Abel et al., (see also Abel & Blanchard, 1976) contend that this measure assesses a "proclivity to rape."

The second factor assessed in the first phase of the research was labelled "Attitudes Facilitating Violence." This was measured by the Rape Myth Acceptance (RMA) and Acceptance

290

of Interpersonal Violence (AIV) scales developed by Burt (1980). These scales were embedded within many other items so that the subjects would not be aware of their specific focus. Burt (1978, 1980) theorizes that certain attitudes about rape and about violence contribute to the commission of rape and similar crimes.

The second phase of the research was held several days after each subject completed the first phase. In this second phase, aggression was assessed. However, subjects were completely unaware of the relationship between the two phases of the research but believed that they were participating in two completely unrelated experiments. This procedure eliminated the possible role of "demand characteristics." In this second phase, subjects were angered by a woman (a confederate) and given the opportunity of ostensibly punishing her with aversive noise. Also, subjects were later asked about their desire to hurt the woman with the aversive noise (Baron & Eggleston, 1972).

The results showed that the measures assessed in the first phase successfully predicted aggressive behaviour in the second phase of the research. This was apparent both in correlational data and in the results of an analysis using "causal" modeling with latent and manifest variables (Bentler, 1978, 1980; Bentler & Bonnett, 1980; Joreskog & Sorbom, 1978). Using the "causal" modeling approach, a latent variable named "Sexual Arousal to Rape" was operationally defined by the two assessments of the "rape index." A second latent factor, named "Attitudes Facilitating Violence," was operationally defined by the RMA and AIV scales. A latent factor labelled "Aggression Against Women" was operationally defined by the levels of aversive noise and levels of the reported desire to hurt the woman. The model constructed had "causal" paths from the Sexual Arousal to Rape and from the Attitudes Facilitating Violence factors to the Aggression Against Women factor. This model was tested by the LISREL IV PROGRAM (Joreskog & Sorbom, 1978). The model was found to successfully represent the data and both of the "causal" paths to aggression were found to be significant, indicating that better prediction of laboratory aggression could be achieved from information derived from assessing sexual arousal to rape and attitudes regarding violence than on the basis of either of these factors individually. Together, the Arousal to Rape and the Attitudes Facilitating Violence factors accounted for 43% of the variance of the Aggression Against Women factor.

Malamuth and Check (in preparation) recently attempted to replicate and extend one aspect of the above findings-- the prediction of aggression on the basis of scales measuring attitudes about aggression. In addition to the RMA and AIV scales, they administered to male undergraduates a scale

291

specifically developed for this research which assessed General Acceptance of Violence (GAV). The results indicated that the RMA and AIV scales but not the GAV scale successfully predicted aggression against women. These data are in keeping with other findings in our research program that suggest that male aggression against women may be affected by processes that differ from those that affect male-male aggression.

These findings provide support for the construct validity of the nomological network described above. The data may be especially pertinent to the debate concerning the external validity of laboratory assessment of aggression (e.g., Berkowitz & Donnerstein, 1982). In providing support for the construct validity of the various measures used in the research program described in this chapter, it is hoped that these data will encourage further empirical work in this area with particular emphasis on the development of testable theoretical models of the cultural and individual factors that cause aggression against women.

ACKNOWLEDGEMENT

I would like to thank the Social Sciences and Humanities Research Council of Canada for their generous support of the research described in this chapter.

REFERENCES

Abel, G.G., Barlow, D.H., Blanchard, E., & Guild, D. The components of rapists' sexual arousal. Archives of General Psychiatry, 1977, 34, 895-903.

Abel, G.G., & Blanchard, E.B. The measurement and generation of sexual arousal in male deviates. In M. Hersen, R.M. Eisler, & P.M. Miller (Eds.). Progress in behavior modification, Vol. 2, New York: Academic Press, 1976.

Baron, R.A., & Eggleston, R.J. Performance on the "Aggression Machine," Motivation to help or harm? Psychonomic Science, 1972, 26, 321-322.

Bentler, P.M. The interdependence of theory, methodology and empirical data: Causal modeling as an approach to construct validation. In D.B. Kendel (Ed.). Longitudinal research on drug use. New York: Wiley, 1978.

Bentler, P.M. Multivariate analysis with latent variables: Causal modeling. Annual Review of Psychology, 1980, 31, 419-456.

Bentler, P.M., & Bonnett, D.G. Significance tests and goodness of fit in the analysis of covariance structures. Psychological Bulletin, 1980, 88, 588-606.

Berkowitz, L., & Donnerstein, E. External validity is more
    than skin deep: Some answers to criticisms of laboratory
    experiments (with special reference to research on ag-
    gression). American Psychologist, 1982, 37, 245-257.
Briere, J., & Malamuth, N. Self-assessed rape proclivity:
    Attitudinal and sexual correlates. Paper presented at
    the Annual Meetings of the American Psychological Associ-
    ation, Los Angeles, August, 1981.
Brown, B.C. Images of family life in magazine advertising.
    New York: Praeger, 1981.
Brownmiller, S. Against our will: Men, women and rape.
    New York: Simon and Schuster, 1975.
Burt, M.R. Attitudes supportive of rape in American culture.
    House Committee on Science and Technology, Subcommittee
    on Domestic and International Scientific Planning Analysis
    and Cooperation. Research into Violent Behaviour: Sexual
    Assaults. (Hearing, 95th Congress, 2nd Session, January
    10-12, 1978). Washington, D.C.: Government Printing
    Office, 1978, 277-322.
Burt, M.R. Cultural myths and supports for rape. Journal of
    Personality and Social Psychology, 1980, 38, 217-230.
Buss, A.H., & Durkee, A. An inventory for assessing different
    kinds of hostility. Journal of Consulting Psychology,
    1957, 21, 343-349.
Carroll, J.L., & Fuller, G.B. An MMPI comparison of three
    groups of criminals. Journal of Clinical Psychology,
    1971, 27, 240-242.
Ceniti, J., & Malamuth, N. Self-assessed rape proclivity:
    Attitudinal and sexual correlates. In preparation.
Check, J.V.P., & Malamuth, N. Can there be positive effects
    of participation in pornography experiments? Journal of
    Sex Research, in press.
Check, J.V.P., & Malamuth, N. The hostility towards women scale:
    Correlations with rape-related variables. Paper presented
    at the Annual Meetings of the American Psychological
    Association, Washington, D.C., August, 1982. (a)
Check, J.V.P., & Malamuth, N. Pornography effects and self-
    reported likelihood of committing acquaintance vs.
    stranger rape. Paper presented at the Annual Meetings
    of the Midwestern Pscyhological Association, Minneapolis,
    May, 1982. (b)
Clark, L., & Lewis, D. Rape: The price of coercive sexuality.
    Toronto: The Women's Press, 1977.
Cronbach, L.J., & Meehl, P. Construct validity in psychological
    tests. Psychological Bulletin, 1955, 52, 281-302.
Donnerstein, E. Aggressive-Erotica and violence against women.
    Journal of Personality and Social Psychology, 1980, 39,
    269-277.
Donnerstein, E., & Berkowitz, L. Victim reactions in aggres-
    sive-erotic films as a factor in violence against women.
    Journal of Personality and Social Psychology, 1981, 41,
    710-724.

FBI Uniform Crime Reports. Washington, D.C.: U.S. Government Printing Office, 1978.

FBI Uniform Crime Reports. Washington, D.C.: U.S. Government Printing Office, 1979.

FBI Uniform Crime Reports. Washington, D.C.: U.S. Government Printing Office, 1980.

Fisher, G., & Rivlin, E. Psychological needs of rapists. British Journal of Criminology, 1971, 11, 182-185.

Freedman, J., & Sears, D. Warning, distraction and resistance to influence. Journal of Personality and Social Psychology, 1965, 1, 262-266.

Giarusso, R., Johnson, P., Goodchilds, J., & Zellman, G. Adolescents' cues and signals: Sex and assault. Paper presented at the Annual Meetings of the Western Psychological Association, San Diego, CA, April, 1979.

Goffman, E. Gender advertisements. Cambridge, Mass.: Harvard University Press, 1979.

Joreskog, K.G., & Sorbom, D.G. LISREL IV: Estimation of linear structural equation systems by maximum likelihoods methods. Chicago: National Educational Resources, 1978.

Kanin, E. Male aggression in dating-courtship relations. American Journal of Sex Research, 1965, 1, 221-231.

Kanin, E. An examination of sexual aggression as a response to sexual frustration. Journal of Marriage and the Family, 1967, 29, 428-433.

Kanin, E., & Parcell, S. Sexual aggression: A second look at the offended female. Archives of Sexual Behavior, 1977, 6, 67-76.

Koss, M., & Oros, C. Hidden rape: A survey of the incidence of sexual aggression and victimization on a university campus. Journal of Consulting and Clinical Psychology, 1982, 50, 445-457.

Malamuth, N. Erotica, aggression & perceived appropriateness. Paper presented at the Eighty-Sixth Annual Convention of the American Psychological Association, September 1978, Toronto, Canada.

Malamuth, N. Rape fantasies as a function of exposure to violent sexual stimuli, Archives of Sexual Behavior, 1981, 10, 33-47. (a)

Malamuth, N. Rape proclivity among males. Journal of Social Issues, 1981, 37, 138-157. (b)

Malamuth, N. Factors associated with rape as predictors of laboratory aggression against women. Journal of Personality and Social Psychology, in press.

Malamuth, N., & Check, J.V.P. Penile tumescence and perceptual responses to rape as a function of victim's perceived reactions. Journal of Applied Social Psychology, 1980, 10, 6, 528-547. (a)

Malamuth, N., & Check, J.V.P. Sexual arousal to rape and consenting depictions: The importance of the woman's arousal. Journal of Abnormal Psychology, 1980, 89, 763-766. (b)

Malamuth, N., & Check, J.V.P. The effects of exposure to
aggressive-pornography: Rape proclivity, sexual arousal
and beliefs in rape myths. Paper presented at the Annual
Convention of the American Psychological Association, Los
Angeles, California, August 1981. (a)

Malamuth, N., & Check, J.V.P. The effects of mass media
exposure on acceptance of violence against women: A
field experiment. Journal of Research in Personality,
1981, 15, 436-446. (b)

Malamuth, N., & Check, J.V.P. Debriefing effectiveness
following exposure to pornographic rape depictions.
The Journal of Sex Research, in press.

Malamuth, N., & Check, J.V.P. Attitudes facilitating violence
and laboratory aggression against women. In preparation.

Malamuth, N., & Donnerstein, E. The effects of aggressive-
pornographic mass media stimuli. In L. Berkowitz (Ed.).
Advances in Experimental Social Psychology, Vol. 15.
New York: Academic Press, in press.

Malamuth, N., Feshbach, S., Fera, T., & Kunath, J. Sexual
arousal as a function of aggressive cues in erotica.
Paper presented at the Annual Meetings of the Western
Psychological Association, San Francisco, April, 1978.

Malamuth, N., Haber, S., & Feshbach, S. Testing hypotheses
regarding rape: Exposure to sexual violence, sex
differences, and the "normality" of rapists. Journal
of Research in Personality, 1980, 14, 121-137. (a)

Malamuth, N., Heim, M., & Feshbach, S. Sexual responsiveness
of college students to rape depictions: Inhibitory and
disinhibitory effects. Journal of Personality and Social
Psychology, 1980, 38, 399-408. (b)

Malamuth, N., Reisin, I., & Spinner, B. Exposure to pornography
and reactions to rape. Paper presented at the Eighty-
Seventh Annual Convention of the American Psychological
Association, New York, 1979.

Perdue, W.C., & Lester, D. Personality characteristics of
rapists. Perceptual and Motor Skills, 1972, 35, 514.

Rada, R.T. Clinical aspects of the rapist. New York:
Grune & Stratton, 1978.

Rada, R.T., Laws, D.R., & Kellner, R. Plasma testosterone
levels in the rapist. Psychosomatic Medicine, 1976,
38, 257-268.

Sherif, C.W. Comment on ethical issues in Malamuth, Heim,
and Feshbach's "Sexual responsiveness of college students
to rape depictions: Inhibitory and disinhibitory
effects." Journal of Personality and Social Psychology,
1980, 38, 409-412.

Tieger, T. Self-rated likelihood of raping and the social
perception of rape. Journal of Research in Personality,
1981, 15, 147-158.

Zillmann, D., & Bryant, J. Effects of massive exposure to
pornography. In N. Malamuth & E. Donnerstein (Eds.).
Pornography and Sexual Aggression. New York: Academic
Press, in press.

295

CONTRIBUTIONS OF AVERSIVE EXPERIENCES TO ROBBERY AND HOMICIDE: A
DEMOGRAPHIC ANALYSIS

Charles W. Turner, Allen M. Cole, and Daniel S. Cerro
Department of Psychology, University of Utah, Salt Lake City, Utah

One of the most fundamental problems confronted in modern
societies is the expression and control of violence. Within the
past century, acts of violence have produced approximately one
hundred million deaths (Elliott, 1972). The destructive capacity
of violence has grown so rapidly in the past 80 years that modern
weapons are capable of destroying every living creature on
earth. In the pursuit of understanding the causes of violence,
we need to distinguish between collective acts of violence (e.g.,
riots and warfare) and individual acts of violence (e.g.,
criminal acts such as murder and robbery). The factors which
precipitate violent acts among groups (collective violence) are
not necessarily the same as the factors which stimulate violence
between individuals. As with collective violence, individual
acts of violence are a major problem for modern societies. Over
the past 80 years, the annual frequency of individual acts of
violence have increased in many modern industrialized societies
(cf. Turner, Fenn, & Cole, 1981). For example, the annual
frequency of violent crime in the United States has risen sharply
in the past 20 years by 300% for homicide and 1000% for robbery
(Uniform Crime Reports, 1960-1979).

Changes in modern societies are not limited to increasing
violence. For example, many nations have experienced a
substantial increase in nonviolent crimes (e.g., theft),
alcoholism, unemployment, pollution, overpopulation, and marital

---

Authors' Note. The authors are indebted to Judith Turner for her
comments on an earlier draft. The research was supported in part
by NIMH funds to the University of Utah.

296

Kaplan, R.M., Konečni, V.J., Novaco, R.W. (eds.) Aggression in Children and Youth
© 1984, Martinus Nijhoff Publishers, The Hague/Boston/Lancaster
ISBN 90-247-2903-3. Printed in The Netherlands

disruption (e.g., divorce). In the United States alone, the number of divorces per 1000 marriage ceremonies increased 83% between 1950 and 1974 (U.S. Bureau of Census, 1950-1974). Similar changes have occurred in most European countries (Goode, 1976; Kenkel, 1977). The birth rate (per 1000 women) has dropped to an all time low (U.S. Bureau of the Census, 1960-1979).

The increasing rate of social problems is sometimes cited as evidence that some modern social institutions such as the family are undergoing increased disorganization (Goode, 1976; Kenkel, 1977). Schulz (1976) proposed that social institutions have not adapted to technological changes. According to this view, some social institutions such as the family may continue to deteriorate if the rate of technological changes remains high. With the disruption of traditional social institutions, young adults often experience high levels of stress when they attempt to leave their parents' home and establish independent lives. Continuing technological changes, Schulz (1976) claims, could lead to high levels of stress that would be reflected in high crime, unemployment, alcoholism, and divorce rates.

We do not deny that modern societies are undergoing rapid change and that many norms, customs, and laws are being challenged. We contend, however, that the recent increases in many important social problems are primarily the result of rapidly fluctuating birth rates over the past 60 years. These changing birth rates have produced marked variations in the number of individuals who are susceptible to major social problems such as unemployment, crime, and divorce. We will try to demonstrate that an individual is most likely to experience these social problems during the transition period from adolescence to adulthood. One effect of an increase in a specific year's birth rate is an increase 18 years later in the number of individuals who will make the transition from adolescence to adulthood.

We provide evidence that some social problems in modern societies are transitory. For example, the high levels of stress on young adults has produced a declining fertility rate (e.g., from 1960 to 1980 in the United States). Due to the declining fertility rate, fewer individuals will be in the critical transition age groups 18 years later (i.e., from 1978 through 1998). As a consequence, the annual frequency of social problems such as crime, unemployment and divorce should decrease from 1978 through 1998. Because there have been cross-national differences in birth rates over the past 60 years, there will also be national differences in the rising and falling rates of unemployment, crime, fertility, and divorce.

The following analysis focuses primarily upon the contribution of fluctuating population pressures to the violent crimes of homicide and robbery. The analysis relies upon data

297

from the United States, but similar analyses could be performed on data in other countries. We have summarized earlier research and provided additional evidence to support five major assumptions which guided our analysis of homicide and robbery. First, we proposed that most murders result primarily from automatic or impulsive actions while most robberies reflect purposive or controlled aggressive acts. Second, although aggressive behaviors are multifaceted phenomena with many antecedent conditions, aggression is particularly likely to to be a learned reaction to aversive life events. Failures to achieve the goals to which one aspires (e.g., task failure or relative deprivation) are aversive events which can increase the likelihood of aggression. Third, aggression is not the only, or even the most likely response to aversive events. Situational and environmental variables can influence whether an individual is likely to respond aggressively to an aversive event. For example, an individual experiencing aversive events is more likely to be aggressive if the environment lowers inhibitions and also contains aggressive cues such as weapons, or aggressive words and film (Turner, Simons, Berkowitz, & Frodi, 1977). The aggressive cues may increase aggression either by eliciting aggressive reactions or by serving as retrieval cues for prior aggressive events (e.g., insults, aggressive models, or aggressive thoughts and feelings). Social learning processes also determine (through direct and vicarious experiences) which members of a society develop aggression as the primary mode of coping with aversive life events. That is, social learning processes produce some personality types (e.g. Type A/B) and some learning environments (e.g., delinquent subcultures) which are particularly likely to influence whether an individual will respond violently or nonviolently to aversive events. Fourth, when young people experience high levels of relative deprivation during the transition from adolescence to adulthood, some may respond violently. For example, revolutions and riots, as well as robbery and homicide become more frequent when young adults experience high levels of relative deprivation. Fifth, fluctuating population pressures (due to birth, death, and immigration rates) have modified the number of individuals who are very susceptible to experiencing aversive life events. As more members of a society experience distress, more of them are likely to act violently; but, the people experiencing the most aversive events are not necessarily the ones most likely to behave violently. In the sections which follow, we have summarized evidence to support these five assumptions.

IMPULSIVE AND PURPOSIVE AGGRESSION

Both robbery and homicide are crimes which involve the threat and use of physical aggression. However, the crimes differ in that most robberies appear to be purposive or planned acts while most homicides appear to be unplanned impulsive acts. Berkowitz

298

(1974, 1982) has proposed that very different processes may be involved in the expression of impulsive and purposive aggression. Other researchers have made a similar distinction with the concepts of hostile and instrumental aggression (e.g., Feshbach, 1964). Bandura (1973) has criticized the hostile/instrumental aggression distinction on the grounds that both behaviors are motivated by the attainment of some goal (achieving an extrinsic goal or avoiding a noxious event): the nature of the goal is simply different for each type of aggression. Hence, Bandura reasoned that both types of behavior should be labeled as instrumental aggression.

In an attempt to resolve this definitional controversy, Zillmann (1979) has proposed that a distinction be made in terms of incentive-motivated versus annoyance-motivated aggression. Incentive-motivated aggression is directed toward the attainment of extrinsic incentives and is characterized by calculated, dispassionate acts (e.g., spreading malicious rumors about a competitor). Most robberies appear to be deliberate acts involving some prior planning with the primary goal of obtaining financial gain rather than hurting the victim, so that these acts might be defined as incentive-motivated aggression.

Annoyance-motivated aggression is directed toward the goal of terminating or reducing noxious conditions. When these conditions produce intense anger, frustration, or excitement, the resultant aggression is characterized by heated, impulsive, emotional reactions (Zillman, 1979, pp 718-725). Most homicides appear to be impulsive reactions following an escalating argument (Newton & Zimring, 1969; Toch, 1969). Such impulsive reactions might be defined as annoyance-motivated aggression.

Regardless of the specific terms that are used, a large number of studies have demonstrated the usefulness of analyzing some aggressive acts as impulsive, automatic processes (cf., Berkowitz, 1974; Turner et al., 1977; Zillmann, 1979). Presumably, an individual might not act violently for the pleasure that s/he anticipates will follow from her/his behavior, nor does s/he act violently because inhibitions against the expression of violence have been lowered. Instead, the aggression results from automatic responses to aversive experiences that an individual is predisposed to make in a given situation (Berkowitz, 1978, 1982).

Intense, aversive experiences predispose an individual toward aggressive responses, and specific environmental stimulation can increase the probability of impulsive aggression from the predisposed individual (Berkowitz, 1982). People learn at a very early age that obnoxious, coercive, or aggressive reactions are effective methods of terminating aversive experiences (Turner et al., 1981). For example, Patterson and Cobb (1973) have investigated aggressive or coercive behaviors in children and

299

compiled extensive evidence that parents frequently but inadvertently produce negative reinforcement--terminate aversive experiences--for their children's obnoxious behavior. That is, when their children are exposed to aversive experiences, parents discover that the resulting crying (or other obnoxious behavior) can be eliminated most readily by removing or terminating the child's aversive experience (cf. Turner & Dodd, 1979). A child with a history of negative reinforcement for obnoxious, coercive behaviors is likely to respond to intense aversive experiences with these obnoxious behaviors in an impulsive fashion (also see Zillmann, 1979, pp. 715-718).

However, violence and aggression are not solely due to impulsive processes. Various cognitive processes can influence an individual's interpretation of the situation and her/his understanding of internal or emotional responses (cf. Konečni, 1975; Novaco, 1979; Rule & Nesdale, 1976). For example, an individual may inhibit aggression if s/he perceives that the aggressive behavior will not achieve desired goals or that aggression is inappropriate (Turner & Simons, 1974) and possibly even dangerous in a given situation. A robber may choose her/his victim primarily by weighing the potential financial gain as compared to the risk of being caught and punished (Gibbons, 1973).

Several researchers have proposed that a major cause of criminal violence is dissatisfaction with economic opportunities (Cloward & Ohlin, 1960; Henry & Short, 1954; Turner et al. 1981). These analyses are based, in part, on a hypothesized link between frustration and aggression. However, individuals react in quite different ways to frustrating or aversive conditions such as economic deprivation. The link between frustration and aggression is not a simple or direct relationship. The research presented in this chapter indicates that aversive economic conditions can increase the probability of homicide and robbery. Before presenting our analysis of homicide and robbery, however, we review some of the factors which mitigate aggressive reactions to aversive events.

AGGRESSIVE REACTIONS TO AVERSIVE EVENTS

Frustration-Aggression Hypothesis

The earliest formal treatment of the relationship between frustration and aggression postulated that frustration was both a necessary and sufficient condition for aggression (Dollard, Doob, Miller, Mowrer, and Sears, 1939). However, it quickly became apparent that the hypothesis was too broadly formulated (Miller, 1941). In fact, in a review of research on the frustration-aggression hypothesis, Berkowitz (1973) argued that: "Contrary to their original argument, the existence of frustration does not always lead to some form of aggression, and the occurrence of aggressive behavior does not necessarily presuppose the existence of frustration (page 2)." Rather than discard the frustration-aggression hypothesis, however, Berkowitz proposed a modification of that early statement: Under certain conditions, a frustrating event increases the probability that aggressive behavior will subsequently appear, and this relationship applies both to humans and to other animal species.

Definitions of Frustration

Much of the debate and research over the years has been directed at the problem of agreeing on a specific definition of the concept of frustration. Some researchers prefer to restrict the concept to an external event, condition, or state (e.g., frustration is defined as "an interference with the occurrence of an instigated goal-response at its proper time in the behavior sequence" (Dollard et al., 1939, p. 7) Other researchers have defined frustration as the internal reaction of an individual to specific events (especially Amsel, 1958; Brown & Farber, 1951; Berkowitz, 1962; and Hokanson & Burgess, 1962). In employing the definition of frustration as an internal state, Berkowitz (1974) has attempted to specify the antecedent conditions which lead to the experience of frustration. Although noxious stimuli and personal insults have been shown to instigate aggression, it is not clear whether these events can be defined as frustrations. Bandura (1973) has proposed that the term frustration be replaced by the construct of aversive events. Thus, insults, painful stimuli, and reductions in the level of rewarding conditions (e.g., extinction) have one property in common--they are all physically or psychologically aversive to the organism. An operational definition of the aversive property of an event can be established by determining whether an organism will work to terminate the event (Ulrich, Dulaney, Arnett, & Mueller, 1973).

Problems of operationalizing and definitions aside, subsequent research demonstrated that frustration (an aversive event) is neither a necessary nor a sufficient condition for aggression. Forms of aggression do occur without apparent frustration (violating the necessary condition) and aggression is not the only or even the most frequent consequence of frustration (violating the sufficient condition). Bandura (1973, 1977, & 1979) has proposed that aversive events produce many different and diverse reactions such as increased striving, depression and apathy as well as aggression.

Cognitive factors can determine whether a particular experience is perceived as aversive, annoying or frustrating. For example, Lazarus (1966) proposed that a distinction must be made between an individual's appraisal of the severity of a potentially aversive event (labeled primary appraisal) and her/his appraisal of the resources available to deal with the event (secondary appraisal).

301

Secondary appraisal is related to Bandura's (1977) concept of self efficacy. Individuals with a strong rather than weak efficacy expectation are more likely to believe that they have resources to control or terminate an aversive event. For example, if s/he is certain of the probable effects of various decisions and courses of action, then s/he can select a course of action which has a high probability of terminating the aversive event. However, if s/he is uncertain about the effects of various actions, s/he is likely to have a weak perceived efficacy in controlling the aversive experiences. Turner et al. (1981) reasoned that individuals differ in their perceptions of whether assertive, achievement, problem solving, or aggressive behaviors are effective in terminating threatening events. For example, children in playground conflicts may learn to stop the threatening behavior of other children either by negotiating solutions to resolve the conflicts or by reciprocating aggression to escalate the conflict. Sometimes escalating aggression can intimidate the other children so that they stop their threatening behavior (Patterson, Littman & Bricker, 1967). When children learn that escalating aggression terminates other people's threatening behavior, they are more likely to use similar strategies in future conflict situations (Patterson et al., 1967).

Even though an individual may not be able to control or terminate an aversive experience, s/he may be able to "blunt" or reduce the intensity of the aversive experience (Miller & Grant, 1979). Turner et al. (1981) have described a variety of strategies for minimizing the intensity of uncontrollable aversive experiences. For example, individuals may use various pleasant or aesthetic stimuli to distract themselves from thinking about aversive experiences. By attending to music, food, television, sexual stimuli, alcohol, drugs, or pleasant thoughts rather than an unpleasant event, an individual can reduce the perceived intensity of an aversive experience. Leventhal's (1970, 1980) distinction between danger control and fear control is similar to the distinction between efficacy and blunting strategies. For example, potentially threatening advertisements which emphasize the health hazards of smoking may cause some individuals to reduce smoking (problem solving-danger control) or to focus on aesthetic stimuli (fear control). Leventhal reasoned that these two strategies are usually incompatible since danger control requires one to focus on the threatening communication while fear control requires one to avoid attending to the threatening communication. According to Leventhal (1980), high self esteem (i.e., high self efficacy) individuals are more likely to use danger control while low self esteem (i.e., low self efficacy) individuals are more likely to use fear control.

Two other types of responses may occur to uncontrollable aversive experiences if blunting/fear control responses are not available for aversive events (Turner et al., 1981). First, an individual may attempt to withdraw from or avoid the event. For example, when adolescents are unable to successfully compete for jobs in the labor force, they may be attracted to juvenile gangs or groups that derogate the pursuit of legitimate opportunities (Cloward & Ohlin, 1960). When an adolescent is unable to terminate or blunt aversive experiences within the family, the teenager may run away from home to avoid these experiences. Second, when an individual cannot terminate, blunt, or avoid an aversive experience, s/he may experience learned helplessness (Seligman, 1975). For example, child neglect may occur when a parent is unable to effectively terminate an infant's distress. The repeated, uncontrollable bouts of crying may eventually cause the parent to "give up" and to stop caring for the child. Both the parent and the child may experience learned helplessness since neither can influence the environment to achieve desired outcomes. This helplessness is likely to produce depression rather than mere indifference (Seligman, 1975).

In summary, aggression is only one of many responses that can occur to frustrating or aversive experiences, and aggression is probably not the most common reaction to aversive experiences. Still, extensive research indicates that aversive experiences increase the probability of aggression. Such experiences can increase aggression in an individual when s/he is also uninhibited and exposed to aggressive cues (Berkowitz, 1974). The research that is presented next specifies some of the conditions in which frustrating and aversive experiences influenced aggression.

Experimental Investigations of the Frustration-Aggression Hypothesis

In criticizing the frustration-aggression hypothesis, Buss (1961, 1966) argued that almost all tests of the theory had confounded frustration with attack. Buss suggested that, at best, frustrations are weak instigations to aggression while attacks or insults can be quite potent antecedents of aggression. Several investigators have reported that frustrations were ineffective in instigating overt aggression from their subjects (Buss, 1961, 1966; Kuhn, Madsen, & Becker, 1967; Taylor & Pisano, 1971).

Berkowitz (1974), however, has proposed that frustrations can produce aggressive reactions, especially if a frustrated individual also is uninhibited and is exposed to aggressive cues (e.g., aggressive words or weapons). Geen and Berkowitz (1967) conducted a study to show that task frustration (failure in completing a task) can lead to aggression. The researchers produced task frustration for one group of subjects by presenting them with an unsolvable puzzle. Some of these frustrated subjects were also verbally insulted by a confederate of the

303

experimenter (ostensibly a fellow subject) when they failed to complete the puzzle successfully. A third group of control subjects was given a solvable puzzle.

The researchers varied the presence or absence of aggressive cues by exposing subjects to an aggressive or a non-aggressive film. Half of the subjects in each of the three frustration groups (including the controls) then observed a seven-minute excerpt from the film Champion which depicts the character played by Kirk Douglas receiving a severe beating in a boxing match. The other half of the subjects in the frustration conditions saw an exciting but non-aggressive track film. Earlier research had indicated that the Champion film produced a specific tendency for subjects who had been insulted to attack an individual associated with the victim of the film (Geen & Berkowitz, 1966; Berkowitz & Geen, 1966). Consequently, the confederate reported his name to be "Kirk" in half of the conditions, thereby ostensibly establishing a connection between himself and the film victim. In a subsequent learning situation, actually a modification of the Buss (1961) procedure, the subject was instructed to train his partner (the experimenter's confederate) on a task by giving him electric shocks.

Geen and Berkowitz (1967) found that the task-frustrated subjects who also had seen the aggressive film were more willing to deliver intense electric shocks to their partner when he was associated with the film victim than subjects in the control conditions. However, the task-frustrated subjects were less willing to harm their high cue-valued partner than the insulted subjects. Although the results demonstrated that task-frustrated subjects are more aggressive than non-frustrated subjects, the relative weakness of task frustration contrasted with insult as an antecedent of aggression may be that laboratory subjects normally experience strong inhibitions about expressing aggression. Increased aggression then would be observed after task frustration only within those limited situations in which inhibitions are low.

Geen (1968) extended the findings of the Geen and Berkowitz (1967) study by separating the insult and the task frustration. Subjects met a confederate of the experimenter who ostensibly was chosen arbitrarily to be a learner in a teaching machine project. The subject was to be the teacher by administering shock of intensity "2" to the confederate whenever he made an error. During the training, the experimenter either verbally "reinforced" the aggression or did not so reinforce the subject (by comments to the subject, such as "Good," or "You're doing fine."). Subsequently, the subject was asked to solve a puzzle which was used to produce the frustration manipulations. Some of the subjects were given a "solvable" puzzle but before they finished they were interrupted by a confederate who prevented them from finishing the puzzle (personal frustration). Another group of subjects received a solvable puzzle and upon completion were insulted by the confederate (insult). A final set of subjects was given the solvable puzzle and permitted to complete it while seated alone. The subjects then observed the prize fight film used in previous studies (Berkowitz & Geen, 1966; Geen & Berkowitz, 1967). This research had shown the film to be essential for producing differences among treatment conditions (partially by lowering inhibitions of subjects). The results indicated that subjects were more likely to aggress against their partner in the task frustration condition than in the untreated control conditions. Geen interpreted his findings in the light of two previous studies. Although task frustration may not be a strong antecedent of aggression in all situations, task frustration can lead to strong attacks in situations where there are aggressive cues.

Frustration, arousal and aggressive stimuli. Geen (1968) suggested two possible mechanisms for the increased aggression following frustration. Presumably, frustration produces physiological arousal. Apparently, insult produces a higher level of arousal than task frustrations. The strong aggressive cues in the situation may elicit only covert or implicit aggressive responses (especially in highly inhibited college students). However, the increased arousal created by frustration might energize these weak responses so that they would be displayed overtly.

Extrapolating from Schachter's (1964) research, Geen (1968) suggested an alternative explanation to the one advocated earlier by Geen and Berkowitz (1967). Insulted subjects might be most likely to have clear and unambiguous cognitions concerning the particular source of their arousal. A subject might have recognized from past experience that an arousal state following an insult is a state of "anger" and that the behavior elicited by the emotional state is to be focused upon the original source of that state of anger (when it is safe to do so). Task-frustrated subjects, Geen reasoned, would have had less clear cognitions concerning the specific source of their arousal state and would be less likely either to define their emotion as anger or to associate the anger with their partner. Personally-frustrated subjects (who were not insulted) would have known that the source of their failure (and hence their arousal) was their partner and might have had conflicting cognitions about their partner. These subjects might have thought, "Even though he did cause me to fail, he does seem to be a friendly, non-hostile person." Consequently, the subject might have been less likely to label his current arousal as a state of anger with a specific target.

Geen and O'Neal (1969) attempted a further test of Berkowitz's theory (arousal amplifies aggressive responses) by manipulating "arousal" independently of frustration. If frustration produces an arousal, and if the aggressive cues in the situation evoke implicit aggressive responses, then an arousal source not directly associated with an arousing confederate should produce an increase in aggression following an exposure to aggressive stimuli. However, according to Schachter's theory of emotion, if this arousal was produced in such a way that it could not be attributed to the confederate, the subject would not be able to interpret his arousal as "anger produced by the confederate" and so he should not be particularly aggressive. Consequently, Geen and O'Neal first exposed subjects either to the Champion film or to a neutral sports film. After the film the subject evaluated his partner's performance on a previous task by giving him electric shocks. Half of the subjects evaluated their partners while being exposed to a non-aversive white noise. The other half of the subjects were not exposed to the white noise.

The experimenters assumed, from principles of activation theory, that the subject would experience increased arousal due to the white noise. According to activation theory (Lindsley, 1951; Malmo, 1959), any sensory input has nonspecific effects which can produce behavior change by modifying a general state of arousal. The experimenters expected the white noise/arousal manipulation to interact with the implicit aggressive responses presumably elicited by aggressive cues associated with the fight film. Computation of the total volume of shock given by the subjects (intensity x duration) produced the expected interaction. Subjects who had seen the fight film and who had been exposed to the white noise gave significantly more intense shock than subjects in any of the other conditions, which did not differ significantly from each other. One might predict from Schachter's (1964) theory of emotion that subjects would be influenced by the aggressive film to label the white noise induced arousal as a state of anger and the anger could have led to the aggressive reactions. However, the subject's self ratings of anger which were obtained after the white noise induced arousal and film treatments but before the shock dependent measures, permit an assessment of this hypothesis. There were no significant differences in subject's ratings of anger. Hence, the condition differences in aggression apparently were not due to differences in subject's perceptions of anger. One possible explanation for the subject's increased aggression is Berkowitz's theory of implicit aggressive responses activated by the arousal state of the white noise.

A separate experiment by Berkowitz and LePage (1967) demonstrated a similar relationship between aggressive cues, arousal, and aggression. Subjects either were or were not angered by their partner (again a confederate of the experimenter). A rifle and a revolver, two badminton racquets, or neutral objects were lying on a table near where the subject was to give an evaluation of his partner. Angered subjects who saw the weapons displayed more aggression against their partner

306

than subjects who had not seen aggressive stimuli. However, those subjects exposed to the weapons who were not angered by their partner did not display any more aggression than subjects who saw the neutral objects. If subjects had merely become more relaxed by the presence of the weapons (i.e., by a more informal definition of the situation) and thus displayed more aggression, the facilitating effect should have appeared for angered and non-angered subjects alike.

There are at least three explanations of how aggressive cues such as weapons can increase the probability of aggressive behavior. First, the frequent pairing of firearms with real or symbolic aversive events may produce a classical conditioning bond between aggressive cues and aggressive behavior (Berkowitz, 1974). Systematic observatiuons of crime drama television programs indicated that drawn weapons had a high rate of appearance (3-4 times per hour) and a strong contingent association with physical aggression (80%) (see Turner et al., 1977; Wilson & Higgins, 1977). Subsequent exposure to a cue may elicit weak classically conditioned responses which are intensified in frustrated, uninhibited subjects (Berkowitz, 1974). Secondly, weapons in media portrayals of violence are frequently paired with real or symbolic termination of aversive experiences. The weapons may serve as discriminative stimuli for positively or negatively reinforced aggressive behaviors (Ellis, Weinir, & Miller, 1971). Finally, the development of an associative bond between firearms and modeled aggression can increase the likelihood that firearms serve as retrieval cues for previously witnessed modeled aggression (Turner & Goldsmith, 1976). All three explanations suggest mechanisms by which exposure to firearms can increase the risk of aggression (Leyens & Parke, 1975; Turner et al., 1977). The instigating effects of aggressive cues are strongest if a cue occurs while someone is experiencing an aversive event.

Firearms, especially handguns, play a particularly important role in contributing to homicide in the United States; approximately two-thirds of all homicides result from firearms (Newton & Zimring, 1969). First, firearms are particularly lethal as compared to other weapons such as knives or blunt instruments. Secondly, firearms are readily available to most Americans; approximately two-thirds of American households contain at least one fireamrm. Thirdly, handguns are easily concealed so that they can be carried by an individual without being detected until the weapon is drawn. Finally, as indicated above, firearms can stimulate impulsive aggressive reactions especially for individuals who have been highly distressed. The contribution of firearms to homicide is revealed in the statistics which show that 75% of homicides occur when a relative or acquaintance attacks the victim following an argument between the two (Newton & Zimring, 1969). Nearly 2/3 of all homicides occur when the victim is attacked with a firearm while 1/4 of the deaths result from attacks by knives. Detailed interviews with the killers suggest that the attacks were the result of a temporary impulse, and the attackers had not expected to kill the victim (Toch, 1969).

Newton and Zimring (1969) compiled extensive evidence on the use of firearms during robberies. Approximately 35% of all robberies (in 1967) were committed with firearms while 15% were committed with other weapons such as a knife. Since financial gain was the primary incentive, the robbers rarely killed their victims. Victims were killed in .6% of firearm robberies and .15% of other robberies (Newton & Zimring, 1969). Still, killings during robberies accounted for 15% of all homicides in 1967 in Chicago (Newton & Zimring, 1969). Robberies also accounted for most of the homicides which occurred between strangers. In approximately 75% of all homicides, the victim is a friend, family member, or acquaintance of the attacker. In most acquaintance killings, an escalating argument or altercation rather than robbery was the immediate precipitating cause of the crime (Newton & Zimring, 1969).

The Type A Behavior Pattern and Impulsive Aggression

Although aversive experiences such as task failure can increase the likelihood of aggression from some uninhibited individuals, these experiences do not always stimulate aggression. One personality attribute which may help to explain individual differences in aggression is the Type A or coronary prone behavior pattern. The Type A pattern has attracted wide attention because it is associated with cardiovascular dysfunction. Extensive research has demonstrated that individuals with the Type A pattern are twice as likely to experience coronary heart disease as individuals with the Type B pattern--defined as the relative absence of Type A characteristics (see Dembroski, Weiss, Shields, Haynes, & Feinleib, 1978; Jenkins, Rosenman, & Zyzanski, 1974).

Glass (1977) has proposed that the increased coronary proneness of Type A's may be due to their physiological responses to aversive experiences. Several studies indicate Type A's display elevated blood pressure when they experience a threat to their control. Elevated blood pressure has been linked to atherosclerosis, a disease process of the arterial system, and Type A's are more likely to experience advanced atherosclerosis. Atherosclerosis frequently results in obstruction of the coronary artery (leading to myocardial infarctions) or to obstructions of the carotid artery (leading to strokes). If Glass (1977) is correct in his reasoning, then the long term effects of the emotional reactivity of Type A's is an acceleration of arterial disease. This disease is one of the leading causes of death in modern industrialized societies (cf. Dembroski et al., 1978).

An analysis of Type A behavior pattern can help to account for individual differences in aggressive reactions to aversive experiences. As contrasted with Type B's, the Type A behavior pattern is characterized by three components: excessive achievement striving, impatience or time urgency, and hostility (Glass, 1977). Extensive research documents that Type A individuals react emotionally when they encounter a threat to their control. Task failure represents a threat to their control, especially if the failure implies a lack of competency that could lead to continuing loss of control. Under these conditions Type A's display exaggerated behavioral and emotional responsiveness (termed hyper-responsiveness). If the loss of control over an aversive experience persists, Type A's are likely to display learned helplessness (termed hypo-responsiveness, Glass, 1977).

Several investigations have provided evidence for the occurrence of these behavioral components of the Type A behavior pattern. For example, Burnam, Pennebaker, and Glass (1975) demonstrated excessive achievement striving in Type A's by showing that they worked near capacity on a seemingly important task even though these individuals did not have a deadline for completion of the task. Other evidence suggests that Type A individuals focus their attention on a task and ignore any cues which they think might interfere with their task performance (Mathews & Brunson, 1979; Strube, Turner, & Patrick, 1981). Glass, Snyder and Hollis (1974, Experiment II) demonstrated that Type A's displayed greater impatience and irritation than Type B's during a cooperative task in which their partner interferred with their performance. Carver and Glass (1978) and Strube, Turner, Cerro, and Stevens (1982) also demonstrated that Type A's were more aggressive than Type B's following a failure experience.

Some researchers have found that Type A's display greater time urgency than Type B's. For example, Type A's underestimate the passage of a minute (Burnam et al., 1975) and they are more likely to arrive early for appointments (Gastorf, 1980). Moreover, Type A's appear to become impatient and restless when they have to perform slowly or to wait between performances (Glass et al., 1974, Experiment I; Glass, 1977).

One possible reason for the Type A/B difference is that Type A's are more likely than Type B's to focus their attention on the immediate or salient task. If the task is very frustrating and unsolvable, the greater focus of Type A's on the task should make their failure experience more salient so that they may be more frustrated than Type B's. Type B's appear to distribute their attention more evenly across several channels of information: the task, internal cues, and environment stimuli (Strube et al., 1981). When soothing stimuli (e.g., complex music) appear in the environment, Type B's are able to use the soothing stimuli to reduce the aversiveness of failure on a task (i.e., blunt the aversive cues of the experience). Consequently, they perform better and feel better when soothing music is played. However, Type A's will not listen to the music so that they forfeit the potentially soothing nature of the environmental stimulation.

In summary, Type A's are more likely to display both problem solving and aggressive behavior in response to aversive experiences. If these activities fail to terminate the aversive experience, the Type A's are likely to experience learned helplessness. Type B's are likely to use blunting as a strategy to cope with aversive experience.

Weapons Effect Revisited

Turner, Layton, and Simons (1975) demonstrated the Weapons Effect in a naturalistic experiment in which horn honking was employed as the measure of aggression. Subjects were obstructed at a signal light by pick-up truck which did or did not have a rifle displayed in the rear window. A bumper sticker with the word "vengeance" was employed in half of the conditions to make the rifle's aggressive connotation more salient (see Berkowitz & Alioto, 1973). We reasoned that the aggressive connotation of a rifle is less apparent than a handgun. Handguns are purchased primarily for self defense while a rifle has many uses. We proposed that a rifle would have to appear in an aggressive context (e.g., bumper sticker) for the aggressive connotation to be salient enough to have an instigating effect on aggression. The results indicated that the rifle produced a stimulating effect on honking only with the aggressive bumper sticker and only for drivers of new cars. Drivers of old cars seemed to be intimidated in the presence of the aggressively connotated rifle. Based on the research of Doob and Gross (1968), Turner et al. (1975) speculated that the age differences of the automobiles might have been perceived as a status difference between the subject and the aggressive target.

Turner, Simons, Fenn, & Layton (1982) have also reported an effect of automobile age differences in subjects' reactions to an aggressive cue. One of three bumper stickers varying in aggressive connotation was attached to the back of cars: "Up against the wall, M. F.," (aggressive connotation), "One step for man, one step for mankind," (neutral connotation), and "Have a nice day," (friendly connotation). The research was conducted in 1972-1973 and the aggressive slogan was widely publicized at the time as an expression of anti-establishment attitudes. New car drivers honked more than old car drivers to the aggressive slogan. The non-aggressive bumper stickers did not produce differential responding for new and old car drivers.

The previously cited research on the Type A behavior pattern suggests an alternative explanation for the aggressive reactions of new versus old car drivers. The lower frustration tolerance,

310

impatience, and hostility of Type A's may contribute to the effect of vehicle age. That is, Type A individuals may avoid driving old cars that could break down due to mechanical problems. In addition, Type A's are more emotionally aroused than Type B's when they are impeded in commuter traffic (Stokols, Novaco, Stokols, & Campbell, 1978). Finally, the impatience of Type A's may cause them to be easily irritated when they are obstructed at signal lights. Type A's are more likely than Type B's to display punitive behavior when they are frustrated by another person's slow behavior (Carver & Glass, 1978; Strube et al., 1982). In short, Turner et al.'s (1975, 1982) findings for automobile age differences in aggression might have occurred because new cars are likely to be driven by Type A individuals. These individuals may be more frustrated by the traffic obstruction and also be more willing to respond hostilely to the obstruction.

To summarize, then, frustration in the classical sense is neither a necessary nor a sufficient condition for aggression. Conceptualized as an aversive event, frustrating-aversive events do increase the likelihood that aggression will be used to terminate the event. But, aggression is neither the only nor the most likely response to aversion. Its employment as a coping response can be mediated by increased inhibition levels against aggression (e.g., fear of retaliation) and previous direct and vicarious reinforcement for the termination of aversion by aggression. The additional presence of aggressive cues in the environment, such as firearms, can also facilitate impulsive aggression as a response to an aversive event. Personality differences (e.g., Type A/B) may also modify the likelihood of aggressive or nonaggressive reactions to frustrating-aversive events.

THE ROLE OF RELATIVE DEPRIVATION IN VIOLENT BEHAVIOR

Aversive events can increase the probability of aggression, but several social learning variables influence whether the event actually produces overt aggression. The concept of relative deprivation describes one type of aversive event which is related to aggression.

Extensive research by economists, sociologists, and psychologists has documented that an individual's relative level of success or reinforcement rate is an important determinant of her/his satisfaction with life's opportunities (Crosby, 1976). People compare their achieved level of success to the performance and outcome standards to which they aspire. When people fail to achieve their aspiration level, they experience relative deprivation. The aspiration level depends upon such factors as previous success in achieving performance or outcome standards, the success of similar other people in achieving similar aspiration levels, immediate pressing biological needs (e.g., hunger, pain) and environmental constraints on performance (e.g., natural disasters). An individual with a low aspiration level is not as likely to experience relative deprivation or to be dissatisfied with a particular (i. e., objective) achievement level as someone with a higher aspiration level. Consequently, a person's relative rather than objective achievement level becomes the more important factor in determining that person's overall satisfaction; the greater the adverse discrepancy between aspiration and achievement levels, the greater the dissatisfaction (Crosby, 1976).

An individual's aspiration level depends partly upon the achievements of her/his reference group and partly upon her/his prior accomplishments. The reference group is usually composed of similar other individuals such as one's family and peers. The accomplishments of the reference group provide one comparison standard against which an individual evaluates her/his own accomplishments. That is, most individuals aspire to achieve as much or more than the reference group. If an individual thinks that her/his accomplishments are below the level of the reference group (hence, below the aspiration level), then s/he is likely to feel relatively deprived.

Relative deprivation can also occur when one's current accomplishments (or outcomes) are below previous levels. Fluctuating economic conditions frequently produce relative deprivation. As economic conditions improve, an individual's income is likely to improve and her/his aspirations begin to rise along with the improving conditions (Davies, 1969). However, during an economic recession, many individuals experience a drop in their income and some even lose their jobs. These individuals experience relative deprivation since their current income does not meet the expectations formed during the earlier more affluent period. When the onset of the recession is abrupt, people are not able to "lower their aspirations" as quickly as their income declines. Hence, they experience relative deprivation. However, if the recession develops slowly, the individual may be able to anticipate the bad economic conditions and lower her/his expectations or aspirations as the economic conditions deteriorate. Hence, these individuals would be less likely to experience relative deprivation.

Abrupt reductions in opportunities such as those occurring during a recession can be described by the principles of extinction and fading. Extinction refers to an abrupt reduction in reinforcement rates while fading refers to a more gradual reduction in reinforcement rates. Ulrich et al. (1973) have shown that extinction is a reliable source of aggression in many species of animals. Fading is much less likely to instigate aggressive reactions. An abrupt, unexpected recession produces conditions analogous to extinction while a gradual, expected

312

recession produces conditions analogous to fading.

Relative Deprivation, Revolutions, and Riots

Davies (1969) proposed that a number of major national revolutions or riots were partly instigated by a rapid increase in relative deprivation following a sudden economic recession (e.g., USA - 1776; France - 1789; USSR - 1919; China - 1949). The revolutions in these countries were preceded by a period of gradually improving economic conditions. However, shortly before the revolution, these countries experienced an abrupt economic recession. Davies (1969) reasoned that the improving economic conditions led to rising aspirations which could not be achieved during the recession. However, Davies noted that relative deprivation is not the only factor which increases the risk of revolutions. For example, the world wide depression in the 1930s produced high levels of relative deprivation from 1930 to 1935, but this period did not lead to revolutions in many modern societies (Davies, 1969).

Schuck (1976) analyzed short- and long-term deprivation as predictors of revolutions in 114 countries for the years 1961 to 1965. He found that the effects of deprivation depended upon several other variables such as perceived governmental legitimacy, coercive force (i.e., police and army) loyalty, and the perceived legitimization of violence as a method for producing political change. Schuck's findings indicate that relative deprivation is only one of several variables which contribute to the risk of revolutions.

Teenage and Young Adult Relative Deprivations

Sears and McConahay (1969) found that participants of a 1965 riot among black youths in Los Angeles (Watts area) were primarily well-educated youths from middle class, stable families living in good housing conditions. However, these youths did not have access to attractive jobs. Sears and McConahay reasoned that these youths experienced relative deprivation because their income and job opportunities were below that of similarly educated white youths. The most deprived youths were not the ones most likely to participate in the riots. Presumably, uneducated youths from low income, disrupted families had lower aspirations so that they were not as dissatisfied with the same low achievement levels as the better educated youths.

During a recession, young adults (16-19 years of age) are the ones most likely to experience both relative and objective deprivation. These individuals have the least employment experience of any members of the community. They are likely to be the first fired or the last hired during a recession. For example, during the 1974-1975 recession in the United States, the unemployment rate for 35- to 55-year-olds rose from 2% to 4%

313

while the unemployment rate of 16- to 19-year-olds rose from 14%
to 20% (Turner et al., 1981). The unemployment rate for
non-white males rose to 50%. These figures indicate that
recessions are most likely to impact employment opportunities for
young, non-white youths. The aversiveness of the objective
deprivation (i.e., unemployment) may be intensified by relative
deprivation (i.e., other groups are not unemployed).

Easterlin (1968) has analyzed some of the factors which have
contributed to the experience of relative deprivation in young
adults. One important factor in the perception of relative
deprivation is the discrepancy between the resources one has
while living with one's parents as a teenager and what one has
while living at one's own home as a young adult. The resource
discrepency includes such basic commodities as clothes,
automobiles, housing conditions, food, vacation expenses, health
care and occupational opportunities. Most young adults have
lower incomes but higher costs than their parents for basic
commodities such as housing and maternity costs. For example,
young adults may have to purchase supplies for their house, such
as furniture and dishes. Since most young adults have access to
reduced quality and quantity of basic commodities when they leave
home, they experience relative deprivation during the transition
away from their parents' home. Youths leaving home during a
recession experience two types of relative deprivation: (1)
deprivation due to the family transition, and (2) deprivation due
to high unemployment rates in young adults (Turner et al., 1981).

The size of relative deprivation depends partly upon the
abruptness and partly on the size of the decline during the
transition away from their parents' home (the family of origin).
One potential indicator of relative deprivation for young adults
16 to 19 or 20 to 23 is the unemployment rates in these groups as
compared to the unemployment rate of their parents. Easterlin
(1968, 1973) reasoned that the experience of deprivation (e.g.,
unemployment) would be more severe if one's peers or parents did
not experience similar difficulties.

Periods of high relative deprivation may lead to diverse
reactions from young adults, including problem solving,
achievement behaviors, blunting reactions, withdrawal and
avoidance behaviors, or learned helplessness reactions (Turner et
al., 1981). These periods of high relative deprivation may also
contribute to aggressive crimes such as robbery and homicide.
Not all youths are likely to act aggressively, but the greater
the number experiencing relative deprivation, the greater the
chance that some will act aggressively.

Legitimate Opportunities and Relative Deprivation

Youths pursue many alternative paths to achieve the goals to
which they aspire. Cloward and Ohlin (1960) analyzed a number of

factors which influence whether legitimate or illegitimate methods are pursued for achieving goals. Both cultural and structural barriers can limit access to legitimate opportunities. For example, education has been one of the major vehicles for upward mobility in industrialized societies. If a youth grows up in a social group that deemphasizes education, s/he is likely to achieve limited educational training. This lack of education can serve as a barrier to legitimate opportunities. Immigrants from nonindustrialized areas frequently have been slow to identify the relationship between educational attainment and social mobility. Hence, the children of these immigrants are more likely than other members of the society to encounter barriers to legitimate opportunities (Cloward & Ohlin, 1960; Toby, 1958). Even when children of low income families desire advanced educational training, they may feel compelled to seek work immediately rather than to pursue educational opportunities because of the economic pressures on their family (Cloward & Ohlin, 1960).

Barriers to legitimate opportunities would have greater impact on males than females and on adolescents than adults (Cloward & Ohlin, 1960). That is, males are more likely than females to seek employment and to have primary responsibility for supporting a family. Similarly, during adolescence, youths are confronted with career decisions. Individuals who experience barriers to legitimate opportunities are more likely to experience discrepancy between aspiration levels and perceived opportunity for achievement. Some of these individuals become vulnerable to pressures toward delinquent subcultures if they view the illegitimate opportunities as a more probable pathway to financial success (Cloward & Ohlin, 1960).

Since an economic recession has its greatest unemployment effect on teenagers searching for their first job (Turner et al., 1981), teenagers in a recession may experience greater pressure toward delinquent subcultures than teenagers of other time periods. Unskilled teenagers tend to be the last applicant hired and the first person fired during a recession. Those individuals attempting to obtain their first job are the least likely to have skills and this condition makes them unattractive to employers. These unemployed, unskilled youths may be tempted toward delinquent subcultures during a recession. Participation in a delinquent subculture increases the risk of being arrested and having a criminal record. A criminal record may serve as another barrier to legitimate opportunities. Thus, those youths who attempt to enter the labor force during a recession may experience long-term difficulties in making the transition from adolescence into adulthood in pursuit of legitimate opportunities.

Short and Strodtbeck (1974) examined delinquent and nondelinquent behaviors in juvenile gang members and their findings indicate that relative deprivation can contribute to delinquent subcultures which foster violent behavior. After more than six months contact with the urban, male gangs, observers rated each gang member on how frequently he had engaged in any of 69 delinquent and nondelinquent behaviors. The investigators' factor analyzed the behavioral categories and isolated two "nondelinquent" and three "delinquent" factors. The delinquent factors were identified as follows: Factor 1 involved acquisitive and destructive conflict (fighting, assault, robbery, concealed weapons); Factor 4 was described as retreatist's behaviors (sexual deviancy, pot, narcotics); and Factor 5 was described as authority protest behaviors (driving without a license, joy riding, public nuisance, auto theft, alcohol use, runaway from home). The two nondelinquent factors were identified as follows: Factor 2 involved stable street corner activities (team or individual sports, social activities, sex, gambling); Factor 3 reflected stable maturity oriented behavior (heterosexual activity, sexual behavior, work experience). Approximately 10% of the gang members had criminal records resulting from their delinquent activities described by Factors 1, 4, and 5.

Short and Strodtbeck (1974) also found that the gangs could be characterized by their perceptions of whether they thought they had access to legitimate opportunities. As a group, those gangs which thought they did not have access to legitimate opportunities were more likely to participate in delinquent activities and to have police records. However, the gang subculture also contributed to delinquency. The individual differences in delinquent behavior within the gang could not be predicted by the differential perceptions of access to legitimate opportunities. Moreover, police records within the gang could not be predicted by individual perceptions of access to legitimate opportunities. Short and Strodtbeck's findings suggest three separate factors which may contribute to delinquency: (1) The perception of lack of access to legitimate opportunities led some youths to be attracted to delinquent gangs. (2) Once an individual was in the gang, the delinquent subculture led some individuals in the gang to commit delinquent acts (independently of the youth's access to legitimate opportunities). (3) Some individuals were arrested for delinquent acts and the police records served as a further barrier to legitimate opportunities.

To summarize, one important determinant of criminal behavior is the development of criminal subcultures associated with delinquent gangs. Criminal subcultures are most likely to emerge in environments where youths perceive their access to legitimate opportunities to have been blocked. These obstructions can produce a disparity between the opportunities that youths desire and the resources that they can actually achieve (i.e., relative deprivation). If youths have much higher aspirations than they can readily achieve through legitimate opportunities, these youths may be tempted to join criminal subcultures where illegitimate opportunities may exist for achieving aspirations.

Robbery and Criminal Subcultures

Robbery is a common form of illegitimate activity committed by members of criminal subcultures (Gibbons, 1973). The robbers rely upon coercion or threat of violence although they rarely actually use force since the primary incentive appears to be financial gain. However, approximately 15% of all homicides are committed during robberies (Newton & Zimring, 1969). Usually the robber relies upon a surprise confrontation to avoid apprehension during the act. Approximately one-half of all robberies are acts of desperation that are committed with little planning and skill. These crimes frequently lead to the apprehension of the offender. The remaining robberies are carefully planned and may be executed with such great skill that apprehension of the offender is very unlikely.

Gibbons (1973) described three types of individuals who may resort to robbery as a means of achieving their aspirations: the professional, the semi-professional, and the "one-time loser." The professional is a highly skilled craftsman who carefully plans and executes robberies and frequently reaps large sums of money. These individuals are usually from low income, deteriorated, urban neighborhoods which contain many criminal activites. Many professional criminals have parents and siblings with criminal careers. These individuals are likely to be the product of delinquent gangs or peer groups who have been expelled from school and who have little experience with legitimate employment.

The semiprofessional robber is a relatively unskilled, unsuccessful, part-time criminal who relies primarily upon crude physical force rather than careful planning and execution. According to Gibbons (1973), most of these individuals believe that they have few alternatives to criminal careers. They view the entire society as corrupt and blame it for their difficulties so that they experience little guilt for their criminal conduct. Although the semiprofessional robbers come from similar social, economic, and family environments as do the professional criminals, they have primarily associated with unskilled, delinquent offenders. Thus, the semi-professional robbers usually have not had contact with or been trained by successful, professional criminals.

The one-time loser label characterizes a large number of individuals who commit isolated but serious criminal offenses (Gibbons, 1973). These individuals have little contact with delinquent gangs. Their crimes are frequently acts of desperation which are committed with little planning or skill.

317

Much of this criminal behavior is never reported to the police. When their crimes are reported, these individuals are not very skillful in avoiding apprehension, and they frequently are caught and serve long prison sentences for a single crime.

These observations clearly indicate that many factors, including one's family, physical, and social environment, influence an individual to commit a robbery. When youths think that they do not have access to legitimate opportunities, they may pursue illegitimate paths to achieve their aspirations. Another important factor is the exposure to a criminal or delinquent subculture that may provide the training and the encouragement for delinquent acts. An economic recession decreases access to legitimate opportunities so that more youths may be tempted by delinquent subcultures which foster violent crime.

STUDY 1

The previously cited research indicates that one important type of frustration is economically based deprivation. When individuals aspire to higher income but the aspiration cannot be met, frustration and dissatisfaction is a common experience. However, the people most deprived are not necessarily the ones most likely to act aggressively. Intense deprivation is more likely to lead to apathy or learned helplessness than aggression (Bandura, 1973; Seligman, 1975; Turner et al., 1981).

Turner et al. (1981) have demonstrated that fluctuations in the age-specific rate of homicide over the past 60 years can be explained by fluctuating levels of relative deprivation. The periods from 1930-1935 and 1970-1980 were times with high levels of relative deprivation and age-specific homicide rates. The period from 1945 to 1965 was a time of unusually low relative deprivation and homicide rates. Turner et al. (1981) based their analysis on data aggregated across the 16 to 34 age groups. These data could not be used to establish whether the age groups experiencing the greatest relative deprivation were also the groups most likely to commit homicide.

We have attempted to evaluate the effects of unemployment-based deprivation on age-specific homicide rates by using the annual age-specific rates of unemployment from 1958 to 1979. Unemployment rates can be misleading indices. For example, an individual must be seeking work in order to be considered as unemployed statistically. When youth become discouraged about seeking legitimate opportunities, they may stop looking for a legitimate job. Hence, these discourage individuals would not be considered unemployed in official statistics. Nevertheless, these unemployed youths may be particularly likely to seek employment in an illicit economy,

318

such as drug dealing or robbery. They may be extensively involved in crime even though they appear not to be unemployed in official statistics.

Despite the shortcomings of unemployment figures, the statistics can serve as an estimate of the percent of youths in an age group who are without employment. We obtained the U. S. Department of Labor (1958-1979) estimates of annual rates for unemployment for ages 16-19, ages 20-23, and the total unemployment rate for each year from 1958 to 1979.

Easterlin (1973) reasoned that one important measure of relative deprivation is the contrast between parent and youth income or employment opportunities. We developed separate indices of relative deprivation for teenagers (16-19 age range) and young adults (20-23 age range) for each year from 1958 to 1979. The indices were obtained by subtracting the annual percentage of middle-aged unemployment (estimating parents' unemployment) from the percentage of teenage or of young adult unemployment.

To obtain age specific rates of homicide and robbery, we used the Uniform Crime Reports (1958-1979) of the F.B.I. statistics on the number of individuals arrested in each age group for each year between 1958 and 1979. Many police agencies did not report local crimes to the F.B.I. before 1958. However, the number of agencies has been increasing since 1958. To adjust for the shifting number of reporting agencies, the annual F.B.I. age-specific arrest rates were modified to provide approximate age-specific arrest rates for all U. S. police agencies. Such an adjustment was made by multiplying the F.B.I. statistics each year by the following ratio: total U.S. population divided by population in police districts reporting to the F.B.I.

The unemployment rates in each of the age groups 16-23 were used to predict the number of arrests in each age group for robbery and for homicide for each of the years 1958-1979 (U.S. Dept. of Labor, 1958-1974). Although we were primarily interested in explaining the age-specific rates of the crimes of robbery and homicide, direct estimates of the ages of offenders were not available. The only information available to estimate the age of offenders is the age of those arrested. For some crimes, statistics on the age of arrest may not accurately reflect most of the offenders since very few of the offenders are ever arrested. For example, aproximately one third of burglaries are reported to the police (Gibbons, 1973), and 18% of the reported burglaries were solved by the police in 1975 (Uniform Crime Reports, 1975). Hence, only 6% of all burglaries were ever solved by the police. The individuals who were arrested may not be a representative sample of all burglars. That is, unskilled burglars may be most likely to be apprehended while skilled burglars may avoid arrests. Homicide has a very high solution

319

rate with approxiamtely 80% of all murders leading to the arrest
of an offender (Gibbons, 1973; Uniform Crime Reports, 1975).
Approximately two thirds of robberies are reported (Gibbons,
1973) and 27% of these were solved by the police in 1975 (Uniform
Crime Reports, 1975). Thus, arrest statistics should be a good
estimate for homicides but the arrest measures may be less
accurate for estimating characteristics of robbers since a much
smaller proportion (perhaps 20%) are arrested by the police.

The annual rates of relative deprivation (parent minus youth
unemployment rates) and objective deprivation (youth unemployment
rates) were correlated with the homicide and robbery arrest rates
from 1958 to 1979. The observations were divided into the age
groups 16-19 and 20-23 since unemployment data are available only
for these age groupings (U. S. Dept. of Labor, 1958-1979). Among
16- to 19-year-olds, relative deprivation was much better than
objective deprivation in predicting robbery [r^2 = .58 VS r^2 =
.35, F (1, 80) = 43.81, p < .001] and homicide [r^2 = .43 VS
r^2 = .21, F (1, 80) = 30.88, p < .001]. Among 20- to
23-year-olds, relative deprivation was marginally better than
objective deprivation for predicting robbery [r^2 = .13 VS r^2
= .10, F (1, 80) = 2.75, p < .10] and homicide [r^2 .105 VS $\bar{r}^2$
= .067, $\bar{F}$ (1, 80) = 3.40, p < .10].

The results of these analyses indicate that the annual
fluctuations in robbery and homicide arrest rates, within an age
group, are directly dependent upon the experiences of relative
deprivation in that age group, especially for the 16- to
19-year-olds. Among 20- to 23-year-olds, both relative
deprivation and objective deprivation are only weakly related to
arrest rates. As more members of a society experience distress
due to relative deprivation, more of them are likely to act
violently, especially 16- to 19-year-olds. We need to examine
some of the demographic changes which are occurring in modern
societies in order to account for changing rates of violence.
Fluctuating population pressures due to birth, death, and
immigration rates have modified the number of individuals who are
maximally at risk for experiencing aversive events such as
relative deprivation.

DEMOGRAPHIC CHANGES AND VIOLENT CRIME

Modern societies are currently undergoing a number of major
transformations. Rapidly fluctuating population characteristics
have contributed to many of the current societal problems (e.g.,
crime, unemployment, divorce, riots). Recent measures of the
rates of these problems have resulted from the increasing numbers
of individuals in certain age groups who are at high risk for
impact by these social problems. For example, the learning
environments of children and the economic and social environments
of young adults have been substantially influenced by the effects

of population fluctuation over the past 50 years (Turner & Dodd, 1979). However, the precise relationship between demographic factors and anti-social behavior appears to be highly complex and poorly understood. The following section describes recent research projects which attempted to relate demographic factors and relative deprivation to homicide and robbery rates.

Major changes are occurring in modern society which have produced changes in family structure. For example, annual crime, divorce and unemployment rates have climbed dramatically in the past decade, while the birth rate has dropped to an all-time low (U. S. Bureau of the Census, 1960-1979). Accompanying these demographic changes are major modifications in norms and values. Sex roles appear to be rapidly changing and women are entering the labor market at an increasing rate. Divorce laws have been greatly liberalized (Goode, 1976; Kenkel, 1977), and factors such as the smaller size of families, the availability of day care centers, and the increased ability of women to compete successfully in the labor market have had a major effect not only on the divorce rate but on society in general (Kenkel, 1977).

Some researchers have argued that the modern family as a social institution is disintegrating (see Kenkel, 1977; Yorberg, 1973), possibly because it is unable to adapt to technological changes (cf. Schulz, 1976). Hence, the changing family could be seen as a causal factor in the high divorce rate and other social problems. An alternative view is that the American family itself is responding to societal change instead of acting as a cause of social change. The rising divorce rate is seen by some observers as evidence of healthy changes in values and expectations among young people (Kenkel, 1977; Yorberg, 1973). Regardless of one's perspective, rather significant changes have occurred in modern societies, and the family institution is involved in much of the change.

Turner and Dodd (1979) noted that many of the changes which are occurring in the United States are also occurring in other societies. Divorce has risen in most western European nations since 1910, often at a rate higher than that of the United States (Goode, 1976; Kenkel, 1977). The divorce and birth rates of the Soviet Union have closely paralleled those of the United States from 1964-1974 (Coser, 1974). Such cross-national similarity in societal change suggests the role of a universal factor. One possible factor is the population variable.

For many years demographers have realized that the birth rate has a major impact on the entire economic and social structure, including industry and commerce, education and politics (Whelpton, 1932). For example, the fluctuating U. S. birth rate has been related to crime and delinquency, alcoholism and drug addiction, and political alienation (Hauser, 1971). Still, the relationship of population to social change is not a simple one.

321

Although the birth rate affects economic conditions, the reverse is also true since economic conditions can affect marriage, divorce, and birth rates (Thamm, 1975; van de Walle, 1972).

Heer (1975) described the societal impact of the birth rate on the labor force, patterns of consumption, political attitudes, welfare, and the women's rights movements. Although demographers have noted the influences of the population for some time, attempts to relate specific demographic factors, such as birth rate, to specific social behavior have been infrequent. Using national data, we have completed two research projects (Cole & Turner, 1977; Dodd, Cole & Turner, 1977) relating fluctuations in the birth rates and relative deprivation to fluctuations in the crime rate.

Crime Rates as a Function of the Post World War II Baby Boom

Not all individuals in the populations are equally at risk for committing criminal offenses. While most serious crimes are committed by males aged 15-24, each class of crime can be characterized by different age specific risk values. For example, the modal age of arrest for robbery and aggravated assault is 18 years, while the modal age is 16 for burglary and 21 for homicide (Uniform Crime Reports, 1965-1978). The number of arrests in 1974 within each of the age groups 10-65 is reported in Figure 1 for homicide and robbery. These data indicate that the maximal ages of risk for committing homicide and robbery are the 16-23 age groups. Other crimes are characterized by younger or older ages (e.g., vandalism or gambling). The increased frequency of crime over the past 20 years can be explained, in part, by the increased numbers of individuals in the specific age groups for which the risk of crime is highest (Ferdinand, 1969; Cole & Turner, 1977; Turner et al., 1981; Wellford, 1973).

Cole and Turner (1977) noted that there have been major fluctuations in the U.S. birth rate from 1920 to 1975. During the Depression of the 1930s, the birth rate dropped substantially, probably due to the effect of the Depression on marriage rates as well as upon the unwillingness of married couples to increase the size of their families. Following the Depression, the birth rate began to climb slowly, then skyrocketed in 1946, immediatley following World War II. The birth rate continued to climb markedly until 1957 when it leveled off; and since 1960 it has dropped steadily. A major contributor to the birth rate fluctuation has been the expanding and contracting family size with larger families occurring between 1920-30 and 1950-60. Fluctuations in mortality and migration rates are minor as compared to the birth rate fluctuation. Thus, previous birth data provide an estimate of the number of individuals in a population for any given year and age group. That is, since the birth rate was quite low during the 1930s, one

322

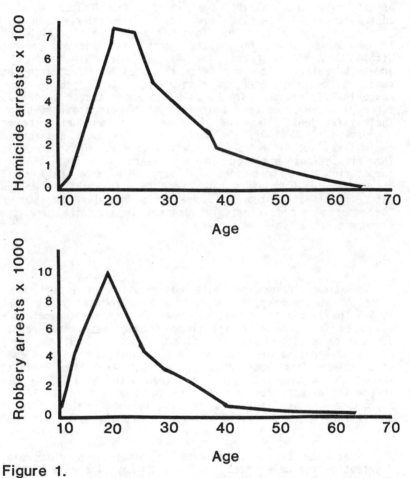

Figure 1.

Frequency of arrests for homicide and robbery by age groups 10–65 for 1974 (U.S.).

can assume that the relative number of 20-year-olds during the 1950s was also low (1930 + 20 years). Likewise, the high birth rate following WWII produced a "population wave" which has greatly inflated the numbers of young adults in modern societies.

The results of Study 1 indicated that relative deprivation in the 16-19 age groups is a good predictor of homicide and robbery arrest rates within the age group. One factor which has contributed to the annual level of relative deprivation is the size of the age group (i.e., cohort size). The size of a cohort is dependent upon prior birth, death, and immigration rates. Within the United States, the factor which has produced the greatest variation in cohort size has been the fluctuating birth rate. Since most teenagers obtain their first job in the age range 16-18 (Taeuber & Taeuber, 1971), their access to the labor force partly depends upon how many individuals are competing for their first job. Since the birth rate was low during the great depression (1930-1940), the number of individuals competing for their first job 16 years later was also low. Thus, competition for first jobs was low in the years 1946 to 1956. The competition for first jobs was very high from 1963 to 1980 because of the high birth rates from 1947 to 1963. Unemployment rates increased for the 16-19 age group from 1963 to 1980 while the rates remained relatively constant in the other age groups (Turner et al., 1981).

STUDY 2

We attempted to assess the contribution of cohort size to unemployment, robbery, and homicide rates for the years 1958 to 1979. The lagged birth rate was used to estimate the cohort size of males for any given age group in any year. The analysis focused on males since they commit almost all of the violent crimes of homicide and robbery. A path analysis was performed in which cohort size was used to estimate relative deprivation (based on unemployment rates) and then both variables were used to predict arrest rates for robbery and homicide in the 16-19 and 20-23 age groups. Measures of relative deprivation, homicide, and robbery rates for 16-19 and 20-23 were the same as for Study 1.

First, the lagged birth rate was used to predict relative deprivation for males aged 16-19 and 20-23. The male birth rate in 1950 provided an estimate of cohort size of males aged 20 in 1970 and males aged 25 in 1975. Next, the lagged birth rate and relative deprivation were used as independent variables in a multiple regression equation to estimate robbery and homicide arrest rates for ages 16-19 and ages 20-23 during the 1958-1979 time period. The standardized regression coefficients served as path coefficients in the path analysis (Kerlinger & Pedhazur, 1973). The results of the analyses are presented in Table 1.

The results indicated that the lagged birth rate (cohort size) accounted for a significant amount of variance in the relative deprivation measures (ages 16-19, $\underline{B}$ = .72, $\underline{p}$ < .001; ages 20-23, $\underline{B}$ =.28, $\underline{p}$ < .01). When the contribution of relative deprivation was removed from cohort size, the residual measure still accounted for a significant proportion of variance in robbery arrest rates (ages 16-19, $\underline{B}$ = .70, $\underline{p}$ < .001; ages 20-23, $\underline{B}$ = .92, $\underline{p}$ <.001) and homicide arrest rates (ages 16-19, $\underline{B}$ = .70, $\underline{p}$ <.001; ages 20-23, $\underline{B}$ = .92, $\underline{p}$ < .001). When the contribution of cohort size was removed from the relative deprivation, the residual measure predicted only a small proportion of the variance in robbery arrests (ages 16-19, $\underline{B}$ =.25, $\underline{p}$ < .05; ages 20-23, $\underline{B}$ = .06, $\underline{p}$ < .10) and homicide arrest rates (ages 16-19, $\underline{B}$ = .16, $\underline{p}$ <.10; ages 20-23, $\underline{B}$ = .06, $\underline{p}$ < .10).

The present findings indicate that the strong association between relative deprivation and violent crime obtained in Study 1 appears to be explained by the cohort size measure. When cohort size is removed, the relative deprivation measure becomes a weak predictor of violent crime. These findings can be explained by assuming that the cohort size measure is responsible for the link between relative unemployment and violent crime. That is, the high birth rate in the period from 1947 to 1957 led to an increasing number of young people competing for a limited number of jobs 16 to 19 years later. Since all of these individuals could not be assimilated into the labor force, the unemployment rate on the 16-19 age groups increased at a much faster rate than the total population. Thus, these youngest age groups experienced increasing levels of relative deprivation (based on unemployment) as compared to the total population.

The effects of cohort size on violent crime was not limited to its contribution to relative deprivation. Even when the relative deprivation measure was partialed out of cohort size, the residual measure still predicted a highly significant proportion of the variance in crime rates. Thus, the relative deprivation measure is not redundant with cohort size in accounting for the variance in arrest rates. Easterlin (1973) has proposed that income measures should be used in addition to unemployment as a measure of relative deprivation for young adults.

Forecasts of Violent Crime

The regression equations of Study 2 can be used to forecast the number of violent crimes on future dates by using estimates of cohort size and relative deprivation. The lagged birth rates provide an estimate of the number of individuals (cohort size) that will be in a given age group in a given year (e.g., 1965 births estimate the 20-year-old cohort size in 1985). The level

Table 1

Summary of Path Analyses with Cohort Size and Relative Deprivation

Predicting Robbery or Homicide Arrest Rates

for Age Ranges 16–19 or 20–23

Dependent Variable	Age 16–19		Age 20–23	
	Cohort Size	Relative Deprivation	Cohort Size	Relative Deprivation

Robbery

Relative Deprivation	$.72_a^{***}$		$.28_a^{**}$	
Robbery	$.70_b^{***}$	$.25_b^{**}$	$.91_b^{***}$	$.06_b^{*}$
	$(.89^{***})$	$(.76^{***})$	$(.93^{***})$	$(.36^{**})$

Homicide

Relative Deprivation	$.72_a^{***}$		$.28_a^{**}$	
Homicide	$.70_b^{***}$	$.16_b^{**}$	$.92_b^{***}$	$.06_b^{*}$
	$(.81^{***})$	$(.66^{***})$	$(.94^{***})$	$(.32^{**})$

Note. The cell entries in the cohort size columns estimate the path coefficients for the direct effect of cohort size on relative deprivation and each violent crime either for the age range 16–19 or 20–23. The path coefficients in the relative deprivation columns estimate the direct effect of relative deprivation on each crime. Numbers in parentheses are zero-order correlation coefficients.

[a] df = 1, 80.

[b] df = 1, 76.

$*p < .10.$

$**p < .05.$

$***p \ll .01.$

of relative deprivation could be estimated by computing youth or teenage minus parent percent unemployment. Of course these values are currently unknown, but different forecast functions can be estimated for each of several possible levels of relative deprivation (e.g., youth minus parent unemployment percent equal either 1% or 10%). Using the cohort size estimates and the 1% or 10% relative deprivation levels, forecast values were estimated from the regression equations of Study 2 for homicide (Figure 2) and robbery (Figure 3) arrest rates for individuals aged 20 years for the years 1980-1985. These forecast values indicate that the level of homicide can be expected to decline substantially over the next 5-10 years regardless of whether relative deprivation levels range from 1% to 10%. However, the robbery rates depend heavily upon relative deprivation levels. Hence, robbery can be expected to increase or to decrease over the next few years, depending upon how current economic conditions impact unemployment rates and how the changing birth rates influence the number of individuals who are competing for jobs.

Relative Deprivation and Fertility Rates

The present findings are consistent with Easterlin's (1973) analysis of fertility rate changes over the past 40 years. Easterlin proposed that the fertility rate shifts are primarily due to changing levels of relative deprivation experienced by young adults following the transition away from their parents' household. High relative deprivation is associated with low birth rates while high birth rates occurred during periods of low relative deprivation. That is, when young adults' income or employment rates are nearly as high as their parents, then there occurs a period of and high fertility and low homicide rates. The negative association between annual fertility rates of women aged 15 to 45 and homicide rates/1000 males aged 16 to 34 are reported in Figure 4. The age of greatest risk for committing a homicide (for males) or having the first child (for females) is in the 18 to 24 age range. The fluctuating levels of divorce closely approximate the homicide rates for the years 1930-1979. As young people experience greater difficulties in making the transition into independent adult life, they are likely to display a wide variety of reactions which can be detected in measures of increased unemployment, increased age of first marriage, increased probability of divorce, increased violent crime, and decreased liklihood of having children.

The experience of deprivation appears to depend more upon relative than objective deprivation. For example, youths leaving home during the years from 1970-1980 have experienced high levels of relative deprivation but low levels of objective deprivation. These individuals have access to a better quality and greater quantity of commodities than their parents experienced when they left home in the years from 1947-1960. However, young parents from 1947 to 1960 came from homes which did not have very many

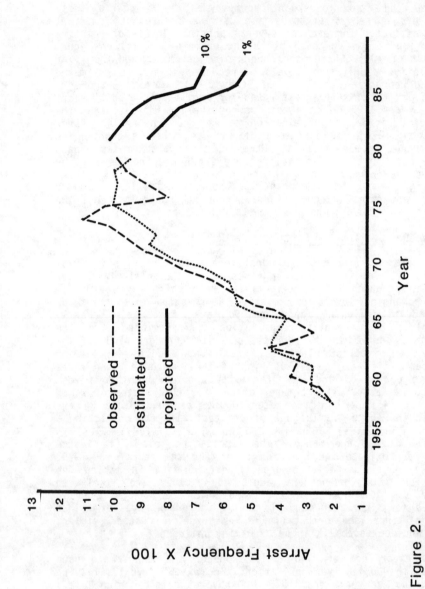

Figure 2. Observed, estimated, and projected frequencies of homicide arrests for 20 year olds(1958–1985). Estimates and projections are based on birth rates (lagged) and relative deprivation.

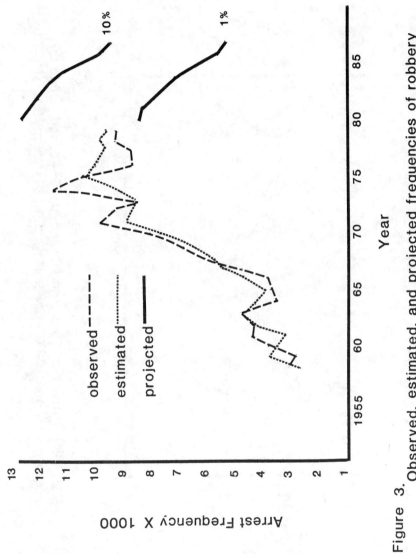

Figure 3. Observed, estimated, and projected frequencies of robbery arrests for 20 year olds (1958–1985). Estimates and projections are based on birth rates (lagged) and relative deprivation.

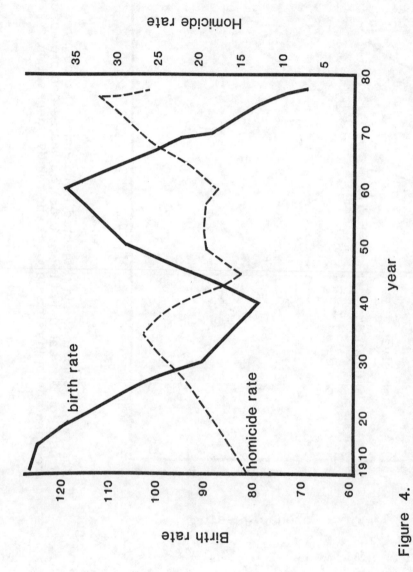

Figure 4. U.S. birth rates per 1000 females aged 15–45 and homicide arrest rates per 100,000 males aged 15–34 from 1910–1977

330

commodities because the commodities were inaccessible during the great depression from 1930 to 1940 or during World War II (1940 to 1945). Hence, the young parents from 1947 to 1960 easily obtained as many or more luxury commodities than their parents. Young parents in the years from 1947 to 1960 had higher levels of objective deprivation but lower levels of relative deprivation than young parents in the years from 1960 to 1980.

Easterlin (1968) reasoned that young parents before 1960, at least in the U.S., had very favorable job opportunities while also having low aspiration levels for commodities. Hence, these young parents had substantial excess income which could be used to spend on children. Apparently, these young parents were more willing to have children. Hence, the birth rate increased from 1947 through 1957 but then declined from 1960-1978. After 1960, competition for jobs began to increase as children born after 1947 began to reach the age of competing for jobs. Moreover, the labor market within the United States after 1960 was not as lucrative for young adults since countries devastated by World War II had rebuilt their economies and were competing with American businesses after 1960. The young people leaving home in the 1960s experienced greater competition for jobs while they also had very high aspirations for commodities (Easterlin, Wachter, & Wachter, 1978). That is, their parents had been able to accrue these commodities during the 1950s when economic conditions were very favorable, and these young people had become used to the commodities in their parents' homes (Easterlin, 1973). When these young adults left home, after 1960, they could not acquire similar items because of the competition among their peers for jobs and housing. This competition meant that young adults had to pay high prices for their new homes. Most young adults purchase their first home while they are 25-30 years of age. Young adults born in 1945-1950 reached the age of buying a home in the period from 1970-1980. Since there was a rapid increase in the number of births from 1940 to 1950 throughout the world, the number of individuals competing for housing also increased dramatically from 1970-1980 in all countries. In the United States, the value of loans for houses increased from 300 billion dollars in 1970 to one trillion dollars in 1980 (Casey, 1981). Most of the increase in loan values probably resulted from increased prices due to increased competition for housing among young adults. For example, the value of an average home increased three fold from 1970 to 1980.

Young adults in the United States aspire to the present living arrangements of their parents, not the living conditions which their parents experienced when they left home. Because of the high aspiration levels which could not be achieved, young people began to experience higher and higher levels of relative deprivation from 1960 to 1980. According to Easterlin (1968, 1973), the declining birth rate was one response of young people to the increasing relative deprivation. As the birth rate

331

declined from 1960 to 1979, the number of 16-year-olds who will compete for their first jobs will decrease from 1976 to 1995. However, competition for first homes should not begin to decline until after 1985. Young people born after 1960 should have less competition for jobs and houses than their parents. This reduced competition should lead to lower levels of relative deprivation when these young adults attempt to leave their parents' home and to establish their own homes.

Cross-national Differences in Relative Deprivation

A different pattern of birth rate and homicide rates occurred in European countries, especially those devastated by World War II than in North America. Although young European parents during 1947-1960 also came from homes without commodities, the disrupted economy made it difficult for young parents to obtain good jobs or housing. Hence, young parents had little excess income and they avoided having children, in part by using abortion as a birth control measure but also by delaying the age of marriage until economic conditions improved. Although a brief increase in the birth rate occurred from 1945-1950, the birth rate remained low throughout most of the 1950s. Hence, the number of young people competing for jobs 16-20 years later (1970-1980) was smaller in these countries than in the United States. In summary, the experience of relative deprivation for young adults in the United States was quite different than for most European countries. As a consequence, the patterns of crime, birth rates, marriage age, divorce, and unemployment are also quite different across the various countries.

Industrialized countries differ from non-industrialized countries in the way that relative deprivation among young adults influences birth rates. In non-industrialized countries, the birth rate was low in the depression (1930-1940) as with most countries. The birth rate increased substantially after World War II and remained high for more than 30 years (1945-1975). Either young parents in these countries did not experience relative deprivation or relative deprivation did not impact birth rates in the same way as it did in industrialized societies. In non-industrialized, agricultural countries, children can contribute to the family income by working in the fields. Children are not as great a financial liability as in non-agricultural societies. In industrialized societies, children usually do not have the skills necessary for work in factories or shops. Children in industrialized societies become a financial liability rather than an asset as in agricultural societies. In summary, the pattern of relative deprivation related to crime and birth rates from North America or from Europe may not be generalizable to other societies.

SUMMARY

The present chapter focused primarily upon the violent crimes of robbery and homicide. We presented evidence that relative deprivation in teenagers and young adults would be perceived as an aversive event which would increase the probability of these violent crimes. However, in order to understand the effects of relative deprivation, several other factors which modify the risk of violent behavior must also be considered. First, an individual's aspiration level (derived from prior experiences and the reference group) can influence whether an individual perceives a particular economic condition as aversive. Second, individuals also differ as to whether they use violent or nonviolent resources to cope with an aversive situation. Personality differences (e.g., Type A/B) can modify achievement levels (influencing relative deprivation) and predispositions toward aggressive reactions. Third, environmental cues can modify the probability of aggressive reactions from uninhibited individuals experiencing aversive events. For example, aggressive cues (words, weapons, or films) can modify the probability of aggressive reactions. Fourth, social learning experiences can modify the risk of the violent crimes of robbery and homicide. When individuals believe that they do not have access to legitimate opportunities, they may be particularly likely to be attracted to delinquent subcultures. These subcultures offer illegitimate opportunities to achieve one's aspirations. Delinquent subcultures are particularly likely to foster violent solutions for aversive experiences. Professional and semi-professional robbers frequently acquire their trade from the training of delinquent subcultures.

During an economic recession, young people (aged 16-23) are likely to be the last hired and the first fired. Hence, a recession has the greatest effect on the unemployment opportunities of young people (especially teenagers). These unemployed youths may be particularly likely to be attracted to delinquent subcultures since legitimate opportunities are not available to them. Once an individual has been attracted to the subculture, delinquent acts originating within the juvenile gangs can lead to arrests and criminal records. A criminal record can serve as a further barrier to legitimate opportunities. Consequently some of these youths persist in criminal careers since they are unable to pursue legitimate opportunities.

Violent crime is particularly likely to be committed by individuals in the age groups between 16 and 23. Individuals in these age groups are in transition from their parents' home to their own independent households. Fluctuating birth rates have modified the probability of violent behavior by influencing the number of individuals in the 16-23 transition age groups. The cohort size can influence violent crime by (at least) two different processes. First, as more individuals enter the violence-prone age groups, more individuals are likely to experience relative deprivation. Approximately 80% of the variance in violent crime from 1958 to 1979 can be explained by the size of the cohorts in the violence-prone transition groups.

Cohort size can contribute to violent crime by a second factor. As the cohort size increases, competition also increases for scarce resources such as jobs and housing. The high birth rate from 1946 to 1960 increased the proportion as well as the frequency of individuals who were unemployed 16-23 years later. With a larger cohort, a higher percentage of individuals will be unable to satisfy their aspirations through legitimate employment.

Young people leaving home from 1960-1980 have experienced another type of relative deprivation which their parents did not experience. That is, young adults have more expensive tastes for commodities than their parents had when they were in the transitional age groups. Teenagers living with their parents between 1946 and 1960 had fewer luxury commodities than teenagers from 1960 to 1980. Young people in transition from their parents' home from 1965 to 1980 have expensive tastes (or aspiration levels) which can not be achieved because of the intense competition for jobs and housing in their age group. The high levels of relative deprivation have produced a number of symptoms of distress such as violent crime, family conflict and divorce, and unemployment. However, another important response to the high levels of relative deprivation has been declining fertility rate from 1960 to 1980. Since fewer children were born after 1960, fewer will be in the 16-23 transitional age groups to compete for jobs and housing between 1976 and 1998.

If these observations are correct, then the current high levels of relative deprivation may be of short duration. The forecast equations that we have developed (see Figures 2 and 3) indicate that the annual frequency of homicide should decline by 35 to 40% (depending upon the unemployment rate) from 1980 through 1985 as the size of the 16-23 age group declines. Robbery may increase or decrease depending upon the unemployment rate. However, since cohort size is so strongly associated with relative unemployment (see Table 1), the declining birth rate after 1960 should lead to declining rates both of relative deprivation and of robbery. Finally, as the relative deprivation levels decline, the fertility rate may increase. A rising birth rate could lead to a repetition of current problems 16-23 years later unless careful planning can mitigate the effects of relative deprivation on youths in transition from home.

REFERENCES

Amsel, A. The role of frustrative nonreward in noncontinuous reward situations. Psychological Bulletin, 1958, 55, 102-119.

Bandura, A. Aggression: A social learning analysis. Englewood Cliffs, N. J., Prentice-Hall, 1973.

Bandura, A. Social learning theory. Englewood Cliffs, N. J.: Prentice-Hall, 1977.

Bandura, A. The social learning perspective: Mechanisms of aggression. In H. Toch (Ed.), Psychology of crime and criminal justice. New York: Holt, Rinehart & Winston, 1979.

Berkowitz, L. Aggression: A social psychological analysis. New York: McGraw-Hill, 1962.

Berkowitz, L. Control of aggression. In Betty M. Caldwell & H. Ricciuti (Eds.), Review of child development research, Vol. 3. New York: Russell Sage, 1973.

Berkowitz, L. Some determinants of impulsive aggression: Role of mediated associations with reinforcements for aggression. Psychological Review, 1974, 81, 165-176.

Berkowitz, L. Whatever happened to the frustration-aggression hypothesis? American Behavioral Scientist, 1978, 32, 691-708.

Berkowitz, L. The experience of anger as a parallel process in the display of impulsive, "angry" aggression. In R. G. Geen & E. Donnerstein (Eds.), Aggression: Theoretical and empirical reviews. New York: Academic Press, 1982.

Berkowitz, L., & Alioto, J. T. The meaning of an observed event as a determinant of its aggressive consequences. Journal of Personality and Social Psychology, 1973, 28, 206-217.

Berkowitz, L., & Geen, R. G. Film violence and the cue properties of available targets. Journal of Personality and Social Psychology, 1966, 3, 525-530.

Berkowitz, L., & LePage, A. Weapons as aggression-eliciting stimuli. Journal of Personality and Social Psychology, 1967, 7, 202-207.

Brown, J. S., & Farber, I. E. Emotions conceptualized as intervening variables--with suggestions toward a theory of frustration. Psychological Bulletin, 1951, 48, 465-495.

Buss, A. H. The psychology of aggression. New York: Wiley, 1961.

Buss, A. H. Instrumentality of aggression, feedback, and frustration as determinants of physical aggression. Journal of Personality and Social Psychology, 1966, 3, 153-162.

Burnam, M. A., Pennebaker, J. W., & Glass, D. C. Time consciousness, achievement striving, and the Type A coronary-prone behavior pattern. Journal of Abnormal Psychology, 1975, 84, 76-79.

Carver, C. S., & Glass, D. C. Coronary-prone behavior pattern and inter-personal aggression. Journal of Personality and Social Psychology, 1978, 36, 361-366.

Casey, D. R. That tricky housing market. Parade Magazine, Salt Lake Tribune, April 5, 1981.

Cloward, R. A., & Ohlin, L. E. Delinquency and opportunity. New York: Free Press, 1960.

Cole, A. M., & Turner, C. W. Effects on crime rates of changing birth orders during the post World War II baby boom. Paper presented at the Western Psychological Association meeting, Seattle, Washington, April, 1977.

Coser, L. A. Some aspects of Soviet family policy. In R. L. Coser (Ed.), The family: Its structures and functions (2nd Ed.). New York: St. Martin's Press, 1974.

Crosby, F. A model of egoistical relative deprivation. Psychological Review, 1976, 83, 85-113.

Davies, J. C. The J-curve of rising and declining satisfactions as a cause of some great revolutions and a contained rebellion. In H. D. Graham & T. R. Gurr (Eds.), Violence in America. New York: Signet Books, 1969.

Dembroski, T. M., Weiss, S. M., Shields, J. L., Haynes, S. G., & Feinleib, M. (Eds.), Coronary-prone behavior. New York: Springer, 1978.

Dodd, D. K., Cole, A. M., & Turner, C. W. Effects of post World War II baby boom on U. S. Divorce rate. Paper presented at the American Psychological Association meeting, San Francisco, CA, August, 1977.

Dollard, J., Doob, L., Miller, N., Mowrer, O., & Sears, R. Frustration and aggression. New Haven: Yale University Press, 1939.

Doob, A. N., & Gross, A. E. Status of frustration as an inhibitor of horn-honking responses. Journal of Social Psychology, 1968, 76, 213-218.

Easterlin, R. A. Population, labor force, and long swings in economic growth. New York: Columbia University Press, 1968.

Easterlin, R. A. Relative economic status and the American fertility swing. In E. Sheldon (Ed.), Family economic behavior. Philadelphia: J. B. Lippincott Co., 1973.

Easterlin, R. A., Wachter, M. L., and Wachter, S. M. Demographic influences on economic stability: The United States experience. Population and Development Review, 1978, 4, 1-21.

Elliott, G. Twentieth Century book of the dead. New York: Scribner, 1972.

Ellis, D. P., Weinir, P., & Miller, L. Does the trigger pull the finger? An experimental test of weapons as aggression eliciting stimuli. Sociometry, 1971, 34, 453-465.

Ferdinand, T. Reported index crime increases between 1950 and 1965 due to urbanization and changes in the age structure of the population alone. In D. J. Mulvihill & M. M. Tumin (Eds.), Crimes of violence. Appendix 3, 1969, 145-152.

Feshbach, S. The function of aggression and the regulation of aggressive drive. Psychological Review, 1964, 71, 257-272.

Gastorf, J. W. Time urgency of the Type A behavior pattern. Journal of Consulting and Clinical Psychology, 1980, 40, 299.

Geen, R. G. Effects of frustration, attack, and prior training in aggressiveness on aggressive behavior. Journal of Personality and Social Psychology, 1968, 9, 316-321.

Geen, R. G., & Berkowitz, L. Name-mediated aggressive cue properties. Journal of Personality, 1966, 34, 456-465.

Geen, R. G., & Berkowitz, L. Some conditions facilitating the occurrence of aggression after the observation of violence. Journal of Personality, 1967, 35, 666-676.

Geen, R. G., & O'Neal, E. C. Activation of cue-elicited aggression by general arousal. Journal of Personality and Social Psychology, 1969, 11, 289-292.

Gibbons, D. C. Society, crime, and criminal careers: An introduction to Criminology (2nd ed.). Englewood Cliffs, N. J.: Prentice-Hall, Inc., 1973.

Glass, D. C. Behavior patterns, stress, and coronary disease. Hillsdale, N. J.: Erlbaum, 1977.

Glass, D. C., Snyder, M. L., & Hollis, J. F. Time urgency and the Type A coronary-prone behavior pattern. Journal of Applied Social Psychology, 1974, 4, 125-140.

Goode, W. J. Family disorganization. In R. K. Merton and R. Nisbet (Eds.), Contemporary social problems (4th ed.). New York: Harcourt, Brace, Jovanovich, 1976.

Hauser, P. M. On population and environmental policy and problems. In N. Hinricks (Ed.), Population, environment and people. New York: McGraw-Hill, 1971.

Heer, D. M. Society and population (2nd ed.). Englewood Cliffs, N. J.: Prentice-Hall, Inc., 1975.

Henry, A. F., & Short, J. F., Jr. Suicide and homicide. New York: Free Press, 1954.

Hokanson, J. E., & Burgess, M. The effects of status, type of frustration, and aggression on vascular processes. Journal of Abnormal and Social Psychology, 1962, 64, 446-449.

Jenkins, C. D., Rosenman, R. H., & Zyzanski, S. J. Prediction of clinical coronary heart disease by a test for the coronary-prone behavior pattern. New England Journal of Medicine, 1974, 290, 1271-1275.

Kenkel, W. F. The family in perspective (4th ed.). Santa Monica, CA: Goodyear Publishing Co., 1977.

Kerlinger, F. N., & Pedhazur, E. J. Multiple regression in behavioral research. New York: Holt, Rinehart, and Winston, 1973.

Konečni, V. J. The mediation of aggressive behavior: Arousal level versus anger and cognitive labeling. Journal of Personality and Social Psychology, 1975, 32, 706-712.

Kuhn, D. Z., Madsen, C. H., Jr., and Becker, W. C. Effects of exposure to an aggressive model and "frustration" on children's aggressive behavior. Child Development, 1967, 38, 739-745.

Lazarus, R. S. Psychological stress and the coping process. New York: McGraw-Hill, 1966.

Leventhal, H. Findings and theory in the study of fear communications. In L. Berkowitz (Ed.), Advances in experimental social psychology, Vol. 6. New York: Academic Press, 1970.

338

Leventhal, H. Toward a comprehensive theory of emotion. In L. Berkowitz (Ed.), Advances in experimental social psychology, Vol. 13. New York: Academic Press, 1980.

Leyens, J. P., & Parke, R. D. Aggressive slides can induce a weapons effect. European Journal of Social Psychology, 1975, 5, 229-236.

Lindsley, D. B. Emotion. In S. S. Stevens (Ed.), Handbook of experimental psychology. New York: Wiley, 1951.

Malmo, R. B. Activation: A neurological dimension. Psychological Review, 1959, 66, 367-386.

Matthews, K. A., & Brunson, B. J. Allocation of attention and the Type A coronary-prone behavior pattern. Journal of Personality and Social Psychology, 1979, 37, 2081-2090.

Miller, N. E. The frustration-aggression hypothesis. Psychological Review, 1941, 48, 337-342.

Miller, S. M., & Grant, R. P. The blunting hypothesis: A view of predictability and human stress. In P. O. Sjoden & S. Bates (Eds.), Trends in behavior therapy. New York: Academic Press, 1979.

Newton, G. C., & Zimring, F. E. Firearms and violence in American life. Washington, D. C.: U. S. Government Printing Office, 1969.

Novaco, R. W. The cognitive regulation of anger and stress. In P. Kendall & S. Hollon (Eds.), Cognitive-behavioral interventions: Theory, research, and procedures. New York: Academic Press, 1979, 241-285.

Patterson, G. R., & Cobb, J. A. Stimulus control for classes of noxious behaviors. In J. F. Knutson (Ed.), The control of aggression. Chicago: Aldine, 1973.

Patterson, G. R., Littman, R. A., & Bricker, W. Assertive behavior in children: A step toward a theory of aggression. Monographs of the Society for Research in Child Development, 1967, 32, (5 Serial No. 113).

Rule, B. G., & Nesdale, A. R. Emotional arousal and aggressive behavior. Psychological Bulletin, 1976, 83, 851-863.

Schachter, S. The interaction of cognitive and physiological determinants of emotional state. In L. Berkowitz (Ed.), Advances in experimental social psychology, Vol. 1. New York: Academic Press, 1964, 49-80.

Schuck, J. R. Paths to violence: Toward a quantitative approach. In A. G. Neal (Ed.), Violence in animal and human societies. Chicago: Nelson Hall, 1976.

Schulz, D. A. The changing family: Its function and future. Englewood Cliffs, N.J.: Prentice-Hall, 1976.

Sears, D. O., & McConahay, J. B. Participation in the Los Angeles riot. Social Problems, 1969, 17, 3-20.

Seligman, M. E. P. Helplessness: In depression, development, and death. San Francisco: W. H. Freeman & Co., 1975.

Short, J. F., Jr., and Strodtbeck, F. L. Group processes and gang delinquency. Chicago: The University of Chicago Press, 1974.

Stokols, D., Novaco, R. W., Stokols, J., & Campbell, J. Traffic congestion, Type A behavior, and stress. Journal of Applied Psychology, 1978, 63, 467-480.

Strube, M. J., Turner, C. W., Cerro, D. S., & Stevens, J. H. Interpersonal aggression and the Type A coronary-prone behavior pattern: Hostility or instrumentality? Unpublished manuscript, University of Utah, Salt Lake City, Utah, 1982.

Strube, M. J., Turner, C. W., & Patrick, S. A. Type A-B attentional responses to aesthetic stimuli. Unpublished manuscript, University of Utah, Salt Lake City, Utah, 1981.

Taeuber, I. B., & Taeuber, C. People of the United States. Washington, D. C.: U. S. Government Printing Office, 1971.

Taylor, S. P., & Pisano, R. Physical aggression as a function of frustration and physical attack. Journal of Social Psychology, 1971, 84, 261-267.

Thamm, R. Beyond marriage and the nuclear family. San Francisco: Canfield Press, 1975.

Toby, J. Hoodlum or businessman: An American dilemma. In M. Sklare, (Ed.), The Jews: Social patterns of an American group. Glencoe, Illinois: Free Press, 1958.

Toch, H. H. Violent men: An enquiry into the psychology of violence. Chicago: Aldine Publishing Co., 1969.

Turner, C. W., & Dodd, D. K. The development of anti-social behavior. In R. L. Ault (Ed.), Selected readings in child development. Santa Monica, CA: Goodyear Publishing Co., 1979.

Turner, C. W., & Goldsmith, D. Effects of toy guns and airplanes on children's anti-social free play behavior. Journal of Experimental Child Psychology, 1976, 21, 303-315.

Turner, C. W., Fenn, M. R., & Cole, A. M. A social psychological analysis of violent behavior. In R. B. Stuart, (Ed.), Violent behavior: Social learning approaches to prediction, management, and treatment. New York: Brunner/Mazel, 1981.

Turner, C. W., Layton, J. F., & Simons, L. S. Naturalistic studies of aggressive behavior: Aggressive stimuli, victim visibility, and horn honking. Journal of Personality and Social Psychology, 1975, 31, 1098-1107.

Turner, C. W., & Simons, L. S. Effects of subject sophistication and evaluation apprehension on aggressive responses to weapons. Journal of Personality and Social Psychology, 1974, 30, 341-348.

Turner, C. W., Simons, L. S., Berkowitz, L., & Frodi, A. The stimulating and inhibiting effects of weapons on aggressive behavior. Aggressive Behavior, 1977, 3, 355-378.

Turner, C. W., Simons, L. S., Fenn, M. R., & Layton, J. F. Inhibiting and instigating cues for aggression in naturalistic settings. In G. V. Caprara, & P. Renzi, (Eds.), Experimental research on aggression. Rome: Bulzoni Editore, (1982) in press.

Ulrich, R., Dulaney S., Arnett, M., & Mueller, K. An experimental analysis of nonhuman and human aggression. In J. K. Knutson (Ed.), The control of aggression. Chicago: Aldine Publishing Co., 1973.

Uniform Crime Reports. Washington, D. C.: U. S. Government Printing Office annual editions, 1957-1979.

U. S. Bureau of the Census. Historical statistics of the United States, colonial times to 1970, bicentennial edition. Washington, D. C.: U. S. Government Printing Office, 1975.

U. S. Bureau of the Census. Statistical abstract of the United States. Washington, D. C.: U. S. Government Printing Office, annual editions, 1881-1979.

U. S. Department of Labor, Bureau of Labor Statistics. Manpower Reports. Washington, D. C.: U. S. Government Printing Office, annual editions, 1958-1979.

van de Walle, E. Marriage and marital fertility. In D. V. Glass & R. Revelle, (Eds.), Population and social change. London: Edward Arnold, 1972.

Wellford, C. F. Age composition and the increase in recorded crime. Criminology, 1973, 11, 61-70.

Whelpton, P. K. The future growth of the population of the United States. In G. H. L. J. Pitt-Rivers (Ed.), Port Washington. New York: Kennikat Press, 1932.

Wilson, M., & Higgins, P. B. Television's action arsenal: Weapon use in prime time. United States Conference of Mayors, Washington, D. C., 1977.

Yorberg, B. The changing family. New York: Columbia University Press, 1973.

Zillmann, D. Hostility and aggression. Hillsdale, N.J.: Erlbaum, 1979.

APPENDIX

INSTITUTE PARTICIPANTS

Mr. Gennaro Accursio
Via dei Mille, 1
University of Rome
Institute of Psychology
Rome, ITALY

Dr. Peolo Alcini
Via Ugo Ojetti, 392
Rome, ITALY

Mr. Antonio Arto
Instituto di Psichologia
00139 Roma
Piazza Deli 'Ateneo Salesiano
Rome, ITALY

Dr. Cathie Atkins
Department of Community
  Medicine
University of California,
  San Diego M-022
La Jolla, CA 92093
USA

Ms. Hasida Ben-Zur
University of Haifa
Mount Carmel
Haiffa, ISRAEL

Dr. Patrizio Bernini
Istituto di Psichiatria
Universita di Roma
Viale dell 'Universita 30
Rome, ITALY

Dr. Massimo Biondi
Istituto di Psichiatria
Universita di Roma
Viale dell 'Universita 30
Rome, ITALY

Dr. Sonia L. Blackman
3405 Mt. Vernon
Riverside, CA 93507
USA

Ms. Zehra Kaya Diler
Istanbul Devlet Munendislik
ve Mimarlik Akademisi
Petrol Sitesi Blok 32
Daire 16 Levent
Istanbul, TURKEY

Dr. Jonathan Bloom-Feshbach
National Research Council
2101 Constitution Avenue
Washington, D.C. 20418
USA

Dr. Sally Bloom-Feshbach
Office of Senator Riegel
1207 Dirkson Senate Office Bldg.
Washington, D.C. 20418
USA

Dr. Christiana de Caldas Brito
Via Ernesto Basile
41/B
00128
Rome, ITALY

Dr. Luciana Carilla
Istituto di Psichiatria
Universita di Rome
Viale dell 'University 30
Rome, IRALY

Mr. Allen Cole
Department of Psychology
University of Utah
Salt Lake City, UT 84112
USA

Mr. Massimiliano Conte
Largo a Beltramelli
1/A
00151
Rome, ITALY

Dr. Carla Conti
Istituto di Psichiatria
Universita di Roma
Viale dell 'Universita 30
Rome, ITALY

Dr. Archangela di Tolla
Piazza Vulture 15
Rome, ITALY

Dr. Tamara Ferguson
Department of Psychology
Catholic University of
  Nijmegen
Nijmegen, HOLLAND

Dr. Laura A. Foster
30 Gloria Drive
San Rafael, CA 94901
USA

Dr. Juan Pastor Freitez
Viale Appio Claudio, 285
Palazzine C
Interno 31
00174
Rome, ITALY

Ms. Shirley French
University College
P. O. Box 78
Cardiff CF1 1XL
UNITED KINGDOM

Dr. Walter Gallotta
V Cattedra Di Clinica
  Psichiatric
Dell 'Universita 30
Rome, ITALY

Mr. Hugh Gault
Orchard Lodge Regional
  Resource Center
William Booth Road
Anerley, London
UNITED KINGDOM

Dr. Mervyn D. Gilmour
Southern Education Board
The Mall, ARMAGH
N. Ireland, UNITED KINGDOM

Dr. D'Imperio Guiseppe
Via Domenico Panaroli 41
00172
Rome, ITALY

Dr. Alice Healy-Fesno
L.A. County Dept. of Education
9300 E. Imperial Highway
Downey, CA 90242
USA

Dr. Michael Katzko
Payensweg #8
6523 MB Nijmegen
HOLLAND

Dr. Barbara G. Lenssen
Sangre de Christo Comm.
  Mental Health Center
Rt. 1, Box 92
Santa Fe, NM 87501
USA

Ms. Gabi Loschper
Projekt Okopsychologies
Universitat Munster
Schlaunstrasse 2 D-440
Munster
WEST GERMANY

Dr. Peter Marsh
Department of Social Studies
Oxford Polytechnic
Headington, Oxford
UNITED KINGDOM

Dr. A. Massarelli
Lungamare Paolo Toscanelli
72-Ostia Lido
Rome, ITALY

Ms. Lynne Novaco
Youth Services Program, Inc.
2803 Royal Palm Drive
Costa Mesa, CA 92627
USA

Dr. Carolyn M. Owen
School of Education
California State University,
  Long Beach
Long Beach, CA 90840
USA

Dr. Giovanna Pennacchi
University Pontificia
  Salesiana
Via Peolo Bemtivoglio 29B
00165
Rome, ITALY

Dr. Patricia Polovy
New York City Board of
  Education
2017 Coleman Street
Brooklyn, NY 11234
USA

Dr. Susan Rose
Albert Einstein College of
  Medicine
Psychology Department
1300 Morris Park Avenue
Bronx, NY 10461
USA

Dr. Barbara Sarason
Department of Psychology
University of Washington
Seattle, Washington 98105
USA

Mr. Peter Toy
College Militair Royal
  de St-Jean
Dept. of National Defense
MLM Dept.
Saint-Jean, Quebec
CANADA JOJ IRO

Dr. Yoel Yinon
Bar-Ilan University
Department of Psychology
Ramat-Gan, ISRAEL

Belson, W.
269, 274, 279
Bem, D.
53, 68, 259
Benedict, B. D.
220, 243
Bennett, S. M.
146, 161
Bentler, P. M.
291, 292
Berberich, J. P.
176, 191
Berger, M.
134
Bergin, A. E.
135
Berkowitz, L.
2, 6, 7, 8, 9, 10, 13,
19, 22, 25, 28, 29, 33,
34, 36, 42, 50, 68, 138,
139, 156, 157, 248, 259,
261, 262, 282, 284, 292,
293, 295, 298, 299, 300,
301, 303, 304, 305, 306,
307, 310, 335, 337, 338,
339, 341
Berlyne, D. E.
86
Bern, D. J.
48, 63
Berndt, T. J.
149, 153, 156
Berry, C. C.
65, 70
Berscheid, E.
147, 160
Best, D. L.
146, 161
Biaggio, M. K.
236, 243
Bibring, E.
93, 101
Bigelow, R.
267, 279
Bijou, S.
199, 207
Blanchard, E.
287, 290, 292
Blaney, N.
202, 205
Blankstein, K.
41

Block, J.
104, 106, 113, 115, 118,
132, 133, 134
Block, J. H.
104, 132, 134
Blum, B.
10, 19, 34
Bobrow, D. B.
228, 243
Bogart, L.
263, 279
Bohn, M. J.
48, 71
Bonnett, D. G.
291, 292
Borden, R. J.
260, 261
Bortner, M.
161
Bourne, P. G.
218, 222, 232, 234, 243,
Bowers, K. S.
117, 134
Bowers, W. J.
66, 72
Bowlby, J.
82, 85
Bramel, D.
10, 19, 34
Brehm, S.
158
Brende, J. O.
220, 243
Brenner, C.
99, 101
Bricker, W.
47, 66, 113, 136, 138, 159,
302, 339
Bridges, ____.
164
Briere, J.
289, 290, 293
Bringmann, W. G.
261
Brock, T. C.
10, 20, 35
Bromley, D. B.
144, 158
Bronson, W. C.
123, 126, 127, 128, 129,
134
Brook, J. S.
144, 161

Kaminsky, S.
  147, 160
Kane, T. R.
  50, 70, 147, 157
Kanin, E.
  281, 294
Kaplan, J.
  70
Kaplan, R. M.
  17, 24, 37, 45, 48, 51,
  66, 207, 264, 265, 274,
  279
Kardiner, A.
  216, 217, 218, 245
Karniol, R.
  151, 152, 153, 158
Karsten, P.
  214, 231, 245
Kassin, S.
  145, 148, 150, 158
Katz, E.
  250, 261
Katcher, A. H.
  6, 43
Keasey, C. B.
  207
Kelley, H. H.
  139, 140, 141, 145, 150,
  151, 158
Kellner, R.
  286, 295
Kendall, P. C.
  71, 176, 188, 190, 246,
  339
Kendel, D. B.
  292
Kendrick, D. C.
  46, 47, 49, 50, 69
Kenkel, W. F.
  297, 321, 338
Kenny, D. T.
  8, 19, 37
Kerlinger, F. N.
  324, 338
Kidd, R. F.
  157
Kim, J.
  237, 245
King, S. H.
  235, 244
Kirshenbaum, H. M.
  7, 8, 19, 35
Kleck, R. E.
  12, 40

Kleinke, C. L.
  146, 158
Klein, P.
  176, 190
Klerman, G. L.
  37
Klein, M.
  96, 98, 99, 102
Klosson, E. C.
  150, 156
Knutson, J. F.
  339, 341
Koblinsky, S. G.
  147, 158
Kohlberg, L.
  106, 116, 135
Kohn, M.
  113, 118, 122, 123, 126,
  127, 128, 129, 130, 135
Konečni, V. J.
  1, 2, 3, 6, 7, 8, 9, 10,
  11, 12, 13, 16, 17, 20,
  21, 22, 23, 24, 25, 26,
  27, 29, 35, 37, 38, 39,
  49, 70, 76, 86, 207, 211,
  230, 245, 300, 338
Koriat, A.
  252, 261
Korn, S.
  146, 158
Kornadt, H.-J.
  74, 77, 80, 85, 86
Koss, M.
  287, 294
Kosturn, C. F.
  20, 40
Kovaric, P.
  263, 279
Kreutzer, M. A.
  164, 173
Kriss, E.
  93, 96, 97, 102
Kuhn, D. Z.
  7, 35, 39, 146, 158, 303,
  338
Kulik, J. A.
  8, 9, 18, 39, 154, 158
Kunath, J.
  282, 295
Kurdek, L. A.
  193, 207
Kushner, H.
  39

355

359

Revelle, R.
341
Riccuiti, H.
335
Ricks, D.
116, 135
Riley, J. W.
250, 251, 262
Riley, M. W.
250, 251, 262
Rivlin, E.
286, 294
Roberts, D. F.
51, 70
Robins, L. N.
122, 129, 136
Robinson, G. L.
224, 235, 246
Rocha, R. F.
17, 41
Roden, A. H.
7, 36
Roe, K.
192, 193, 206
Rogers, R. W.
17, 41
Roodin, P. A.
148, 159
Rose, R. M.
234, 246
Rosenbach, D.
144, 148, 159
Rosenbaum, M. E.
10, 19, 41
Rosenblum, L. A.
162, 174
Rosenfeld, H.
100, 102
Rosenfield, D.
143, 159
Rosenman, R. H.
308, 338
Rosenthal, L.
176, 190
Rosenthal, R.
2, 41, 225, 245
Rosman, B. L.
113, 118, 135
Rosnow, R. L.
41, 261
Ross, D.
7, 33, 50, 68

Ross, L. B.
51, 72
Ross, M.
151, 158
Ross, S. A.
7, 33, 50, 68
Rotenberg, K. J.
144, 145, 159
Rothenberg, B. B.
200, 207
Rubinstein, E. A.
54, 70, 72, 135, 262, 263,
279, 280
Ruderman, A.
155, 157
Rule, B. G.
2, 9, 41, 80, 87, 139,
148, 149, 150, 151, 152,
153, 154, 155, 156, 157,
159, 300, 339
Russell, G. W.
7, 32
Rustin, S.
220, 244
Rutherford, E.
7, 40
Rutter, M.
104, 122, 129, 134, 136
Ryan, E. D.
6, 8, 42
Rybash, J. M.
148, 159
Saccuzzo, D. S.
40, 45, 48, 70
Salt, P.
42
Sandilands, M. L.
7, 32
Sanford, N.
216, 246
Santogrossi, D. A.
255, 261
Sarason, B. R.
182, 188, 191
Sarason, I. G.
46, 72, 80, 85, 87, 176,
177, 182, 191, 217, 224,
235, 240, 246, 248, 249,
255, 260, 261
Sarason, S.
203, 207
Sargent-Pollock, D.
6, 12, 13, 39, 42

CONTRIBUTORS TO THE VOLUME

Prof. Gian Caprara
Universita Degli Studi Di Roma
Facolta Di Magistero
Istituto Di Psichologia
Rome, ITALY

Dr. Norma Feshbach
School of Education
University of California, Los Angeles
Los Angeles, CA   90024
USA

Dr. Seymour Feshbach
Department of Psychology
University of California, Los Angeles
Los Angeles, CA   90024
USA

Dr. Robert M. Kaplan
Department of Community Medicine
San Diego State University
San Diego, CA   92182
USA

Dr. Vladimir Konečni
Department of Psychology
University of California, San Diego
La Jolla, CA   92093
USA

Dr. Hans J. Kornadt
Fachbereich 6 Der Universitat
Des Saarlandes D-6600
Saarbraken, WEST GERMANY

Dr. Jacques Philippe Leyens
Department of Psychology
Universite Catholique
De Louvain
BELGUIM

Dr. Neil M. Malamuth
Department of Psychology
University of Manitoba
Winnipeg, CANADA   R3T 2N2

Dr. Raymond Novaco
Program in Social Ecology
University of California, Irvine
Irvine, CA   92717
USA

Prof. Dan Olweus
N-5274 Bolstadoyri
NORWAY

Dr. Brendan Gail Rule
Department of Psychology
University of Alberta
Edmonton, Alberta
CANADA

Dr. Irwin Sarason
Department of Psychology
University of Washington
Seattle, Washington 98195
USA

Dr. Robert Singer
Department of Psychology
University of California, Riverside
Riverside, CA   92521
USA

Dr. Charles Turner
Department of Psychology
University of Utah
Salt Lake City, Utah 84112
USA